TALK FICTION

FRONTIERS OF NARRATIVE
Series Editor: David Herman
North Carolina State University

Talk Fiction
Literature and the Talk Explosion

IRENE KACANDES

University of Nebraska Press
Lincoln and London

Library of Congress Cataloging-in-Publication
Data
Kacandes, Irene, 1958–
Talk fiction : literature and the talk explosion /
Irene Kacandes.
p.cm. – (Frontiers of narrative series). Includes
bibliographical references and index.
ISBN 0-8032-2738-8 (cloth : alkaline paper) –
ISBN 0-8032-7801-2 (paperback : alkaline paper)
1. Fiction – 20th century – History and criticism.
2. Narration (Rhetoric) 3. Talk shows. I. Title.
II. Series
PN3503.K33 2001 809.3´04–dc21 2001027063

For Philippe

Contents

Preface

As a graduate teaching assistant in a course called "Comedy and the Novel," I had an encounter with a student that has intrigued me to this day. Indeed, in many respects the kernel of this book lies in that interaction (and for this reason I am particularly sorry I have long forgotten the name of the student). The professor had assigned Italo Calvino's *If on a winter's night a traveler*, and just before we began our small-group discussion on the novel, a male undergraduate rushed in and blurted out: "This book was so cool. It was talking to me. I never read a novel before that was about me." I wasn't amused. I was puzzled and annoyed by his reaction. I had read the novel for the first time to prepare for this class and had been thoroughly irritated by it, so the student's enthusiasm alone irked me. My initial hunch about the differences between this student's affect and my own was based on gender: the inscribed reader in Calvino's novel is male, and this student was able to identify with him because he too was a "he"; in contrast, I was put off by yet another instance of the "male" masquerading as the "universal." That the student hadn't overtly noticed the inscription of gender in the text didn't particularly surprise me; after all, it is less immediately apparent in the English translation the class had read than in the Italian original (a topic I take up in chapter 4). But I continued to be perplexed—and initially discouraged—by how a Harvard undergraduate who'd been through an entire semester of a novels course could think that the text actually "was talking" to him or could actually "be about" him. Hadn't I spent a significant proportion of our discussion time in the previous months introducing narratological terms, distinguishing, for example, between the narratee, the inscribed reader, and the flesh-and-blood reader? Ironically, I appeared to have failed as a teacher where this student succeeded, for his conviction that the novel was talking to him eventually taught *me* to revise how *I* read—at least how to read certain novels like Calvino's. More precisely, I realized that this novel aims for readers to have both the student's reaction *and* mine: delight and annoyance, engagement and disengagement, identification and alienation. My frustration turned to pleasure when I started trying to have both reactions simultaneously.

I propose to call *If on a winter's night a traveler* and novels in the same mold "talk fiction," because they contain features that promote in readers a sense of the interaction we associate with face-to-face conversation ("talk") *and* a sense of the contrivance of this interaction ("fiction"). Furthermore, I mean my phrase to signal a mingling of elements from spoken and written communication: these texts contain "talk" in "fiction," as in prose fiction. This hybridity of orality and textuality links the works I'm considering to the eighteenth and nineteenth centuries, when a sense of literature as "but a different name for conversation" had not yet been banned from the developing novel form, a period, too, when literacy itself was becoming a mass phenomenon. It also links talk fiction to the twentieth century through the phenomenon of "secondary orality," a term referring to the resurgence of oral communication made possible by technology like the telephone, radio, film, television, video, and computer. I submit that we can't know whether talk fiction is a response to the talk explosion or a response to the same forces that led to that explosion. In either case, it seems to me that to fully appreciate the communicative hybridity of our age, we need to register the presence (reemergence? persistence?) of oral elements in literature, the verbal form that the twentieth century nevertheless posited as the most unlike speech.

Contrivance connects my phenomenon to its auditory template, "talk radio" and the television "talk show," related genres based on mediated engagement of speakers and interlocutors, not on passive transmission of music, news, or other information. While not arguing for the direct influence of developments in radio or television on prose fiction or vice versa, I do intend "talk radio" to echo in my phrase "talk fiction," because talk radio, television talk shows, and talk fiction all privilege involvement over content—false though the dichotomy may technically be. I propose that this privileging of interaction remains partially unrecognized, even as it characterizes many cultural phenomena of our secondary oral age.

Before I expand my definition of talk fiction, I'd like to contextualize my embarrassingly haughty graduate student posture of judging those readers who do not perceive the impermeable boundaries between the world of fiction and the world in which people actually live as naïve, and, well, illiterate. I now see a connection between such a view of literature (one fostered in many academic environments) and a widespread hostility in contemporary society toward the ubiquitous spoken word. With the exception of media enthusiasts and some professional linguists, I suspect that much of the world's formally educated population fears that secondary orality is threatening print culture, leading inexorably to a decline in literacy. While there are numerous valid reasons that educators and the general public should be concerned about literacy rates and failures to educate subsequent generations, assumptions about the relative value of spoken and written discourse that underlie these concerns hinder appreciation of various phenomena that are products precisely of new shifts between the two. If humans could suspend a long-standing habit of thinking about orality and literacy as dichotomous, we might be able to apprehend emerging forms of communication, with the gains and the losses that their deployment entails.[1]

Talk fiction is one such emerging form. To bring it into focus for myself I had to confront not only personal and societal views of oral and literate culture but also an academic crisis closer to home: a crisis about the role of literary studies in an age of cultural studies. While definitions, merits, and demerits of cultural studies (rightly) continue to be debated, I submit that cultural studies is one of those intellectual developments that shifts our very notions of "literature" and "literary studies." We may eventually reject the term "cultural studies" and coin a new one; we may even refine our practice of interdisciplinarity. Still, I believe that the nineteenth-century German university model of segregated academic disciplines has already been irrevocably undermined. Cultural studies has taught me that cultural phenomena are linked. They cannot be comprehended in isolation, and therefore they must not be analyzed this way. Scholars need to cast their nets widely in trying to describe the links among them. Media philosopher Marshall McLuhan revealed a similar understanding of culture when he argued that the use of radio to broadcast the human voice was bound to produce "new shapes for human experience" (1964: 302). He perceived scholars' resistance to change, marveling at "the universal ignoring of the psychic action of technology" (304). McLuhan himself, of course, created curiosity about "the psychic action of technology," and media studies—necessarily interdisciplinary—now thrive in many universities of the "global village."[2]

In my view, an interdisciplinary model does not imply abandoning either the close study of literary texts or the tools that have been developed to understand how prose fiction works.[3] Rather, lessons from cultural studies call for exploring the way prose fiction responds not only to internal developments like the use of stream of consciousness or present-tense narration but also to various types of forces in the world in which literature, like other cultural products, is created and consumed. Therefore, a cultural studies approach to prose fiction works of the twentieth century requires special attention to how literature might be responding to secondary orality, a task not yet undertaken, I suspect, because of the propensities mentioned above to denigrate talk and to venerate (and thus isolate) literature. Bakhtin's campaign to categorize prose fiction as one of several "speech genres" (1986), Pratt's project to define literature as "speech act" (1977), and more recently, Fludernik's attempt to derive narratological categories from features of "spontaneous conversational storytelling" (1996) are three examples of previous literary investigations that have tried to overcome the traditional dichotomization of orality and textuality. I offer this study in a similar spirit, and yet I distinguish it from these through its cultural and historical specificity. Its major claims are not about speech or literature in general, but rather about a particular trend in contemporary prose fiction. I suggest that from the current vantage point of cultural studies, available maps of the twentieth-century novel (Realism-Modernism-Postmodernism; x-y-z) don't help us navigate well enough anymore through certain features of the cultural landscape. We have to frame different questions and then redraw the maps. To push my topographical metaphor one step further, I'm not suggesting that the continents have shifted but rather that there are mountain ranges and deserts, or, better still, roads through the mountains and deserts that people have been using but which we haven't charted yet. Identifying talk fiction may help us chart some of them.

During my first pedagogic journey through novelistic territory, I was waylaid and forced to notice that *If on a winter's night a traveler* addressed my student in a different fashion than that of other novels we had read in the course. That student did not feel addressed just in the sense of encountering a topic he found interesting. He felt addressed in the sense of being the interlocutor. He experienced "properly managed" writing as a conversation in which he had a personal stake: the novel was talking to him, and it was about him. His reaction and particularly his choice of the word "talk" prompted me to ask myself in what sense reading could be like conversation. The answer I eventually came up with after apprentic- ing in sociolinguistics is that in the case of certain texts, reading can be considered "talk as interaction."[4] By talk as interaction, I mean conversa- tion as a "turn-taking system." "Turns" or "moves," as understood by Erving Goffman and other sociolinguists, are not necessarily verbal but rather are characterized by their expression of *orientation to exchange*. Specifically, Goffman thinks of the first move, the "statement," as reveal- ing "orientation to some sort of answering to follow." The second move, or "reply," is characterized by "its being seen as an answering of some kind to a preceding matter that has been raised" (1981: 24). Along these lines, in many cultures, clapping one's hands together functions as "re- ply" (applause) to the presentation of an entire story or play as "state- ment." Similarly, gesturing to one's bare wrist with a quizzical look on one's face functions equivalently to uttering the words "Do you have the time?" And the shaking of one's head side to side replies as effectively to the issue that has been raised as the verbal response "No."

Using a framework of talk as interaction to reconsider twentieth- century prose fiction, I seek texts I can classify as "statements," in Goff- man's sense of oriented to an answering. What I mean here by the text as statement, as the first part of the conversation, are texts that in toto or in part ask for their readers to react to them in certain ways. Such texts do not suppress "telling" to promote "showing," to use the terms given wide currency by Henry James and his collaborator Percy Lubbock that sub- stantially influenced the way we drew our first maps of twentieth-century prose fiction; rather, they reveal their "addressivity," as Bakhtin puts it. When such texts are read by flesh-and-blood readers like my student or myself, who find themselves feeling something, something like being the audience for this text, something like wanting to display the "orienta- tion" the text seems to be asking for, readers can be said to be respond- ing, or "replying" in Goffman's sense. In the type of analysis I propose, to do something (feel something, think something) *and* to identify that something as an appropriate reply to the text-as-statement, constitute reading as interaction, or as Talk (with a capital T to mark this sense of the word). It could be argued that all texts, literary and nonliterary, reveal their addressivity by virtue of being written down, and that all reading involves having a response. But, in the spirit of cultural studies, my concept of Talk is only intended to apply within an historical context in which to write and read literature self-consciously as communication that aims for effects in the real world must be viewed as going against the grain, as going against the hegemony of a twentieth-century aestheticist view of literature as art for art's sake.

Reading prose fiction as a turn-taking system like conversation helps me notice texts from numerous moments and places that haven't received much attention to date and to perceive roads between these texts and some others that are more well known. The contribution of this study is to connect such texts to each other not so much through content or national tradition or literary movement or style or narrative technique, as through the type of orientation to exchange they exemplify, as through the type of interaction they create between themselves and their readers, as through the type of response they seek outside the writing and reading transaction. Focusing on prose fiction as Talk allows me to ask what cultural work such interaction does in our secondary oral age. My various answers to this question allow me not only to group certain texts among those I have identified as talk fiction that seem to do similar work but also to relate these groupings to extraliterary cultural developments.

I think of these groupings as modes of Talking. The modes I will discuss in this book are "storytelling," "testimony," "apostrophe," and "interactivity." In accordance with a view of secondary orality as a widespread phenomenon, I assume there must be other modes that can be identified by experts with cultural knowledge different from my own. For now, I will present my four modes in an order that foregrounds my defining criterion of interaction. That is to say, I examine these modes along an axis of increasing exchange; each subsequent mode demands greater effort on the part of the reader to recognize the call of the text to interaction or to carry out the interaction itself.

My study unfolds in five chapters. In the first chapter, I define my concept of talk fiction by exploring the general notion of talk as interaction and by developing more fully the restricted notions of "statement," "reply," and "Talk" introduced briefly above. I review current

conceptions of secondary orality and suggest how they help us understand the communicative hybridity of our age. I look at talk radio and the
television talk show to illustrate mediated interaction, a structural characteristic these genres share with talk fiction.

Each of the next four chapters takes up one of my talk fiction modes;
each strives to illuminate the nature of "orientation to exchange" in
that mode by discussing the historical or cultural circumstances to which
it responds and by closely reading several literary texts. In chapter 2,
"Storytelling: Talk as Sustenance," I propose that some late-twentieth-
century novels address their readers as if they were not only auditors but
also as if those reader-listeners were committed to sustaining the relationships extended to them by the narrators. I use the term "storytelling"
to signal the connection of these texts to the oral exchange of stories
whose intimacy and immediacy they try to reproduce in their own fashion. While my suspicion is that every culture in the twentieth century
registers the shifting relationship between orality and textuality, I have
chosen my examples from two cultures that particularly employ talk for
passing on cultural and historical knowledge that sustains community:
the Modern Greek and the African American. This preoccupation with
oral communication is apparent in late-twentieth-century texts like
Kóstas Tachtsís's *The Third Wedding Wreath* and Gloria Naylor's *Mama
Day* through the relationship each establishes with the reader, an engaged listener who will in turn become a teller. I foreground these
relationships with reference to nineteenth-century texts like Dimítris
Vikélas's *Lukís Láras* and Harriet Wilson's *Our Nig*, where the narratorial
clamor for response exposed a belief that creating a relationship between
text and reader was even literally a matter of life and death. Our associations with storytelling as a primary form of human interaction and the
vital—in the sense of both basic and life-sustaining—demand on the
reader to "listen" suggest to me that the storytelling mode should be
considered first.

In chapter 3, "Testimony: Talk as Witnessing," I propose that novels
from a wide array of societies over the course of the century have tried to
respond to trauma inflicted through war, brutal regimes, and interpersonal violence by witnessing to these rampant acts of aggression. The
nature of trauma itself requires modifying notions of telling and listening to reflect that constructing a narrative about the trauma is a collab-

orative task between witness-victim and cowitness-enabler. Whereas in my storytelling mode, readers are called through direct address to listen (receive the story) with the proper attitude, Talking in my testimony mode is more difficult to decipher; readers must first recognize the text as a call to testify, and then they must interpret the evidence in an act of cowitnessing that creates the story of the trauma for the first time. Testimony to the presence of trauma can take the form of mimetic textual performance of traumatic symptoms (for instance, repetition, elision, absence of inside views within the narrative) or of the "telling" itself (for instance, uncompleted, unpublished, or misunderstood texts whose lack of success is subsequently interpreted—witnessed to—as testimony to trauma). Specifically, I offer a schema of "circuits of witnessing" that accounts for testimony at the levels of the story, the discourse, and the production and reception of the text. I briefly illustrate these circuits with a wide range of familiar twentieth-century texts (from Woolf's *Mrs. Dalloway* to Camus's *The Fall* to Atwood's *The Handmaid's Tale*), and then offer a more sustained treatment of one less well known novel, Gertrud Kolmar's *A Jewish Mother*, to show how the various circuits interrelate to produce Talk between text and contemporary reader.

My fourth chapter, "Apostrophe: Talk as Performance," borrows from the rhetorical figure for turning away from one's normal audience to address someone or something who by reason of absence, death, inanimateness, and/or mere convention cannot answer back. Though apostrophe has been extensively discussed in the context of oratory and lyric, no one has remarked its systematic use in some recent narrative fiction, where a first-person narrator (inscribed or effaced) tells a story primarily through address to a *you*, who does not reply. Apostrophe is a particularly apt metaphor to describe a type of talk fiction, since the content of the message being delivered is rarely as important as the relationships created by the complicated enunciative situation. Structures of address are mobilized not to promote a verbal reply by the specified addressee (who, besides, may be incapable of speaking) but rather to promote an emotional response in actual readers. Whereas identifying the text as "statement" in the testimony mode provides a hermeneutic challenge to readers, in the apostrophic mode, readers face the perhaps even more difficult task of recognizing the address as double, as simultaneously for and not for them. They can choose to step into the role of the addressee, while recognizing that they are performing a script written for someone else. I describe actual and inscribed reader responses to the apostrophic *you*'s in Jane Rule's *This Is Not for You*, Michel Butor's *Change of Heart*, Günter Grass's novella, *Cat and Mouse*, Julio Cortázar's "Graffiti," and John Barth's "Life-Story." I conclude by returning to the text that launched my search for talk fiction: Italo Calvino's *If on a winter's night a traveler*. My readings illustrate how apostrophe—address that is not quite address—delivers another kind of message, a message about various blocks to intimacy in postmodern societies and how to redress them.

In chapter 5, "Interactivity: Talk as Collaboration," I sketch out what appears to be the endgame of talk fiction. Late-twentieth-century innovations in communication technologies have spawned an era of interactive storytelling. Technology facilitates the orientation to exchange that I have been tracing in prose fiction in the twentieth century, leading to even greater activity on the part of readers. If we think of the role of the reader in the apostrophic mode as scripted and performed, in the interactive mode, the scripting itself requires the activity of both participants to the Talk, the traditionally named "writer" and "reader." I begin this chapter with a brief analysis of Julio Cortázar's pioneering novel *Hopscotch*, in which readers are invited to create their own text by assembling the chapters in one of two orders. Of course, to invite reading in an order other than the conventional start to finish is to open the door to reading in any sequence whatsoever, and thus *Hopscotch* can be considered the forerunner to cyberstories that are "told" only when the "reader" selects and orders—and even writes. I conclude with a consideration of computer hypertexts and interactive video—modalities through which the very concepts of book, writer, and reader begin to vanish, as does therefore my concept of talk fiction.

Like authors of most cultural study projects, I make large claims about the phenomena I'm considering. I attempt to support those claims by reading a particularly broad range of texts in complexly developed contexts. My choice of specific novels and stories was guided above all by selecting those that most clearly illustrate the mode I describe in each chapter. But I also purposely selected examples that might be less familiar to some readers, hoping to support my thesis that the talk phenomenon is a widespread one. My corpus prompts two provisos, one practical and one more substantial. As for the practical, wherever possible I have used published translations of non-English texts to facilitate my audience's independent evaluations of my readings. Still, there are occasions when such translations do not follow the original text closely enough to illustrate my point, in which case I have included both the original language and my own translation of it. As for the more substantial issue related to my corpus, as varied the literary traditions from which I have selected, my examples are limited by my own primarily Western training. I hope that scholars will seek Talk in prose fiction from cultures not represented in this study, and I will welcome any additional modes or modifications they may propose.

Prefaces often mention the origins of the study at hand, and this one has been no exception. But in sharing my encounter with the undergraduate who "talked" with Calvino, I have admitted only the most explicit prod to developing the concept of talk fiction. I want to conclude by briefly mentioning a more personal source of my study, because I believe it provides some insight into my fascination with orality and textuality and into what has come to feel like an obsession with certain types of literary texts.

I have always wondered why my family members tell stories the way they do. Even as a youngster, I noticed how each of us tends to connect many things with the telling of an anecdote, quotidian or extraordinary. No one in my family tells a short story. We never go directly to the event but rather set the scene with detailed explanations of the people involved and how we know them. If one of us wants to relate a feeling or an idea, we always seem to embed it in a story: how I came to have that feeling or idea. While I, as much as any other member of my family, engage in this behavior (for instance, I knew I would open this preface by telling the story of how I came to the idea of talk fiction), I also find myself somewhat embarrassed by it.

At the time I began investigating the dynamics of orality and literacy, I believed I was following a strictly intellectual concern. Yet it wasn't long before I realized the extent to which this search addressed my dilemma about family speech style. I recall the sense of relief I felt after reading Deborah Tannen's comparative analyses of Athenian Greek and Californian American women's reactions to the same silent film (1980, 1982a).

Although my own parents were raised in rural Greece and I in suburban New York, the participants in Tannen's study matched closely enough to intrigue me, indeed closely enough for me to identify with all of them.

In evaluating their responses to the question What happened in the movie? Tannen remarks several sets of differences that organize along cultural lines. Whereas Americans discussed the film as a film, recounting details, reconstructing the temporal sequence, and using technical cinematic terms to do this, the Greeks tended to offer explanations of the events and characters in the film, omitting the movie frame and details that didn't contribute to their philosophizing. Americans focused on *message content* to display their analytic skills to the interviewer, while the Greeks used *personal interaction* to display their storytelling skills. Even though everyone gave their answers orally to an interviewer, Tannen suggests that the Americans were deploying "literate" strategies they had learned at school and that they associated with an interview situation, whereas the Greeks deployed "oral" strategies they had learned at home and that they associated with interpersonal communication. (Tannen and others connect focus on "message" with literate culture and focus on "relationship" with oral.) Tannen concludes that "insofar as any verbal performance is an exercise in presentation-of-self, it seems that the Americans were concerned with presenting themselves as sophisticated movie viewers and able recallers, while the Greeks were concerned with presenting themselves as acute judges of human behavior and good storytellers" (1980: 55). While I find these markers of oral and literate strategies ultimately too simplistic, Tannen's work helped me understand how, as a member of both cultures, I was judging my family's storytelling strategies by American criteria I had learned outside the home. And yet when it came to conversing, like the Greek women in Tannen's study, I would tell stories in the style of my relatives.

The Greek civilization, of course, has known writing for millennia. Nevertheless, because of historical circumstances, like the centuries-long Ottoman occupation (with its repression of Greek schools), to name the most prominent one, oral strategies have played a large role in shaping and preserving the culture of modern Greece. As I educated myself about debates over the nature of orality and literacy generally, I began to notice that features cited to explain the presumed poor quality of Modern Greek prose fiction are characteristics associated with oral storytelling, for example, episodic structure (Tziovas 1989).[5] I was in-spired to search for oral elements in Greek prose, not to compare it against more "literate" traditions and pronounce it inferior, but rather to characterize more precisely its unique qualities as a written genre de-veloping in a culture with high "residual orality," as Walter Ong has it (1982: 68–69). While the exact results of that investigation have been published elsewhere and are not directly relevant here (Kacandes 1990, 1992), I mention this previous direction of my research because my love of Greek prose with its "oral residue" led me to frame the broader ques-tion behind this book about the *hybridity* of prose fiction written in other (all?) cultures of our secondary oral age. I found myself shifting from a more mechanical evaluation of "literate" and "oral" qualities of a par-ticular novel to an investigation of the cultural values it expresses and the cultural work it does. As a result, I began to see textual strategies that seemed to recruit readers into relationship, into forms of interaction with works of prose fiction that potentially had consequences beyond the actual reading experience. I began to think of the secondary oral cultures in which these texts were produced not primarily as cultures where the spoken word can be heard anywhere, any time, but as ones in which the main characteristic of speech—that it brings participants into relation-ship—becomes privileged in almost all forums of life. This is why Talk became the organizing principle of my study. Talk fiction fills the same function as speech: it creates relationships and elicits interaction.

I think of this book as a celebration of talk in all its senses. Like Tannen's Greek interview subjects, I am aiming to tell a good story. And I look forward to you talking back.

Acknowledgments

This is a book about writing and reading as interaction, something without which this book never could have been written. It is also a book about stories, and since I tell quite a few anecdotes in the main text, I will try to restrict the length of the ones I tell here. I have been fortunate to teach a large number of very smart students at Harvard University, the University of Texas at Austin, and Dartmouth College; their reading agendas have concretely contributed to what I read and how I think about literature. I particularly want to single out the students in Donald Fanger's "Comedy and the Novel" course and Susan R. Suleiman's "Author, Text, Reader" seminar at Harvard, where the specific seeds for this study were planted in me as a graduate teaching fellow; and the students in my Comparative Literature 39 class, "Trauma and Prose Fiction," at Dartmouth, where I rehearsed the model of narrative witnessing that informs chapter 3.

Developing the skills to write this book has taken many years. I want to thank Dorrit Cohn for teaching me how to read closely and Susan R. Suleiman for modeling how to risk who one is and enjoy it. Madeline Maxwell, Jürgen Streeck, and the late Robert Hopper of the College of Communication at the University of Texas at Austin generously invited me to join the Monday afternoon viewing group, where they introduced me to the tools of conversation analysis and inspired me to consider the insights of sociolinguistics in the context of literature. For first suggesting I read the work of Walter Ong, I am indebted to Margaret Alexiou; and for stimulating conversations on orality and literacy I thank Dina and Joel Sherzer. The Society for the Study of Narrative Literature has been a hospitable place to learn more about narratology and to try out ideas: Jim Phelan, Peter Rabinowitz, and Gerry Prince need to be singled out for their helpful feedback on this project. For culturally specific explorations of what is at stake in "talk," I thank my father John G. Kacandes and my friend Michael Hanchard. My first introduction to the Modern Greek texts I analyze in chapter 2 came through the erudite and kind late George P. Savidis; my mother Lucie N. Kacandes helped me

xxi

puzzle through the meaning of several critical Greek phrases. My journey into cyberspace would not have been possible without the guidance of my computer-savvy friends, David Bush, Alfred Dupraz, and Marc Comina. My thanks, too, to Sebastian for demonstrating the use of a joystick and for answering all my questions and to Keith for patiently explaining the thrill he finds in *Unreal*.

Concrete aid for writing this book came from Dartmouth College, most especially in the forms of a Burke Research Award and a Junior Faculty Fellowship. Research help from Lauryn Zipse, Laura Montague, Linda Williams, Susan Stiles, and Audrey Choi greatly enriched the historical dimension of the project. My thanks to Gail Vernazza for technical help. Invitations to lecture from the Modern Greek Study Group of the Center for Literary and Cultural Studies and the Department of Comparative Literature at Harvard University, the Public Lecture Series at Davidson College, the Department of German Studies at Indiana University, the Women's Studies Research Seminar at the University of Texas at Austin, and the Humanities Forum at Dartmouth College propelled this project forward at critical stages. Series editor David Herman and humanities editor Virginia Wright-Peterson showed an early enthusiasm for the project that has made my interaction with University of Nebraska Press enjoyable and productive from beginning to end.

I would like to thank Michael Rubiner for his kind permission to reprint a portion of "T. S. Eliot Interactive," which originally appeared in the *New York Times Magazine* (18 June 1995). I would also like to thank the editors and anonymous readers who helped me work through earlier versions of some of the arguments made in this book. The commitment to text-reader interaction in Modern Greek novels discussed in chapter 2 was originally rehearsed in "Orality, Reader Address, and Anonymous 'You.' On Translating Second Person References from Modern Greek Prose" (*Journal of Modern Greek Studies* 8, no. 2 [1990]: 223–43) and in "The Oral Tradition and Modern Greek Literature" (*Laografía: A Newsletter of the International Greek Folklore Society* 9, no. 5 [1992]: 3–8). A shorter reading of Kolmar's novel than that which appears in chapter 3 was published in "Narrative Witnessing as Memory Work: Reading Gertrud Kolmar's *A Jewish Mother*" (*Acts of Memory*, ed. Mieke Bal, Jonathan Crewe, and Leo Spitzer [Hanover, 1999], 55–71). The ideas of "literary performative" and "narrative apostrophe" that are discussed in chapter 4 were first floated in "Are You in the Text? The 'Literary Performative' in Postmodernist Fiction" (*Text and Performance Quarterly* 13 [1993]: 139–53) and "Narrative Apostrophe: Reading, Rhetoric, Resistance in Michel Butor's *La Modification* and Julio Cortázar's 'Graffiti'" (*Style* 28, no. 3 [1994]: 329–49).

As I hope to convince you in the chapters ahead, some of us cannot write without readers who are very much present to us; I could not have written this book without those friends and colleagues who were willing to be interlocutors for me: Kit Belgum, Susan Brison, Scott Denham, Mary Desjardins, Gerd Gemünden, Mary Jean Green, Linda Haverty-Rugg, Lynn Higgins, Alexis Jetter, Monika Kallan, Amy Lawrence, Jennifer Levin, Agnes Lugo-Ortiz, Diane Miliotes, Adam Newton, Annelise Orleck, Graziella Parati, Jonathan Petropoulos, Ivy Schweitzer, Leo Spitzer, Andrea Tarnowski, Tom Trezise, Janet Whatley, and Mark Williams. Robyn Warhol and Mary Lou Kete, the members of my writing group in Burlington, and Lisa Moore, Marianne Hirsch, and Susanne Zantop read my drafts with a level of attention that even Pulitzer Prize winners would be lucky to get; this book is simply better written and more interesting because of their input. The flaws that remain can be no fault of theirs.

The emotional support that allowed me to complete this project came from many of the people acknowledged above, but most especially from Nora Pirquet, my church family, my nuclear family, and from the *famille suisse* into which I married. John, Lucie, Maria, Steve, Tina, Georgia, Tom, Regina, and Peter, et Mireille, Alfred, Marie-Claude, Christine, et Anne-Marie, your tasty meals, encouraging conversations, and simple faith that I had something interesting to say kept me going at times I truly would have preferred to stop. Half and Susanne Zantop encouraged me in this and other endeavors with the pride of parents and the confidence of best friends. They would have enjoyed celebrating the appearance of this book. Finally, I thank Philippe Carrard, whose good ideas inform every aspect of this project, and whose wit and love sustained me in ways that cannot be adequately described here.

TALK FICTION

1

SECONDARY ORALITY
Talk as Interaction

It is in talk alone that we can learn our period and ourselves. In short, the first duty of a man [*sic*] is to speak; that is his chief business in this world; and talk, which is the harmonious speech of two or more, is by far the most accessible of pleasures. It costs nothing in money; it completes our education, founds and fosters our friendships, and can be enjoyed at any age and in almost any state of health.—ROBERT LOUIS STEVENSON, "Talk and Talkers"

The premise of this book is that literature, like other institutions, shapes and is shaped by shifting forms of communication. The major shift of the just completed twentieth century has been identified colloquially as the "talk explosion" and professionally as "secondary orality." In my view, the most important consequence of this oral resurgence has been an as yet unfully recognized privileging of the interactive component of communication. In the preface I proposed "talk fiction" as a label for works of twentieth-century narrative literature that promote a sense of relationship and exchange in readers that we normally associate with face-to-face interaction. I connect "orientation to exchange" in these texts to sociolinguistic definitions of conversation as a "turn-taking system" to bolster my contention that some literature, in this sense, anyway, truly does talk. I use the word "fiction" in my titular concept denotatively to signal the restriction of my study to prose fiction, but also connotatively to evoke the useful pretenses, the "fictions," on which the broader idea of secondary orality and the narrower idea of talk fiction rely. On the surface of it, my modes of talk fiction, "storytelling," "testimony," "apostrophe," and "interactivity," sound like four quite distinct phenomena. In this chapter I follow the thread of "talk as interaction" that ties these modes together by (a) creating a context for and fleshing out the sociolinguistic definition of talk introduced in the preface; (b) identifying the place of interaction in notions of secondary orality; (c) illustrating talk as interaction in familiar secondary oral genres, namely, in talk radio and the television talk show; and (d) demonstrating what "talk as interaction," my Talk, can mean in prose fiction.

"Talk"

Baby talk, grown-up talk, girl talk, self-talk, street talk, small talk, shop talk, black talk, straight talk, double-talk, hot talk, bad talk, cheap talk, talk about town, talk of the party, talking-to, talking back, talking up, talking down, talking out, talking over, talking big, talking dirty, talking sense, talking turkey, talking garbage, talking shit, talking story, talking cure, talking book, talking head, talk radio, talk show, alltalk, confrontalk, talk EXPLOSION. Talk, talk, talk. We use the word all the time, but what does it mean?

For the purposes of this study, I follow Robert Louis Stevenson and others in understanding the term "talk" as referring first to the ubiquitous situation of the mundane exchange of words between two or more people. In summoning this model, I foreground the interactional element of language, as well as its immediacy, its topicality, and its reciprocity. Further, I aim to align myself with those scholars who believe that conversation is the foundation for other forms of communication and that "the same dialogic principle governs relations within and among *written* words as within and among spoken utterances" (Holquist 1985: 83).[1]

An interactional conception of language developed over many routes, through and between disciplines such as psychology, philosophy, anthropology, sociology, and certain lines of inquiry within linguistics. My study relies most explicitly on a tradition that can be plotted from Harold Garfinkel, Dell Hymes, and Erving Goffman to Harvey Sacks, Emanuel Schegloff, and Gail Jefferson. Sociologist Garfinkel developed an intellectual approach known by the awkward but descriptive name "ethnomethodology," and was committed to understanding daily life "from within" actual social settings. He believed that past and present interactions, not the words of language, lie at the heart of communicating (1967). Hymes is associated with a hybrid of anthropology and sociology often referred to as the "ethnography of speaking." Among other things, he proposed the development of a field called "comparative speaking," along the lines of comparative religion or comparative zoology (see Hymes 1962, 1974a, 1974b; Bauman and Scherzer 1974; Tedlock 1983; Sherzer 1992). Goffman, of course, was the premier investigator of "face-to-face interaction"; he made apparent the unspoken rules of common-place behavior.[2] Sacks and Schegloff (Goffman's students), along with Gail Jefferson, founded "conversation analysis," a discipline in which transcripts from unstaged, unscripted conversations can be analyzed at the most minute level to determine how verbal interaction proceeds in specific contexts.[3] All these approaches reject the materials of traditional linguistic analysis, artificial data like the statement "the cat is on the mat."[4] They listen instead to the word spoken in situ. Data are gathered mainly from interpersonal encounters unelicited by researchers and are analyzed for the interconnection of mundane conversation, social structure, and culture. Why? Because, as ethnographer Moerman puts it, in a formulation with which many practitioners of these disciplines would probably be comfortable, "language itself is mute. Anyone interested in how a view of the world is shared, recognized, maintained, or socialized within a community must attend to language made public and socially compelling, must attend to talk" (1988: 103).

By attending to talk, these sociolinguists shifted notions of conversation toward the interactional. Three aspects of this shift particularly inform my project: the building blocks of talk are not words or sentences but rather "turns" or "moves"; the roles of speaker and listener are conceived as equally integral "participants"; and the activity itself is defined not so much by what gets produced (the content of the speech) as by participants' perceptions of what is going on.

Baldly, participants take turns. A more elegant definition of talk in the idiom of conversation analysis characteristically emphasizes interaction and reciprocity: "Talk is designed to reflect back on prior turns and project ahead to future ones, and we interpret talk as if it is tied in some way to prior and future turns" (Nofsinger 1991: 3). The basic principles of turn organization were first outlined by Sacks, Schegloff, and Jefferson in their foundational 1974 article, "A Simplest Systematics for the Organization of Turn-Taking for Conversation." Specifically, conversation analysts define "ordinary," "natural," or "spontaneous" conversation as "instances of speech exchange organization with variable turn order, turn size, and turn content peculiar to a given occasion and the participants involved" (West and Zimmerman 1982: 515). Sacks and Schegloff further proposed the useful concept of "adjacency pair," observing that "a current action (a 'first pair part' such as a greeting or a question) requires the production of a reciprocal action (or 'second pair part') at the first possible opportunity after the completion of the first" (as summarized in Goodwin and Heritage 1990: 287). That the absence of a second pair part will be noticed confirms that it is expected. Conversation analysis posits that adjacency pair organization is "an elementary framework through which conversational participants will inevitably display some analysis of one another's actions" (Goodwin and Heritage 288). From this perspective, a first turn is always produced not only with the traditionally named "receiver" in mind but also with the idea that the receiver will quickly take a turn as "speaker." Sacks's terms "participant" and "party" facilitate a reconceptualization of the roles of "speaker-sender" and "listener-receiver," particularly with regard to "independence" and "activity." In the view of conversation analysts, speakers are not sovereigns imposing what they have to say on passive listeners. Rather, "hearers are active participants in the process of building a turn at talk, and their action, or nonaction, can lead to substantial modifications in the sentence the speaker is in the process of producing" (Goodwin and Heritage 293).

Goffman derives concordant notions of talk through the Wittgensteinian concept of "games."[5] The components of these games are "moves" that "may sometimes coincide with a sentence and sometimes with a turn's talk but need do neither" (Goffman 1981: 24). That is to say, for Goffman, talk is not completely dependent on words. He departs, further than conversation analysis originally did, from the standard linguistic notions of questions and answers, statements and replies, even away from exclusively verbal utterances. He appropriates from linguistics the terms "statement" and "reply," only to redefine them for his own purposes. Goffman defines "statement" as "a move characterized by an orientation to some sort of answering to follow" and "reply" as "a move characterized by its being seen as an answering of some kind to a preceding matter that has been raised" (24). These definitions, like those cited above, identify talk by its characteristic of mutual focus, that is, by its participants' orientation toward exchange, or to put it yet another way, by its participants' perception that they are interacting with each other. For my work, Goffman's understanding of the attitude of participants is critical: a reply is constituted not by "being" an answering, but by "being seen" by participants as an answering. As with Sacks and Schegloff's notion of the adjacency pair, a second pair part may never actually materialize, but that would not change the fact that a statement in Goffman's sense displays orientation to an anticipated response.

Goffman repeatedly and humorously illustrates that nonlinguistic acts are often more appropriate replies to statements than are verbal utterances: we would be baffled by someone responding "yes" to the query "Do you have the time?" and then walking away. Similarly, around the table we are more likely to expect to receive the salt than to be told "yes, I can pass it" and to receive nothing. An oral response to "On your mark, get set, go" or "The test begins now" would be self-defeating (Goffman 36–40; see also Goodwin and Heritage 298). In all these examples, a combination of verbal and nonverbal actions or nonverbal actions alone can function effectively as second pair parts; the actions of giving the time (by looking at one's watch and then verbally announcing it, by showing one's wristwatch, or by gesturing to the lack of one), passing the salt, or starting the race or test reveal the respondents' thorough orientation toward the "matter that has been raised" by the speaker.

Although sociolinguists often use the terms "talk" and "conversation" interchangeably, I have chosen the term "talk" for my central concept to avoid the more strictly verbal connotations of the word "conversation" and to foreground the idea that interaction matters. In this I follow Goffman's hypothesis that "What is basic to natural talk might not be a conversational unit at all, but an interactional one" (48). The interactional unit may contain any number of smaller elements (even "turns" in the conversation analytic sense), but the length of the interactional unit will depend on appropriate orientation to the matter that has been raised, not on an abstract unit of speech such as the sentence nor on change of speaker. Goffman's illustration of this point is particularly relevant for my study. In the case of oral storytelling, as in the performance of a play, he suggests, the "answering" will take the form of appreciation "not for the last sentence uttered but rather for the whole story and its telling" (42).[6] This example points to one more feature of Goffman's model that informs my own project to view some literature as

Talk. The participants in talk should not be thought of as "speaker" and "respondent," "unless we keep in mind that they refer not to individuals as such, but to enacted capacities" (Goffman 46). In the cases just raised of oral storytelling or the theater, the enacted capacity of "speaker" may be one or more persons relating the story or performing the play.[7] The complementary enacted capacity of "respondent" may be a single listener or a group of varying size orienting to the "statement" (story, play) as an audience. The instance of self-talk further illustrates the utility of this more capacious conception of participants since both roles of "speaker" and "respondent" are enacted, but a sole individual makes all the moves (Goffman 80).

These definitions and examples have brought me far from my baseline of talk as the mundane conversational exchange of words between two or more people. However, exchange—more precisely now, orientation to exchange—remains central. I appear to have set myself up to make the argument that the interactional unit of talk fiction would be the production (writing) and consumption (reading) of the literary text. I do mean this, though this applies to all fiction, indeed to all writing. I want to define talk fiction as something much more narrow. Goffman and conversation analysts have expended much effort in specifying the modifications from spontaneous conversation for other kinds of speech-exchange systems, such as visits to the doctor, telephone calls, or television news interviews.[8] I undertake my project to specify how orientation to exchange is expressed in some twentieth-century narrative literature in a similar spirit. But before I proceed with describing talk fiction as a turn-taking system within a specific historical and cultural context, I need to pose a question about that context: Why is an understanding of talk as interaction like that just laid out so alien to our culture that we need specialists to propose and explain it? The answer lies in two issues that go hand in hand, those of medium and communicative era.

Spoken-Written Wor(l)ds, aka The Age of Secondary Orality

So far, I have used "secondary orality" as a descriptive term for an age—our age—of technological innovation that enables the spoken word to reemerge as the dominant form of communication. To be sure, oral speech has always been the dominant method of communicating in terms of numbers of minutes per day in which it is used by numbers of people. But the term "secondary orality" is meant to reference (among other things) the proliferation of modes for the conduct of oral speech, as well as the displacement through those modes of written or printed communication, for instance the diminution of personal letter writing through use of the telephone.[9]

To expand this parsing of the term: secondary orality derives from diachronic approaches to the study of human communication, in which societies are assumed to progress from an exclusively oral mode of communication ("primary oral") to one based on writing (and therefore "literate," "textual," or "chirographic"). A subsequent oral age, which privileges speech, serves as an addendum to this model. Simply put, we hear more speech during our waking hours than our parents, grandparents, and great-grandparents presumably did. But how does this inundation of speech affect us? To what extent is the "word" a whole "world"? Assuming that the medium of communication does shape the mentality of those using it over time, what mentalities result from our hybrid ways of communicating? To rephrase my question from above, if we are "oral" once again and interaction is such a basic component of oral communication, why is an understanding of talk as interaction not obvious to us?

The short answer to this last question is that we are not "oral" once again, we are "secondary oral" for the first time, only very recently having "woken up to the presence of orality as a contemporary fact in our midst" (Havelock 1986: 118). Within a diachronic oral-literate schema, the designation "secondary" refers not only to its chronological sense of coming after something else (that is, secondary orality comes after a primary oral and a literate stage) but also to the idea of being "auxiliary" or "subordinate." That is to say, secondary orality could not come into being without the written word, both because the technologies that facilitate the resurgence of the spoken word rely on written language for development and some levels of operation, and also because the changes in mentality associated with literacy—for example, individualism, self-consciousness, and a sense of communication as transfer of information—endure in this communicative age.[10] On this score, the expression "secondary orality" is opaque, only indirectly signaling the *literate* components of the phenomenon. Intentionally or unintentionally ignoring the dependency of secondary orality on literacy and the literate mentalities that continue to shape contemporary societies constitutes what I styled in the opening of this chapter a certain "fiction." Though inelegant, my phrase "spoken-written" may be more descriptive for our age.

To get one step closer to the effects of the related technology and talk explosions, I want to briefly consider the ideas of Wallace Chafe, who, though not particularly interested in the diachronic schema introduced above, does illuminate the differences medium can make. Chafe launches his analysis from the observation that the dependence of speaking on sound and of writing on sight has a variety of consequences (1994:42).[11] One of the most striking is differences in tempo of production and reception of language: "while speaking and listening necessarily proceed together at the same speed, writing and reading deviate from that spoken language baseline in opposite directions, writing being much slower and reading somewhat faster" (1982: 37; also 1994: 42–43). Chafe and others attribute the spontaneous quality of speech and the "worked over" quality of writing to these disparate tempi. Whereas ideas tend to develop as they are enunciated, writers typically revise sentences many times before they are read by someone else (Chafe 1994: 43).[12] Sound of any kind quickly fades away, and the unassisted human voice does not carry very far in space; writing, depending on the exact materials used, can be transported and can last, in some cases, even for millennia. Finally, in terms of medium, talk in its conversational form is not of a predetermined length. Breath is an immediately renewable resource, and as Chafe observes, speaking seems to be natural to human evolution. Writing and reading, on the other hand, must be laboriously learned and are highly dependent on resources external to the bodies of writers and readers (1994: 43–44).[13]

These physical facts—at least until the invention of the microphone and subsequently derived technologies for voice pick-up, a proviso to which I will return—bear upon interaction. Speakers and listeners share a common time and space, whereas writers and readers most often do not. Speakers and listeners can be said to collaboratively produce speech, in that speakers are not only aware of the identity of the audience but also of its developing reaction to the speech. Of course, in the case of written communication, too, writers must have an audience in mind (Ong 1982: 177). But there is typically a lack of immediate interchange between writer and reader, and therefore the reader presumably influences what is written less than the listener what is spoken. Although both speakers and writers may intend specific addressees, due to what Chafe calls the evanescence of speech and the transportability of writing (1994: 42), the speaker is less likely to have unknown hearers than the writer to have unknown readers. An awareness of consumption by unknown readers perhaps plays a larger role for writers in many situations than an awareness of unknown listeners for speakers. (Is this a source of the attraction of eavesdropping?) Since speakers and listeners share the same physical environment at the time the language is produced, that language itself generally has a closeness to the immediate physical and social situation, a characteristic Chafe terms "situatedness." Written language, on the other hand "is usually desituated, the environment and circumstances of its production and reception having minimal influence on the language and consciousness itself" (44–45).

At first glance, Chafe's characterizations make sense. But, as I have already felt compelled to interject, we recognize them only as long as we bracket technologies developed in the last century that have changed the speed of writing and the evanescence of speech. For example, while most people write by hand more slowly than they speak, contributing to the "worked over" quality of the text produced, many writers using keyboards join professional stenographers in achieving speeds of speech. Among my student speed-typists, there are some whose writing assignments read as less-thought-through than their verbal contributions in class sound, especially when they do not take advantage of electronic word processing's possibilities for easy revision. Similarly, assumed lack of shared space and time (and therefore of a communal sense) between writers and readers is challenged not only by (ancient) blackboards but more especially by electronic chatrooms that provide a "surface" for reciprocal writing for immediate consumption by an individual or a group. Conversely, microphones, loudspeakers, telephones, two-way radios, and tape recorders—to name just a few relevant technologies— allow for physical and/or chronological *separation* of speakers and listeners. Chafe's justification for excluding technology's effects from the descriptions he develops—that "the properties of spoken language must have reached their present stage long before the telephone was ever thought of" (44)—seems untenable when we consider how quickly and effectively technology helps develop new motor skills.[14] No contemporary culture is either purely oral or purely literate, and I agree with Dimitris Tziovas that the "relationship between orality and textuality is not one of rigid opposition, but rather one of intrication and enfolding" (1989: 321; see also Tannen 1982a: 3). To better familiarize ourselves with the "intrications" and "enfoldings" of our age, we can turn to Walter Ong, one of very few scholars to concern himself with the effects on the human mind of specific types of "technologizing of the word," most notably, of handwriting, printing press, *and* electronic word processing.[15]

To begin with, Ong explains how one sign of the current continuing grip of literacy is our obsession with "media." For, the very term "medium" reveals a sense of communication as "a pipeline transfer of units of material called 'information' from one place to another" (1982: 176). Our "willingness to live with the 'media' model shows chirographic conditioning." That is to say, literate cultures regard speech as "more specifically informational than do oral cultures, where speech is more performance-oriented, more of a way of doing something to someone" (177). Of course, Ong is not denying the effects of medium; rather, he is cautioning that the media model obscures what he considers most distinctive about (all) human communication: "the capacity of human beings to form true communities wherein person shares with person interiorly, intersubjectively" (177).

Ong's search for how this sharing occurs has led him to hypothesize about primary orality—something no literate can truly know—about literacy, and, most relevant to our purposes here, about secondary orality (his description of this last highlights its hybrid character). On the one hand, electronic word processing creates more written texts, reinforcing the mentalities of literacy, what Ong calls a commitment of the word to space, sequentiality, and closure (for example, 135–36). This literate understanding of the word contrasts with that of primary oral cultures, where the spoken word is "an event, a movement in time, completely lacking in the thing-like repose of the written or printed word" (75). On the other hand, the spoken word proliferates through technology; it becomes available to more people over larger amounts of space and longer periods of time. I quote at length Ong's analysis of the effects of hearing more talk:

Secondary orality is both remarkably like and remarkably unlike primary orality. Like primary orality, secondary orality has generated a strong group sense, for listening to spoken words forms hearers into a group, a true audience, just as reading written or printed texts turns individuals in on themselves. But secondary orality generates a sense for groups immeasurably larger than those of primary oral culture. . . . In our age of secondary orality, we are group-minded self-consciously and programmatically. . . . Unlike members of a primary oral culture, who are turned outward because they have had little occasion to turn inward, we are turned outward because we have turned inward. In a like vein, where primary orality promotes spontaneity because the analytic reflectiveness implemented by writing is unavailable, secondary orality promotes spontaneity because through analytic reflection we have decided that spontaneity is a good thing. We plan our happenings carefully to be sure that they are thoroughly spontaneous. (136–37)

In addition, then, to literacy's legacy of privileging information and the individual who "communicates" it, secondary oral cultures display features known to characterize primary oral cultures: a strong communal sense, desire for participation, and love of spontaneity. What distinguishes these features in a secondary oral culture from these features in a primary culture is a mental capability developed through literacy: self-consciousness.

I want to extend Ong's analysis by adding that the "self-consciousness" and "analytic reflection" to which he points can be sporadic and short-lived. That is to say, at least from the perspective of the early twenty-first century, what is most striking about the rise of secondary orality in the twentieth century is the propensity of individuals to "forget" the planning that went into making the happening "spontaneous," to cite Ong's oxymoron. To put it another way, the technology that brings us the spoken word becomes invisible to us. Or, to return to my earlier formulation, we forget the "secondary" in secondary orality, creating for ourselves a partial fiction that the happening "is" spontaneous or the interaction "the same as" face-to-face. Such "slippage" or "forgetting" is illustrated in the anecdote of my student's sense of "talking" with Calvino's *If on a winter's night a traveler* that I related in my preface. But in order to facilitate my analysis of the more specialized case of literary secondary oral genres, I want to turn next to the more familiar, if not necessarily apparent, case of radio and television talk shows. Though what follows can by no means be an overview of the history of broadcasting nor even of the specific form of the talk show, a pause over certain aspects of those histories reveals a bizarre combination and/or alternation of self-consciousness and naïveté about technology that I propose is characteristic of many secondary oral phenomena and that can serve as a helpful backdrop for the kind of reading procedures I am proposing in this book.

Talk Radio, Talk Show

Long before the development and proliferation of specific formats known as "talk radio" and the television "talk show," the earliest days of radio provide support for Ong's thesis that secondary orality generates relationships—or at least a sense of them. In articles with titles like "The Social Destiny of Radio" and "Radio Dreams That Can Come True," journalists in the 1920s marveled at the ability of radio to bring Americans together: "How fine is the texture of the web that radio is even now spinning! It is achieving the task of making us feel together, think together, live together." Another commentator saw radio "spreading mutual understanding to all sections of the country, unifying our thoughts, ideals, and purposes, making us a strong and well-knit people." The same writer supports his view by citing the hundreds of letters a day that Newark station wjz received in 1922 from "illiterate [*sic*] or broken people who are for the first time in touch with the world about them" (as quoted in Douglas 1987: 306). For some listeners, like the author of "It's Great to Be a Radio Maniac," the thrill of knowing he was "connected" to others in far-flung places outweighed the substance of the contact: "To me no sounds are sweeter than 'this is station soandso' " (as quoted in Douglas 1987: 307). This sense of being part of a group is the prominent feature distinguishing early radio from the prior development of the telephone.[16]

Early radio history also provides support for Ong's claim of self-consciousness about this new kind of interaction. In contemporary commentator McMeans's view (1923), radio listeners thought of themselves as an audience "totally different in several ways from anything before known" (as quoted in Douglas 1987: 312). One appreciative listener praised the fact that he could be part of a crowd and yet remain at home: "This vast company of listeners . . . do not sit packed closely, row on row, in stuffy discomfort endured for the delight of the music. The good wife and I sat there quietly and comfortably alone in the little back room of our own home that Sunday night and drank in the harmony coming three hundred miles to us through the air" (as quoted in Douglas 1987: 308). He and the wife consider themselves part of a "vast company" and yet they are happy to be "alone." Another early fan of radio celebrated listeners' "control" over speakers: "With radio we, the listeners, will have an advantage we have never had before. We do not even have to get up and leave the place. All we have to do is press a button, and the speaker is silenced."[17] I find the exact formulation revealing: again, the radio listener thinks of himself as part of a group, "we"; furthermore, he does not say that "we" stop listening but rather, "the speaker is silenced" —as if the fact that he longer hears it must mean (as in face-to-face interaction) that the speaker has stopped speaking.

Though Bruce Bliven might sound to us like an early technophobe, he was pinpointing already in 1924 one of the major differences between secondary and primary orality when he worried about the effect of this separation of listeners and speakers: "so much listening without seeing" had "upset one of nature's subtle biological balances" and had created "what might be called 'a hunger of the eyes' " (as quoted in Douglas 1987: 312). Others remarked the transformed relationships between the speakers and listeners from the producer's perspective: the lack of immediate feedback since speaker or performer could neither see responses on listeners' faces nor hear laughter, booing, silence, or applause. Absence of this kind of contact caused anxiety mixed with excitement about this "greatest audience ever assembled by any means for any purpose in the history of the world" (as quoted in Douglas 1987: 312).

I want to pause next over a quotation from media guru Marshall McLuhan, who in the 1960s awards radio a special place among early technology: "Even more than telephone or telegraph, radio is that extension of the central nervous system that is matched only by human speech itself. Is it not worthy of our meditation that radio should be specially attuned to that aboriginal mass medium, the vernacular tongue?" (1964: 302). Presumably, the radio can function synecdochically in interpersonal communication because both the radio and the human voice send sound via the airwaves. But what draws my attention most about this pronouncement is that in making the synecdoche, McLuhan obscures the differences between face-to-face interaction and communication mediated through technology, even as he celebrates the technological. For McLuhan, the radio is an *extension* of the central nervous system. He even seems to anthropomorphize radio by saying that it is *specially attuned* to the human tongue.

The specific formats known as talk radio and the television talk show best make apparent the hybridity of secondary orality hinted at in the examples above. In order to make my own argument about the parallel between some narrative fiction and broadcast media most clear, I will need to offer a fairly full description of the form. This is perhaps the appropriate point to acknowledge that my term "talk fiction," my excursion into talk radio and talk shows, and perhaps even my quoting of McLuhan will be a red flag for some of my readers.[18] I'm raising the specter of the talk show nevertheless to foreground the concept of secondary orality and to provoke consideration of the inevitable influence of media upon each other. Though I am uninterested in tracing any direct influence by the broadcast media on the production of specific literary works, I do aim to point out the common privileging of interaction over content in talk radio, talk shows, and talk fiction.[19] In this era when many children learn to view television at a much younger age than they learn to read, when televisions and radios are tuned in for more hours a day than most people are at work or school, how could the mass media not play a role in how we read and write? I intend not to undermine our appreciation of literature as a distinctive form of communication but rather to challenge the notion that it is somehow a sacrosanct one that responds only to internal formal developments.[20]

For those of us who grew up with radio and television, Goffman once again helps us perceive the specific functioning of the mundane. In his analysis of radio broadcasting, he identifies three main modes of "announcing," that is, "all routine talk into a microphone" (1981: 232). He names the first mode "action override," where the action in question is of primary concern to the audience, as in sportscasting, for example, and "the talk of the announcer is only a means to that end" (234).[21] His second category is "three-way announcing," where a host conducts a conversation with one or more persons in the studio and a studio audience and/or broadcast audience listen in (234). "Direct" radio, in which the announcer speaks to the individual listener at home as if in a tête-à-tête is his third category (235). With this last term, Goffman is referencing direct address in speech, an analogy that also applies to the moment in cinema and television when actors or announcers look directly into the camera. The television medium in particular has a propensity for direct address, which Sarah Kozloff suggests gives such a strong impression of interpersonal exchange that some viewers even answer back (1992: 81).[22] Robert C. Allen terms direct address television's "rhetorical mode," which in contrast to the "cinematic mode" does not pretend the viewer isn't there, but rather "simulates the face-to-face encounter by . . . acknowledging both the performer's role as addresser and the viewer's role as addressee [and attempting] to persuade the actual person watching at home that he or she is the 'you' to whom the addresser is speaking" (1992b: 117–18; see also Shattuc 1997: 73). In other words, this mode explicitly acknowledges the communicative circuit that underlies all uses of the media but remains implicit in many.

Though Goffman seems disinterested in the historical development of radio, it is worth noting that his latter two categories of announcing, "three-way" and "direct," qualify as what is now widely referred to as "talk radio" and not just "radio talk," the title of his study.[23] To describe the genre more fully, one needs to add the additional category of "call-in," shows or segments of shows in which a radio host engages in fresh talk with an individual over the phone—and on the air—in the context of an extended "conversation" with other callers and silent listeners. Many television talk-show formats combine a segment of Goffman's "three-way" announcing, with guests and hosts interacting and studio and home audiences only listening, and a subsequent segment of "call-in," where the studio audience reacts to the talk of the first segment and creates fresh talk based on the subject introduced. These may be linked by moments of direct address.[24]

Talk shows—I will use this term alone when I refer to both the radio and television formats—have enjoyed nothing short of a meteoric rise (and partial fall) in the last few decades in the United States. Radio talk shows became so popular, and therefore lucrative, that exclusive "all-talk stations" developed in the 1970s.[25] The talk format has made serious inroads into TV as well, beginning in the 1960s and expanding through the mid-1990s, when talk shows surpassed soap operas as the dominant daytime form and proliferated in late-night programming (Shattuc 1997: 1–9). Some hosts like Rush Limbaugh and Oprah Winfrey have become household names. Even sportscasts and newscasts, shows with content to transmit, have come to rely more and more on a conversational format to deliver their information.[26] Thus over the history of the radio and television media, which roughly overlaps with the period whose fiction I want to reevaluate, there is a fairly continuous expansion of—though by no means complete takeover by—forms that stage interaction between producer of speech and consumer of speech.

The particular structural feature of talk shows most relevant to talk fiction is what Goffman calls "the presence . . . of absent addressees" (321), an oxymoronic phrase worth pausing over. What makes the talk of broadcast different from ordinary conversation is the physical absence of its addressees. Goffman explains: "Because talk is learned, developed, and ordinarily practiced in connection with the visual and audible response of immediately present recipients, a radio announcer must inevitably talk *as if* responsive others were before his eyes and ears" (241). To bring this into dialogue with Goffman's conception of talk reviewed above, the talk of the radio host must display orientation to exchange with absent addressees. That is to say, what makes talk shows qualitatively different from broadcasting, say, music, today's price of internet stocks, or a movie, is that while music and so forth may be "sent" with the intention of being "received" by willing listeners/consumers, the talk of the talk show is itself *produced as address* to those absent receivers. To overstate the case with a phrase meant to echo McLuhan's most famous dictum: the interaction is the content. In television (and some radio) talk shows, there is typically a studio audience that is an audio and/or visual part of the spectacle, some of whose members become actual participants in the conversation. But these shows are produced not so much for these present addressees as for the exponentially more numerous absent addressees, the listener-viewers at home, in the car, at work, at the beach. These displaced listener-viewers are "present" to the speakers—they are in mind even when not directly addressed—as the talk is constructed. Though there may be a daily topic organizing the show, the main attraction seems to be this multi-tiered, multi-located conversation.[27] The idea that a talk show is about interaction rather than delivery of information is another feature that links it to primary orality. Ong refers to this as the "person-interactive context" of orality and suggests that the privileging of the interpersonal component over the informational ("object-attentive") context may cause irritation to literates by "making all too much of speech itself . . . overvaluing and certainly overpracticing rhetoric" (1982: 68). This privileging of interaction over content may partially account for the strong negative judgments talk shows elicit from social commentators who consider themselves the guardians of literacy.[28]

Radio talk shows, as even more obviously talk shows on television, "need real people" (Bogosian 1988: xv). There are real hosts, real talk-show guests, real callers, real people in the studio audience, real people in other locations listening. Yet talk shows also rely on "fiction"; they have what Murray Burton Levin calls a quality of "contrived authenticity" (1987: 19). It bears reminding ourselves here that when television hosts or guests appear to be looking directly at us, they are actually staring into the lens of a camera. Another fiction is immediacy; though it may seem spontaneous and simultaneous, the interaction between those "real people" who conduct radio or television talk is, in fact, highly mediated. Many (unheard, unseen) people and much machinery facilitate this conversation between speaker and receiver. The talk which is thereby disseminated is not even as "fresh" as it's meant to sound. To cite the most obvious example, almost all "live" radio talk shows have a multiple-second delay to allow the station to delete any obscenities beyond the accepted standards of the station, its sponsors, and financial backers (Bogosian xv). *Donahue* was aired live in many markets for years, but most television talk shows are taped several weeks before they are broadcast. Jane Shattuc points out that most shows do not actually write or even subsequently edit conversations, yet their spontaneous quality is nonetheless "highly regulated through the host's selections, prior coaching, and the general production process of camerawork, miking, and segmentation" (1997: 6; see also 73). Another type of fiction is that the "audience at home" is a part of the conversation *in the same way* that the hosts and guests or studio audience are part of it. A great deal of verbal juggling is required to keep up this conversational pretense, especially as hosts have to change footing repeatedly, switching from one-on-one with a caller, to address to the viewers at home, to exchange with a studio guest, and so on (see Goffman 1981: 235–37; Shattuc 73).[29]

With these "fictions" in mind, we can now return to the idea of the talk show as a hybrid communicative form. It contains face-to-face interaction: real people speak to one another; but the show effects and disseminates those conversations through technological mediation, self-consciousness, and pretense. Though he does not use the same framework, Wayne Munson concurs with this analysis, calling the talk-show format a bizarre combination of paradigms of the traditional and the modern worlds: "talk" and "show"; the format "links conversation, the interpersonal—the premodern oral tradition—with the mass-mediated spectacle born of modernity" (1993: 6). Even though media experts point out that we really do not (yet?) know very much about how radio and television get consumed (Shattuc 48), they still make pronouncements about what audiences experience. Eric Bogosian, author of the play and star of the movie *Talk Radio*, hypothesizes that the popularity of the talk shows depends on audiences' attraction to "realness." When a caller dials in to a radio talk show or when Oprah or Ricki Lake speaks with members of the studio audience, we, the nonparticipating but "present" audience, can ascertain with our own ears and/or eyes that those are humans talking to one another. Other folks want to listen to those people, according to Bogosian "because they might hear some small tidbit of genuine emotion" (xvii). Similarly, Shattuc suggests that the draw of television talk shows is "the ultimately uncontrollable: real people without scripts" (73). Audiences are not lured as much by a desire to understand social or personal problems (that is, content), Shattuc maintains, as by a desire to identify with the participants (that is, emotion, relationship) (95). Again, creating identification is set in motion by the talk hosts' awareness of the "presence of absent addressees"; as Goffman puts it, "the remote (and studio) audience is treated as if it were a ratified participant, albeit one that cannot [always] assume the speaking role" (234). It may be the attractiveness of being treated as a part of the conversation, in addition to the witnessing of real emotion mentioned by Bogosian, that first gave talk shows their large audiences.

Participation is key to the evolution of the genre. In the 1990s, talk shows (especially those occupying a late-night time slot) attracted their audiences not so much with the promise of "talk" as of "show": these audience members, according to Shattuc, are not as concerned about witnessing authenticity and real emotion as they are about "reveal[ing] the performance behind the notion of truth." They foreground much of the contrivance by themselves participating and putting on the most outrageous parts of this show (160–61). The partial "fall" of talk shows to which I alluded at the beginning of this section may in fact be related to mediation. For example, there has been negative publicity about manipulation of guests and audiences, what, drawing again on the framework introduced above, we might call an intentional obscuring on the part of producers of the mediated aspects of the "talk."[30] And yet, Shattuc's analysis reminds us that we should not make easy assumptions about who manipulates whom. In my own experience as a listener-viewer of talk shows I recognize that there are brief moments when I feel as if Dr. Laura is judging *my* behavior or Oprah is chiding *me* to pay attention because *I* really need to hear this part. More frequently, however, I am keenly aware that I am one of myriad other individuals listening and/or viewing, that most of what I hear and see is carefully calculated to make us each feel interpellated, and that the emotions of hosts, guests, and callers might just as well be fabricated as genuine. I attribute both my moments of identification and my self-consciousness about those moments to my secondary oral conditioning.

How did radio and television get this way? What is the history of the lure of these mediated and vicarious forms of "participation"? While it would take me too far from my topic of talk fiction to recount in detail the development of broadcasting talk forms in all their specificity, it is worthwhile mentioning that some critics, relying on Habermas's notion of the public sphere, connect the talk show with the general rise of participatory talk practices and the multiplication of "talk spaces" in the West, such as the coffeehouse, the philosophical society, literary circles, and lyceums (Munson 20–26; Shattuc 87–88).[31] For a more precise origin of audience participation in the media, Shattuc points to seventeenth-century broadsheets that were themselves "descendants of such oral traditions as the town crier, gossip, and folk tales" (15). Munson starts with eighteenth-century magazines whose titles reflected their close connection to oral practice, for example, *Tatler, Town Talk, Tea Table, Chit Chat* (20). Both analysts identify the talk shows' direct antecedent as late-nineteenth-century women's advice columns and service magazines that specifically fostered participation by inviting individual response to contests, surveys, advice columns (Munson 21–22; Shattuc 3, 26–28). Foregrounding exchange was one way to get more people into the conversation—and into the mass marketplace. In Munson's interpretation: "The disruptions of modernity, which took people from an ethic based on localism and self-sufficiency to one of spectatorship and consumption, were eased by the magazines through the rear-view mirror of nostalgic participatory practices. . . . As modernity broke with the past, it also had to ease the transition for its now anonymous consuming subjects" (24). Levin offers a more specifically class-based analysis of talk radio, maintaining that "Working-class listeners are often encouraged to participate by the host, who assumes that their natural estrangement will provoke a barrage of civic complaints and expressions of mistrust from others. Working men and women may be emboldened to participate by the absence of video, which relieves them of the shame that bourgeois society imposes on the unfashionable and less well educated" (16). Shattuc continues to follow this thread—though she does not subscribe to Levin's classist assumption about shame—when she connects the specific forms of television talk shows with the "larger shift brought on by identity politics in the second half of the twentieth century" (91). In the tumultuous 1960s, she argues, "Participatory talk shows were where common people could express frustration with the impersonal state and society" (35).

Of course, talk fiction, unlike talk radio and talk shows on television, is not a mass phenomenon, nor is it as commercially successful. Although there is some literature that has massive audiences, no reading public today compares with the size of the TV audiences of today's most—or even less—popular talk shows. To cite just one illustrative set of data: whereas a typical John Grisham novel sells three million copies in toto (Goodstein 1998), an Oprah Winfrey audience averaged nine to ten million viewers a day in 1986 (Shattuc 39).[32] (Unfortunately for their authors, the texts I'll be discussing sell many fewer copies than Grisham novels.) Another immediately apparent difference between talk shows and talk fiction resides in their audio and visual qualities. Radio and television can reproduce the human voice with a fidelity that allows for the transmission of tone, volume, pitch, and so forth.[33] And the television image is more than adequate to pick up gestures and facial expressions of participants. Thus sounds and images in face-to-face communication and in broadcast communication are registered as quite similar—albeit not identical—in simple physical terms. Print can disseminate static images, but of course not voices, though several theories of reading suggest that we create sounds in our head when we read (Ong 75). There are other important semiotic differences between talk shows and talk fiction to which I turn in the next section. But my point here is that participants' sense of interacting and yet being at least to some extent self-conscious about that interaction are common to both talk shows and talk fiction and link them to each other and to secondary orality. Having created, I hope, an unfamiliar backdrop for a discussion of twentieth-century prose fiction, I now want to pursue printed Talk.

Talk in Fiction

As far as my investigations uncover, linguist Robin Tolmach Lakoff was one of the first scholars to elucidate specific ways in which the oral mode is being incorporated into the written in North American culture. In a 1982 article titled "Some of My Favorite Writers Are Literate: The Mingling of Oral and Literate Strategies in Written Communication," Lakoff considers a wide variety of contemporary written texts. In her examples, which range from placards in crowds to newspaper and magazine articles, and from college-student essays and comics to novels by Thomas Pynchon and Tom Wolfe, she remarks nonstandard uses of quotation marks, italics, ellipses, capitalization, and orthography. To quote Lakoff's analysis of this last: "special spellings are used not simply as a guide to pronunciation, but as a way of indicating, 'Since this representation is different from the "formal" forms of written language, it is to be taken as "oral," i.e., immediate, emotional, colloquial' " (253).[34] What she identifies as "new" in writing affects the oral in two specific ways. On the one hand, Lakoff suggests that nonstandard typography and orthography serve as a guide to the sounds of speech (for example, capitals as volume, italics as rise in pitch, ellipses as silence or hesitation, misspellings as actual pronunciation of words). On the other, that a current practice deviates from traditional practice itself communicates that this writing is trying not to be writing, but presumably its "opposite": speech.

Lakoff attributes the proliferation of these features as one type of sign of the general "shift in our society from a literacy-based model of ideal human communication to one based on the oral mode of discourse" (240). She offers several other examples of this shift into secondary orality, though she does not use the term. For instance, whereas signs of forethought, a feature usually associated with the written, used to be valued and therefore considered desirable in writing as in speech, we are now suspicious of speech that sounds rehearsed; we value spontaneity— or what sounds like it—in both speech and writing (245).[35] According to Lakoff, we are not completely comfortable with any of these changes, even though they seem to express our preferences, because "the borrowing of a device from one medium into another is always overdetermined: it carries with it the communicative effect, or 'feel,' of one medium into another (the metacommunicative effect) and at the same time attempts to utilize the language of one mode to communicate ideas in another (the communicative effect). It is no wonder that this sort of translation can create confusion in readers (or hearers), and can also create in them very strong feelings—typically negative" (251–52). Lakoff offers her analysis to address this negativity—not by denigrating literacy, but by identifying these new practices as attempts to "come to terms with the future" (259–60).

I find Lakoff's argument extremely helpful and recapitulate it here for two purposes. First, I want to emphasize that the particular communicative change on which she focuses, what she calls the "mingling" of oral and written communicative strategies is of course not a fact, but a fiction to which we agree. Written texts do not now "speak," but because they are doing something different from custom *we let them function for us* as spoken interaction. Though Lakoff never draws attention to this point, her argument implies active reading. Her examples do not constitute speech in some ontological sense: they are not oral, they are *to be taken as* oral. It is *readers* who may interpret them as templates for the sound of speech or as spontaneous and emotional, and therefore like speech. Readers' activity and pretense play important roles in the talk shows described above and in what I call talk fiction, too, though I judge the activity involved in reading talk fiction as necessarily more self-conscious, and the pretense of a different nature.

Accordingly, my second purpose in citing Lakoff's observations is to distinguish the specific written phenomena she is describing from the ones I am treating, beyond the fact that she deals with various types of writing, whereas I deal only with prose fiction. I take Lakoff's "borrowing of a device from one medium into another" to mean a substitution of one sign system for another, say, italics for a rise in pitch or capital letters for such emotions as excitement, anger, and hysteria. The italics and the capitals signal: "to be taken as 'oral.'" My corpus may contain some of the borrowing that interests Lakoff. But the strategies I focus on do not involve substitutions to be interpreted as imitations of qualities of speech. (I am not interested in representations of dialect, for example.) Talk-fiction texts are not "translations into writing which we understand through reference to speaking" (Lakoff 247). Rather, they mobilize textual strategies that reveal orientation to exchange between text and reader. That is to say: I call my phenomenon Talk neither because the written page sounds like oral speech nor even because it signals difference that should be interpreted as informal or spontaneous—and therefore as resembling speech more than writing—but rather because talk fiction performs what many experts identify as the central function of speech: it creates relationships and invites interaction.[36] Readers must be self-conscious about this hybridity and about interacting with a written text for the reading experience to constitute Talk. I will return to this issue below.

In presenting sociolinguistic definitions of talk in the first section of this chapter, I suggested that the concept of the interactional unit invites consideration of the production of a literary work by an author as a "statement" that asks for the "reply" of being read. After all, literature is written with the intention of being read by someone, even if only by the author who then wants it destroyed, as Kafka purportedly did. But I also suggested, following Ong, that this interactional unit in fact applies to all writing and doesn't help us specify anything about literature, much less about some twentieth-century prose fiction.

Describing talk fiction requires time and space, and I try to give each mode its due by discussing it in its own chapter to illuminate the way a set of texts has responded not only to secondary orality as broadly sketched out above but also to more specific, though still widespread, cultural phenomena: the changing forms of transmission of cultural/historical knowledge (chapter 2, "Storytelling"); the infliction of trauma (chapter 3, "Testimony"); and attempts at intimacy in societies that for various reasons promote alienation (chapter 4, "Apostrophe"). The signs and extent of interaction in each mode vary; in some cases the initial situation of enunciation invites the reader to consider the entire discourse as displaying orientation to exchange. In others, specific textual features elicit a distinct response from the reader. In all cases, the texts aim to provoke some kind of reaction in the reader's world, that is, in the world outside the text. Without undermining the specificity of the talk fiction modes I analyze in subsequent chapters, I want to adumbrate how Goffman's conception of talk can be applied to narrative fiction.

Traditional narratological models of the narrative communication system draw arrows from a real author to a fictional narrator of a story to a fictional receiver of the story, the narratee, to a real receiver of the story, the reader.[37] Narrators and narratees may be more or less perceptible, and there may be additional narrators and narratees embedded in a given text.[38] But in all such models, narrators and narratees are considered intrinsic to the text, whereas "the real author and real reader are outside the narrative transaction as such, though, of course, indispensable to it in an ultimate practical sense" (Chatman 1978: 151). Thinking of talk fiction as a turn-taking system invites two important modifications to such schemas. First, if we take seriously Goffman's concept of the producers of statements and replies as "enacted capacities," there is no justification for keeping narratological levels distinct.[39] And second, the ideas of turn-taking and of moves as not necessarily verbal invite the addition of a set of arrows pointing in the opposite direction, from the real reader back toward the author-narrator.

I can now offer the following description of the basic talk fiction communicative circuit: the initial moves, or "statements," are constituted by the discourse or segments of the discourse, in the sense of the words, punctuation, and even blank space that communicate the story of the literary work. I will refer to these statements as "texts." Texts-as-statement are produced by flesh-and-blood authors through narrators who enunciate them. Like traditional narratology, I will refer to this participant in the Talk as the "narrator," but with the understanding that the real authors as well as the characterized or uncharacterized narrators together constitute the "enacted capacity" responsible for producing texts-as-statement. These texts ask for replies from real readers, the other participant in the Talk. By "reply" I do not mean just the action of reading the text. I mean specific "answerings" to specific matters that have been raised by the text as statement. These may be constituted by the feeling of an emotion, the making of an intellectual connection, the speaking of an utterance, the passing on of a story in the real world beyond it, or the completion of another type of action in the physical world. What distinguishes this communicative circuit from any other literary one is the self-conscious perception by readers that they are formulating a reply invited by some feature of the text. On this point, I again take my cue from Goffman: a reply is constituted not by "being" an answering, but by "being seen" by participants as an answering.

This model of Talk immediately elicits a few observations. First, a conglomerate author-narrator as "speaker" implies only one interactional unit: a statement and a reply to that statement. The participant-narrator as I have defined it cannot then take another turn in response to the participant-reader's reply.[40] It should be noted, however, that a given work of prose fiction may be constructed as a series of interactional units.

Second, the participants to the Talk are not symmetrical. The enacted capacities that produce texts-as-statement are only partly animate—human authors to whom, in any case, real readers normally have no access, including their attitudes toward exchange. What real readers do have access to, in some sense, are nonsentient narrators through whom authors' orientation to exchange is expressed. Conversely, real readers' answerings may be guided by the way the text depicts narratees. But strictly speaking, narratees are part of the "statement," not the "reply." Author-narrators cannot directly control what real readers do, nor can they adjust their statements to real readers' developing responses.

Third, as real readers ourselves or as scholars thinking about talk fiction, we don't have (much) access to the "answerings" of other real readers. What we can examine is the author-narrator's call for response, the text, Goffman's statement. This is why I refer to "*text*-reader interaction" rather than to author-reader or narrator-reader interaction, even though, within my own framework, the participants are author-narrators and readers. In the chapters that follow I will categorize these calls into different modes of talk fiction on the basis of the type of reply they seek. I can and will occasionally report on real readers' responses by pointing out my own readings or those of others, like my student, who felt he had talked with Calvino, or by presenting data from literary history, like published reviews, or lack thereof.

Fourth, though any one reader lacks access to all other readers' responses, my study is predicated on a reading of my corpus as intending real effects on real readers. Recall once again Goffman's definition of reply as a move "characterized by its being seen as an answering." Talk fiction requires active readers. Whereas for Lakoff's corpus the main activity involves interpreting textual sign systems for speech sign systems, in mine, active readers interpret what they might be feeling, thinking, or doing *as a reply to the move of the text*.[41]

A sense of responding to the text should ring familiar to lovers of the early novel. This can be the place only to remind rather than demonstrate that literature in general and the novel in particular were in earlier epochs thought of as communication between authors and readers. To return to the epigraph from Sterne's *Tristram Shandy* with which I launched my preface, "Writing, when properly managed (as you may be sure I think mine is) is but a different name for conversation" (127). Sterne and his readers may have been eager already in the mid-eighteenth century to make fun of this idea. But to frame the joke, I contend, is to have entertained the idea of writing and reading as conversation. Over several centuries, refinement of print technology, changes in the mentalities of the cultures in which the novel form thrived, and internal developments of the genre loosened this sense of contact and exchange.

To understand why Talking with texts today necessarily involves self-consciousness on the part of readers, I want to review two of the numerous steps along the way between those seventeenth-century broadsheets to which Shattuc points and Calvino's novels, "moments" that promoted eradication of a view of the novel as genuine communication between authors and readers. In this context I'd like to recall Tziovas's metaphor of the "intrications and enfoldings" of orality and literacy cited earlier. Attitudes toward the communicative status of fiction change neither instantaneously nor completely. Novels were not vehicles of communication one day and autonomous aesthetic objects the next, nor have they been uniformly considered one or the other within a given culture at a given time.[42] Conversely, though the term may be a recent invention of my critical vocabulary, talk fiction did not burst onto the literary scene at a specific moment. Rather, it developed over the course of the twentieth century in response to cultural and historical circumstances within a broader context of a burgeoning secondary orality that privileges interaction generally, as well as to specific literary-critical prohibitions against fiction as communication. Furthermore, by no means do all contemporary novels Talk.

The first "moment" I'd like to consider involves the relationships of authors to readers of fiction in the eighteenth century. Much intelligent research has been done into how the increasing efficiency of printing and the development of trade publishing, circulating libraries, serial publication, and newspapers loosened further the connection between storyteller, story, and listener begun by the advent of writing and accelerated enormously by the invention of the printing press.[43] Technological, economic, and social organizational innovations contributed to and, indeed, created a wide readership for fiction. As Christopher Flint argues, however, this readership developed at the price of a "referential belief system, predicated on the evidential aura of an authentic manuscript, by which a fiction frames its empirical status" (1998: 214). Specifically, Flint sees reflected in the content and structure of eighteenth-century (mainly English) stories narrated by "speaking objects," real authors' concerns about the amount of mediation between author and reader, the unpredictability and heterogeneity of readership, and commodity culture. In describing the functions of these speaking-object narrators, Flint writes: "the power to tell stories is compromised by the subjection of the [speaking object] storyteller to systems of social, economic, and material exchange that delimit its identity. . . . To some degree, the narratives do prevent the author from being drawn into the kind of public vortex that necessarily envelops the text. . . . But the protection the surrogate provides is nonetheless a sign of the author's vulnerability" (221). Although Flint emphasizes transformations in relations between author and text, the changes he details affected all dyads of literary communication: texts and readers, authors and readers, readers and authors. Literary relations, like increasingly international financial transactions, were becoming anonymous (223).

Admittedly, Flint focuses on only one type of fiction, and we would have to investigate much more widely to discover the extent of anxieties about transformations of literary relations and to deduce the persistence of an attitude toward literature as communication. The important work of Robyn Warhol on reader address reveals the nineteenth century to be a period of further transition when authors used narrators *to obfuscate and emphasize* the boundaries between their fictions and the world of lived experience (1989: 44). As we will see in the next chapter, some talk fiction utilizes the same strategies as Warhol's engaging narrators "by implying or even asserting that author, reader, and characters are all present simultaneously on the same diegetic plane" (204). What then is "new" and "distinct" about talk fiction? Why is it not merely a continuation of some strains of eighteenth- and nineteenth-century prose fiction? My answer to these questions is modeled on the distinctions between primary and secondary orality or face-to-face conversation and talk shows. They share qualities but are not identical; the second element in these pairs resembles the first through filters of self-consciousness about mediation and pretense. In the case of talk fiction, this self-consciousness involves choosing to interact despite my second "moment": the early-twentieth-century triumph of art for art's sake, that is, of what we might style "the most literate" of moments in the history of the novel, when practitioners and theorists advocate elimination of all overt signs of fiction as communication.

We might associate the idea of the literary text as an autonomous aesthetic object most closely with Modernism, the New Critics, and poetry. But we can trace to Flaubert the seeds of analogous attitudes for the novelistic genre, that is, a privileging of "impersonal," "objective," or "dramatic" narration over "any mode that allows for direct appearances by the author or his [sic] reliable spokesman" (Booth 1961: 8). In the history of the Anglo-American novel this position is most forcefully presented by Henry James, in prefaces written for the revised publication of his novels (begun 1907; see James 1962) and then reiterated and synthesized by his younger friend Percy Lubbock. In the latter's 1921 study *The Craft of Fiction*, Lubbock praises the technique of *Madame Bovary*, for example, commenting, "the art of fiction does not begin until the novelist thinks of his story as a matter to be *shown*, to be so exhibited that it will tell itself. To hand over to the reader the facts of the story merely as so much information—this is no more than to state the 'argument' of the book. . . . [I]n fiction there can be no appeal to any authority outside the book itself" (1957: 62). By privileging "showing" over "telling," James and Lubbock contributed further to the loosening of author and reader from each other and from the literary text detected already by Flint in eighteenth-century novels. Needless to say, the idea that a story "will tell itself" would be ludicrous to sociolinguists like

28

Goffman.[44] And yet the allure of the view that literary art should "be, not do" has been so strong that it has affected both what is written and how people read since the early twentieth century. Jane P. Tompkins describes this legacy of Modernism as an eradication of a sense of literature's ability to "accomplish social tasks," such that we no longer think of writing or reading it "as a means of carrying out social transactions" (1980: 210).

I have proposed we call post-Modernist prose fiction that aims to have effects in the real world—or to return to my framework, to interact with readers—"talk fiction."[45] To summarize now the fuller context in which talk fiction develops: the transformations that accompany the development of new communication technologies (secondary orality), most notably the ubiquitous privileging of interaction, offer competing pressures on the novel form to literary theoretical injunctions to show, not tell. If overt reader address is rare in the direct wake of Modernism's "idealist, aestheticist line of thinking" (Warhol 1989: 195), it nonetheless self-consciously reemerges—in some works—in the second half of the century.[46] I treat this reemergence in my next chapter, calling it "storytelling," to suggest both its connections to and distinctions from its ancestors in previous centuries. Twentieth-century prose fiction develops additional strategies to promote readers' orientation to exchange. Although I am not trying to connect my other modes to earlier narrative forms, I place testimony, apostrophe, and interactivity under the same talk-fiction umbrella as reader address—my storytelling—because they solicit a similar text-reader interaction; they too should be counted as part of the general resurgence of the spoken wor(l)d I have been examining in this chapter.

I agree heartily with Tompkins that modern readers have forgotten how to read literature "as a means of carrying out social transactions." To date, most reader-response criticism is interested in reader response as a *psychological* process, not as the interactional one for which talk fiction provides evidence. My readings of some twentieth-century prose fiction as talk fiction could be considered a variety of reader-response criticism, however it is one that takes the idea of response literally. Unlike the other types of criticism we have come to identify by this term, I am exploring the response—Goffman's and my "reply"—as designated quite specifically by the enunciating strategy of the participant-narrator through the text-as-statement, not as residing in the subjective will of an individual reader. In other words, I am arguing for talk fiction as a textual and interpretive phenomenon. Indeed, one of the most important insights I have borrowed from sociolinguistics is that "statement" and "reply" are interdependent.

To be sure, as we have learned from Stanley Fish, interpretive communities behave differently, and thus I am not claiming that all actual readers provide the reply constructed by the text. The reader can resist the invitation to Talk by ceasing to read or by merely refusing to provide the reply. But my interpretive community is not a resisting one. It seeks to perform the intended reply sought by the text-as-statement. Or, more exactly, my interpretive community posits that there is such a thing as an intended reply to the statement, and it tries to describe that reply and give it. By doing so, such nonresisting, active readers Talk with the text. Most fundamentally, they embrace the idea of providing an answering to the text, even as they remain aware that Talking departs from received reading strategies and that it is not to be confused with face-to-face interaction. Accordingly, my last goal in this chapter is to begin to suggest how readers can train themselves to "hear" novels as statements in Goffman's sense. In doing so, I will address the most fundamental difference between talk fiction and face-to-face interaction or talk fiction and other secondary oral genres like talk shows: the signs of orientation to exchange.

In oral speech, desire to make an initial move, that is, to say something, may be signaled by the hopeful speaker's touch, gaze, and/or inbreath. In talk fiction the participant-narrator has no such corporeal resources. The equivalent gesture is use of deictics, in Gerald Prince's sense of "any term or expression which, in an utterance, refers to the context of production of that utterance" (1987: 18). In conceiving of talk fiction as a turn-taking system I have expanded the traditional notion of deixis from specific words like "I," "you," "here," "now" to any literary strategy that can be interpreted as signaling a text's orientation to an answering.[47] In my storytelling and apostrophic modes, the texts-as-statement do use traditional deixis, the pronouns of ordinary conversation: "I" and "you." In my testimony mode, I count as deictics in my expanded sense any number of textual features from (a) typographical markers like ellipses or blank space, (b) narrative indirection like absence of quoted speech or quoted interior monologue, (c) avoidance of certain words, and even (d) deferral of publication, because they can all signal request for the reply of cowitnessing to the presence of trauma. In my final case of interactivity in computer hypertexts, I consider menu option icons, highlighting, and underlining "deictic equivalents" because they signal the need for an "answering" that involves readers making choices. Because of the obvious way in which pronouns of address "refer to the context of production of the utterance" in which they appear, I would like to discuss the second person here, postponing my exploration of other forms of deixis to their respective chapters.[48]

As linguist Emile Benveniste has observed, to address someone using the second person is to recognize her/his ability to become a subject, to switch places and as an "I" talk to a "you." In Benveniste's formulation: " 'you' is necessarily designated by 'I' and cannot be thought of outside a situation set up by starting with 'I' " (1971: 197). The use of "you" thus effects two conditions for Talk: the existence of participants and orientation to exchange. Still, not every use of "you" in spoken speech or prose fiction elicits response. To elucidate my category of talk fiction, it would be helpful to borrow from conversation analysis once again, in this instance to distinguish between "addressees," "hearers," and "recipients." For conversation analysts, addressees are the persons to whom speakers explicitly address their speech, hearers are any persons who hear the speech, and recipients are hearers who orient toward the speech (Goodwin and Heritage 1990: 292). The Talk of talk fiction texts involves exchanges that are created when readers consider themselves addressees by acting as hearer-recipients in the sense just designated. Often this opportunity is marked explicitly by an untagged pronoun of address—a "hey you," so to speak—that the "dear reader" accepts as a call to her/himself.

As literates we have been taught to recognize that we cannot be the intended addressee in certain circumstances. Readers routinely identify the discourse included within quotation marks or their typographical equivalents as address to a different addressee, as an exchange of already designated (other) participants of elsewhere and of another time. Quoted dialogue in texts cannot be instances of Talk in the sense I am developing it here. For similar reasons, quoted storytelling does not constitute Talk, though virtually all of the texts I am analyzing contain embedded storytelling situations that may serve as negative or positive

31

models for the reply the text seeks from its readers. In Conrad's *Heart of Darkness*, for example, Marlowe and his audience constitute an instance of embedded storytelling: the time, the place, and the participants are determined. But the narrating "I" that tells about Marlowe telling his story addresses himself to an unspecified "you"—no quotation marks, no name, no description—that an actual reader of *Heart of Darkness* may choose to become, thus entering into a relationship of listener to that "I," and in the terms of my study, becoming a hearer-recipient who Talks with the text. In other words, the "you" must be "available" to readers, who can then choose to enact a conversation with the text by considering the address as a personal address, thereby becoming a participant in Goffman's terms, or in conversation analytic terms, a recipient.

In sum, the use of "you" automatically implies relationship between two parties, and instances of it in fiction that are not designated as quoted dialogue or embedded storytelling invite actual readers to enter into a relationship with the participant-narrator through the text. To be sure, there are certain pretenses involved here: similar to talk-show audiences, being the "recipient" of talk fiction requires taking the text-as-statement as emanating from an enacted capacity with whom one can interact *and* taking this statement as a call to oneself, even when one realizes that one is personally unknown to the "speaker" and cannot be the sole technical "addressee," because others can answer the same call as a call to themselves. It is precisely self-consciousness about the type of interaction one is engaged in (awareness of being one of Goffman's present-absent addressees) and about being part of a group engaged in the same activity that connects talk fiction to secondary orality in general and to talk shows in specific. In brief, this is the lesson my student taught me about reading Calvino: I could choose to become recipient of the text's "you-reader," even as I remained aware that I didn't quite fit the bill; in choosing to become a recipient anyway, I Talked with *If on a winter's night a traveler.*[49]

In this chapter I have argued that there are moments in history when forms of communication are pushed to the fore and that we are experiencing one of them. I will turn now to a series of texts that have not received appropriate attention in canonical approaches to twentieth-century prose fiction. With Talk and deixis in mind, I hope that you will become a recipient of my "hey, you" by noticing features of this prose fiction that you would not have noticed otherwise.

2

STORYTELLING

Talk as Sustenance

A word is a bridge thrown between myself and another. If one end of the
bridge depends on me, then the other depends on my addressee.
—MIKHAIL M. BAKHTIN

I call my first mode of Talk "storytelling" since the "moves" involve the
recital, reception, and passing on of stories. Specifically, the "statement"
of these texts should be thought of as the narrators' entire recital of the
story, and the "reply" as the readers' proper reception and eventual
retelling of that story. The deictics that guide us to this understanding are
the personal pronouns we are familiar with from pre-twentieth-century
reader address: "I" ("we") and "you." I am taking up storytelling first
because of our associations with oral storytelling as a basic form of
human interaction (Nofsinger 1991: 162), and more specifically because
the call for response is the easiest to identify among the four types I
present in this study, indicated as it is by direct address: "you." This is not
to say that the activity of replying is itself automatic, passive, or trivial. As
in my epigraph from Bakhtin, the authors of these works of talk fiction
want to create bridges—relationships—that can only be sustained when
"speaker" and "respondent" are equally active. The phrase "dear reader"
never appears, in part, I surmise, because readers are posited as listeners
who are as "present" as the tellers, to paraphrase a point made by Gayle
Jones (1991: 161). For this reason, too, I use the term "storytelling" to
make a bridge to (primary) oral cultures where telling stories is an activity of serious purpose. As Ong explains, putting information vital to
the survival of a people into a narrativized form allows it to be more
easily memorized and passed on (1982: 34, 140). I am spelling these
points out at the beginning, because the sense of readers as active par-

ticipants and of stories as accomplishing social tasks is not necessarily familiar to us secondary oral creatures.

To demonstrate how novels of my storytelling mode reassert a notion of literature as interactional, I will read two twentieth-century texts, Kóstas Tachtsís's *The Third Wedding Wreath* (*To tríto stefáni* 1963; 1970) and Gloria Naylor's *Mama Day* (1988), whose "statements" call for readers to "reply" by listening with the proper attitude, which implies acceptance of the responsibility to hand on the story. To understand the full import of the demand for attentive, respectful listening it will be necessary not only to consider these texts in rather great detail but also to consider two nineteenth-century texts in their respective traditions— Dimítris Vikélas's *Lukís Láras* (1879) and Harriet E. Wilson's *Our Nig* (1859; 1983)—to whose calls for the creation of community, I would suggest, Tachtsís's and Naylor's novels are responding.[1] Given the privileged role of storytelling in this chapter, I will share a few stories, reflect on the purposes of storytelling revealed in Vikélas's and Wilson's nineteenth-century novels, and then present the kind of storytelling Talk found in Tachtsís and Naylor.

Anthropologist John B. Haviland offers the following anecdote from his early fieldwork:

> In 1968 I spent a summer in a Maroon community in Suriname, where the people spoke a Portuguese based Creole called Saramaka. My host and primary teacher, Captain Mayòo, had high hopes that I would learn something of both the language and the history of his village, Kadjoe. One afternoon he summoned me and my tape recorder in order to speak to me in a formal manner. My halting Saramaka, unfortunately, was not up to the task of responding to him appropriately, and shortly after he began my clumsy responses forced him to grind to a halt. Unperturbed, he signalled me to put the tape recorder on pause for a moment. Walking out to the street, he grabbed the first man he saw, and dragged him in to sit beside me. He was going to tell *me* a few things, he told the dragooned passer-by, but he needed a competent *listener* to be able to talk at all. Once he had the necessary verbal lubricant, he went on to declaim to me (and to my machine) for nearly an hour. (1986: 258–59)

This anecdote foregrounds the premise that telling simply cannot occur without proper listening. I suspect that Haviland's Saramaka may not have been good enough even to know exactly what it was Mayòo said to the "dragooned passer-by"; in Roman Jakobson's terms they don't fully share the linguistic code (1960: 356). In any case, it seems unlikely that Mayòo expressed his dilemma to the recruited listener in terms resembling those used by Haviland in this anecdote. Nevertheless, Haviland's training clues him in to the way a listener is not just a passive receiver; his own "clumsy responses" stop Mayòo, who, despite a predetermined agenda, cannot "tell" without active listening. In Mayòo's culture, a cipher in the form of the anthropologist's body will not do for a listener. Even if Mayòo's intended addressee is Haviland, to tell his story at all he needs a capable hearer with whom he shares similar talk behavior. In the terms of conversation analysis introduced in the previous chapter: Haviland is the addressee and a hearer, but he doesn't have the skills to be a recipient. Or to use Goffman's framework: he doesn't know how to give the reply that shows he is oriented to Mayòo's discourse as statement.

Change of scene and characters: one of my father's tasks when he was growing up in a small and desperately poor mountain village in Greece after the German invasion in World War II was to watch a herd of goats. Their favorite place to graze was in the village cemetery because that was the spot with at least a bit of vegetation. Occasionally, older women would come to the grave sites—which were multiplying—and talk to their dead, usually relating family news and village gossip. Out of boredom, and probably curiosity, my father would try to overhear these recitals as he kept an eye out for the goats. One widow was particularly faithful to her dead spouse, and as a result she ran out of things to say. Fortunately for her, around that time the Nazis dropped leaflets on the village. The woman couldn't read, but she picked up a flier and proceeded with it to the grave of her husband. With the paper in front of her she began to make up stories about the villagers. My father couldn't read the flier either, because, he reported, it was written in German. When he took a copy to someone to decipher, he found out that it was a warning to the local population that ten Greeks would be executed for every German found dead. I don't know whether the widow ever found out what the writing on the paper meant, but she continued to hold it in her hand and tell stories, thus trying to entertain her dead spouse—and succeeding to entertain my eavesdropping father—for several more weeks.

One of my many reactions when I first heard my father tell this story was amazement at the power of the spoken word that allows people to feel connected even across the divide of the living and the dead. This woman didn't need the normal "verbal lubricant"; she could "talk" to her absent husband. Or, as I came to understand it, she could talk to him because in her view, he was not absent; her addresses resuscitated him and therefore he was a present listener.[2] What pertains most here is how storytelling—evidently unwittingly in this case—can transform death threats into life-sustaining narratives. The widow probably needed those time-outs in the cemetery as much as my father needed her stories to keep going under the stress of their wartime routines. My wonderment extends also to the way orality and literacy are completely enmeshed in this scene and in the culture in which it took place. The woman is functionally illiterate and yet she knows that paper can talk. With the flier in her hands, she feels empowered to narrate; the paper somehow authorizes her to frame stories that perform the same function as the gossip she brings from her actual daily life.

I am, of course, borrowing this idea of talking paper from the trope of the Talking Book in the African Anglo-American tradition, a trope I would like to revisit because the scenario of a primary oral individual witnessing someone reading offers a unique opportunity to consider what might happen if we believed we could interact with books. The earliest textual sources for this trope appear to be from seventeenth-century accounts of the encounters between Spaniards and Incas (Gates 1988: 149–50).[3] But in the African Anglo-American slave narrative context, the first known treatment surfaces in *A Narrative of the Most Remarkable Particulars in the Life of James Albert Ukawsaw Gronniosaw, an African Prince, as Related by Himself,* first published in 1770 and appearing in numerous editions throughout the English-speaking world in the following decades. An uncannily similar occurrence is reported in the longer autobiography of Olaudah Equiano (1789; 1995: 68), and variations on the refusal of a book to talk are set into first-person narratives by John Marrant, Ottobah Cugoano, and John Jea.[4] The way Gronniosaw describes his encounter with books displays most clearly the points I would like to make about bringing oral ways of knowing into the literate communicative situation, so it is Gronniosaw's version I will quote and discuss here.

After being traded into slavery, Gronniosaw is transported to Bar-

bados on a Dutch ship. In recounting the voyage, Gronniosaw describes
the following scene:

> [My master] used to read prayers in public to the ship's crew every Sab-
> bath day; and when first I saw him read, I was never so surprised in my
> whole life as when I saw the book talk to my master; for I thought it did, as
> I observed him to look upon it, and move his lips.—I wished it would do
> so to me.—As soon as my master had done reading I follow'd him to the
> place where he put the book, being mightily delighted with it, and when
> nobody saw me, I open'd it and put my ear down close upon it, in great
> hope that it would say something to me; but was very sorry and greatly
> disappointed when I found it would not speak, this thought immediately
> presented itself to me, that every body and every thing despised me
> because I was black. (1774: 16–17)[5]

This scene has been thought of as the archetypal encounter of an oral
man and the emblem of literate culture: the book. Henry Louis Gates Jr.'s
perceptive analysis rightly proceeds from the perspective that we are
reading Gronniosaw's recollection and that at the point Gronniosaw
wrote his memoirs, he could not only read but also had steeped himself in Western literary tradition. Once he is literate, neither he—nor
we—can ever fully recover his preliterate mind-set (see Ong 1982: 12).
Nevertheless, what I find most striking about this anecdote is precisely
something we might expect from a (primary) oral individual for whom
information is only ever communicated between speakers, through the
medium of voice. Gronniosaw does *not* interpret what he sees before him
as an egotistical act wherein the man is doing something with/to the
book that literates would describe as a subject acting on an object: the
man reads the book. Gronniosaw interprets what is going on before him
as an intersubjective, relational act: the book and the man are speaking.
This aspect appears to attract him the most, since he then answers the
"call" of the book with the "reply" of opening it and listening. What
Gronniosaw transfers from the oral situation that informs his weltan-
schauung to the literate situation he is witnessing for the first time is
that reading, like talking, brings individuals into relationship (Nofsinger
1991: 3). This directly counters the view held by literates that literacy
individuates (Ong 1982: 69, 74). Gronniosaw's attitude and actions, however, do not result in an exchange similar to the one that he believes he
has just witnessed between the book and the captain. Not being able to

read is therefore also interpreted as a relational problem: "every body and every thing despised me because I was black." Gronniosaw does not know what kind of "being" the book is, but he is profoundly aware that he is excluded from having a relationship with this being because of his race (see Gates 1988: 137).

Reversing this exclusion becomes his raison d'être. His long-term response to this encounter is not only to learn to read but also to assimilate into the Western (white) community. Directly prior to relating the incident with the book, for example, he explains how relieved he is when the gold chains and adornments of the dress in which he leaves his African home are replaced by clothes "in the *Dutch* or *English* manner" (16). Later steps on this road to assimilation include converting to Christianity and taking a white, English wife. He demonstrates his accomplishment "by narrating a text of a life that charts his pilgrimage to the shrines of European culture" (Gates 139, 145). Though Gates argues that this process comes at the price of obliterating the traces of his black African past (138), I would like to suggest that Gronniosaw's emphasis on being in relation to others, which gives poignancy to the recital of his first encounter with reading and to his memoir as a whole—over and over he presents the people he has met and interacted with—is one way in which at least a single element of his black African *oral* past survives. This is literacy "with a difference," where relationship is privileged and necessary for communication—indeed for life itself.

I now have the pieces in place to return to the specific subject at hand: the storytelling mode of talk fiction. In these texts, the presence of the listener is not just a convention but a necessity for the telling of the tale. The listening required for such tales must constitute a response that brings teller and listener into relationship. And whereas relationship leads to sustenance and survival, its failure to materialize threatens the existence of the teller and of the community. To understand the import of the storytelling mode in late-twentieth-century texts I will look at two specific moments from the Greek and the African American literary traditions during which—as in my anecdotes—sustaining adequate, concrete response in a literate environment was paramount. I am not assuming that Naylor and Tachtsís modeled their novels directly on *Our Nig* and *Lukís Láras*—though it is probable that each knew the earlier work—but rather that the central issues in the twentieth-century texts echo those of the nineteenth-century texts. I also do not assume that the modern Greek and African American cultures are the only secondary oral cultures that privilege relational strategies (see Jones 1991: 192). Indeed, as I have suggested in my previous chapter, this privileging of interaction seems to be an as yet unfully recognized feature of secondary orality itself. I consider these particular examples, rather, because their calls for community are so poignant. On the other hand, I do not want to gloss over the fact that much of their poignancy stems from their status as works of "minor literature" in Deleuze and Guattari's sense of the revolutionary potential of what a minority group manages to create within a major literary tradition (1986: 16–27).[6] In any case, I am beginning with two nineteenth-century texts because they prepare us to "hear" the "statement" of my twentieth-century talk-fiction examples. In other words, to understand what those stories are really about, we need to understand what was at stake in the tradition to which each returns. I will begin with the chronologically later *Lukís Láras* (1879), since it takes up forms of communication so explicitly, and then turn to the more subtle call of *Our Nig* (1859).

Bridging the Literacy Gap: Addressing the "Reader" in *Lukís Láras* and *Our Nig*

Although the first-person narrators of these novels are excruciatingly aware of the differences between writing a story and telling one, each tries to bridge the "literacy gap," the distance in time and space between writers and their readers, through direct address to those readers in an effort to create sustaining relationships of intimacy. Literacy is used in the service of community, not of individualism. These narrators are "engaging narrators" in Warhol's sense of encouraging actual readers to identify with the narratee (1989: 31).[7] In contrast to the talk-fiction texts I will examine in the next section, these narrators can and do assume that their readers understand what constitutes proper listening, even though they do not assume that their audiences will necessarily engage in it. As we will see, the talk-fiction texts must school and transform their readers by modeling competent listening.

Dimítrios Vikélas's tale of the Greek revolution, *Lukís Láras*, was first published in serialized form in 1879 in *Estía*, arguably the most important literary periodical in the Greek world of its time. It was re-published in book form shortly thereafter, and several new editions and translations appeared in rapid succession, including a highly readable (and faithful) English translation in 1881 by John Gennadius, like Vikélas, a Greek living in England. Lukís Láras, the novel's eponymous protagonist-narrator, feels he should record his experiences as a youth during the historic period of the Greek War of Independence.[8] Despite his stated intentions to tell his own story, relationships to others prove central to the theme and form of the novel. The novel is not so much a recital of individual heroic feats as the story of trying to preserve family and community under extraordinary conditions.[9] Or rather, the individual feats detailed are feats accomplished with the goal of preserving personal relationships. The conclusion of Lukís's tale dramatically illustrates this when Lukís chooses to ransom orphaned Déspina from the Turks who had abducted her with the treasures he has recovered from his abandoned family estate, instead of securing his own financial welfare. Just as Déspina can think only of him, screaming "Lukí, Lukí," he can think only of her and of restoring her to her rightful relations with Greeks in general and with his family in particular.[10]

In terms of form, Lukís's tale is filled with narrative digressions and reader address that similarly reveal the priority of relationships. Lukís addresses his "reader" (*anagnósti*) using the singular/informal second-person pronoun *esí*.[11] In some passages Lukís seems to imagine this reader as a compatriot, as an ethnic, social, and economic peer who knows the world in which Lukís grew up; in others he seems to assume that his reader is unfamiliar with the places and even general events Lukís describes. In one passage, which I describe in greater detail below, Lukís explicitly states that he writes his story for posterity, specifically for future members of the Greek community in England.[12] I suggest that the overall frequency and urgency of reader address in this text cannot be explained by convention. The presence of the "reader" is not just a trope but a necessity for the telling of this tale about relationships. Although Lukís makes numerous references to his activity of *writing*, his repeated addresses to the reader resemble oral calls, functioning phatically in Jakobson's sense of checking that the channel of communication is open (1960: 335); Lukís wants to know his reader is "present" and "listening."

Apologetic addresses as well as references to the production of the tale were common in the sentimental fiction of the period, and they are one sign that Vikélas knows and controls contemporary conventions.[13] But I suggest that Lukís's need for connection also explains his frequent narrative wanderings. He pleads his case early in the novel in a passage about digression in the form of a reader address:[14]

> Excuse, reader, these digressions. My pen, obedient to the impulses of an old man's heart, finds pleasure in loitering over the accumulated recollections of my sufferings and earlier impressions. My intention is to limit myself to the narrative of my own adventures in life. Yet the life of each one of us constitutes but a small unit, closely bound up with the total of the circumstances which encircle us. How am I to separate, in each instance, the vicissitudes of my insignificant self from the rush of the all-pervading whirlwind which carried me along!
>
> For this reason, and because I am an old man, perhaps I shall not always succeed in avoiding such digressions while writing my reminiscences. (1881b: 19)

Relationship with others is a compelling, natural priority, as Lukís's metaphors of the circle and the whirlwind suggest. Lukís cannot tell a single story—his own—in part because he cannot disentangle himself from his community.

Lukís delivers this message in a form that entangles him with his "reader." I use quotation marks here because, while Lukís is conscious of himself as a writer and of his audience as readers, he attributes qualities to his narration and its reception that belong to the oral communicative situation. Most importantly, Lukís seems to consider the narration of his tale and its reception contemporaneous, as if it were being verbally recounted.[15] This becomes most apparent in the continuation of the apology to the reader for digressing; I quote again the linking sentence:[16]

> For this reason, and because I am an old man, perhaps I shall not always succeed in avoiding such digressions while writing my reminiscences. But neither are you, good reader, under an obligation to peruse them to the end. When you were a child, and your nurse related to you her tales, she did so in order to gratify not only your curiosity, but also her own impulse [*anángi*] which prompted her to repeat them. Sleep may have come over you sometimes. Yet she continued her tale, and you awoke just in time to listen to the finish. That is why you perhaps remember the beginning only and the end of many a fairy tale, though you may not know how the

recollection of the middle portion has failed you. But my story has no
particular beginning or end of its own; so that *you may fall asleep even
now: you will not interrupt me.* (1881a: 25–26; 1881b: 19–20; my emphasis)

Lukís associates old age (the writing self) with childhood (the oral/aural
self). His nursery analogy emphasizes the oral character of his tale and
implies that he, like the nurse, wants to tell this story regardless of the
listener's commitment to hearing it. The word translated by Gennadius
as "impulse" is *anángi*—"need"/"necessity"—in the original Greek.
Lukís does need the reader, however, even if only as a prop (recall Haviland's anecdote; see too Ong 1982: 34). But I would not interpret Lukís's
main intent as expression of solipsism, false modesty, or mere adherence
to the sentimental convention of self-disparagement. Rather, by conveying these thoughts in the second-person singular, Lukís not only enters
into relation with the reader in the present moment by engaging him in
"dialogue" but also assumes that the reader is like him—he creates a
coalition, displaying engagement and solidarity (Brown and Gilman
1960: 257–58).[17] Lukís wants to empathize with the reader's (potential)
boredom, and he asks the reader to reciprocate by empathizing with an
old man who wants to indulge his memory rather than curb it.

The bedtime scene Lukís evokes adds one more characteristic to this
probe of the nature of storytelling: the telling of the story is salutary to
both the teller and the listener *because* the listener falls asleep. One, if not
the primary, goal of this kind of storytelling is to allow the child to sleep.
And the child falls asleep not only because of the sounds and rhythms of
the story being told but also because of the ongoing physical presence of
the one doing the telling; the story's content has little to do with this part
of the experience.[18] Therefore, by raising the model of bedtime storytelling, Lukís is raising in another guise his point about connectedness. He
and his reader do not have corporeal proximity, but through his nursery
metaphor he reminds his reader of this feature of storytelling.

The oddest feature of this passage is its seeming confusion of the oral
and literate storytelling situations. First Lukís displays awareness of the
reading contract; it is true that readers are under no obligation to read to
the end of a novel. Lukís, however, then shifts to the scene of oral storytelling by introducing the metaphor of the child and nursemaid, and it is
in this context that he concludes by inviting the reader to sleep while he
narrates! If the reader sleeps, he cannot read, and if he does not read, he

does not receive the story. Of course, Lukís and Vikélas know this. And they also know that Lukís can *write* without the reader's participation, just as the nurse can keep speaking while the child sleeps. But again, while reader or child sleeps, the story is not being communicated. Lukís's odd invitation to fall asleep must also be seen as a disguised appeal for attention. By making the analogy to the sleeping child, nursemaid, and missed story, Lukís implies that reading is linked to writing as incontrovertibly as attentive hearing to oral recital for communication of the whole story. In sum, Lukís is warning the reader that he actually *can't* write without (imagined) active listening and that the import of the story will not come across to reader-listeners if they are not attentive to the entire telling. In other words, Lukís draws upon and brings to the attention of his readers both oral and literate behaviors: the intimacy and copresence of oral storytelling and the attentiveness to content of literate communication.

This issue of how best to communicate a story's full import figures prominently in another instance of reader address in the novel. In recounting his family's flight from their home during the Turkish ransacking of Chios, Lukís describes a point at which his family was still in hiding while other families were being discovered, dragged into the streets, and attacked. Lukís's group hears the marauders coming closer. Lukís interrupts the scene to comment on his narration of it:

> Hear them approach, did I say [*Tus ikúomen, légo, plisiázondas*]? It is but an abstract and cold expression. But how can I adequately describe the horror of these events [*ton akusmáton*]? It is for you, reader, to supplement the insufficiency of my narrative by imparting life into the scenes, and by vivifying the impressions which my memory now reflects. It is one thing to read [*állo n'anayinóskeis*], comfortably seated in your room, of devastations in a distant or unknown country, and at a bygone time, and another thing to hear [*ke állo n'akúeis*] that your acquaintances, and your relatives, and friends, and countrymen, are massacred or carried into slavery; that homes familiar to you, and which you visited but the other day, are burnt and pillaged. (1881a: 63–64; 1881b: 64)

Lukís begins this passage similarly to others in which he seems just to be disparaging his narrational skills. He cannot describe the scene adequately and so requests the reader's assistance. Lukís knows his reader is distanced from what he narrates in more ways than one. He understands modern reading practice: years after the described events, his reader sits alone quietly closed off in a room, so as not to be disturbed, so as not to hear anything.

Indeed, hearing could be considered the main subject of this passage, for it is the phrase "hear them approach" that causes Lukís to interrupt his narrative. Focus on hearing is sharpened by Vikélas's diction; Lukís uses the word *akúsmata*—literally, "the things heard"—for what has happened (Gennadius translates *akúsmata* as "events"). Lukís cannot *write* the "things heard" adequately, so he asks the reader to *read* the "things heard" adequately.[19] But even while proposing this idea, Lukís becomes infuriated and shifts his frustration from the inadequacies of writing to the inadequacies of reading. Reading, he decides, is ineffective: one thing to read, another to hear! The Greek original of this formulation is entirely in the second person. A more literal translation would be: one thing for you to read (*n'anayinóskeis*), quietly sitting in your room . . . and another for you to hear (*n'akúeis*). . . . That is to say, by directly addressing the reader here, Lukís redresses his problem with written storytelling: he calls the reader and makes the reader hear something too. This use of reader address is a literate strategy in the service of relational (oral) goals.

Lukís seems obsessed by the need to eradicate distance. He scolds both the reader and himself as he continues this passage:

> It is a widely different thing [from *reading* about devastations in a distant country] to be told by name that such and such a friend has been killed and his wife made a slave; that she was seen dragged along by a savage Turk, wailing, and in despair. You know her voice; you have heard her often talk to you merrily, and you fancy that you now listen to her rending, piteous screams, that you see her, with upturned head and dishevelled hair, being led into captivity, into shame. And you think of her husband and her children! You are yourself near at hand, with your aged mother and your virgin sisters, and you expect, from one moment to another, to see her iniquitous persecutors appear before you. Ah! may God spare you such experience! (1881b: 64–65)

Again, Lukís's use of the second person and the present tense locate the reader in the scene.[20] By doing so, Lukís would put the reader through the same experience now that Lukís had then. Because in that particular moment of the Revolution, Lukís "vivified" for himself. He used what he had heard and what he was hearing to *see* what was happening beyond his view and to personalize it. He doesn't want to think only of himself, nor does he want to think of the victims as strangers. He imagines he feels their pain by bringing to mind his connection to them. Those who are suffering are people he knows. Lukís's wish at the conclusion of this passage that the reader be spared such experiences is duplicitous, as least to the extent that it follows his efforts to put the reader precisely in this situation. It is duplicitous, too, in that Lukís's attempt to effect a sense of connectedness to the events he relates underlies his entire narrative project.

Adequate telling and adequate listening are crucial to Lukís because he believes that a whole nation's existence depends on the story of the Revolution being passed on. As we have seen, Lukís actively tries to promote successful "passing on" not only by writing effectively himself but also by programming the listener to the correct response. His struggle to find the right way to tell this story is Herculean, not so much—as he protests—because he is a bad writer but rather because on some (mainly implicit) level Lukís knows that forms of communication themselves are rapidly shifting in his society:

> And when, in a few years, the generation of our War for Independence [*i yeniá tu agónos*] shall have passed away, and the recital of our reminiscences by word of mouth [*ton proforikón paradóseon i mnimónefsis*] shall have ceased, our grandchildren will not easily realise with what sacrifices and what tortures their well-being [*evimería*] and our national regeneration [*anayénnisis*] have been purchased. Therefore I should wish that more of the survivors of that time would write their memoirs. (1881a: 106–7; 1881b: 117–18)

While Lukís and his generation still cherish *telling* stories, he has realized that oral transmission can no longer guarantee preservation of the history or wisdom of his people. Lukís, our troubled narrator, exhorts others to write, as he does. What Lukís fears will die out with the old men is "the recital of our reminiscences by word of mouth." Gennadius's translation tries to unpack the key elements of Vikélas's rich phrase but inevitably leaves out several. The original Greek here—[*i mnimónefsis*] *ton proforikón paradóseon*—might be translated more literally as "the commemoration of oral traditions." To understand the gulf between Gennadius's translation and mine and, more importantly, to fully appre-

45

ciate what Lukís fears losing, we need to look at each word. *Mnimónefsis* has the same root as "memory" (*mními*) and can mean the quotation or mention of something (Gennadius's "recital"), but it can also refer to the more specific activity of memorization, learning by heart. Furthermore, the word can mean (as I have translated it above) commemoration or celebration. In this sense, *mnimónefsis* connotes religious ritual. What has been recited or memorized or commemorated are *proforikís paradósis*. Lukís uses the words in the plural. The adjective means "oral" or "verbal." The fundamental meaning of the noun *parádosis* is "giving" or "handing on," hence Gennadius's choice of "reminiscences by word of mouth [that which is handed on orally]." But the word *parádosis* also commonly means "tradition" or even "teaching." So what is at stake in Lukís's view are not just the individual stories of private citizens, but, more threateningly, the extinction of whole traditions and teachings, of oral storytelling itself, of a whole (oral) way of transmitting knowledge. Lukís even implies that without knowing how they got there, younger and future generations of Greeks risk not only their private well-being and prosperity (*evimería*) but also their ethnic identity; they might lose the whole nation that had been reborn (*anagénnisis*) as a result of the sacrifices of their forebears. Lukís's concern obviously takes on even greater urgency in a diasporic context. Spatial distance to the scenes recounted and residence in a foreign country compound the challenge of the chronological gap.

Lukís's proposed solution, as we have seen, is to write, even though writing is a struggle for him. But the additional point I find compelling about the passage quoted above is Lukís's humility. His plea implies that if only *he* writes, Greeks are doomed. But if all survivors write—if writing becomes a communal priority—traditions might be saved in this less familiar medium.[21] Lukís's call through a written text for more written texts that can preserve community accrues resonance when we consider the novel's paratext, Gérard Genette's term for all those elements that surround the text itself: jacket blurbs, title pages, dedications, forewords and prefaces, notes, afterwords, and so forth (1997).

In the original serial publication of Vikélas's novel, as well as the first book edition in Greek, the author published a preface in which he accounts for the origin of his tale and expresses a wish that others will enjoy it. I quote it in full here:

46

Those of our countrymen who have resided in England will easily recognise the old Chiote merchant, who is here concealed under the name of Lukís Láras. Often have I heard him relate the vicissitudes of his early years; and it was at my suggestion that, towards the close of his life, he undertook to write his memoirs. When, a few years ago, he died, his manuscript notes were found amongst his papers under cover, addressed to me. In publishing them now, I wish they may be read by others with as great an interest and pleasure as I experienced whenever I listened to the narration of the old gentleman. (1881b: 1)

In an actual reading of the text, Vikélas's juxtaposition of oral and written narration here would foreground what is already familiar to us from passages of his narrator. Like Lukís, he is concerned about the efficacy of literate transmission. Vikélas hopes his written version will in some way mimic the oral performances he says he has heard from the "authentic" Lukís. We are also familiar through our experience of similar conceits in numerous European eighteenth- and nineteenth-century novels with Vikélas's claim that the first-person narrative that follows has resulted from the author's mere editing of a preexisting autobiographical manuscript.[22] In my view, what gives poignancy to this otherwise conventional preface is its relation to the passage in the text we just examined, and to another piece of the paratext, albeit to that of its English translation, Gennadius's introduction.

To begin with the former, assuming that scholarly research is correct and that though there was an historical personage on whom Lukís was based, the shape, style, and details of this story are Vikélas's creation (1881b: xi), Vikélas calls not once, but twice for translating oral stories into written ones. In the preface he says it was he who asked "Lukís" to write down his life story, and then within the main narrative he has his protagonist issue the same call for fellow Greeks to write down their stories. This might appear to be some kind of solipsistic game on Vikélas's part—a *mise en abîme*, to be more precise—were it not for the fascinating document we have in Gennadius's introduction to his 1881 translation of Vikélas's novel.

Gennadius begins, "The translation into English of a modern Greek tale is a literary enterprise so unusual, not to say unprecedented, that it seems to call for some explanation, if not for apology" (1881b: v). Gennadius responds to what he assumes will be the protests of English readers by producing justification for the translation and their perusal of it. His arguments run the gamut from the utility of his translation for learning the Modern Greek language to the literary merits of this particular text (xxiii–xxiv). In the process of justifying his translation, Gennadius produces one of the first histories of modern Greek prose fiction (xiv–xxii). On the one hand, Gennadius, like Vikélas and Lukís, demonstrates that he knows the literary game by playing it according to its English rules: of course the English should disdain a modern Greek novel. On the other, I count his very acts of translating *Lukís Láras*, bringing it before the English public, and documenting that there in fact was a substantial modern Greek literary tradition in the nineteenth century *as a response to Lukís-Vikélas's call for the sustenance of community through writing*. In his own way, Gennadius is carrying out the task assigned by Lukís-Vikélas to all Greeks of his generation by insisting on the existence of a contemporary idiom and of texts in that idiom, and by making more widely available this particular Greek text calling for preservation of community and more Greek texts.[23] Thus Gennadius, like Lukís-Vikélas, writes to accomplish extraliterary goals. This feature ties the text taken as a whole to the function of storytelling in oral cultures and prompts a comparison to African American Harriet Wilson's accomplishment of telling the story of Frado in *Our Nig*. But whereas Gennadius's translation constitutes a piece of evidence that Lukís-Vikélas received the kind of response he called for, available historical evidence reveals that Frado-Wilson tragically did not succeed in rallying a black community of writers and readers, at least not in her lifetime.

Like the trope of the Talking Book, Harriet E. Wilson's *Our Nig* is a text that has greatly enriched our understanding of African American literature in recent years. Much important and creative research has been done on Wilson's work, starting with Henry Louis Gates Jr.'s substantive introduction to the second edition (1983), which began the restoration of this text to its unique place in the history of African American letters. I want to focus here on the "call" to readers Wilson and her supporters make in and through the text and to detail the desired response, explaining how "relationship," as in the case of Gronniosaw, fails to materialize in the immediate wake of the call. Wilson's narrative does not contain the kind of extended reader address we find in *Lukís Láras*. Nevertheless, taken as a whole, *Our Nig*, too, seeks and addresses a responsive readership that will work to create extratextual relationships. Focusing on personal pronouns in the title, the preface, the text, and the appendix, one can discover numerous clues to the complexities of community building in antebellum New England.

Wilson titles her text *Our Nig; or, Sketches from the Life of a Free Black, in a Two-story White House, North. Showing that Slavery's Shadows Fall Even There.* The title page says that it is authored "By 'Our Nig.'" Published in Boston by Geo. C. Rand and Avery in 1859, the book states on its copyright page that it was registered in the clerk's office of the district court of the district of Massachusetts by "Mrs. H. E. Wilson." The text seems to have undergone only a single printing and languished in almost complete obscurity until the second edition of 1983. Gates's research established, among other things, that the author signing herself "Our Nig" was in fact the woman who had registered the text, Mrs. Harriet Wilson, a black widow residing in Boston at the time of publication, the main features of whose life overlap with the main events recounted in the narrative (1983, esp. xiv–xvii).

Even these bare facts hint at the baffling question of genre for *Our Nig*. Wilson's text is probably best described as a hybrid form, between autobiography and fiction.[24] Features pointing to the text as prose fiction include the fact that the narrative is told in the third person—with a few exceptions, which will be discussed below—and the fact that the work's structure, characterizations, and plot comply to a great extent with conventions of the sentimental and gothic novel.[25] Perhaps even more convincing is recently discovered biographical information which verifies that several elements of the story were not drawn directly from Wilson's life (see White 1993: 41–45). On the other hand, the many points at which the life of the protagonist and the life of the author do overlap support the idea that this is autobiography thinly veiled by third-person narrating pronouns and pseudonyms. Even this veiling breaks down, as in the use of first-person pronouns in the first three chapter titles (for example, "A New Home for Me") and in a reference to "my narrative" in the final chapter. Additionally, there are structural features such as the title and appendix that resemble nineteenth-century slave autobiographies. Robert Stepto has helped us understand how important it is to think of these elements as integral parts of the narratives and to see how their function was not only to authenticate the former slaves' accounts but also, in literary terms, to "create something close to a dialogue—of forms as well as voices" (1991: 3–4). Although Harriet Wilson was not technically a slave, she would have had similar reasons for wanting to include a plurality of voices and forms. The authenticating apparatus of *Our Nig* consists of two main parts framing the narrative: a "preface" signed "H. E. W." and an appendix consisting of three testimonials or endorsements, the first by someone calling herself "Allida," the second by a "Margaretta Thorn," and the third initialed "C. D. S." I will begin with Wilson's preface and Thorn's testimonial since their addresses/addressees are the most explicit.

Like Vikélas's preface to *Lukís Láras*, Wilson's follows some common conventions, beginning with an apology for her inadequate writing skills: "In offering to the public the following pages, the writer confesses her inability to minister to the refined and cultivated, the pleasure supplied by abler pens." But even in continuing her self-disparagement by calling her narrations "crude," she defends herself by saying that she is not writing for the pleasure of the refined and cultivated. Like Vikélas, his narrator Lukís, and Gennadius, Wilson's apologies and adherence to convention are subverted by nonconventional goals. I quote the remainder of the preface in full:

> Deserted by kindred, disabled by failing health, I am forced to some experiment which shall aid me in maintaining myself and child without extinguishing this feeble life. I would not from these motives even palliate slavery at the South, by disclosures of its appurtenances North. My mistress was wholly imbued with *southern* principles. I do not pretend to divulge every transaction in my own life, which the unprejudiced would declare unfavorable in comparison with treatment of legal bondmen; I have purposely omitted what would most provoke shame in our good anti-slavery friends at home.
>
> My humble position and frank confession of errors will, I hope, shield me from severe criticism. Indeed, defects are so apparent it requires no skilful hand to expose them.
>
> I sincerely appeal to my colored brethren universally for patronage, hoping they will not condemn this attempt of their sister to be erudite, but rally around me a faithful band of supporters and defenders.
>
> H. E. W. (3)

Wilson's need to write the book to support herself and her child might be the element that stands out the most at an affective level.[26] But for my purposes here, more remarkable features of this preface may well be the way Wilson carries out a criticism of white abolitionists while seeming to deflect offense, and more remarkable still, the subtle address of her appeal for support of her general political and specific personal goals *to a peer constituency*. Like her bracketing of refined and cultivated pleasure seekers at the opening of her preface, Wilson, as I see it, turns from white abolitionists as well.[27] The only direct address she makes in this preface is to "my colored brethren"; she is asking fellow blacks to buy her book and to "rally around" her as "a faithful band of supporters and defenders." She envisions something like that which Lukís enjoys in his old age: a circle of peers who share experience and a vision for a communal future. While abolitionists may be "our good anti-slavery friends at home," she is sister only to her "colored brethren." Furthermore, like the use of "our" in the title, and in the appendix (to which I will turn shortly), Wilson's use of the first-person plural possessive pronoun establishes insiders and outsiders, actors and those acted upon: we blacks are over here, so to speak, our good antislavery friends (those we choose) are over there. Despite denigrating herself, Wilson demonstrates her authorship and authority by emphasizing her control of the material that follows in the main narrative: "I have purposely omitted"; "My humble position and frank confession of errors will . . . shield me." She effectively pre-empts judgment coming from outside by saying that those who would exercise it against her have "no skilful hand."

The relationship between writer and addressee is reversed in Margaretta Thorn's endorsement in the appendix: "To the friends of our dark-complexioned brethren and sisters" (138). Thorn issues a challenge to this audience when she repeats her formulation with slightly altered wording in her closing request: "those who call themselves friends of our dark-skinned brethren" (140). If you really are a friend, she implies, you will buy this book. Thorn's use of "our" functions similarly to Wilson's in the phrase "our good anti-slavery friends" in that she creates two groups: we are here, and "our dark-complexioned brethren and sisters" are over there. Although Thorn uses filial appellations for blacks (in contrast to Wilson, who does not use them cross-racially), Thorn appeals to a white audience and implies her and their alterity to the author of *Our Nig*. In sum, both Thorn and Wilson are engaged with two groups: colored and abolitionist whites. And both imply that there can and does exist friendship between them. But whereas Thorn emphasizes that all belong to one family, Wilson maintains distance by including only colored people in the community she would create through her book.

The third testimonial does not address anyone directly, though its author casts the net for readers widely by stating, "I hope *no one* will refuse to aid her in her work, as she is worthy the sympathy of *all Christians, and those who have a spark of humanity in their breasts*" (140; my emphasis). Gates assumes that this writer could be white, since this endorser mentions the difference in color between this endorser's skin and the author's: "Although her complexion is a little darker than my own, . . ." But, as Gates also points out, the initials C. D. S. were a common abbreviation in the period for "Colored Indentured Servant" (xix–xx). He or she could thus have been a racial peer to Wilson, though the very presence of this endorsement implies that its author is in a superior socioeconomic position to her.[28] "Allida," author of the first and longest endorsement, does not address anyone directly either but urges "all the friends who purchase a volume" to "remember they are doing good" (137). Although the identity of none of these authors has been subsequently established and nothing they say proves they are white, at the very least, we can gather from what they write that none, like Wilson, is trying to address an exclusively black community. We have no reason to question their support for the author of *Our Nig*, or for blacks in general, since all demonstrate their friendship through the content of their testimonials and the very fact that they give them to Wilson to publish in her volume. Still, the contrast to Wilson persists. That Wilson herself was aiming for building community among blacks is supported not only by the preface but also by her title and her story.

To turn back to the title, anyone who has tried to teach this text or has even told acquaintances about it has already confronted Wilson's audacity in naming her work "Our Nig." Today, one finds oneself immediately explaining that the text is by a black author, indeed one who controlled rhetoric so skillfully that she even signed the text " 'Our Nig.' " What did it mean to audiences at the time it was published? In Gates's view, "Harriet E. Wilson allows these racist characters to name her heroine, only to *invert* such racism by employing the name, in inverted commas, as her pseudonym of authorship. . . . Transformed into an *object* of abuse and scorn by her enemies, the 'object,' the heroine of *Our Nig*, reverses this relationship by *renaming herself* not Our Nig but 'Our Nig,' thereby transforming herself into a *subject*" (1983: li). Gates plausibly accounts for the shift in significance from the first usage (in the title) to the second (in the signature). But we can mine Wilson's title page even further for what it tells us about the intended audience(s) and the author's possible goals. Specifically, I'd like to pause over the juxtaposition of "our" and "nig."

It takes a huge leap to imagine a white abolitionist audience that could be comfortable with Wilson's title, for to begin with a first-person possessive pronoun without quotation marks implies a relationship between the one who enunciates it, that is, the "I" of the reading subject, and the object being possessed: my and yours/others = our + Nig. In the North of Wilson's day, the word "nig" or "nigger" for a black person was derogatory, even if it was in circulation (Gates 1983: li), and for this reason it would presumably be shunned by white abolitionists. Of course even the subtitle announces one of Wilson's goals as revealing that "slavery's shadows" fall in the North, and a reading of the text shows that those who profess to be abolitionists can be hypocrites who engage in racist behavior. Indeed, new research on the likely prototypes for the white family in the novel, the Bellmonts (historically, the Haywards), builds a strong argument that they had ties to abolitionism and most likely considered themselves abolitionists; but their abolitionist beliefs did not prevent them—at least some of them—from mistreating their black servant.[29] Wilson's main title, in other words, forces the white reader to utter what would be considered a racist statement in an abolitionist milieu. Those who do not want to say "our" in conjunction with "nig" must in a sense refuse to read. We do know that readership for Wilson's novel was tragically small, though no one has yet proven why. It does not take extravagant logic, however, to assume that the title may have put off some white readers who might normally have bought literature presumably supporting the abolitionist cause.[30]

What if, on the other hand, as I have already proposed, we assume that Wilson writes for a black audience, an audience of free blacks like herself? Her subtitle, after all, makes clear that she is not relating the narrative of a slave, slavelike though her protagonist's existence might have been, but rather "Sketches from the Life of a *Free Black*." I propose that the word "Nig" can then function as a sign of recognition: someone else like me. Instead of drawing the reader into a collective of racist whites, the first-person plural phrase would place the (black) reader into a peer collective of blacks, the kind of peer collective Wilson hopes for in her preface. Lest my interpretation seem anachronistic, I point out that such a solidaristic use of the word "nigger" appears in Wilson's novel. In the very first chapter, "Mag Smith, My Mother," Wilson has Jim, a free black, wondering out loud to himself whether the scorned and destitute white Mag would marry him:

> After the usual supply of fuel was prepared, Jim returned home. Full of pity for Mag, he set about devising measures for her relief. "By golly!" said he to himself one day—for he had become so absorbed in Mag's interest that he had fallen into a habit of musing aloud—"By golly! I wish she 'd *marry* me."
>
> "Who?" shouted Pete Green, suddenly starting from an unobserved corner of the rude shop.
>
> "Where you come from, you sly nigger!" exclaimed Jim.
>
> "Come, tell me, who is 't?" said Pete; "Mag Smith, you want to marry?"
>
> "Git out, Pete! and when you come in dis shop again, let a nigger know it. Do n't steal in like a thief." (10)

Though Jim is annoyed that he's been overheard, there is no sign that his use of the word "nigger" in this scene is malicious. To the contrary, that Jim uses the word once to refer to Pete ("Where you come from, you sly nigger!") and once to refer to himself ("let a nigger know it") enhances the reader's sense that the two know each other well and are comfortable with teasing each other. It is perhaps critical to the benign valence of the word that the two men are alone; there are no whites present who could seize on the term and "hear" it differently.

Most uses of the word "nigger" in the novel refer to the mixed-race daughter of Mag and Jim, Frado, and any number of other scenes show how the term in the mouths of whites is meant to dehumanize the protagonist and separate her from people who could be her (cross-racial) peers. When Frado first goes to school, for instance, Mary Bellmont sets the tone by exclaiming that she is ashamed to be seen "walking with a nigger." The other children immediately take up the word and the sentiment, shouting, "See that nigger" and "I won't play with her" (31). Although, under the influence of their teacher, the schoolchildren stop ostracizing Frado and even come to treasure her and her antics, verbal (and physical) abuse only gets worse in the Bellmont household. How the word "nigger" inflicts harm on the girl is revealed through another eavesdropping scene. James, Mary's older brother and a sympathetic, if ineffective, friend to Frado, overhears her complaining to her dog Fido in the barn. Frado's words are communicated to the reader when James narrates the scene to his Aunt Abby, another impotent white friend of Frado's. James reports to Aunt Abby that Frado says to her dog, "Work as long as I can stand, and then fall down and lay there till I can get up. No mother, father, brother or sister to care for me, and then it is, You lazy nigger, lazy nigger—all because I am black! Oh, if I could die!" (75). Frado's lament reminds us of Gronniosaw's when the book refuses to speak to him; both feel themselves despised and cut off from human relationships because of the color of their skin. Particularly relevant to our analysis of the valence of this epithet is that of all the horrible beatings Frado has received, it is the barb of being called "lazy nigger" by her white mistresses that she complains about in a private moment of agony, a situation in which presumably she utters her most honest thoughts.[31] While verbal insults must not be the only thing that makes Frado want to die, they are what she singles out here.

Based on these and other uses of the word "nigger" in the text, I conclude that, from the perspective of a black audience reading a text by a black author, the title page could function inversely from how it functions for a white audience. For black readers, the unmarked use in the main title of the phrase " 'Our Nig' " could be read as: "[A Story about] One of Our Own." Whereas the inverted commas around the author's use of the phrase as a pseudonym at the bottom of the page could be thought to mark the phrase as one from the mouth of someone not part of our collective, that is, whites. "Our Nig" in its second appearance on the title page could signal to the black audience: this is authored by one who is/was called by (white) others "our nig." To be sure, we don't need to choose between these readings. As Du Bois has taught us, African Americans have had to develop double vision and double consciousness; the minority group has to know how to read through majority lenses (1903; 1961). Black readers could have discerned both meanings, as Wilson could have intended both. Additionally, if Wilson really wrote the book to raise money to support herself and her child—research supports this claim—she needed any sympathetic readers she could find.

What I find remarkable is that her concrete, urgent financial reasons to sell as many copies as possible did not deter her from two challenging goals that would have an impact on readership. As we have already examined in the preface and title, Wilson uses sophisticated rhetorical strategies, addressing black and white audiences to different ends: appealing to black readers to constitute themselves as a community of equals she had never enjoyed or even witnessed; and appealing to a white audience to deliver a message about hypocrisy that could only make them uncomfortable. It may well have been her sense of how likely a white audience was to take offense at her message about Northern racism that enforced her desire for a sympathetic black audience. In any case, we can better appreciate the challenges she faced in achieving these goals by reviewing the elusive character of Frado/Wilson's black husband.

It is not until the twelfth and final chapter, "The Winding Up of the Matter," that Frado meets Samuel, a black man, whom she marries after a very brief courtship. He abandons her several times, finally dying of fever in New Orleans and leaving her to raise their child. I maintain, however, that the manner in which this affair is presented in Wilson's text mitigates Samuel's offense. His relationship to Frado, for example, is described as a natural outcome of the meeting of two lonely colored people. Wilson achieves this sense of fate by embedding the narration of the courtship in a series of rhetorical questions: "as people of color were rare there, was it strange she should attract her dark brother; that he should inquire her out; succeed in seeing her; feel a strange sensation in his heart towards her; that he should toy with her shining curls, feel proud to provoke her to smile and expose the ivory concealed by thin, ruby lips; that her sparkling eyes should fascinate; that he should propose; that they should marry?" (126). The answer, of course, is no, it was not strange.

Wilson employs several additional strategies to impede a negative view of Samuel. The entire narration of Frado's relationship with him constitutes only one part of one chapter. As profound an influence as the failed marriage with Samuel may have had on Frado, in terms of sheer space given to the narration of causes of misery in her life, the brutality of life with the white Bellmonts overwhelms abandonment by her black husband. Indeed, it is Frado's preoccupation (obsession?) with the Bell-monts that concludes even this chapter and thereby the novel. In a brilliant reversal of the trope of the slave hunter as bloodhound who will never stop trying to find the escaped slave, Wilson closes by remarking that though the Bellmonts may have forgotten her, Frado "will never cease to track them till beyond mortal vision" (131).

More specifically effecting an exoneration or at least mitigation of Samuel's culpability for his treatment of Frado, the narrator points to the character we already know and empathize with, Frado, as the source of the attraction: "was it strange *she* should attract her dark brother" (my emphasis). Frado, not Samuel, is the subject of the sentence; she is the starting point, so to speak, for the chain of events that will eventually leave her an impoverished single mother. The narrator also deflects some blame from Samuel to Frado by implying that Frado fooled herself into thinking she knew him better than she actually did at the time they married (127). Furthermore, the narrator repeats more than once that when they are together, he does take good care of her (127, 128). Perhaps one could use the issue of assigning responsibility to explain the reap-pearance of the (narrator's) first-person voice at this point in the text, where the opening sentence of this chapter reads, "A few years ago, within the compass of *my* narrative, there appeared often in some of *our* New England villages . . . " (126; my emphasis). The narrator places herself in the scene in which these events transpire. Still, nothing ob-structs our view to the facts that Samuel abandons Frado several times and that she must struggle to sustain herself and their child as a result. From this perspective, the one specific experience of "black community" described in the novel is a disaster for Frado.

As the much greater harm done to Frado by the Bellmonts minimizes the portion of her misery caused by Samuel, the characterization of abolitionists in this chapter also contextualizes Samuel's behavior. Sam-uel is introduced, you may recall, by way of reference to others like him: "professed fugitives from slavery, who recounted their personal experience in homely phrase, and awakened the indignation of non-slaveholders against brother Pro" (126). Abolitionists, in other words, are painted as Northern whites who would listen to any lie that allows them to feel better about themselves by criticizing Southern whites. When Samuel reveals the truth to Frado, that is, that "he had never seen the

South," he characterizes his "illiterate harangues" as "humbugs for hungry abolitionists" (128). Again, Samuel's duplicity reflects worse on abolitionists than on himself or other blacks. He (merely) feeds a hunger they have for "illiterate harangues," as long as Southerners are blamed and abolitionists left unscathed.[32]

Abolitionists' inability to detect lies or even their desire for them seems relatively benign, if hypocritical, compared to the one direct description of abolitionist "interaction" with blacks. This indictment of abolitionists is made even more scathing by its insertion into the narrative at the point when Frado must search for work to support herself and her child after Samuel's death from yellow fever, that is to say, at the point when Samuel can no longer be blamed for not taking care of her because he is dead. Frado heads to Massachusetts, the state most identified with the abolitionist cause, but where she, as a free black, has "strange adventures": "Watched by kidnappers, maltreated by professed abolitionists, who did n't want slaves at the South, nor niggers in their own houses, North. Faugh! to lodge one; to eat with one; to admit one through the front door; to sit next one; awful!" (129). It is one thing to give public audience to a black who criticizes Southern whites, but quite another to let "niggers in their own houses."[33] Wilson makes a brilliant move between the first and second sentences in this passage. By using interjections and avoiding personal pronouns, the second sentence could be a first-person proclamation of these racist sentiments—quoted monologue, as opposed to reported speech. As in the case of her title, by omitting quotation marks here, Wilson forces the white reader into a rhetorical performance of the hypocrisy she would uncover and criticize. To read this line is not to read that someone else says, "Faugh! to lodge one; to eat with one; to admit one through the front door; to sit next one; awful!" but to "utter" it oneself.

I have interpreted Gennadius's introduction, as well as his translation, as a response to Lukís/Vikélas's call for preservation of Greek history, tradition, and community through writing. If we look to the paratext of Wilson's novel, we can say that she issues a similar call for a communal response. The paratext, however, also hints at the lack of response or rather at the lack of the hoped-for response. I have already pointed out how hard it is to hear the various voices of *Our Nig*'s paratext as engaged in harmonious conversation; their agendas are too divergent. Specifically, none of the authors of the testimonials takes up Wilson's call in the preface for a black community, widening the circle instead to include "friends" of blacks and all "Christians."[34] While Wilson seeks to embed her story in a black community, her text can only come into the world embedded in white voices or at least voices that call for cross-racial community. The first endorsement, that of "Allida," about which I've said little so far, also gives us reason to believe that Wilson's other goal (of delivering a message about Northern racism) wasn't getting through either, for Allida makes the story of abandonment by Frado's black husband rather more central than Wilson. In Allida's recital, despite Frado's awful treatment at the hands of whites in the early part of her life, once she moves to W——, Mass. and meets Mrs. Walker, she is happy, "truly happy." Allida even reports that her health begins to improve (133). But meeting the man who becomes her husband irretrievably reverses her fortunes; the narration of this "reversal" takes up most of the space of Allida's testimony. My point here is not that Allida wasn't sincere in her affection for the "real Frado" or in her desire to help her but rather that she doesn't give the inscribed response. She doesn't "get" Wilson's point that the greatest crime committed against Frado is hypocrisy on the part of (some) Northern whites, not on the part of (some) Northern blacks who act duplicitously because that seems to be what whites want from them, and who therefore become duplicitous as a way to sustain themselves. On this point, at least, Margaretta Thorn comes closer when she calls the author "indeed a slave, in every sense of the word; and a lonely one, too" (139).

In sum, then, it seems to me that Wilson cannot have been sanguine about the chances of her story of Northern racism getting through to a white abolitionist audience. Then again, after her experiences with her husband, neither can she have been sanguine about being supported by a community of blacks. As Wilson's story itself so poignantly illustrates, there simply weren't that many black people in the areas of New England in which she had been living, and those who did live there were under enormous pressure to secure their own survival.[35] Vikélas's character Lukís, for one, would have understood how great the odds were against developing community under the conditions circumscribing the lives of many blacks in antebellum New England. In looking back at the period of his own troubles from the comfort of his community in London, Lukís laments how impossible it was to think about others during the Revolution: "encircled by adversities," each "thought of his own safety, and had no leisure to inquire into the condition of others" (Vikélas 1881b: 115). It is only once they are out of harm's way—"when we rested our wearied heads, without the fear of a sword held ready over us, when we sat at the doorstep of a hospitable refuge which no Turk's shadow could darken"— that they begin to reconstitute a community (116). Even though Wilson's story is not set during an officially declared war, the circumstances she recounts show how hard it must have been for blacks who were literally and figuratively fighting for their lives to have the "leisure to inquire into the condition of others."

Unfortunately, historical evidence indicates that Wilson's call for community through *Our Nig* did go unheard. Unlike the trajectory of slave narratives, *Our Nig* does not end in freedom, in this case the hoped-for economic freedom. Most tragically on the human level, Wilson did not raise enough money from the sale of her novel to retrieve her son from foster care and nurture him herself. Ironically, it is the death certificate of her son that became the critical link in proving the existence of Harriet Wilson and her authorship of the novel (Gates 1983: xii–xiii). Eric Gardner's research has uncovered no record of free blacks offering support, either materially by purchasing Wilson's text or emotionally by creating or offering a community of which she could be part (1993: 227). Furthermore, so few copies of *Our Nig* were sold that it does not seem to have had much of a verifiable effect on the immediately subsequent development of African American literature. This provides all the more reason to follow Debra Walker King when she concludes that "Wilson's appeals for support demand that we do many more revisions" of the ending today (1997: 44).

To do such a revision in our age would require letting ourselves be lodged together in some kind of intersubjective world, not of the normal world of conversation Goffman was describing with this phrase but a world created by erasing the boundaries between reality here and literature there. Readers would have to believe the book's "you" actually calls them, and they would have to be ready to respond. This includes the reader-listeners' realization that they cannot be passive consumers of an entertaining fiction but that they are instead part of the community constituted through the storytelling. With such knowledge comes the responsibility of passing on the story. This proper listening attitude includes recognition of the price of sustaining community: in Maya Angelou's unforgettable phrase, you have to remember that you've been paid for. You've been paid for by Lukís and his compatriots, by black slaves and black indentured servants like Frado, by writers like Vikélas and Wilson. Adopting such an attitude toward a literary text requires displacing the attitude, reviewed in the previous chapter, that art is supposed to "be, not do." Twenty-first-century readers can be schooled into these various "*responsibilities* of listenership" (Stepto 1986: 306) by talk fiction, two examples of which we are now ready to take up.

"Responsibilities of Listenership" in *The Third Wedding Wreath* and *Mama Day*

In twentieth-century texts of my storytelling mode, direct references to the production of the story are gone. Absent, too, are tales of found manuscripts and explicit directions to readers in paratextual forewords or afterwords about how to understand the main text. But I contend that to read these texts as Talk is to discover extratextual communal goals similar to those of Vikélas and Wilson. Talk-fiction texts of my story-telling mode reveal orientation to an answering—that is, they reveal themselves as statements—in two ways. Most obviously, they use traditional deixis, displaying awareness of a communicative circuit by addressing their readers with "you"—although not with the even more obvious "you reader" of my nineteenth-century examples. These calls may appear intermittently throughout the text, as in Tachtsís's novel, or they may appear in the frame, as in Naylor's. In either case, that readers should consider the whole text as statement (and not just the sentence in which the deictic appears) is conveyed by the second, less obvious move of the text-as-statement: telling stories that are about creating relationships and communities through storytelling. In other words, these texts embed negative and positive models of listening and listeners in the stories themselves. To "reply" to texts of my storytelling mode, readers have to feel the vocative force of the narrators' "you"—they have to feel that they are addressed by it, *and* they have to be willing to enter into an intimate relationship with the storyteller and the communities effected and affected by the stories told. As would-be respondents to the statements of these texts, we can learn to listen by deciphering the lessons learned by the narrators and narratees, the tellers and the listeners, in the novels. At first glance, the process of learning to listen appears to unfold as a battle between two characters who "represent" oral and literate cultures, respectively. In *The Third Wedding Wreath*, Nína originally appears as the literate character and Ekávi (Hecuba) with her unwieldy, episodic stories as the archetypal oral creature. In *Mama Day*, George's way of understanding the world is based on logic learned "mainside," whereas Cocoa has been schooled by familial and communal oral traditions of the island that is on no map, Willow Springs. As in my father's anecdote about the widow and in Lukís's about the nursemaid, however, proper response ultimately involves a profound entanglement—a marriage in Tachtsís's metaphor—of oral and literate culture, not a triumph of one over the other. I would go so far as to say that these two examples of my storytelling mode are parables about learning how to recognize oneself and how to operate as a secondary oral creature. For this reason, it will be necessary to recount a fair amount of what occurs in the novels and how they are narrated to understand their Talk.

Kóstas Tachtsís's novel *The Third Wedding Wreath*, first published in 1963, is narrated by a bourgeois Athenian named Nína who recounts the events of her life and those of an older friend named Ekávi (Hecuba) before, during, and directly after World War II. Nína narrates retrospectively during the civil war into which Greece plunges after the world war, and after Ekávi's death and Nína's marriage to Thódoro, one of Ekávi's sons. (Their marriage serves as source for the titular concept. In marrying him, Nína dons her third wedding wreath.[36]) Despite the serious events recounted, the novel can be uproariously funny. Both Nína and Ekávi engage in battles with their children that are so extreme they seem comical. In the context of the entire novel, however, these conflicts and the narration of them fulfill the serious function of creating and cementing vital relationships. The novel's high level of invective also signals its connection to oral culture, which Ong characterizes in part as "agonistically toned" (1982: 43–45). In other words, I contend that Tachtsís's main purpose is not to entertain—though he is not uninterested in entertaining—but rather to examine what is at stake in storytelling for individuals, families, and communities.

Unlike Vikélas's Lukís, who refers repeatedly to the (difficult) activity of writing, Nína never mentions explicitly the form of transmission of her story; she neither refers to herself writing nor to someone out there who must be reading. Similar to Lukís, however, Nína does reveal her total orientation toward receivers of her story. Using plural second-person forms (which in Greek means either that she is addressing more than one person informally or one person or a group formally), Nína continually appeals to assumed auditors for sympathy and understanding. Composing a large portion of Nína's narration are her quotations of Ekávi's own stories to Nína. Thus in Tachtsís's novel, as in Naylor's, there are numerous embedded examples of telling and listening that readers have to decipher.

As character and as narrator, Nína thinks of herself as well educated. In her youth she was a good student, and even wanted to go on to study law, though this dream is foiled by her mother's ideas of women's role in society (1985b: 37). As an adult, she loves to read "serious books," in contrast to those around her like Thódoro, her third husband (186), or María, her daughter, whom she picks at for reading pulp fiction (208, 244). She knows who Freud and Nordau are, unlike her friend Ekávi, who panics when her son in prison wants her to send him books by these authors (185). Nína uses numerous classical allusions, referring to the story of Odysseus and Polyphemos (12), to Teiresias (28), or to Medusa, an epithet she uses repeatedly for her daughter (for example, 48). Literary topoi influence how she thinks about her life. She frequently uses phrases that she associates with prose fiction. For instance, when she narrates seeing her first love at a distance long after their relationship had been forbidden by her family, she comments, "For a moment I wanted to speed up my pace so I could catch a glimpse of his face, but as they say in novels, my feet would not obey me" (34). When she marries her third husband, Nína reports feeling like she is "marrying the hero of a novel which I'd read and reread years before" (58). That novel would be the novel of her mother-in-law's life. But, of course, she's never read anything by or about Ekávi, she's only listened to Ekávi tell countless anecdotes about her own life and the lives of those connected to her, like Thódoro. This repeated listening to Ekávi's stories, in Nína's view, is like reading and rereading a book; after she has known Ekávi for a few years she believes she can predict her behavior: "I could read her like a book by

63

then" (175). However, through even longer acquaintance with Ekávi, Nína will come to revise her framework of thinking about interpersonal relationships as reading, as a subject acting on an object, to recall my analysis of Gronniosaw.

A huge portion of the discourse that makes up the novel is Nína's quotation of Ekávi telling those stories by which Nína thinks she has come to know her. What kind of storyteller is Ekávi? Like Lukís, she makes frequent references to her listener, and she often "digresses" to tell about incidents in the lives of other people that would seem to be related at best tangentially to what she started talking about. After Nína quotes her for the first time, Nína comments, "Et cetera, et cetera" (my translation; 1985a: 66; 1985b: 62), implying not only that the stories are indeed endless but also that there isn't much individuality to them.[37] Ekávi herself is aware of digressing, but again, like Lukís, she believes it always serves a purpose. After one long sequence in what had started out as a story about losing her husband to another woman, but ends up about her daughter being healed from a severe fever through her mother's intercessions to a saint, Ekávi justifies her parenthesis by explaining to Nína, "If I'm unraveling this whole history, it's to tell you that this same Saint Anastasía who saved my Xéne from certain death once again gave me the warning sign that I would lose my husband" (74). Ekávi is at her most entertaining as a storyteller, Nína thinks, when her life is the most tumultuous (245).[38] Perhaps most importantly, Ekávi is shown to be both a good listener and a good storyteller (9). Nína is particularly jealous that her own husband—the second one, Antóni—seems to have enjoyed Ekávi's company so well because of her qualities as listener and teller (256).

And what kind of interlocutor is Nína? When the two women first become acquainted, it is clear that Nína spends numerous hours listening to Ekávi recite the details of her earlier life. Several times when Nína quotes Ekávi's stories, she quotes herself providing the goad, indicating, among other things, that she's heard the story before. The following setup is typical of storytelling in their early relationship: "Many times, when we had company in the afternoons and the talk would come around to failed marriages and divorce, Ekávi would get all excited and launch into a harangue, laying down the law. . . . 'Her first cousin turned her husband's head!' I would butt in to give her the right encouragement.

'Come on, Ekávi, tell us about it; it'll pass the time! For my part, you know that I never tire hearing you tell about it' " (75–76). This is a perfect example of what Genette calls iterative narrative: many similar events are narrated once (1980: 116). Naturally, the afternoon's storytelling can't have been exactly the same each time, but Nína emphasizes the similarity and the repetition through her summary statement, indicating that if she's a frequent listener to Ekávi's stories, she's not necessarily a good one in the terms set up by the novel as a whole—and therefore also in the terms necessary for understanding its Talk. Initially, letting herself be entertained seems to be Nína's chief reason for spending so much time with her new friend ("it'll pass the time!"). When Ekávi has just recited a heartrending sequence about how she discovered her two grandchildren abandoned in their ice-cold house by her daughter Eléni, and how she subsequently decides to take one of the children home with her—not by chance the grandson—leaving the granddaughter behind, Nína interrupts not to show empathy with the tough decision nor even to express horror that she left the other child behind but rather to comment on an irrelevant detail—that Ekávi knew how to play the mandolin (140).

In a sequence of scenes that constitutes one of two major turning points in the women's relationship and therefore in the novel, Nína revises her opinion of Ekávi and her stories and—most importantly for our purposes here—her posture as interlocutor. The Italian invasion of Greece and the imminence of war with the Germans create particular stress for Nina and how she copes with her life. She realizes, for example, that reading doesn't do her much good; it hasn't prepared her to deal with war (198), and it doesn't help her to understand human nature (204). During this period Nína comes to realize that being in relationship with Ekávi is more important than always agreeing with her opinions, something that Ong might describe as a newfound appreciation for the "person-interactive" component (1982: 68). One day after Nína has argued with Ekávi about politics (specifically about the Greek dictator Metaxás who has just died), Nína tries to take her afternoon siesta, but her guilty feelings about the fight with her friend prevent her from falling asleep. She thinks to herself:

> Metaxás isn't anything to me [*o metaxás the mu ínai típota*]. One's died, ten will take his place. Whereas Ekávi is one of my own [*ínai dikós mu ánthropos*]. For me she's more important than a hundred Metaxáses. I

remembered the stories which she had told me about Davíko, things which I'd listened to then as if they were fairy tales [*paramíthia*], stories which belonged forever to the past, which wouldn't have any consequences, but which now suddenly took on retrospective, as they say, meaning. (my translation; 1985a: 215; 1985b: 222).

Nína's words here are obviously a reference to the famous soliloquy in *Hamlet* in which the protagonist muses about the actor who plays the character of Queen Hecuba (Ekávi) of Troy: "What's Hecuba to him, or he to Hecuba?" (Act II, Scene 2, line 559). Here Nína realizes that Metaxás isn't anything to her, whereas Ekávi means everything to her; she's one of Nína's own, literally "her person" (*dikós mu ánthropos*). And Nína's relationship with Ekávi is constituted by and through their oral exchange of stories.[39]

Nína's use of a Shakespearean intertext gives meaning to her epiphany in quite an abstract, and, indeed, literate way. Whereas for the actor—or Hamlet for that matter—Hecuba is a remote historical character among the vanquished—only known through literature—for Nína, Hecuba (Ekávi) is a flesh-and-blood woman who tells her the story of her life in person, who shares her world and her friends. Nevertheless, Hamlet launches his muse because the actor seems so engaged with Hecuba; whereas Nína, despite quotidian contact, has let this Hecuba and her life seem like myth to her and let a politician, whom she probably only "knows" through the newspaper—and who, furthermore, is now dead—get in the way of her relationship to her friend. By having his protagonist-narrator learn such an important lesson in this particular way, Tachtsís provides a brilliant illustration of the marriage of oral and literate values, reminding us of Tziovas's hypothesis, cited in the previous chapter, that "the relationship between orality and textuality is not one of rigid opposition, but rather one of intrication and enfolding" (1989: 321).

What Nína learns here is not only the value of her individual relationship to Ekávi but also the value of (oral) stories for building community. Previously she'd thought of everything Ekávi told her as fairy tales (*paramíthia*), made-up stories that have no value for the present other than as entertainment to "pass the time," as she says. Previously, Nína scorned the past, or at best discarded it as quickly as she possibly could. Thus a certain portion of Ekávi's narrating for Nína must truly have been "digressions." By coming to understand the importance of her relationship to Ekávi, Nína also achieves clarity about the relationship of pieces of the story that before seemed irrelevant or at best irrevocably linked to the past. Now these links hold "retrospective meaning." It's not irrelevant to our analysis that Nína tags this phrase with "as they say" (*ópos léne*), not "as they say in novels." This is a lesson one learns from other people, not from books. As if to solidify her revised attitude toward Ekávi and story-telling, directly after having this epiphany, Nína is trying to read *Anna Karenina*, but she can't concentrate on the novel. Now the real-life stories of Ekávi's younger, troubled son, Dimítris, his Jewish fiancée, Viktória, and her angry father, Davíko, genuinely interest her (223). In subsequent scenes too, Nína seems to have lost the desire and satisfaction that she previously derived from reading (for example, 259).

Further promoting Nína's reevaluation of her own relationship to books and learning as well as to Ekávi and Ekávi's relation to literacy are encounters the two have together with the actual literati of Greece. A few years after Metaxás's death and Nína's subsequent epiphany, but still during the war, Ekávi starts to take Nína with her when she goes to retrieve the rations to which she is entitled as mother of a journalist. (Thódoro, Ekávi's older son whom Nína will eventually marry, is working as a journalist in the Middle East at this point, and Nína's second husband, Antóni, has died.) Although Nína does need and appreciate the food she receives there, she insists that she goes mainly "for the company" (271). And what company! Nína comments:

No, I hadn't been brought up in an unrefined environment, but it was the first time I'd found myself in such close proximity to a world I'd always dreamed of entering. And in that world I was discovering, again for the first time, an altogether new and different Ekávi, lively and full of good humor as always, but with a completely new air about her, one that placed her much higher socially than I'd ever suspected before. The journalists would address her with respect and ask with real interest for news of Thódoro. And she, amid those clanish and demanding intellectuals, behaved as if she were perfectly at home with them. (272–73)

Whatever ignorance Ekávi may have had about Freud and Nordau, she is comfortable in the world of Palamás, Várnalis, and Tscharúhis, some of the heavyweights of Greek arts at the time.

What puts Ekávi on level ground with these famous artists and thinkers is her use of language, her ability to tell stories. During one particular expedition to the food distribution center, Nína is racking her brains to try to remember the name of a woman she recognizes waiting in line next to them. Whereas Nína silently thinks about it, Ekávi strikes up a conversation with her. As they're leaving, Nína asks Ekávi if she knows who it is. She doesn't. When Nína finds out the celebrity's identity from somebody else and tells Ekávi, her friend replies, "Who cares who she is, it's all the same to me!" (273). Ekávi's reply echoes the Shakespearean intertext of Nína's epiphany, but here it shows that Ekávi already knows where she stands in relation to other people. She doesn't need to know people's official titles or public reputations to be interested in them. Nína, on the other hand, still has something to learn, about her friend, about relationships, and about storytelling. She revises her opinion of Ekávi yet again, commenting, "Of course I'd always admired her gift of the gab [*to légein tis*], but when I saw her holding a conversation on an equal basis with the great Spanoúdi [the most eccentric and brilliant music critic of the day] and having her in stitches with her stories, I began to wonder whether I hadn't perhaps underestimated good old Ekávi" (273).[40] As her comments reveal, Nína is wrapped up with the celebrity of these people; even her relationship to Ekávi could be shifted by "connections." Ekávi, in contrast, takes famous people at face value. She judges them by their willingness and ability to interact with her as conversation partners, though she does seem happy to impress Nína in the process. As through the fight over the politician Metaxás, once again, interaction with Ekávi leads Nína to a reevaluation of her worldview.[41]

If one thinks of Nína and Ekávi as trading places in relation to the literate world through their experiences at the Journalists' Cooperative—Ekávi being the one at ease with the people of the world of books, and Nína being the outsider—subsequent developments in the plot can also be thought of as the two women trading places in their relationship to oral storytelling and its vital activity of keeping people alive through the relationships stories create. This switch is effected through events leading to Ekávi's death, which is itself precipitated by the arrest, imprisonment, and death of Ekávi's beloved youngest child, Dimítris. Throughout their lives, Ekávi and Dimítris had argued, but conflict in Ekávi's oral framework, anyway, means interaction and therefore life.[42] Consequently, the beginning of Ekávi's end could be traced to the first time

Dimítris refuses to fight back.⁴³ The two had been sparring once again about the son's behavior with his (now) wife, Viktória. The three live under one roof to save money (Viktória has been disowned by her family for marrying a Christian). Nína drops in for a visit at this inauspicious moment, overhears mother and son cursing each other, and tries to slip away. But when Dimítris refuses to respond to his mother's last round of invectives, Ekávi turns to the escaping Nína and announces, "I want to die." Nína has grown accustomed to Ekávi's extreme formulations, but when she hears this pronouncement, she shudders (*anatríhiasa*): "It was one time she wasn't play-acting; it wasn't just words, her heart was in it" (278). When Viktória subsequently disappears, the ultimate is at stake for Dimítris. He races to their former home in Thessaloniki, but it is too late, for her, for him, and consequently for Ekávi as well. Viktória has been rounded up with other Jews for transport to Auschwitz, and, according to Nína, Dimítris turns back to drug use "like a man who's falling from the top of a building head first" (280). He ends up arrested for petty thievery and is placed in a prison hospital for consumptives, where Ekávi tries to supplement the starvation diet as well as she can. Mother and son get into a new fight, this time over his sister Polixéni's marriage to a policeman,⁴⁴ and by the time Ekávi decides to make up and visit again, Dimítris has been dead for three days.⁴⁵

We hear nothing of how Ekávi feels about her son's death, but when Ekávi and Nína search for Dimítris's grave, her friend reports "she'd gotten thinner than she ever had even during the worst famine of '41. Her back was stooped, her face had a wild look, and even the locks of her hair, always sensitive to the slightest breeze, were now like tangled pieces of fine wire." What worries Nína the most about Ekávi's condition, however, is her silence: "During the whole afternoon I don't think she spoke more than two or three words. I expected wailing dirges and the beating of her breast, and this silence terrified me" (my translation; 1985a: 278; 1985b: 285). To give Ekávi some time alone at the grave site and to calm her own anxiety, Nína wanders among the wildflowers: "It was the first time I'd been outside of Athens since the beginning of the war. I'd almost forgotten nature existed. . . . My breast seemed to swell with a feeling of well-being [*idoní*] I had almost forgotten existed in life" (286). This walk revitalizes her, and her chest swells because nature blows breath and sensation back into her. (The word "*idoní*," which Chioles translates as "well-being," has the same root as "hedonistic" and in Modern Greek connotes sensual pleasure.) This mini-rebirth seems to come at the expense of Ekávi, but in fact it allows Nína to become the interlocutor her friend needs before she can do her mourning and come back to life, at least temporarily, herself.

As the two begin their journey home, Nína tries to make conversation about the beauty of the pine trees mercifully still standing despite the need for fuel during the war:

> It's time I thought to myself, to pull her out of that depressing silence. If she continues that way, she'll either get sick or she'll go mad. Let her cry for pity's sake, let her wail at last! Ekávi and not crying! I thought it so strange. But I never imagined for a moment that what I said would raise such a storm. Suddenly, she began to shriek and howl. All the tears she'd been holding back in the past few days poured out in a flood, as though some dam had broken:—"My son! My child! Do these pine trees live, my son! They live and rule the world, my boy! It's only you who's dead and gone [*Móno esí mu péthanes*]!" . . . I just let her cry and cry. And when we got up to start walking again, her face had lost something of that wild look it had before. (1985a: 279–80; 1985b: 287)

There are several features of this interaction that point to changes in the relationship between the two women. Most obviously, they have traded places as mourner and comforter. When Nína's second husband, Antóni, had died, it was Ekávi who was saying to the unnaturally silent Nína: "Nína! Don't take it like that! Let yourself go, talk! Scream! Cry out!" (232). Though Nína feels that Ekávi was her only true comfort during the difficult period after Antóni's death, she was not able to scream and cry, explicitly rejecting an oral, external component of mourning (237). Therefore, perhaps the aspect of Nína's behavior that is the most uncharacteristic when the tables are turned after Dimítris's death is that she is able to let Ekávi cry. She is able to be the recipient of Ekávi's talk without judging it, indeed she realizes its therapeutic function. Mourning, like Ekávi's apostrophe to Dimítris, involves making, sustaining, and cherishing relationships and telling stories. Ekávi not only models these behaviors for Nína, she specifically assigns her the responsibility of becoming a storyteller—the teller of Ekávi's story.

Releasing her grief reawakens Ekávi's love of life. Nevertheless, the loss of her beloved Dimítris has put her on the road to her own end, since "no matter where she went, she would always be walking on his grave" (292). When she knows her death is imminent, she has her daughter Polixéni summon Nína to her bedside:

> Suddenly she waved her hand impatiently towards Polixéni who was standing beside me, as if she wanted to get rid of her. Polixéni left the room in tears, the two of us were alone. — "Nína . . . I don't want to die . . . You remember when I said to you I want to die? . . . I don't want to die now . . . I want to live to see my elder boy . . . Maybe he's the only one of my children who loved me a little . . . He was loud and rowdy, I know . . . But he never said a harsh word to me . . . He may have my blessing. . . . And if I die . . ." — "Shh!" I said, "you're not going to die. In a few days you'll be up and at it! . . ." She tried to smile, as if to say: you don't believe what you're saying, I know. — "But if I die," she said again, "I want you to promise me that you'll tell him everything . . ." — "What do you want me to tell him?" — "All the things they did to me [*aftá pu múkanan*]. . ." — "You have my word."
>
> Her face relaxed. She sank back on the pillows as if a great weight had been lifted from her bosom, and she began the same rumbling snore. (1985a: 286–87; 1985b: 294; Tachtsís's ellipses)

On the most superficial level, this scene merely adds to the seemingly endless roller coaster of Ekávi's love-hate relationships with her children. Dimítris is gone now, she feels mistreated by Polixéni and her husband, and she's fought yet again with her daughter Eléni, so she posits Thódoro as the only one who really loved her. But what is important to us here is that Ekávi cannot rest until she knows her story will go on by being passed on. Nína is to tell Thódoro "what they did to me." Although it is plausible—and is indeed Nína's interpretation in the immediate aftermath of her death—that by this phrase Ekávi means Polixéni and her husband's role in "causing" Dimítris's and her own deaths, the very generality of Ekávi's terms allows for a broader interpretation of what she is supposed to pass on as "all the things that have happened in my life."[46] Nína, then, has promised to tell Ekávi's story, and she has promised to tell it to someone whom Ekávi, at least, thinks will be a good, because empathetic, listener—her elder son.

Ekávi's death follows shortly after she extracts this promise from Nína, but Nína does not have a chance to fulfill her pledge immediately since Thódoro's return from the Middle East is delayed. Once he is back in

Athens, Thódoro shows no interest in becoming a listener to this story. On the contrary, though he starts to pay attention to Nína, she practically ignores him, saying that she was perturbed because he did not ask her about the death of his brother or mother. Even if he had asked, she comments, "I wouldn't have told him anything of what I knew. In spite of my word to her, I was determined never to open my mouth. The best thing, I told myself, was to let the past lie where it was" (309). Again, Nína takes a narrow interpretation of her task; she believes she had promised to tell about the events immediately prior to Ekávi's death, the quarrels between mother, son, daughter, and son-in-law, and she also reports her desire to disregard the past. But that Nína has in fact fulfilled her promise to Ekávi by telling all of Ekávi's story is testified by Nína's narration itself: a whole novel filled with stories, including, of course, the events leading up to Ekávi's death. Nína's discourse proves that she of all people is, or has become, unable to let the past "lie where it was."

We now have the information needed to understand the Talk of *The Third Wedding Wreath*. As I proposed initially, this kind of Talk can only be detected through the "whole story" in the sense of the entire story told within the novel, as well as how the story is told—in other words, its narration. Readers who want to reply properly to the novel's entire discourse as "statement" need to respond by becoming the kind of listener Nína has become to Ekávi, which includes seeing how all the episodes are connected and accepting the responsibilities of passing on the story.

As I mentioned at the outset of this section, Nína never describes her narration as writing. To the contrary, Nína always uses expressions of speech to refer to her own enunciation, and just as importantly, implies that her interlocutors speak back. Expressions like "I don't want to say" or "now that we're talking about it" or "you'll say" fill the novel and can be thought of as inscribed "statements" to which readers who want to Talk with the text will respond by feeling addressed, thus reaffirming their status as attentive listeners. Nína's little interrogations of herself by the listener[47] and even the absence of phrases referring to her activity as "writing" or her interlocutors as "readers" could also be thought of as statements to which actual readers reply by reaffirming their sense of themselves as present and attentive listeners. These individual "statements" remind readers to consider the entire novel as a statement to be responded to as well. Like Goffman's example of the theater, there should be reactions along the way, but the applause at the conclusion is a reply to the entire play as statement.

Similarly, readers who want to Talk with the text need to make connections between the story told and the telling of the story, as I have done above when I proposed generally that the novel models proper listening through Nína's development or that Nína fulfills her promise to tell Ekávi's story. Another instance of such connections would be the statement (in its common usage as well as in my specific Talk sense) that Nína makes about why she is remembering all this now: "Ah me, I remember such a string of things now [*Ah, éna-éna ta thimámai*]! Everytime she upsets me, it all comes back, my mind dredges up all that I've been through in my life. It's hard to choose what memories to bring up first [*Ti na protothimitheí kanís*]" (1985a: 39; 1985b: 34). If the reader-listeners put this passage together with the very opening, in which Nína is cursing out her daughter, María, they will realize that the series of memories that makes up the novel must have been initiated by this argument (María had been picking on her stepfather, Thódoro; she must then have taken down photographs, including one of her stepfather's mother, Ekávi; her mother must have rehung the portraits, so that the daughter in retaliation insults the mother-in-law by calling her a washerwoman). Making such a connection would constitute a reply because the nature of the argument that slips out in the first pages provides verification that Nína has changed.

A reader who has listened properly to the whole story responds in part by recognizing the fight and the book as signs of Nína's ability to finally mourn Ekávi, again, precisely by remembering the past—something she had been unable to do directly after Ekávi's death. This is a connection that Nína makes in a very late passage in which she identifies her reactions to María's insults with this special love of Ekávi: "It just had to be like that, all these years gone by before I could really mourn for her; before I could really realize that, apart from poor papa, I'd lost the only other person in the world who really understood something of what was in my heart, who taught me a thing or two in this life. That's why I get so furious now when I hear that anthropoid monster insulting her" (314).

Furthermore, the very ferocity of the exchanges between Nína and her daughter will remind reader-listeners of Ekávi's innumerable clashes with her own children. Attentive reader-listeners might also connect the beginning to the very end in which Nína says she would consider a fourth marriage just to spite María. No matter how vicious the insults between either mother and child sound, in Ekávi's value system, which, as the opening and closing imply, Nína now accepts, what is important is inter-action itself. As long as the insults fly back and forth, the connection between the two is strong. And relationship means life itself—"survival," even after death.

Another act of Nína's confirms that she has learned this lesson. The day Ekávi's children divvy up their mother's possessions, Thódoro fi-nally breaks down and cries. But his mourning is brief and private. Nína says to herself, "Poor Ekávi. You used to say that when they lost you, they would come and scratch at your grave with their fingernails. That too was one of your delusions. The truth is that the living forget. Woe to him who dies" (my translation; 1985a: 307; 1985b: 314). The content of Nína's thought is about forgetting. But her very act of apostrophizing her friend enacts the opposite. It shows that Nína has not forgotten her, and, in-deed, by "speaking" to her is still in relation to her. Ekávi's photo on Nína's living-room wall is a symbol for this relationship that still goes on. But even more importantly, Nína's entire discourse, represented by the novel we hold in our hands, tells the story of this relationship; no matter "how" Nína produces it, the very utterance of the story demonstrates the connection between the two women. Nína can make connections be-tween events now that she couldn't make or had forgotten when Ekávi was alive, because on some level at least, she now knows that all these events belong to one story, a story of a community that includes her (a lesson that is critical to Naylor's *Mama Day*, as well).

In addition to making the connections between the stories told within the novel and the novel's discourse as a whole, to listen properly, readers have to realize their role in this communicative circuit. Nína never refers to readers as such, I wager, precisely so that they can think of them-selves—like Nína had to learn to think of herself when listening to Ekávi's stories—*as part of the story*. The repeated foiling of the separation of literate and oral behaviors in the story and minimal reference to the production and reception of the discourse should discourage readers from thinking of the story as myth—or "just a novel"—and of themselves as shut up in the little room of Lukís's reader. Nína's frequent appeals to nonspecified "you's" function as open invitations to pick up the book, to come over for coffee and gossip, to don the wedding wreath and to become part of the family. As Ekávi's story becomes Nína's own story when she marries the "hero of the novel," Ekávi-Nína's history can become ours if we take up Nína's calls and listen. In such a communicative circuit, Nína is not talking to herself (as she frequently quotes herself as having done in the past); she is talking to us. That Nína's addresses are all plural further indicates that any individual reader should think of her/himself as one of many, as part of a community. In the interpretive community of this kind of storytelling, the level of invective in these stories is not just for entertainment, nor merely to remind us of the (positive) reevaluation of orality, as I stated at the outset, though many of Nína and Ekávi's outbursts are outrageous enough to solicit mirth, and it is indeed true that the novel highly values oral culture. Rather, the intensity of the arguments, as well as their content, can serve as a reminder of the price people pay for being connected.

What happens when the generation that actually witnessed foundational events is gone? If Lukís is right that societies depend on stories being passed on to subsequent generations, we need to "hear" the stories of Nína's and Ekávi's families not as the stories of a bunch of crazies but as a story of the struggle for family and community in the face of forces like war, foreign occupation, famine, poverty, antisemitism, homophobia, and drug abuse that pull at the network of the relationships that make up the independent, if fragile, Greece that Lukís's crew had fought so hard to create and that Ekávi and Nína's generations fought so hard to sustain. If we look to Nína as a model, we will reply to *The Third Wedding Wreath* by making these connections and repeating these stories.

I want to conclude this chapter with a look at Gloria Naylor's 1988 novel *Mama Day*, because it illustrates even more explicitly than Tachtsís's novel *Talk* in the service of community. As reviewed above, Harriet Wilson makes a plea in *Our Nig* for her black brethren to not only buy her book but to "rally round and support her." The historical evidence suggests that she had few readers at all and that what few she did have did not in any way constitute a community. As if in answer to Wilson, Naylor depicts a community of free, self-sustaining, landowning blacks, the community of Willow Springs. And through what is perhaps the most remarkable feature of *Mama Day*, she not only assigns the reader a similarly crucial role as Wilson does in sustaining community but she also crowns the reader with success in carrying out this role, that is, in learning of and passing on the foundational stories of this black community. To understand the text-as-statement and the answering toward which it is oriented, we will again need to look at the inscriptions of tellers and listeners and of telling and listening in the novel, because, as in *The Third Wedding Wreath*, in *Mama Day* characters and readers must learn that what may seem to be different stories are in fact all part of the one story that is necessary to sustain the community.

There are two main discourse situations in *Mama Day*: a communal "we" that addresses itself to the novel's readers, who, as in *The Third Wedding Wreath*, are addressed as "you" and never referred to as "readers" per se; and a series of apostrophes between the deceased George Andrews of New York City and his still-living wife, Ophelia Day, also known as Cocoa, Baby Girl, and child of Grace (her mother's name). The frame story and the apostrophes between Cocoa and George occur in 1999 in Willow Springs, an (invented) island off the coast of South Carolina and Georgia that is completely owned by its African American residents, the descendants of slaves freed by Bascombe Wade at the request of the woman he loved, Sapphira.[48] The "conversations" between Cocoa and her deceased (but not absent) husband, George, have taken place many times before, we are told, near the Day family cemetery overlooking the Sound (10, 310). This particular performance of their exchange, which we "overhear," is clearly indicated as taking place in the same year as that in which the community voice of Willow Springs explicitly addresses us, the readers (see 10). What George and Cocoa "say" to each other is about a "summer fourteen years ago when she left, but he stayed" (10).[49] More precisely, George and Cocoa review their courtship, which begins in 1981, and their first and only trip together to Willow Springs in 1985 when Cocoa is put under a spell by Ruby and when George dies trying to save her life. These apostrophes between the lovers are interspersed with sections that, like the frame story, are narrated by the communal Willow Springs–"we" but that are also highly focalized (in Genette's sense) through Cocoa's great-aunt, Miranda, also known as Mama Day.

Both the frame story and the embedded communal sections are narrated in the present tense, whereas the apostrophes are mainly narrated in the past. In the sections interspersed with the exchange of apostrophes between George and Cocoa, the "we"-narrator fills in additional information about the context of George and Cocoa's relationship but from the time frame of the unfolding events—that is, the first sections of these embedded "we"-narratives take place in 1981. To state it otherwise, both types of sections are telling one story, but George and Cocoa's apostrophes relate the material retrospectively, whereas the interspersed communal voice narrates simultaneous to action. At the moment after George and Cocoa have reviewed to each other (in August 1999) how they met (in August 1981) and how Cocoa lost the job for which George was hiring because she was going to Willow Springs to visit her great-aunt and grandmother (13–33), the sections of this other narrative level describe, from the perspective of August 1981, the preparations by Cocoa's grandmother and great-aunt in Willow Springs for the events of Baby Girl's (Cocoa's) visit (33–52). In other words, the embedded sections narrated by the communal "we" deliver information, especially dialogue that could only very awkwardly and implausibly be quoted in the apostrophes (for example, 178–83). The next apostrophe (by George to Ophelia) picks up where the communal "we" leaves off and narrates George's receipt of a letter that Ophelia (forced by Mama Day) sends to George telling him of her interest in the job, how George got Ophelia a different job, and how they subsequently begin their romance.

As George and Ophelia's review of their life together progresses—and they do review in a mainly chronological, orderly fashion—the embedded narratives progress with them, moving through the events of 1981, the events of the young couple's courtship and marriage, and the events not only of the fateful summer of 1985 when George dies but also of the aftermath of his death, including the closing of the young couple's home in New York and Cocoa's return to Willow Springs. They conclude at the end of 1985 with Candle Walk and specifically with Mama Day's visit to the family cemetery, where she tells George not to worry, because "One day she'll hear you, like you're hearing me" (308). There is always a gap between the time level of the embedded stories and of the delivery of the apostrophes, except for the opening section and the very brief closing one, which like the apostrophes are iterated in August 1999.

That explanation seems complicated, and the novel's structure *is* complex. But I have taken pains to describe it first because it teaches us the most important lesson about storytelling in this novel, a lesson that Cocoa expresses to George in the very last of the lovers' apostrophes: "there are just too many sides to the whole story" (311). A reply of proper listening to Naylor's novel-as-statement involves trying to make sense of even more voices than those in Tachtsís's. Fortunately for Naylor's readers, they too will get help in learning how to hear the "whole story" through numerous positive and negative models of listening. As in *The Third Wedding Wreath*, these models originally seem framed in terms of literacy: those who grew up or went to live "mainside" ("on the other side of the bridge" from the island) are bad listeners, and characters associated with the "oral" world (residents of Willow Springs) are good listeners. In another parallel to Tachtsís's novel, ultimate success in hearing the whole story in/of *Mama Day* involves the coming together of the characters and characteristics associated with orality and literacy.

At first glance, George, the engineer/businessman from New York, seems to be the opposite of everything Willow Springs represents, including good listening and consequently what the community considers valuable knowledge. When George is confronted with the challenge of learning how to live with Cocoa, he buys books about women's physiology (141) and takes out his slide rule and graph paper to calculate space allotment for each of their wardrobes (145). Once he is on the island, faced with Dr. Buzzard's cheating at cards or Cocoa's debilitation (after the curse from Ruby), George continues to believe that logic is the solution to every problem (208–13; 260). George has been raised to believe in himself and what he can see. "Only the present has potential" and "rely on yourself" are the mottos that have been ingrained in him by the Wallace P. Andrews Shelter for Boys where he was raised.

On the island, in contrast, proper listening gives Day family members access to the past, present, and future. When Cocoa and Miranda go to clean the family graveyard, for example, they can hear the voices of the dead: "No headstone for Jonah Day. He waits under a blanket of morning glory vines tangled among the sweet peas. They know he's there, 'cause they listen: Some of my brothers looked like me and some didn't. But it wasn't for me to ask Mama" (151). Good listeners can also learn about the future, as when Miranda hears, while she works on a quilt for the couple, that Cocoa and George won't be coming to visit this summer or the next (138); or when Cocoa hears that she will break George's heart (223–24).

Of course not all stories are for everyone to hear or to hear fully (except for the reader—a point to which I will return). Miranda, for instance, does not always listen as well as she would like to, and she reproaches herself for not listening sooner and better to Bernice and therefore for not realizing how powerful her desire to bear a child was (84).

The difference between the way "mainsiders" and "islanders" listen is paralleled by differences in seeing and telling. The contrast in seeing is illustrated dramatically when Cocoa begins to deteriorate at an even faster rate than she has so far. George, who has been working frantically on the bridge (so he can take Cocoa to a doctor mainside), yells at her grandmother, "And she needs help badly. . . . Have you seen her?" And Abigail responds, "I don't have to see her" (289). Abigail knows through her belief system about the ravages Ruby has worked on Cocoa; she doesn't need visual confirmation. Similarly, George comes up short against the Willow Springs communication standard for telling. In one of Cocoa's apostrophes to George about an earlier stage in their relationship when they were first getting to know each other, she complains that she "talked" to George, whereas George just "conversed" with her:

> I had told you about where I grew up. I painted the picture of a small rural community and my life with Grandma and Mama Day. . . . I did open up fully to share my feelings about my father running off and my mother dying so young. I talked to you about loneliness—all kinds. . . . I talked and talked, but getting you to say anything about yourself was like pulling teeth. Oh, you'd hold a conversation. . . . But you'd never talk about your *feelings* surrounding any of that . . . what you didn't understand is that I thought you didn't trust me enough to share those feelings. A person is made up of much more than the "now." (126–27)

Of course, that Cocoa can "tell" this to George fourteen years after his death shows that George has learned to listen and in turn tell. But this learning only takes place after his intense contact with other members of the Willow Springs community besides Cocoa, a situation somewhat analogous to Nína's apprenticeship with Ekávi.

One event that had particularly befuddled the rational George is the community's behavior around the death of Little Caesar, the beloved son eventually born to Bernice and Ambush. In the "standing forth" ceremony, all members of the community talk to the dead: "Always addressing the coffin, and sometimes acting as if they expected an answer back."

George the mainsider remarks their attitude as "Dry eyed and matter of fact" (268). They talk to the dead child about what he did when they first saw him and what he'll be doing when they see him next. Miss Reema tells him, "When I first saw you . . . you were wearing a green bunting, being carried in your mama's arms. You had a little fuzzy patch of hair on your head and your mouth was open to let out a squall. I guess you were hungry. And when I see you again . . . you'll be sitting at my dining table, having been invited to dinner with the rest of my brood" (268). In other words, standing forth erases distance between the living and the dead through direct address and through the implication of a continuity between past, present, and future. They may be sad, but they can be "matter of fact," too, since their view of relationships is not circumscribed by death. Because George delivers this thought in an apostrophe to Cocoa fourteen years after his own death, we see that George has learned to erase the barriers he saw the members of Willow Springs erasing on the day they buried Little Caesar; he has learned how to talk and listen across the divide of the living and the dead.

Although George witnesses another modus vivendi by virtue of being in Willow Springs and participating in events like the standing forth ceremony, it is ultimately his love for Cocoa that effects the major transformation in his own life—his transition from this side of life to the other, and more importantly (in the value scheme of the book), from individuality into community. In my view, it is critical that the resolution of Cocoa's crisis involves both George and the Days. As this realization first dawns on the older Days, Abigail asks Miranda, "How bad is it gonna be?" And Miranda answers:

"How bad is hate, Abigail? How strong is hate? It can destroy more people quicker than anything else."

"But I believe there's a power greater than hate."

"Yes, and that's what we gotta depend on—that and George."

"That boy is from beyond the bridge, Miranda." Abigail's voice is bitter. "We ain't even got his kind of words to tell him what's going on."

"Some things can be known without words."

"With or without, how is he gonna fight something he ain't a part of?"

"He's a part of *her*, Abigail. And that's the part that Ruby done fixed to take it out of our hands."

"George ain't never gonna believe this, Miranda. Go to him with some mess like this, and he'd be sure we were senile."

80

"That's right. So we gotta wait for him to feel the need to come to us. I'll have to stay out at the other place. And when he's ready, head him in my direction."

"That boy'll never make it, Miranda."

"Don't sell him too short too early. He'd do anything in the world for her." (267)

This passage pits George's worldview against the Days'. Abigail's worrying about not having "his kind of words" underscores the gulf between them. But this passage also shows that these two worlds meet in their love for Cocoa who "done tied up her mind and her flesh with George" (265). In this passage and the many others that describe the attempts to bring George to the "other place," it becomes clear that saving Cocoa requires the coming together of those who love her, of those who up to this point have been representatives of oral and literate cultures, or of supernatural and rationalistic ones. At this point in the story their differences are framed in terms of communal versus individual values. Dr. Buzzard is the one who scolds and schools George and convinces him that he needs to believe—and not just in himself:

"That's where folks start, boy—not where they finish up. Yes, I said *boy*. 'Cause a man would have grown enough to know that really believing in himself means that he ain't gotta be afraid to admit there's some things he just can't do alone. Ain't nobody asking you to believe in what Ruby done to Cocoa—but can you, at least, believe that you ain't the only one who'd give their life to help her? Can you believe that, George? . . .

'Cause if you can bring yourself to believe just that little bit, the walk you'll take to the other place won't be near as long as the walk back over to that vat of tar." (292)

George does take that walk—twice, in fact. But he can't quite save Cocoa "Mama Day's way." That way, Willow Springs's way, involves connecting up through another person, in this case Mama Day, to all the believing that's gone before, in other words, becoming part of a human ancestral network (285, 294–95). Yet George doesn't quite save Cocoa "his way" either, at least not through logic and engineering, not by going mainside, as he first thinks fit. George is able to save Cocoa through love and connection: "I was to get over to that house, because I was not going to let you go" (301). This way will cost him his life—or at least his corporeal life—in the process.

Much is made of George doing it "his way" (Miranda's words, 302) by critics and even in the novel. Yet the novel also shows that George's last actions—his walk to the other place, his massacre in the henhouse, his last hug with Cocoa, his death—bind him to the community of Willow Springs and the Day family for eternity. When Miranda apostrophizes George during that first Candle Walk after his death, she makes it clear that George has given to the community, and not just by saving their Baby Girl. He has also opened memories for the community, specifically about Candle Walk itself, the event connected with the founding of Willow Springs as a community of free, landholding blacks. She explains to him:

> I can tell you now about this here night. You done opened that memory for us. . . . It weren't about no candles, was about a light that burned in a man's heart. And folks would go out and look up at the stars—they figured his spirit had to be there, it was the highest place they knew. And what took him that high was his belief in right, while what buried him in the ground was the lingering taste of ginger from the lips of a woman. He had freed 'em all but her, 'cause, see, she'd never been a slave. And what she gave of her own will, she took away. I can't tell you her name, 'cause it was never opened to me. That's a door for the child of Grace to walk through. And how many, if any, of them seven sons were his? Well, that's also left for her to find. And you'll help her, won't you? she says to George. One day she'll hear you, like you're hearing me. And there'll be another time—that I won't be here for—when she'll learn about the beginning of the Days. But she's gotta go away to come back to that kind of knowledge. And I came to tell you not to worry: whatever roads take her from here, they'll always head her back to you. (308)

George is now connected; he can hear Mama Day, and she promises him that Cocoa (the child of Grace) will one day hear him too, proof of which we readers have in the apostrophes exchanged between the two. Cocoa will be the recipient of much critical knowledge about the community. But it's important to note that Mama Day posits a special role for *George* in Cocoa's acquisition of that knowledge. In other words, it's no longer possible to separate George's world or way of knowing from Cocoa's and Willow Springs's. There's only one way now, and all knowledge will come through Cocoa, the daughter of Willow Springs but also the wife of George of mainside. She has gone away in the past and will need to do so again in the future before she can learn still-buried secrets; and she will learn these secrets in part because she had "done tied up her mind and her flesh with George," and he with her by dying for her sake.

To understand the correctness of Cocoa's behavior (and accept it as a model for our own), we need to look at another member of Willow Springs who also went mainside but who did not achieve Cocoa's success. That character is "Reema's boy," one of the most unforgettable in Naylor's novel, even though he is mentioned only briefly:

> the one with the pear-shaped head—came hauling himself back from one of those fancy colleges mainside, dragging his notebooks and tape recorder and a funny way of curling up his lip and clicking his teeth, all excited and determined to put Willow Springs on the map.
>
> We was polite enough—Reema always was a little addle-brained—so you couldn't blame the boy for not remembering that part of Willow Springs's problems was that it got put on some maps right after the War Between the States. And then when he went around asking us about 18 & 23, there weren't nothing to do but take pity on him as he rattled on about "ethnography," "unique speech patterns," "cultural preservation" and whatever else he seemed to be getting so much pleasure out of while talking into his little gray machine. He was all over the place—What 18 & 23 mean? What 18 & 23 mean? And we all told him the God-honest truth: it was just our way of saying something. (7)

Narrated from the perspective of the community of Willow Springs, it's not surprising that Reema's boy is always referred to in just that way. Though he may have become a scholar for the outside world, in the world of Willow Springs he can have an identity only through his relationships. We never find out his given name; he will always be his mother's son: Reema's boy. He seems susceptible to getting things wrong just because he's been "mainside." But since, as we've seen, Cocoa's been mainside and still becomes a good listener, that can't be his fatal flaw. Rather, he talks to his machine instead of to people, and he doesn't remember his community and its history. The narrative voice keeps reiterating, "Why didn't he just ask?"; "When he was running around sticking that machine in everybody's face, we was sitting right here— every one of us—and him being one of Reema's, we woulda obliged him" (8). The voice then goes on to list who was available for the asking and what they would have been willing to tell him (8–9). The behavior that

is outlined for Reema's boy involves cultivating interpersonal relationships, visiting folks at home, drinking ice water or tea with them, listening to the stories of their lives. The narrating voice describes what some
anthropologists (who learned their subject better than Reema's boy) call
the "communal function"—the use of talk as a "means for linking individuals into communities of shared identity" (Philipsen 1989: 79). In
Willow Springs, as in Greece and most other places, people's lives are
intertwined in complex ways that make answering just one question—
"what 18 & 23 mean"—difficult. What Reema's boy could have asked but
did not were things that would show this full context: "He coulda asked
Cloris about the curve in her spine that came from the planting season
when their mule broke its leg, and she took up the reins and kept pulling
the plow with her own back. Winky woulda told him about the hot tar
that took out the corner of his right eye the summer we had only seven
days to rebuild the bridge so the few crops we had left after the storm
could be gotten over before rot sat in. . . . Naw, he didn't really want to
know what 18 & 23 meant, or he woulda asked" (8). He could have heard
it all, but didn't, though the communal voice holds out the possibility
that he could still learn, by just watching "Cocoa any one of these times
she comes in from Charleston" (10).

The communal voice of the narrator then expands on this counterexample. Cocoa knows proper storytelling behavior:

> She goes straight to Miss Abigail's to air out the rooms and unpack her
> bags, then she's across the road to call out at Mama Day, who's gonna
> come to the door of the trailer and wave as Cocoa heads on through the
> patch of dogwoods to that oak grove. She stops and puts a bit of moss in
> her open-toe sandals, then goes on past those graves to a spot just down
> the rise toward The Sound, a little bit south of that circle of oaks. And if he
> was patient and stayed off a little ways, he'd realize she was there to meet
> up with her first husband so they could talk about that summer fourteen
> years ago when she left, but he stayed. And as her and George are there
> together for a good two hours or so—neither one saying a word—Reema's
> boy coulda heard from them everything there was to tell about 18 & 23.
>
> But on second thought, someone who didn't know how to ask wouldn't
> know how to listen. (10)

So Reema's boy needs to watch, to be patient. What he would see if he
could stand still and watch would be Cocoa tending to relationship. She

airs out her grandmother's house, and she greets her great-aunt. She shows respect for tradition by putting moss in her shoes. She goes to the place where she and George can talk. And she believes that they can communicate. Within this society, these acts and attitudes function phatically, in Jakobson's sense quoted earlier; they establish that the lines of communication are open. The seemingly paradoxical fact that Cocoa and George communicate everything without words ("neither one saying a word"), I would argue, underscores how completely she—and anyone who can imitate her—is oriented toward exchange. Cocoa and George's relationship is a rather extreme illustration of Goffman's idea that statements and replies do not have to be verbal.

Cocoa has grown into proper listening and telling, for in the direct aftermath of her husband's death, Cocoa was *not* capable of hearing him. Like Nína with regard to Ekávi, Cocoa had had to learn first how to stop grieving for herself before she could begin to grieve for him (304, 307, 309). Once this kind of mourning is learned, she can be open and oriented toward George in a way that allows her to hear him, even from the far side of life. Cocoa's developed listening skills are evident through the series of apostrophes between her and George that make up the bulk of the discourse we read. That series constitutes one sign that Cocoa is *changed* by learning to listen, by participating in this kind of storytelling.

In the novel's final passage (August 1999), Cocoa becomes bound to her own community in an even more profound way than by "hearing" George: Cocoa and her ancestress Sapphira see each other. The narrating voice remarks Cocoa's transformation: "It's a face that's been given the meaning of peace. A face ready to go in search of answers, so at last there ain't no need for words as they lock eyes over the distance" (312). This exchange of looks with her foremother points toward the day prophesied by Mama Day when Cocoa will be able to hear even more "sides of the whole story"—not the narrow story of what happened the summer George died, but the story of the community of which those events are just a small part. Cocoa will learn the foundational stories of Willow Springs, including, for example, the name of the woman with whom she has locked eyes—Sapphira—something not to be opened to Mama Day, though she is privy to the knowledge that it will be revealed to her great niece (308).

As I've mentioned, the novel is framed by sections narrated by a first-person plural voice situated in Willow Springs in August 1999, addressed to an unspecified "you." This date should attract our attention, especially when we realize that the voice emanates from what was the future for Naylor's first readers in 1988:

> Think about it: ain't nobody really talking to you. We're sitting here in Willow Springs, and you're God-knows-where. It's August 1999—ain't but a slim chance it's the same season where you are. Uh, huh, listen. Really listen this time: the only voice is your own. But you done just heard about the legend of Sapphira Wade, though nobody here breathes her name. You done heard it the way we know it, sitting on our porches and shelling June peas, quieting the midnight cough of a baby, taking apart the engine of a car—you done heard it without a single living soul really saying a word. (10)

This passage is framed by a contrast between us and the misguided son of Reema: "And he coulda listened to them the way you been listening to us right now" precedes it, and "Pity, though, Reema's boy couldn't listen, like you, to Cocoa and George down by them oaks—or he woulda left here with quite a story" immediately follows it. There are several aspects of this model of storytelling that have a direct impact on an understanding of Talk in *Mama Day*.

Whereas in our nineteenth-century novels the narrators express desire for their readers to be like listeners, and in Tachtsís's novel our act of listening is implied by the numerous second-person pronouns and the absence of mention of reading, here the narrator explicitly tells us we are *hearing* the story. It would be a standard setup for writer and reader to be in different places and to engage in their respective activities at different times, but hearing a story when you are in a different time and place than its teller is bizarre—unless the story is broadcast or recorded and replayed, of which there are no indications here.

Furthermore, this passage tells us that no one narrates this story. So how is it that we "hear" it? We hear it the same way the communal narrator "knows it." And how do they know it? They know it by virtue of being members of the community, by "sitting on our porches and shelling June peas, quieting the midnight cough of a baby, taking apart the engine of a car"—all the simple things that constitute communal daily life. They know the story by being in the place where it occurred and by behaving as part of the community whose history it is. Being part of the community means being part of a fabric of relationships (unlike Reema's boy, who forgets to tend to them). So to reverse the logic, readers who are told in no uncertain terms that they can "hear" the story must have become members of the community by erasing the differences between their lives and the lives they read about, a situation analogous to the way Cocoa erases the line between herself and George.

This passage also posits a difference between "knowing" a story and "hearing" one. The community members know; the novel's addressees hear. "Knowing," in this context at least, does not extend to being able to put it into words, whereas "hearing" does (since addressees learn "the legend of Sapphira Wade," although "nobody here breathes her name"). Mama Day doesn't know her name. At the moment the story concludes, even Cocoa doesn't know her name. Yet reader-addressees learn it. We even get a family tree of the Days and the complete "Bill of Sale" of Sapphira, along with a map of Willow Springs, in the paratext—that part of the text that is received only by the readers, not by the narrators or narratees, nor by characters in the text proper.[50] That is to say, we get the whole story.

In the value system of Willow Springs, this implies that we, the novel's addressees, are the best listeners. But as in Lukís's strategy of telling us it's alright to fall asleep because we won't miss anything important—whereas, of course, we actually have to pay close attention if we want to get the whole story—I suggest that the strategy of the communal "we" here is to crown us preemptively with success to make us even more aware of what it is we actually have to do to achieve that success. To "hear" everything without anyone telling us anything, that is, to Talk with *Mama Day*, we have to reply to the story by fulfilling all the responsibilities of listenership. And through attention to the positive model of Cocoa and the negative one of Reema's boy, we have all the pieces we need to know what these responsibilities are. We know that we need to be willing to think of ourselves as part of the community by attending to relationships and asking the right questions, and we know that our special success in "hearing" the whole story carries with it the responsibility of passing on what we have heard.

And what is the story we are meant to pass on here? It is a story about creating and sustaining the relationships that build community. In Bakhtin's metaphor that serves as the epigraph to this chapter, it is about words as bridges between individuals. Indeed, bridges and linked hands serve as ubiquitous symbols for the novel's theme. To express this same idea in terms closer to the Talk framework of my study, *Mama Day* is about learning how to say "Thou" in Martin Buber's terms or about learning how to "orient toward exchange" in Goffman's. When one fully recognizes the subjectivity of the other, one cannot possess the other. This lesson ties all the plots of Naylor's novel together: that of George and Cocoa, of Bernice and her beloved son, "Little Caesar," and of Ruby and Junior Lee. Loving in this way leads to community, as when Bascombe Wade realizes that "his belief in right" means not only that he has to free his slaves but, even more importantly, that he cannot possess Sapphira—this knowledge leads to the creation of Willow Springs as an independent, self-sustaining community of free landholding blacks.[51] In this context, I think it is very important to note that there are no prescriptions for the race of the addressees, the "you" to whom the communal "we" of the novel addresses itself. I suggest that this absence of racial prescriptions functions analogously to the communal "we" crowning us with success as the best listeners at the outset or to Lukís's invitation to fall asleep. Ultimately these moves challenge us to confront the very issue that is elided, in this case, race. Whoever—black, white, or other—respects the history of Willow Springs *as a community that is distinguished precisely by the race of its members* can "join" the community by hearing and passing on its story. In this sense, too, I think *Mama Day* must be seen as a response to the call of *Our Nig*.

Prose fiction in my storytelling mode suggests that, like that widow in my father's village, we can be in relationship to people who are on the "other side" of life or on the "other side" of the literary transaction by believing that we can be in relation to them, by listening properly, and by passing on the stories we thus hear.

3

TESTIMONY

Talk as Witnessing

> No, don't forget. Don't erase it.
> You can't erase it. But make it into a story.
> —GRAHAM SWIFT, *Waterland*

We mostly remember Walter Benjamin's 1936 essay, "The Storyteller," for its claim that the rise of the novel comes at the expense of storytelling. I want to recuperate here Benjamin's contention that the communicability of experience is decreasing. Specifically, Benjamin points to a historical event that numerous cultural analysts of his time and ours consider a watershed in Western civilization: the Great War and its aftermath. In Benjamin's passionate formulation:

> never has experience been contradicted more thoroughly [*nie sind Erfahrungen gründlicher Lügen gestraft worden*] than strategic experience by tactical warfare, economic experience by inflation, bodily experience by mechanical warfare, moral experience by those in power. A generation that had gone to school on a horse-drawn streetcar now stood under the open sky in a countryside in which nothing remained unchanged but the clouds, and beneath these clouds, in a field of force of destructive torrents and explosions, was the tiny, fragile human body. (1969: 84; 1977: 439)

And the fragile human psyche, I append. Though Benjamin does not use the word, he is describing the phenomenon of "trauma" in its recently coined sense of psychic woundings.[1] He notes that "men returned from the battlefield grown silent"; the novels some of them eventually wrote about the war appeared with a ten-year delay and communicated "anything but experience that goes from mouth to mouth" (84). Later in his essay, Benjamin connects such novels with "information," facts that expend themselves and are disconnected from the lives of teller and reader (88–90).

While Benjamin never makes clear whether he means to denigrate all novels through this comparison, the premise behind my study is that "experience" is still exchanged through some twentieth-century narratives. In this chapter, I consider novels whose Talk specifically concerns traumatic experience. I call such texts "witness narratives" and their statements and replies "witnessing" and "cowitnessing."[2] While these novels would not count as "storytelling" in Benjamin's sense of offering "counsel" (86) or conveying "the epic side of truth, wisdom" (87), nor necessarily in my sense, which I presented in the previous chapter, of foregrounding attentive listening and passing on of stories, they do demonstrate orientation to exchange. Recognizing testimony as Talk is difficult, however, because the nature of trauma itself demands revised notions of "exchange," "experience," and "story"—and therefore also of "statement" and "reply." I suspect this is why Benjamin read such novels as "information." Accordingly, I will begin with what testifying to trauma means in a psychoanalytic setting, then propose a schema for witnessing in a literary context, and conclude by illustrating my schema with actual works of prose fiction.

Trauma, Narrative, and Memory

The term "trauma" is used in technical and lay literature to refer to both the forces or mechanisms that cause a psychic disorder and the resulting psychic state. In her acclaimed book *Trauma and Recovery* (1992), psychiatrist Judith Herman makes the insightful and polemical move to connect three types of trauma in the first sense, that is, modern warfare, domestic violence, and totalitarian control, whether it be exercised through governments, individuals, or religious cults. Traumatic events, which generally involve "threats to life or bodily integrity, or a close personal encounter with violence and death" (Herman 33), produce victims who share remarkably similar symptoms, trauma in the second sense.[3] Despite decades of encounters with their symptology, trauma victims have been "legitimized" only recently by the American medical establishment through the designation (in 1980) of a specific disease: Complex Post-Traumatic Stress Disorder (PTSD). This syndrome is characterized by the victim's numbness, isolation, and withdrawal, disruption in intimate relationships, persistent dysphoria, self-injury, suicidal preoccupation, depersonalization, hallucinations, amnesia, and re-living experiences or flashbacks (DSM-IV 1994: 424–29).[4]

PTSD appears to be caused by an inability to integrate atrocities into consciousness. According to psychiatrist Dori Laub, "The traumatic event, although real, took place outside the parameters of normal reality, such as causality, sequence, place and time" (Felman and Laub 1992: 69). In Caruth's terms, trauma "occupies a space to which willed access is denied" (1995a: 152). Many accident or assault victims report how the mind—without conscious decision—elides the moment of impact; dissociation of the experience may occur as the trauma occurs (van der Kolk and van der Hart 1995: 168). The infliction of trauma can be hard to predict (and therefore to avoid or detect) because what is traumatic for one person might not be for another (Wigren 1994: 417; Caruth 1995a: 4). Furthermore, the evidence for the trauma may first surface not as a verbal recital of the assault, but as a symptom—as one of the symptoms of PTSD listed above, for example. These symptoms alone may be what announce the psychological state of the victim. The truth will out, so to speak, causing what Herman refers to as the dialectic of trauma: an alternation of reenactment and numbness or remembering and secrecy, where, unfortunately, secrecy often triumphs (1992: 1–2).

Recovery of the victim involves overcoming silence and withdrawal to witness to what happened. That is to say, the victim produces a narrative of the traumatic events. The production of this potentially healing narrative is hauntingly difficult, however, because the event that needs to be narrated may not have been experienced by the victim fully consciously in time. Rather, "[w]hat causes trauma . . . is a shock that appears to work very much like a threat to the body's spatial integrity, but is in fact a break in the mind's experience of time" (Caruth 1993: 25). The victim's recovery requires the translation of this break into what Pierre Janet, student of Charcot's and a contemporary of Freud's, whose work with hysterics at the Salpêtrière was widely admired in the first part of this century,[5] has called "narrative memory," an ability to construct mental schemas that make sense out of experience (Janet 1928). Understanding how traumatic symptoms might be transformed into narrative memory and how the role of the listener-witness functions in this process is crucial to my project of reading as narrative witnessing, a form of Talk.

Van der Kolk and van der Hart, following Janet, distinguish at least three types of memory: "habit memory," which we share with animals and which refers to the "automatic integration of new information without much conscious attention to what is happening"; "ordinary or narrative memory," a uniquely human capacity; and "traumatic memory," apparently also exclusive to humans, but which is not memory at all in the common sense of recalling something that has been learned. Rather, it is a return of the traumatic event as "physical sensations, horrific images or nightmares, behavioral reenactments, or a combination of these" (van der Kolk and van der Hart 1995: 160, 164). Unlike "normal" memory, traumatic memory is inflexible. Perhaps most importantly, traumatic memory "has no social component; it is not addressed to anybody, the patient does not respond to anybody; it is a solitary activity" (van der Kolk and van der Hart 1995: 163). For these reasons, more descriptive terms than "traumatic memory" are "traumatic reenactments" or "traumatic recall." Janet called them *idées fixes* (fixed ideas).[6]

Janet, Freud, and others have emphasized that treatment for such traumatic reenactments involves integrating the "unclaimed experience," to borrow Caruth's phrase (1996).[7] As Janet described the task: "it is not enough to be aware of a memory that occurs automatically in response to particular current events; it is also necessary that the personal perception 'knows' this image and attaches it to other memories" (as quoted in van der Kolk and van der Hart 1995: 167; loosely translated from Janet 1911: 538). Janet, in fact, thought of (narrative) memory itself as action: "essentially," he said, "it is the action of telling a story. Almost always we are concerned here with a linguistic operation quite independent of our attitude towards the happening" (1925: 661). Since the infliction of trauma involves some inability to act, the taking of action by turning the unassimilated experience into a story, seems to promote healing. Specifically, Janet considered his patients healed when they could "tell" about their traumas in different versions, long or short, adding or deleting certain details, depending on whom they were addressing (1925: 661–62, 672–73). These points about Janet's and our current understanding of trauma can be productively reviewed by recounting one of the cases to which he himself referred over and over.[8]

For more than ten years, Janet treated a young hysteric named Irène, who had lost her mother after attending to her almost without rest for a period of sixty days. Irène, however, had no recollection of her mother's death. At the funeral she behaved highly inappropriately, talking and laughing without shedding a tear. At the time she was admitted to the Salpêtrière she could repeat what she'd been told about her mother's death, but she did not remember the events leading to or following this devastating personal loss:

> If you insist on it, I will tell you: "My mother is dead." They tell me that it is so all day long, and I simply agree with them to get them off my back. But if you want my opinion, I don't believe it. And I have excellent reasons for it. If my mother were really dead, she would have been dead in her room, on a specific date, and I who never left her and took very good care of her, would have seen it. If she was dead, they would have buried her and taken me to the funeral. Well, there has been no funeral. Why do you want her to be dead?[9]

Although she had no conscious memory of her mother's death, when Irène found herself in a room positioned at a certain angle to a bed, she would reenact the events of that night, making gestures as if trying to revive a corpse, giving it medications, cleaning its mouth, talking to it. The demonstration was invariable and would last for hours. This case and others like it led Janet to the conclusion that *idées fixes* are a different order of mental activity than ordinary memory in that they can neither be narrativized nor adapted (1925: 663). Traumatic reenactments like Irène's replays incapacitate the victim; Irène, for example, "could no longer work; she could not make up her mind to anything; she had no normal feelings; no interest in her associates" (1925: 658). She was alone and isolated not only from her relatives and friends but from herself. The memory work Janet did with Irène (at first under hypnosis and then by what he called "assimilation") eventually allowed her to change what she said and did. At the point Janet considered her healed, she could tell about her mother's death in just moments rather than in the hours required for her traumatic reenactment of it, and in different versions, depending on the identity of her addressee (1925: 680–81). In other words, Irène was able to take her traumatic *fabula* or "story" (in the narratological sense of the situations and events that make up the plot) and present it as various *sjuzet* or "discourse" (the particular form and order of the telling of those events).[10]

Diverse contemporary psychotherapies for trauma victims similarly work toward the creation of a flexible narrative of the traumatic experience. Wigren details the goals of constructing such a narrative as follows: attention to an experienced sensation, screening various elements of the internal and external environment for relevance to the felt sensation, constructing causal chains, accounting for affect, and drawing conclusions that will guide future behavior and contribute to the ongoing formation of a worldview and a personal identity (1994: 415–16).[11] Exactly how this is accomplished remains a mystery, but it appears that "the traumatized person has to return to the memory often in order to complete it" (van der Kolk and van der Hart 1995: 176).[12]

Because most victims have phobias of the traumatic memory, this revisiting can usually be accomplished only in the presence of a sympathetic, committed listener or other "appropriate social supports" (Wigren 1994: 417).[13] As Laub has argued about his work with Holocaust survivors, the eventual production of the story of traumatic events, of the retrieval of that missing piece of history, necessarily includes the hearer of the story, "who is, so to speak, the blank screen on which the event comes to be inscribed for the first time" (Felman and Laub 1992: 57). Without a witness with whom to construct the story, the trauma will continue to surface as symptom-waiting-to-be-narrated, as unassimilated reenactments like Irène's of the night her mother died, for example. Yet "when the survivor knows he [sic] is being heard," Laub explains, "he will stop to hear—and listen—to himself" (71). Silences and gaps are important to this listening-witnessing process. Laub says "the listener has to let these trauma fragments make their impact both on him and on the witness" (71). And Wigren warns that cowitnesses must pay attention not to fill in the holes themselves, lest the *patient* miss the opportunity to register them as absent, a necessary step to their integration and to general recovery (1994: 418).

From these psychotherapeutic models one could come to the false conclusions that trauma is some kind of silent other of language that awaits verbalization or that there is one, "good" version of the story of the trauma. But numerous trauma victims, researchers, and clinicians warn that there is no "authoritative telling" of the event (Felman and Laub 1992: 171). As Roberta Culbertson realized after numerous attempts to "tell" of her childhood sexual violation: "Whatever I said . . . would indeed be untrue because it would not be what I knew/felt; this had no words" (1995: 189). Caruth astutely observes that the goal of processing trauma is not a simple mastery of facts or achievement of "a knowledge that can see and situate precisely where the trauma lies" (1996: 111). And in a similar spirit, Laub warns that the process is never really complete (75).[14] Thus even Laub's own metaphor for witnessing to trauma as inscription on a blank slate seems misleading in its implications that there is nothing there to begin with, that the listener is passive, and that a coherent text results.

Circuits of Narrative Witnessing

To approach literary narratives *of/as* trauma, in Talk terms as "statement," one would not only identify depictions of perpetration of violence but would also look for signs that the text is oriented to an answering, for deictics, in the expanded sense of any markers of the context of production introduced in chapter 1. In the context of trauma these might be anything that can communicate gaps, silences, and even whole stories that cannot be told or cannot be told fully. Such investigations must therefore consider the levels of the story and discourse, and the levels of the production and reception of the text. Specifically, one must investigate the communicative circuit, the components of which—an enunciator (victim/witness/narrator), a story (the narrative of the traumatic event and its consequences), and an enabler for that story (analyst/cowitness/reader)—are completely enmeshed and interdependent. In extending psychoanalytic concepts of witnessing to narratological analyses of specific prose fiction works, I propose to describe several different, though related, communicative situations. I think of these as a series of circuits. These circuits include traumatized characters trying to witness to themselves, trying to speak of their own trauma to other characters, and trying to speak on behalf of other characters; narrators telling their stories to inscribed readers (narratees); and authors witnessing to their historically contemporary flesh-and-blood readers, as opposed to the inscribed readers who are part of the previous circuit.

Whereas the ordinary, legal use of the verb "to witness" is associated with cognizance of something by direct experience, psychotherapy has shown how the process of "remembering and telling" about trauma is a social act, not an individual one. The social dimension refers both to the interpersonal activity required to allow the story of the trauma to come into being and to the effect of trauma on the societies in which they occur. Coconstruction of the story suggests use of terms like "witness"/ "cowitness" and "testifier"/"enabler" rather than the standard "sender"/ "receiver" or "speaker"/"addressee" of communication theory.[15] The effect of trauma on society suggests consideration of another communicative circuit in which readers at a historical and/or cultural remove cowitness to the stories in the inner circuits by recognizing and explicating their previous, uncompleted attempts at telling the story/ies of individual and collective traumas. Benjamin, as discussed above, perceived his whole generation as transformed by the experiences of war, inflation, and other forms of social violence. As part of that world himself, he perhaps could not perceive its literature as telling stories of traumatic experience, instead calling it "information." Herman reminds us that "[d]enial, repression, and disassociation operate on a social as well as an individual level" (1992: 2). Both Benjamin and Herman would probably agree with Caruth's formulation that "we are implicated in each other's traumas" (1996: 24). This implication bequeaths a role to current readers and hence creates the need for including this outermost circuit of witnessing.

My metaphor of the circuit tries to underscore the point made by theorists of trauma: it is not so much that the analyst/reader "knows" and "understands" a victim who is "ignorant" and "fails." Rather, the presence of the analyst/cowitness/reader completes the circuit and allows the story to come into being, like components of electronic circuits that are properly connected so that the current can flow. The listener has to be there so the survivor can re-externalize the event, "articulate and *transmit* the story, literally transfer it to another outside oneself and then take it back again, inside" (Felman and Laub 1992: 69). Geoffrey Hartman (1996) speaks similarly of *transmitting* Holocaust testimonies, of finding a way in which this kind of story can be passed on, even when we do not fully understand what the experience really was and therefore what it is we are passing on.

With these lessons of psychoanalysis in mind, I summarize here the six circuits of narrative witnessing I propose we investigate to understand literary Talk as testimony. Moving from the depicted individual psyche outward to the literary text in which that depiction occurs to whole societies in which the texts are produced and/or read, these are:

1. intrapsychic witnessing: a character witnesses to the self about the character's own experience;
2. interpersonal witnessing: two characters cowitness to trauma suffered by one of them;
3. surrogate witnessing: two characters cowitness to a third character's trauma;
4. textual witnessing: narrator and narratee cowitness to the trauma of/in the text;
5. literary-historical witnessing: text and its contemporary reader cowitness to the trauma of/in the text;
6. transhistorical-transcultural witnessing: text and its later or foreign reader cowitness to the trauma of/in the text.

This classification calls for a few explanations. First, I want to foreground some of the critical differences between witnessing in a psychoanalytic setting and witnessing in literature. Laub, for example, is communicating his personal experience as survivor, psychoanalyst, and interviewer of victims of the Holocaust. And though he writes about this, the witnessing he describes takes place orally and has various means for retrieving additional information.[16] What I am calling narrative witnessing, in contrast, is either extrapolated from or communicated through the written word. There is no recourse to a clinical setting that might uncover further knowledge than what the novel tells us.[17] This is why we need the kind of schema I have just proposed: circuits one through four help us detect whether we are dealing with the text-as-statement of trauma and hence should reply with the witnessing of circuits five and/or six.

Second, I want to qualify the inclusion of the first circuit, which involves an individual's ability to bear witness to oneself about violence to the self. When this circuit is flowing, that is to say, when the individual can integrate the event, there is no trauma. I include the category nevertheless to mark a first necessary "short-circuit" in communication; in other words, there must be someone who is unable to fully experience an event for trauma to occur and consequently for a schema of witnessing to trauma to be meaningful. Including this category is also useful because after trauma has been inflicted, a connecting of circuit one must occur at some point in tandem with circuit two, a witnessing to the trauma through a sympathetic listener; as Laub has said, "when the survivor knows he is being heard, he will stop to hear—and listen to—

himself" (Felman and Laub 1992: 71). Of course, a breakdown in witnessing could occur at any of the other levels as well. Cowitnesses in more distant circuits would then testify to those incomplete previous attempts at witnessing. Most relevantly for my framework of Talk, literary texts might be produced in a whole society under siege, like Benjamin's. In a society in crisis, it might not be possible for contemporary (potential) readers of a text to recognize the trauma articulated through that text, because those readers exist within the same cataclysmic experience. In these cases, reader-enablers from other societies or at a later time may interpret the contemporary reception of a particular text, the short-circuiting of circuit five, as itself a traumatic symptom; such readers' cowitnessing would constitute circuit six.[18]

Elie Wiesel's pronouncement that our age has given birth to a new literary genre—the genre of testimony (1977: 9)—is well known and eagerly repeated as a truth about our culture, as is Shoshana Felman and Dori Laub's similar argument that the twentieth century is the era of testimony. Perhaps the most oft-quoted sentence from Felman and Laub's widely read 1992 book is the one in which they argue that literature can do work, witnessing, that history cannot do in an age of trauma. Crises of history are translated into crises of literature whereby "literature becomes a witness, and perhaps the only witness, to the crisis within history which precisely cannot be articulated, witnessed in the given categories of history itself" (xviii). I basically agree with Wiesel, and with Felman and Laub, as long as the nature of literary testimony is carefully qualified and, specifically, as long as we do not lose sight of the idea of *translation*. For one thing, we might keep in mind Culbertson's remarks about the naïveté of many current discussions of recuperation of traumatic memory: "narrative, as simply an accounting in time of events in time, limits what can be told, indeed making the truth of body recall appear unintelligible and false, because too disjointed and without context" (1995: 191). In a related vein, Trezise speaks of the "space" between trauma and testimony (1997: 10). And Tal warns against equating representations of trauma and traumatic experience: "Textual representations—literary, visual, oral—are mediated by language and do not have the impact of the traumatic experience" (1996: 15). As reader-enablers, our account of the Talk, that is, our reply of cowitnessing to the text-as-statement of trauma, is even further removed from what Culbertson calls "body recall" than the testimony of the literary text, circuit four.

Finally, I think it is worth acknowledging the recent explosion of trauma studies and stating plainly that the northern Western Hemisphere does not have some kind of exclusive claim to catastrophe in the twentieth century, or in any other century for that matter, even if Westerners have cultivated writing about it. Though it was the Nazi genocide of the Jews that has provided the impetus for much of the current theorization about trauma and witnessing, including my own, it was not the first or only mass trauma, even within the Western geographical and cultural realm, as Benjamin's essay reminds us.[19] Below, I purposefully illustrate the circuits of narrative witnessing with many diverse texts, in the hope that my schema will be tested and qualified by readers who supplement these examples with many more from a still wider range of literary traditions. I have chosen mainly canonical texts to enable my selective pointing. Though I try to tease out distinct circuits in the analyses that follow, it will not always be possible to focus purely on just one, since, again, all are necessarily intertwined through the medium of literary narration itself.[20] For this reason, I conclude by returning to one of my less well known examples, Gertrud Kolmar's *A Jewish Mother*, to show how the various circuits interrelate and how such an analysis produces Talk.

Literary Survey of Narrative Witnessing

1. INTRAPSYCHIC WITNESSING

This circuit involves an individual character's ability to bear witness to the self about experience. When violent events result in psychic trauma, this circuit is broken. The healing of that trauma involves integrating aspects of the experience that have been missed, and this process seems almost invariably to require another person (circuit two). Presumably, at some point during the witnessing process the self must reintegrate the experience by testifying to the self about the occurrence (circuit one). Yet even the experts know so little about exactly how and when this reintegration happens, that it is perhaps not surprising that literary texts rarely (ever?) take up this exact moment. What we do get in prose fiction are countless moments in countless novels illustrating the normal integration of (normal) experience, and not an insignificant number of depictions of the traumatized self.

To illustrate both types with texts contemporary to Benjamin's essay, in an early scene of Joyce's *Ulysses*, Stephen Dedalus takes leave of Mr. Deasy and walks outside: "He went out by the open porch and down the gravel path under the trees, hearing the cries of voices and crack of sticks from the playfield" (29). Although the passage is not narrated in the first person, readers view the scene through Stephen. In narratological terms, it is focalized through Stephen.[21] The use of "hearing" with a direct object leads readers to assume that Stephen recognizes the sounds and can connect them with a concept called "hockey." Our assumption is trivial, and we wouldn't normally pause over a passage like it. In the opening of Woolf's *Mrs. Dalloway*, however, the war veteran Septimus can neither see the cricket players nor even correctly identify the voice of his wife, Rezia, who implores him to look at them: " 'Look,' she repeated. Look the unseen bade him, the voice which now communicated with him who was the greatest of mankind, Septimus, lately taken from life to death, the Lord who had come to renew society, who lay like a coverlet, a snow blanket smitten only by the sun, for ever unwasted, suffering for ever, the scapegoat, the eternal sufferer, but he did not want it, he moaned, putting from him with a wave of his hand that eternal suffering, that eternal loneliness. 'Look,' she repeated, for he must not talk aloud to himself out of doors" (37). The middle part of this passage is focalized through Septimus. What we see through him are not the cricket players but rather a bizarre vision of a world in which Septimus is the beleaguered scapegoat-savior. In other words, this passage, like many others in Woolf's brilliant novel, depicts the disjunction between Septimus's processing of the world around him and those of others, of the nontraumatized, like his wife. Septimus's inability to integrate his war experiences and to get on with a "normal" life in London eventually leads to his suicide, a potentially traumatic experience for his wife, but one which, despite the shock and solicitous shielding of the others around her, Rezia is able to process: " 'He is dead,' she said, smiling at the poor old woman who guarded her with her honest light-blue eyes fixed on the door" (228). (We recall that it took Janet's patient Irène years to be able to realize her mother was dead, underscoring the point that trauma cannot be predicted solely by the event, here, the death of a loved one for whom one has cared for an extended period.)

I'd like now to turn to two texts that come the closest I can find to actually illustrating circuit one. These novels concern themselves with the stage directly prior to witnessing to trauma, prior to the creation of the story of what has happened to the self, when the mind heals by consciously incorporating the traumatic memory into existing mental schemas "that will guide future behavior, and contribute to the ongoing formation of a worldview and a personal identity," as Wigren puts it (1994: 415–16). In neither Christa Wolf's *Patterns of Childhood* (*Kindheitsmuster* 1976) nor Nadine Gordimer's *Burger's Daughter* (1979) are the traumatic events clearly identified. Rather, reader-cowitnesses deduce the infliction of trauma by the main evidence of the unintegrated psyche of the respective protagonists.

The overwhelming task of integrating the self is at the heart of Christa Wolf's *Patterns of Childhood*. Wolf's narrator foregrounds this search for the self through her use of pronouns. She refers to herself as a child attempting to make sense of the totalitarian Nazi world in the third person with "she" and often by her childhood nickname, "Nelly." The interrogative self who is trying to figure out the relationship of her adult self to that child's psyche is addressed directly as "you" (with the German informal-intimate singular pronoun *du*). This is the self that returns to the formerly German town of Nelly's childhood in present-day Poland and then spends almost four years trying to write about it. In struggling with her project to reintegrate herself, the narrator makes a fascinating statement about memory that relates to my first circuit: "It is the person [*der Mensch*] who remembers—not memory. The person who has learned to see himself not as 'I' but as 'you.'" (1980: 118; 1979: 113). Her conception of the "you" necessary for the act of remembering supports the psychoanalytic tenet of the self needing to be a witness to the self. The passage continues with Wolf's protagonist's description of the dream that presumably allowed her to address herself as "you." What the dream shakes loose for the narrator is the realization that she can't protect her childhood self: "That's when you had to realize that you could never again be her ally, that you were an intruding stranger pursuing not a more or less well-marked trail but actually the child herself; her innermost secret that concerned no one else" (1980: 119). To be a *Mensch* would be to be able to remember, to be able to conduct a dialogue by creating an interlocutor, a "you," with whom to witness to what happened. But as the dream and its epiphany reveal, to do this would be to change the relationship to the childhood self. Here, fragmentation and distancing seem to be prerequisites to the potentially healing process of witnessing.

The narrator's search to become a fully integrated person is epitomized by her attempt to understand why certain sentences are connected in her brain. She recalls with certitude that the child Nelly would stare into the mirror and declare: "Nobody loves me." With equal assurance she knows that this pronouncement is connected to one by Goebbels about the Teutonic empire, and yet she reflects: "How can anyone be made to understand that these two completely unrelated sentences are, in your opinion, somehow connected? That, precisely, would be the kind of authenticity you're aiming for, and this trifling example shows you where an actual acceptance of your goal would lead: into the unfathomable [*ins uferlose*], to say the least" (1980: 165; 1979: 155).[22] Like the pronominal splitting of the self, a prerequisite for the search to put together the story seems to be more chaos. The original German phrase *ins uferlose* means literally "into that without boundaries" and is a common expression for "leading nowhere." That the protagonist's belief in the connection of the statements is framed in the form of a question reveals not only her skepticism of others to understand her project but also continued self-doubt about her own ability to figure out the relationship, the "pattern" in the metaphor of Wolf's title.[23]

This self-doubt pervades her search and the novel, such that the first time the narrator refers to herself in the first person—in the closing lines—it is to say, "I don't know" (1980: 406). This "it" of what she doesn't know is precisely whether she has broken the power of the past that has kept her split into an "I," "you," and "she": "And the past, which can still split the first person into the second and the third—has its hegemony been broken? Will the voices be still?" (1980: 406). The fact that the next word of the text is "I" seems to offer hope that the answer is "yes," and yet, again, that "I" is used to express doubt: "I don't know." The narrator's ruminations end with her desire to face what I would call her traumatic past, what she calls "the experience of dreaming" and the "limits of the expressible." As intellectualized as are the terms of the project the narrator has assigned herself, these closing admissions indicate, to me at least, that she is now capable of proper affect, one of the goals of witnessing to trauma. She trusts that what she knows, for instance, about the connection of certain sentences or images in her mind, is not fully expressible. Her conclusion is corroborated by Culbertson's points about the intranslatability of body recall. And the very act of her writing the story of her search functions like a call for a cowitness. In sum, the novel offers a fictional representation of the process of getting to the stage where a trauma victim could try to deal with the past; an oscillation between my first and second circuits of witnessing. Ultimately, *Patterns of Childhood* does not depict the moment of healing, the moment of the connecting of either or both circuits, though Wolf's novel gets as close to the experience as any literary text I have encountered.

In Nadine Gordimer's *Burger's Daughter*, we find another protagonist who is trying to connect childhood and adult experiences. Although Rosa Burger reflects on the process less explicitly than the protagonist-narrator of Wolf's novel, Rosa, too, begins by trying to witness to the self. Rosa's reflections on who she really is take the form of apostrophes not to herself as with Wolf's "you," but to others: in the first section to Conrad, a young man with whom she has lived; in the second to Katya, the first wife of her now deceased father; and in the third to her dead father, Lionel Burger, a white opponent of the South African regime. Rosa's search thus might seem to belong to my second category, witnessing about the self to another. Yet Gordimer's protagonist insists that she would not be able to articulate *anything* if someone else were actually listening. Putting aside for a moment the question of the efficacy of her self-talk, it is clear that, failed or successful, it belongs within the circuit of intrapsychic witnessing. In one of these peculiar apostrophes "to" Conrad, Rosa explains:

> And if I were really telling, instead of *talking to you in my mind* the way I find I do . . . One is never talking to oneself, always one is addressed to someone. Suddenly, without knowing the reason, at different stages in one's life, one is addressing this person or that all the time, even dreams are performed before an audience. I see that. . . . It's just that with me it never happened before. . . . *If you knew I was talking to you I wouldn't be able to talk.* But you know that about me. (16–17; my emphasis)

Rosa's frequently fragmented or truncated statements are just one sign that she is not in fact trying to communicate to someone else: "if I were really telling, instead of talking to you in my mind the way I find I do . . ." (Gordimer's ellipses). Though she speaks using the second person, what

she says in that "speech" is that she wouldn't be able to articulate anything if an addressee could actually hear her. Her apostrophes can't
qualify as interpersonal witnessing since she never testifies to anyone out
loud. Her admission that this kind of "talking in one's mind" is new for
her indicates that she has advanced from some even deeper social isolation ("with me it never happened before"). These internal apostrophes
represent progress, since they do allow her to articulate pieces of her
story, at least to herself. In other words, Rosa imagines an interlocutor
and then occupies that place herself.

This unpolitical daughter of a political martyr comes to view her own
inability to witness as treason. She cannot utter public words about the
wrong that has been done to her (her loss of childhood, her loss of her
father) or, in this racist society, about the wrong that is being done to the
blacks around her. "I do not speak," she accuses herself (200), concluding that "I don't know how to live in Lionel's country" (210). Her decision to abandon South Africa for Europe and a personal private life
signals her inability or unwillingness to learn how to give testimony. And
yet eventually, Rosa does voluntarily return to South Africa, ending up in
prison. These acts themselves seem to testify, even though Rosa continues to refuse to speak aloud. In a characteristically fragmented, private admission, she apostrophizes her dead father, saying: "If I were to
try out telling, which I won't" (350). This statement, like much of the
book, portrays Rosa, like Wolf's unnamed protagonist, teetering on the
border of witnessing; she considers trying to tell but quickly asserts that
she won't. Rosa's final reported act, however, causes one to suspect that
her attempts at intrapsychic witnessing did finally change her: she writes
and sends a letter from prison to Katya (Madame Bagnelli). Gordimer
describes and quotes from Rosa's letter in the last paragraph of the novel:

> In a passage dealing with the comforts of a cell as if describing the features
> of a tourist hotel that wasn't quite what the brochure might have sug-
> gested—*I have rigged up out of fruit boxes a sort of Japanese-style portable
> desk (remember the one old Ivan Poliakoff had, the one he used when he
> wrote in bed) and that's what I'm writing at now*—there was a reference
> to a watermark of light that came into the cell at sundown every eve-
> ning, reflected from some west-facing surface outside; something Lionel
> Burger once mentioned. But the line had been deleted by the prison
> censor. Madame Bagnelli was never able to make it out. (361)

That the letter gets censored and that Katya never reads parts of it may seem to transform Rosa's communication into a futile gesture. However, in the context of her previous, purely interiorized narrative, I suggest, it represents Rosa's first act of testimony: an attempt to witness beyond the self to another living person. Perhaps the attempt alone makes a difference to/for Rosa. Still, a message sent but not received (in the sense that Katya does not read the part about Lionel, and thus cannot know that Rosa has finally been able to articulate a thought about him) makes this letter analogous to Rosa's mental apostrophes. Gordimer's decision to end the novel with the announcement that yet another message does not reach its addressee ("Madame Bagnelli was never able to make it out") leads us to conclude that *Burger's Daughter*, like *Patterns of Childhood*, concerns itself mainly with the psyche prior to healing. Wolf's character struggles to learn how to say "I," and Gordimer's to talk to others out loud. These novels help us appreciate the enormous difficulties for the traumatized psyche to cross the threshold of witnessing.

2. INTERPERSONAL WITNESSING

In this circuit, which also occurs within the story level of the text (in the narratological sense of the events that make up the plot), a character tries to communicate to another character a personal trauma. That other character's listening, her cowitnessing, becomes the means, as Laub puts it, by which the story comes to be.

My first example of interpersonal witnessing is structurally close to the previous one from *Burger's Daughter* in its use of apostrophe; in both novels, the protagonist addresses an absent other, but the act of apostrophizing functions quite differently for each testifier. In Margaret Atwood's *The Handmaid's Tale* (1986), the main part of the novel consists of the Handmaid's present-tense first-person account of her experiences; she addresses this eyewitness report of her life in totalitarian Gilead to an unspecified "you." Whereas Rosa addresses "real" people in her life, but with the dogged determination that these apostrophes must remain private—that is, in her head—the Handmaid believes that the unnamed other, though absent, will certainly "hear" her. Her certitude that her addressee exists somewhere and will empathetically listen enables her to tell her story of indoctrination and institutionalized dehumanization and rape. In Gordimer's text, Rosa uses her mental apostrophes to confirm her feelings. She apostrophizes Conrad, for example, saying: "In fact, only if you believe will it become believable, to me" (196). In Atwood's novel, in contrast, belief springs from the Handmaid toward the other: "By telling you anything at all I'm at least believing in you. I believe you're there, I believe you into being. Because I'm telling you this story I will your existence. I tell, therefore you are" (267). In the repressive society Atwood creates, cowitnessing takes on an existential, not just therapeutic, function. One could paraphrase and explicate the Handmaid's attitude as follows: Even though I don't want to, I tell this story. And because I tell this story, other people, besides the ones who keep me imprisoned here, exist. In other words, whereas the Cartesian intertext is egotistical: I think, therefore *I* exist; the Handmaid's is relational: I tell, therefore *you* are. And it is relationship that is both forbidden in this totalitarian society and yet critical for the second circuit of witnessing. The Handmaid deals with her dilemma by internally willing this circuit into being. That is to say, through her belief that others, an other is alive,[24] she creates a relationship to a cowitness that allows the story of her trauma to be told.

William Faulkner's magisterial and deeply disturbing testimony to American southern racism, *Absalom, Absalom!* (1936), could also be mined for examples of interpersonal witnessing. Faulkner's novel is filled with dark secrets from the past that are transmitted from one character to another.[25] The novel is foregrounded with haunting injunctions to telling and listening through the pathetic and yet irrepressibly determined character of Rosa Coldfield. She simply insists that Quentin Compson hear her story, manipulatively suggesting, "[m]aybe some day you will remember this and write about it," and then more gently, adding: "Perhaps you will even remember kindly then the old woman who made you spend a whole afternoon sitting indoors and listening while she talked about people and events you were fortunate enough to escape yourself when you wanted to be out among young friends of your own age" (6). But Quentin recognizes Rosa's "summons" (7) as the coercive act that it is: "*It's because she wants it told* he thought *so that people whom she will never see and whose names she will never hear and who have never heard her name nor seen her face will read it and know at last why God let us lose the War*" (8).

Although *Absalom, Absalom!* could be used to illustrate any number of points about testimony and cowitnessing, I consider it under the rubric of interpersonal witnessing to raise the issue of how "listening" to trauma narratives can transform the listener. Laub calls the listener "a participant and a co-owner of the traumatic event" (1992: 57). In Faulkner's novel, Rosa's life is directly affected by Sutpen the tyrant (by his suggestion that the two "mate" to see if they conceive, before getting married) and through her role as recipient of the story of others' traumas (most especially, her sister's and niece's). Readers eventually realize that Quentin is also directly touched by the Sutpen legacy and by listening to the story. Quentin's cowitnessing profoundly changes, indeed, eventually hastens the end of his life, a point to which I will return. Although Quentin resists Rosa's choice of him as interlocutor—why tell me about it? why tell me?—he knows even at the beginning of his forced audience to Rosa's recital that on some level her story is his story; it is every southerner's story: "his very body was an empty hall echoing with sonorous defeated names; he was not a being, an entity, he was a commonwealth. He was a barracks filled with stubborn backlooking ghosts still recovering" (9).[26]

More specifically, Quentin's father parses Rosa's choice of Quentin as rooted in the friendship shared by Sutpen and General Compson, Quentin's grandfather. Thus the witnessing, like the trauma, in this story is passed from generation to generation. As Laub suggests about witnesses in general, Quentin has a dual role: he becomes not only a witness by hearing Rosa's story but also a participant, in this case quite literally, by driving Rosa to Sutpen's mansion, where Quentin sees Henry, Rosa's nephew, long a fugitive for having murdered his best friend, his sister's fiancé, and their half-brother, Charles Bon.[27] Through this act, Quentin enters the inner circle of the story; he becomes involved with those "directly" traumatized by Sutpen, or in a larger sense by the holocaust—Faulkner's word—of American southern racism (18). One sign of Quentin's traumatization lies in his compulsion to piece together the Sutpen catastrophe with his college roommate, Shreve. Another is his furious denial, which ends the novel; when Shreve asks him why he hates the South, Quentin counters: " 'I dont hate it,' Quentin said, quickly, at once, immediately; 'I dont hate it,' he said. *I dont hate it* he thought, panting in the cold air, the iron New England dark: *I dont. I dont! I dont hate it! I dont hate it!*" (471). Thus Quentin is not "fortunate enough to escape," as

Rosa believes him to be when she first begins her testimony on that sultry afternoon in her stifling living room in Mississippi.

3. SURROGATE WITNESSING

Also operating within the story level of the text, this circuit involves a character's attempt to witness to other characters about a third character's trauma. This circuit foregrounds the social issues of testimony: How and to what extent can we know the trauma of another person? How can we bear testimony to it? Again, *Absalom, Absalom!* serves as a paradigm, both because it is filled with numerous such attempts and because it illustrates so clearly that some surrogate witnesses succeed where others do not.

In addition to the long sections that render Rosa's testimony to Quentin, the novel devotes several extended passages to Mr. Compson's (Quentin's father's) transmission to Quentin of what he knows about the Sutpen tragedy. The last part of the novel takes place in a dormitory room in Harvard Yard and is an extended reconstruction of the Sutpen family story by Quentin and Shreve. Faulkner draws our attention to the contrast between Mr. Compson's inadequacies as a witness and the boys' success. Faced with the mystery of why Henry would reject Bon as a suitor to his sister, Mr. Compson muses:

> It just does not explain [. . .] we see dimly people, the people in whose living blood and seed we ourselves lay dormant and waiting, in this shadowy attenuation of time possessing now heroic proportions, performing their acts of simple passion and simple violence, impervious to time and inexplicable—Yes, Judith, Bon, Henry, Sutpen: all of them. They are there, yet something is missing; they are like a *chemical formula* exhumed along with the letters from that forgotten chest, carefully, the paper old and faded and falling to pieces, the writing faded, almost indecipherable, yet meaningful, familiar in shape and sense, the name and presence of volatile and sentient forces; you bring them together in the *proportions* called for, but nothing happens; you re-read, tedious and intent, poring, making sure that you have forgotten nothing, made no *miscalculation*; you bring them together again and again nothing happens; *just the words, the symbols, the shapes themselves*, shadowy inscrutable and serene, against that turgid background of a horrible and bloody mischancing of human affairs. (124–25; my emphasis)

Compson's language reveals part of the problem; he is not a sympathetic listener willing to be transformed by the process of listening. Rather, he is the scientist, chemist, and mathematician determined that the elements of his experiment, the pieces of his formula, should perform as he predicts they should.[28] From these fragments, Compson can only glean "information," in Benjamin's sense.

The boys, on the other hand, can piece together the same fragments as a story. They see the events as if they had actually been there. Even clearer than if they had been there, Quentin astutely realizes, because if he had actually been there: "*I could not have seen it this plain*" (238). Quentin's statement reveals that which we have already learned: the trauma consists precisely in inflicting on the victim an inability to absorb the event, to "see."[29] The trauma can only be "seen" through the (later) telling. Quentin and Shreve's reconstruction of the Sutpen family history can serve as a model of collaborative surrogate testimony:[30]

> it did not matter to either of them which one did the talking, since it was not the talking alone which did it, performed and accomplished the overpassing, but *some happy marriage of speaking and hearing* wherein each before the demand, the requirement, forgave condoned and forgot the faulting of the other—faultings both in the creating of this shade whom they discussed (rather, existed in) and in the hearing and sifting and discarding the false and conserving what seemed true, or fit the preconceived—in order to overpass to love, where there might be paradox and inconsistency but nothing fault nor false. (395; my emphasis)

Faulkner's metaphor of marriage underscores the reciprocal nature of listening and speaking required for the boys' reconstruction of the story, the "co" in "cowitnessing," so to speak. The roommates' "immense labor of imagination," in Arnold Weinstein's evocative phrase, is fueled by their youth, by their ability to posit love as a motivating force in the story they are telling, and by their ability to empathetically experience the plight of the victims (1974: 147, 144). In thinking about the night Henry renounces his patrimony, the boys are transformed and transported: "So that now it was not two but four of them riding the two horses through the dark over the frozen December ruts of that Christmas eve: four of them and then just two—Charles-Shreve and Quentin-Henry, the two of them both believing that Henry was thinking *He* (meaning his father) *has destroyed us all*" (417). The roommates are able to testify to Henry's pain by giving him words: he has destroyed us all. Four young men become two young men. But this kind of cowitnessing has a price.[31] For if we allow ourselves to read between novels, as it appears Faulkner wanted us to, then we can add that Quentin will actually pay with his life; I refer of course to Quentin's suicide, which in turn marks, if not traumatizes, his own nuclear family in *The Sound and the Fury*.

Efficacious surrogate witnessing and the price paid for it are also illustrated masterfully in Graham Swift's 1983 tour de force *Waterland*. As in *Absalom, Absalom!* there are numerous dark secrets that affect several generations. And as in Faulkner's South, the larger forces of history lock horns with individual destinies in the English Fens. Swift foregrounds this connection even more explicitly than Faulkner by making his protagonist a history teacher, one who will be sacked for having connected my third circuit of witnessing by telling his students these stories of history and individual fates. Tom Crick knows about the efficacy of storytelling from his parents—his father, Henry, whom he claims descends from a long line of storytellers, and his mother, Helen, whose work with veterans of the Great War teaches her that stories are "a way of bearing what won't go away, a way of making sense of madness" (170). I selected Helen's precept for working with suffering veterans as the epigraph of this chapter because it can serve as a goad to witnessing generally and because it foregrounds the activity necessary to transform traumatic memory: "No, don't forget. Don't erase it. You can't erase it. But make it into a story" (170).

Indeed, the entire novel could be thought of as Tom's institution of his mother's precept. When his wife, Mary, steals a baby whom she believes God has sent her, Tom has to become her surrogate witness, because for Mary, "the happening won't stop . . . she's still in the midst of events . . . which have not ceased" (247–48). So he makes the events of their lives into a story he tells his surrogate "children"—his appellation for his students—until he loses his job, at which point he tells the same stories over and over again to himself (249). Like Quentin, Tom Crick is himself implicated in the events about which he tells. Although there are no indications that this testifying will help Mary (for example, 87), the completeness of Crick's story, his earnest attempts "to put himself into history" (4), the full recitals of Freddie Parr's murder, young Mary's abortion, Dick Crick's suicide, and Tom's role in all three tragedies seem to offer closure as the final missing pieces surface at the book's conclusion.

A dramatic protest by the "Holocaust Club" during the school assembly to bid Crick farewell testifies to the fact that this circuit of surrogate witnessing is indeed completed by Tom's previously passive, uninterested, young addressees. Their feelings crystalize into "a sudden solitary cry, strangely urgent and imperative, devoid of schoolboy insolence: 'No cuts! Keep Crick!'" (252). Even though there is no indication that the headmaster will reverse his decision to let Crick go, this desire for Crick on the part of the students voiced through Price should be interpreted in the context of the novel as a sign that they now understand the value of Crick's kind of "stories" for the present and therefore for themselves. Their newly discovered maturity (underscored by the phrase "devoid of schoolboy insolence") signals that Tom Crick's pupils have become apt cowitnesses who will be capable of transmitting what they have received.

4. TEXTUAL WITNESSING

The fourth circuit occurs at the level of the novel's discourse (the form of the telling of the events that make up the story). It involves the narrator-text's (extrapolated to the author's) attempt to communicate the traumatic experiences of the characters within a novel to what Gerald Prince has called a text's narratees or inscribed readers (1980). This circuit encompasses circuits one through three. Actual readers who want to Talk with the text will need to interpret textual witnessing as the "statement" to which they are to respond. (The "reply" takes place through the fifth or sixth circuit, depending on the reader's historical and cultural relation to the text.) The "deictics" that signal the text's orientation to exchange fall into two categories. Some texts make an explicit request for a cowitness through pronouns of address, similar to the request for listeners in my storytelling mode. Others use textual strategies like narrative indirection, anachrony, ellipses, and repetition to mimic traumatic symptoms, thus calling for cowitnesses' reply of interpreting them as such. (A combination of both types is theoretically possible, in my view, but I have not located an example.)

The most explicit request for cowitnessing to trauma I am familiar with is made in Albert Camus's *The Fall* (*La Chute* 1956). On the one hand, we could certainly analyze this novel under the second circuit of witnessing: one character tells another about a traumatic event he has experienced. Clamence does appear to address a Frenchman, his *cher compatriote,* in the bar, in the streets, and on the waterways of Amsterdam. That this listener "exists" at the story level—that he performs physical actions, asks questions, and makes comments—can be inferred from many things Clamence says. To cite one of myriad instances, toward the beginning of their acquaintance, Clamence asks, "Are you staying long in Amsterdam? A beautiful city, isn't it? Fascinating? There's an adjective I haven't heard in some time" (1956b: 6). The construction of the flow of Clamence's comments here implies that his conversation partner must have replied to his query, "A beautiful city, isn't it?" with something like, "Amsterdam is fascinating." This novel has the feel of a conversation.

However, *The Fall* is not a quoted conversation. Not a single word reproduced in the text emanates from anyone other than Clamence. The novel does not quote someone saying, "Amsterdam is fascinating." This absence leads me to consider Camus's novel under the rubric of my textual witnessing. Since the character of Clamence is also the narrator of the whole text and his interlocutor's position is carved out but vacant, there is "room" for the position of the character of Clamence's addressee to be collapsed with the narratee of the whole discourse. Furthermore, this narratee can be collapsed with the actual reader through the text's incessant second-person address, *vouvoiement* (referring to the second-person formal pronoun *vous* used throughout the original French text). That is to say, the continued call to a "you" who does not actually reply can prompt readers to take up the available second-person pronoun and feel themselves addressed.[32]

Clamence even explicitly invites his addressee-narratee to step into the cowitness's role by insisting on how similar all humans are. We too should share our story: "But just think of your life, *mon cher compatriote!* Search your memory and perhaps you will find some similar story that you'll tell me later on" (1956b: 65). The text concludes with Clamence quite ill in his bed at home, insisting once again on how similar he and his interlocutor are and imploring his addressee to "tell": "Please tell me what happened to you one night on the quays of the Seine and how you managed never to risk your life. You yourself utter the words that for years have never ceased echoing through my nights and that I shall at last say through your mouth: 'O young woman, throw yourself into the water again so that I may a second time have the chance of saving both of us!'" (1956b: 147). Clamence's discourse has been called "a malignant act"

(Newton 1995: 7), and Camus reflected on it as a "calculated confession" by one who hastens to try himself "so as to better judge others" (original book blurb, as quoted in Lottman 1979: 564). From the perspective of trauma, however, this passage can be evaluated more positively as an invitation to cowitness: come, tell my story, let me speak through your mouth.[33] More specifically, Clamence seems aware of the necessity of a cowitness to effect the healing. He is asking the cowitness to help him do precisely what he could not do in the moment of the infliction of the trauma: act. As Janet pointed out, the inflexible traumatic recall, at least in the mind, has to be changed, and the first step in that process is to re-create the scene and change an element in it.[34] Although this will not erase the "fact" of the young woman's death, from a psychological perspective the addressee-narratee's actions could not only allow the story of the trauma to be told, but through that transmission could also begin the social healing that Herman insists needs to be accomplished for the society's general health as well (1992: 1). In this instance, the fact that Clamence finally admits he even wishes he had acted otherwise holds up a value system to readers that is different from the one by which he operated previously, specifically, on the original night of the young woman's suicide. Camus's concept of speaking through "your mouth" is so evocative for me because ultimately it is the very essence of cowitnessing as Talk. Readers must be willing to behave like Faulkner's Quentin and Shreve. With regard to the inscribed scene in Camus, one must add that Clamence's inscribed cowitness does not rush to take him up on the offer (we assume, anyway, since again, we have no independent access to the interlocutor's words or actions). And Clamence himself quickly retracts his openness to cowitnessing by adding: "A second time, eh, what a risky suggestion! Just suppose, *cher maître*, that we should be taken literally? We'd have to go through with it. Brr . . . ! The water's so cold! But let's not worry! It's too late now. It will always be too late. Fortunately!" (1956b: 147). Still, that these words close the novel suggests to me that actual readers can choose to take up the challenge of cowitnessing by "jumping in the water," not by literally jumping into the Seine but by letting themselves feel addressed by the "you" of the text and therefore retelling Clamence's story, including this change of heart.[35]

So one way in which my fourth circuit of witnessing flows is when the narrator directly addresses an interlocutor-narratee, inviting the telling of the story of the trauma by "you yourself uttering the words that I shall at last say through your mouth." A very different form of textual witnessing is illustrated by novels like Monika Maron's *The Defector* (*Die Überläuferin* 1986). Rosalind Polkowski, Maron's protagonist, displays such symptoms of PTSD as insomnia, hallucinations, and social withdrawal. More importantly for my purposes here, the text "tells" her story through fragmentation, flashbacks, achrony, repetition, and elision, narrative techniques that could be said to mimic symptoms of the traumatized psyche. Or rather, if readers interpret these textual features as analogous to traumatic symptoms, those readers are replying to the statement of the text as trauma by cowitnessing.

Maron's novel opens and closes with the image of Rosalind sitting in her apartment, immobile with two lame legs. Rosalind's physical paralysis is never explained; rather, like Gregor Samsa's metamorphosis into a beetle, it is the fantastic assumed "given" that tempts us into interpreting everything that follows as its consequence. It finds echoes throughout the book in myriad images of lameness, amputation, deformation, and decapitation. Rosalind's immobility and disconnectedness find their analogue on the level of the text in stasis and lack of plot. Both Rosalind and the text are "stuck" in the "happening," or the non-happening, as the case may be, like Irène reenacting the night of her mother's death, or Tom Crick's wife, Mary, reenacting the kidnapping of the baby. I have just mentioned one prominent sign of the novel's lack of forward progression: it begins and ends with the same image, and that image is itself an image of immobility. The four intermezzi (*Zwischenspiele*) in Maron's novel can also be interpreted as a performance of the traumatic symptom of social disconnection and immobility. Several critics interpret the stock characters of these intermezzi as unintegrated pieces of Rosalind's psyche; and such an interpretation supports the idea that at the story level, Rosalind suffers from PTSD. But I would also point to them as a sign of the *text's* performance of trauma, and specifically of an inability to tell the story of what happened, to narrate Rosalind's past. The conversations of the intermezzi are non-narrative; they do not report any events, and perhaps most importantly, they cannot be integrated into any (larger) story about Rosalind's life or her paralysis. Thus, though Rosalind begins to offer an initially somewhat chronological account of her early life, order breaks down quickly with the interjection of the first ahistorical and impersonal intermezzo. A reconstruction of Rosalind's history is complicated further, if not completely foiled by the confusion and switching of personal pronouns and tenses, sometimes even in mid-sentence. When actual readers like myself point to textual features like repetition, similar images, interruption of chronology, and confusion of agency and causality and make a connection between them and symptoms of PTSD (for example, social withdrawal, reenactments, depersonalization), instead of, say, between them and structure or aesthetics, they are cowitnessing to the trauma the text performs. Their actions would officially belong to the fifth or sixth circuit.

5. LITERARY-HISTORICAL WITNESSING

This circuit considers how a text communicates to the actual flesh-and-blood readers of the culture and time in which it was written. In many instances it will be the circuit about which later readers will have the least information. I suspect it is an aspect of the texts mentioned here for which most of my readers will have the least information. Still, I think the fact of how, if at all, a text testifies to its contemporary readers can be particularly important in connecting literary representations of trauma to their historical contexts. Shoshana Felman's reading of Camus's *The Fall* through his previous works, especially through *The Plague* and *L'Homme révolté*, and through the controversy surrounding the latter, is a particularly fine example of unearthing literary-historical witnessing. (Felman's act itself belongs to my sixth circuit, since she is a later reader who cowitnesses to the trauma articulated through the text.) I would suggest that it is characteristic for this category that even a summary of these kinds of arguments is too complex to include in a survey, though I hope my readers will reread Felman's analysis in the context of my schema (Felman and Laub 1992: 165–203).[36]

You will recall with regard to my first circuit (intrapsychic witnessing) that if actual trauma has occurred, the circuit is broken: the traumatized individual cannot witness to the self. Similarly, if an entire society has been traumatized—say, Benjamin's post–Great War Germany—the text-as-statement of trauma produced in that society may not be recognizable as such to those who are victims of the trauma, that is, to other members of the traumatized society in which the text was written, the contemporary potential readers of the author. How will we know if circuit five is disrupted? To interrogate art for what it might tell us about trauma in the society in which it was produced, one would obviously begin with depictions of perpetration of violence, but one would also look for lacunae—for stories that can't be told or can't be told fully—for trauma, as we have seen, can only be made "present to consciousness" with difficulty (Felman and Laub 1992: 194). Such an investigation, as I hope I've demonstrated, would operate at the level of the story, but also at the level of the discourse *and*—the aspect I'm foregrounding with this category—at the levels of the production and contemporary reception of the text.

In this context I'd like to introduce the little-known novel by Gertrud Kolmar that I will be analyzing more extensively in the last part of this chapter. Kolmar, the pen name of Gertrud Chodziesner, born in Berlin to bourgeois Jewish parents in 1894 and presumed to have been exterminated upon arrival in Auschwitz in 1943, is known primarily for her poetry. But she also wrote several dramas and prose works in her brief lifetime, including the short novel usually referred to as *A Jewish Mother (Eine jüdische Mutter)*. This story of the brutal rape of a five-year-old child and her mother's subsequent search for the perpetrator was never published in Kolmar's lifetime. That is to say, as far as I know, *there was no contemporaneous reception of the text*, except perhaps by Kolmar's trusted sister, Hilda, who had the manuscript during the war and eventually allowed it to be published in 1965. In other words, there is no fifth circuit of witnessing for this text. That is my point. Though there were not yet any official publishing restrictions against Jewish authors in the late Weimar Republic when this story was written (1930–31), Kolmar did not attempt to publish it. This very absence causes me to ask why. That the novel was not circulated in the Weimar Republic or in Nazi Germany also causes me to reread the text to consider whether it provides any hints about why Kolmar might not have attempted publication. While I will bracket my specific questions and their inconclusive answers until my fuller analysis of the novel, I want to mention here that my activities of remarking the traumatic symptoms or "short-circuit" in circuit five, framing questions about it, rereading the text, and searching for answers belong to the witnessing of my sixth circuit.

6. TRANSHISTORICAL-TRANSCULTURAL WITNESSING

This outermost communicative circuit includes the previous five. A reader from a culture other than the one in which a text was written and/or from a later time period cowitnesses to the trauma articulated in and through the text. For example, a twenty-first-century North American reader-interpreter tries to explicate Kolmar's novel to the interpreter's contemporaries as a symptom of cultural trauma in the Weimar and Nazi periods of which Kolmar was a victim. If the interpreter as cowitness is successful, she points to gaps and silences and in the process produces a narrative about the other circuits of witnessing to trauma; when this circuit is flowing, cowitnessing is a "reply." In cases like that of *A Jewish Mother*, where the text could not testify in the society in which it was written, it is particularly critical for later exegetes to complete the circuit of witnessing. This is what I have begun above and will continue below with my sustained analysis of *A Jewish Mother*, but before continuing with Kolmar I'd like to close this survey section with a negative example of transhistorical-transcultural witnessing from Atwood's *The Handmaid's Tale*.

Although Atwood's novel begins by throwing us directly into the nightmare world of its protagonist-narrator, it ends with great distance to that world through a section called Historical Notes (299–311). Here the reader gets "a partial transcript of the proceedings of the Twelfth Symposium on Gileadean Studies, held as part of the International Historical Association Convention, held at the University of Denay, Nunavit, on June 25, 2195" (299). The transcript records the introduction of a Professor Maryann Crescent Moon of the Department of Caucasian Anthropology and the talk of a Professor James Darcy Pieixoto, director of the Twentieth- and Twenty-First-Century Archives at Cambridge University. In other words, Atwood offers a creative projection of what scholars will be doing in two hundred years. Atwood has stated that she added the epilogue in order to communicate a number of things about Gilead that the Handmaid could not have known, and also to express the author's own optimism that Gilead, like the Third Reich, would not last forever (Ingersoll 1990: 217). The Historical Notes certainly accomplish these tasks, but Atwood is being a bit duplicitous in her explanation. The epilogue functions more compellingly to extend the totalitarian themes of the novel, illustrating how Atwood does not want us to read it. She dislikes these late-twenty-second-century scholars and their attitudes. Her portrayal of them can serve as a negative illustration of my sixth circuit. Although their research has uncovered some helpful information about the origins of the testimony (that it was recorded onto cassette tapes, presumably after the Handmaid's escape from the household, but before actually leaving Gilead), the ironic tone in which these facts are communicated, like the witty place and personal names, carries a message for Atwood's readers about how not to read, or in the framework of this chapter, about the inability to cowitness.

The scholars at the conference show no interest in what the Handmaid actually tells, indicated in part by their obsession with the historical identity of her Commander. Pieixoto's hypotheses about this take up the greater part of his talk. He concludes:

> This is our guesswork. Supposing it to be correct—supposing, that is, that Waterford was indeed the "Commander"—many gaps remain. Some of them could have been filled by our anonymous author, had she had a different turn of mind. She could have told us much about the workings of the Gileadean empire, had she had the instincts of a reporter or a spy. What would we not give, now, for even twenty pages or so of print-out from Waterford's private computer! However, we must be grateful for any crumbs the Goddess of History has deigned to vouchsafe us. (Atwood 1986: 310)

This passage and others mean to lead readers to the conclusion that these scholars have missed the point. Their implicit and explicit criticisms of the Handmaid completely gloss over her pain, over her story, over her trauma—to their minds: "crumbs"! In my terms, they haven't responded to her text as a statement. They miss all the insights her tale *does* provide about her own life and even "about the workings of the Gileadean empire," because they seem interested only in historically verifiable fact, in the most limited political and military events and their agents. Their attitude, like Mr. Compson's, limits their ability to cowitness. They can only read for information and blame their text for not rendering the story.

I read Atwood's epilogue as asking its readers to read against the scholars' reading, so that those readers—we—*can* become cowitnesses. In a variant of the category I've outlined of transhistorical-transcultural witnessing, Atwood offers the intriguing proposition that we who historically "precede" the tale can be more effective cowitnesses than those who come after, if we are able to grasp what's important about the story, that is, if we are able to realize that twenty pages of a computer printout would *not* reveal more about a culture and its upheavals than a lengthy personal narrative of an individual's interactions with her society. If we embrace this attitude, we will be in a better position to cowitness to the Handmaid's narrative as statement. To do so, we have to recognize and read her testimony in all its aspects; we have to orient to her personal experiences as sources of knowledge about a society in crisis. Atwood's "scholars" were not able to do this from their later historical and cultural remove. Readers faithful to my sixth circuit of witnessing would be. In the context of trauma and witnessing, there is at least one other lesson I believe Atwood is illustrating negatively for us through these scholars— their cockiness. Atwood's portrayal of these scholars brings to mind Hartman's warning that because we cannot "know" or "understand" what Holocaust survivors have endured, we can only try to transmit it. *The Handmaid's Tale* can return us to a basic point about literature as a turn-taking system. Within Atwood's novel, the Handmaid creates a cowitness to whom to tell her story *and* whose story she so desperately hopes to hear one day. Pieixoto and his crowd, in contrast, posit themselves as superior exegetes (to the Handmaid) of Gilead; in their estimation, she offers them only crumbs.[37] As we have learned from Quentin, surely distance can offer clarity on some matters. And yet, as we have also learned from Quentin and Shreve's efforts, one can get closest to the story only through a sense of partnership, an attitude I hope to demonstrate in turning to Kolmar below.

Narrative Witnessing as Talk:
Reading Gertrud Kolmar's *A Jewish Mother*

Most readers know Kolmar through her poetic oeuvre, first made widely available in 1955 with the posthumous publication of *The Poetic Work* (*Das lyrische Werk*). Kolmar's prose has been generally regarded as "second-rate" (Shafi 1995: 189) and has often been read only for the light it sheds on her poetry and her biography.[38] The basis of Kolmar's reputation is beginning to change—a point I will take up later in this discussion. Still, her biographers generally tie her to the Wilhelminian world of her birth rather than to the Weimar Republic of her adulthood (for example, Eichmann-Leutenegger 1993). One literary critic argues that the Weimar Republic "remained foreign [*fremd*] to her" (Sparr 1993:

76). In contrast to her more famous, cosmopolitan first cousin Walter Benjamin, she is usually depicted as the rural recluse (Wizisla 1991: 126–27; see too Picard as quoted in Balzer 1981: 168). This assessment, I believe, comes from focusing on her poetry. While it may well have been the case that Kolmar personally "felt at home" (Smith 1975: 9) in the rural atmosphere of Finkenkrug, rather than in the Berlin of her early and late life, my analysis of the short novel she wrote in the closing years of the Weimar Republic, *A Jewish Mother*,[39] demonstrates her sensitivity to the pressures of modern urban life as well as to the beauties of nature.

Although violence can hardly be claimed as an exclusively modern phenomenon, the particular crime at the center of this story, the abduction and rape of a five-year-old girl by a stranger, links Kolmar's novel to twentieth-century urban culture. Furthermore, I suggest that the book is modern, not so much for what it tells, as for what and how it does not tell. Specifically, I interpret the silences of characters in the face of events that overwhelm them, as well as the author's own doubts (deduced in part from her decision not to publish the book), as signs of trauma. My analysis demonstrates how this novel inscribes what Kolmar did not yet fully know of her lived historical relation to the events of her times: of the marginalization of minorities and the escalation of violence against them that would lead, shortly after the novel's composition, to the election of the National Socialist Party in Germany and eventually to the attempt to eliminate the Jews of Europe. I will show how circuits one through five are disconnected and how that disconnectedness is testified to—is responded to as statement of trauma—through my cowitnessing as a later and foreign reader. By completing the sixth circuit, that is to say, by interpreting *A Jewish Mother* as artistically bearing witness to the crisis of increasing violence against women, children, and minorities in the late Weimar period, I am Talking with Kolmar's novel.

A Jewish Mother is set in the cosmopolitan Berlin of the Weimar Republic, the late 1920s to be more precise. Its protagonist, Martha Wolg, née Jadassohn, is an outsider, literally, as a Jew born in an eastern province, and figuratively, as a loner in the urban culture of the German metropolis in which she marries, bears a child, is abandoned by her gentile husband, and struggles to make a living for herself and her daughter, Ursula (Ursa, for short). When her five-year-old child does not return home one evening at the accustomed time, Martha sets off in search of her. Martha's initially casual walk turns into a mother's nightmare. Although she finds Ursula's playmates at a riverbank, her daughter is not among them. Ursa went off, the children report, with a man who said her mother was looking for her. After a frantic evening of questioning the neighbors, a sleepless night, and an agonizing morning, Martha finds her daughter's limp body in an abandoned shed in an outlying garden district, which locals refer to as the "garbage-dump colony [*Siedlung Müllabfuhr*]" (38).[40] The child is still breathing, but her body is blood-soaked. Martha, with the assistance of some alarmed local women, manages to get the unconscious child to the nearest hospital. Several days later, the tortured child is helped to her presumed inevitable death through sleeping powder administered by her mother. Martha swears revenge against the murderer of her child and assumes he is lurking somewhere in Greater Berlin. But she is rebuffed or ignored by those whose aid she seeks: neighbors, the police, a lawyer, a friend of her former husband whom she takes as a lover. Martha's attempt years later to terminate this search for the perpetrator, and concomitantly her role as mother, also proves impossible. Rejected by her lover, she plunges into the River Spree, ending her life with the sense of expiating a crime *she* perpetrated.

A *Jewish Mother*, with its admittedly melodramatic plot, contains numerous potentially traumatic events and situations. These include the child's rape, her poisoning, and her mother, Martha's, suicide, but also the backdrop for these events: Martha's and Ursula's marginalization by the husband's family and by society in general, Martha's experience of her child's rape, and Martha's loss of her child.[41] The text hints that these are all interconnected, creating a sinister portrait of the Berlin in which they occur. The child's rape will serve as my focal point for examining attempted testimony to trauma. This particular event foregrounds one reason why there is no immediately accessible knowledge of violence: the perpetrator chooses as victim a person who cannot speak of the crime. The child Ursula cannot say what happened to her, though the crime is inscribed on her body. My first posited circuit, intrapsychic witnessing, does not flow. Martha, as societal outsider, and in a kind of maternal metonymy, also cannot witness to the crime. Her attempts to find Ursula's violator are in vain partly because no one understands what she is trying to say; some simply refuse to listen or, in psychoanalytic terms, are unable to serve as cowitnesses. Martha's search for revenge therefore results in a reinscription of the trauma on her own body through her decision to commit suicide. To understand this self-erasure, one needs to understand the obstacles Martha faces in processing the violence against her child and herself. Kolmar's text both contains and itself constitutes acts of incomplete or failed witnessing; short-circuits result from a lack of competent tellers and sympathetic listeners. I would like to consider the novel more closely now through my schema of the six circuits of narrative witnessing, reminding my readers that these circuits are intertwined through the medium of literary narration and therefore cannot always be kept strictly distinct, and also that the story I will coconstruct with the text-as-statement constitutes Talk.

1. AND 2. INTRAPSYCHIC AND INTERPERSONAL WITNESSING

In the central crime of Kolmar's work, there is never any doubt that Ursula has been sexually violated; the child is so young and the sexual violence so great that she cannot integrate that experience (circuit one) and is therefore traumatized. Although the crime and the trauma are decodable through the victim's body, the perpetrator and the exact forms of abuse remain unspecified. Several scenes reveal that the child is suffering from PTSD. When a male visitor in the hospital steps toward the child to offer her grapes to eat, for example, Ursula begins to scream and shake (55); in the current terms of the psychiatric diagnostic manual, Kolmar depicts "intense psychological distress . . . or physiological reactivity . . . when the person is exposed to triggering events that resemble or symbolize an aspect of the traumatic event" (DSM-IV 1994: 424). At one point when her own mother approaches her, she seems to reenact the abduction and rape scene (58); this depicts a "dissociative state . . . during which components of the event are relived and the person behaves as though experiencing the event at that moment" (DSM-IV 1994: 424; Janet's patient Irène comes to mind once again). Culbertson summarizes this relationship between trauma and the body more poetically: "No experience is more one's own than harm to one's own skin, but none is more locked within that skin, played out within it in actions other than words, in patterns of consciousness below the everyday and the constructions of language" (1995: 170).

Ursula's experience is indeed "locked within" her skin. The five-year-old child cannot *speak* of that to which her body testifies.[42] Her trauma is never put into narrative form, is never communicated verbally by the victim to a sympathetic listener (circuit two). When Ursula's mother first finds her after her disappearance, for example, the child is unconscious and therefore mute: "Its head hung like a wilted flower. Intact. It was still breathing [*Sein Köpfchen hing wie eine welke Blume. Unversehrt. Es atmete doch*]" (39).[43] After surgery at the hospital, she is placed in a children's ward; we see her next when her mother arrives for a visit: "Ursa lay quietly. From a superficial glance, one would think she was sleeping. But she was breathing with difficulty and her dark face shone on the bluish-white pillow with a pale waxy sheen. Martha's hand twitched. Her hand itched to lift the blanket to see the wound and its dressing. But she didn't dare. She peered into her child. But it didn't sense anything" (47). The child does not appear conscious, much less able to explain. Her wounds could testify to the rape, but they are not seen and therefore don't "speak"; the mother won't—apparently can't—look at them.

During Martha's next visit, she learns that the child by now has tried to tell of her violation. But her speech is avoided, even stifled by those who could have listened.[44] As the elderly, female patient into whose room Ursula is moved explains to the mother: "Yes, last night over there in that ward she screamed so horribly [*so gräßlich geschrien*]. Not that loud, but so . . . you know . . . so awfully it makes you shudder [*so zum Graulen*]. A few of the little girls woke up and began to cry. Because she'd also begun to talk [*reden*]—about this man—you understand. So the nurses moved her. On account of the other children . . . if they hear that . . ." (54). Clearly, this passage is one of several that *do* communicate (to the reader and presumably to Martha and even the old woman) how horrible Ursa's abduction must have been. But it accomplishes this in part by pointing to the internal and external obstacles the victim faces in telling her story coherently. At first Ursula cannot talk. She screams her message (*geschrien*). Then when she does try to articulate it by speaking (*redden*), no one wants to listen, or rather the other children who hear her are too frightened to function as the listener-cowitness Ursula needs. Her attempt to testify to what happened is completely stifled when hospital personnel move her to another room, precisely so she will not be heard. Revealingly, even Ursula's attempted testimony is reported thirdhand via the patient into whose room the child is moved, a woman who could not herself have witnessed the event (of Ursula's efforts to speak) and who seems more concerned about the other children's distress and her own than about Ursula's. This narrative mediation, an aspect that belongs, strictly speaking, to my fourth circuit of textual witnessing, can be considered as yet another way the text renders the traumatic nature of the original crime and concomitantly the child's lack of success in attesting to what happened.[45]

Ursa's chance at recovery through successful interpersonal witnessing is depicted by the text as slim through a juxtaposition to an incident from her mother's childhood. This incident is relayed via an external analepsis—a flashback to an event prior to the beginning of the story at hand (Genette 1980: 49). When Martha's neighbor assures her that Ursa will heal from her wounds and even forget the event, Martha thinks to herself: no, she will never forget. This thought in turn triggers Martha's recollection of a walk home from school during her own childhood:

> She was eight or nine years old. She saw it before her. With a young schoolmate—Lucie Weigeler it was, she remembered that still—she was coming through the Torweg. There the man stood. He hadn't done anything to the children, he just exposed himself shamelessly, and they ran away fast. "What a pig!" Lucie said afterward full of disgust. "He looks like a fine gentleman and is really such a pig." *She* said nothing. Her every limb shook. (43; Kolmar's emphasis)

Martha's recall of the exact name of the schoolmate who was with her and the location of the flasher hint at the intensity of the original experience as well as the clarity of her memory of it: the exactitude of traumatic memory.[46] Yet the text foregrounds in this passage that Martha was unable to *verbalize* what happened to her: she didn't say anything. The next passage describes Martha's continued inability to verbalize her terror. As in the case of her daughter, Ursula, the body speaks of what the tongue cannot: "Then the nights. She couldn't sleep. Because it would come to her. It would shine: the horrible thing, the terrifying thing. It threatened her. Sweat broke out of all of her pores. She burned. She wanted to scream and couldn't and didn't dare move" (43). The passage continues at length, reporting that for more than a year afterward, Martha would have nightmares and was completely unable to talk about the incident with another person—neither with her parents nor even with her friend Lucie, a child who *was* able to name the perpetrator immediately: "what a pig."[47] Martha thus remained isolated in and through her speechlessness and fear. The absence in this passage of quoted interior monologue, the direct quotation of a character's train of thought (Cohn 1978: 12–13), underscores Martha's inarticulateness; she could not put the experience into words even for herself, much less talk about it to other people. In Culbertson's formulation about survivors of personal violation, "she simply cannot make the leap to words" (1995: 169). In evaluating Martha's reaction to this encounter, we are reminded that any specific event "may or may not be catastrophic, and may not traumatize everyone equally" (Caruth 1995a: 4). In other words, to no matter what category of social violation we might assign flashing, it was traumatic for the young Martha. The magnitude of her reaction is communicated by the text to the reader partly through narrative indirection, linguistic avoidance, and euphemism. Martha could not acknowledge its sexual dimension. What she saw remained the threatening but nonspecified "it." She never tells a story about what happened, not even as an adult.[48]

3. SURROGATE WITNESSING

Given Martha's inability to testify for herself, it is not surprising that she cannot serve as recipient of Ursula's story and that she cannot function successfully as surrogate witness for Ursula to others. From the beginning of her search for her daughter, her ineptitude is underscored by descriptions of her as "the trembling wench [*Weib*]" and as "a stammering lunatic [*Irre*]" (28). The child's body cannot testify to the crime, since the mother is unable to cowitness by looking at the wounds. Martha had been equally incapable of "seeing" at the scene of the crime, when she found her daughter in the trash heap the day before (40). Furthermore, she and others around her can only speak of the crime against the child through indirection, and even in their indirection they do not name the sexual nature of the violence. The word "rape" (*Vergewaltigung*) never appears in Kolmar's text. The most explicit word any character uses is *Sittlichkeitsverbrechen* (literally, "morality crime," a standard euphemism for sexual offenses), used once by a nurse to the employee registering the child's arrival at the hospital (40). The crime usually gets referred to as "that" or "it," as in "how on earth is that possible" (40). Significantly, when Martha tries to imagine to herself what happened to her daughter, she uses adjectives and adjectival nouns of ineffability: "that was indescribable, unimaginable . . . this unspeakable thing [*diese Unsäglichkeit*]" (43). The crime against Ursula becomes that which cannot be described nor even imagined; as such it cannot be witnessed to either.[49]

Such expressions can and should be explained in part as social custom in the face of the incommensurability of the crime; they are also well-intentioned attempts to minimize further pain to the victim's mother. The nurse, for instance, does not want the secretary to ask Martha why the child is being admitted because she fears Martha will get even more upset than she already is. But characters' linguistic avoidance must also be interpreted in terms of a larger social pattern that emerges in the novel: characters' inability (refusal?) to witness to what actually happened to the child or in general to witness to injury to someone else. When first questioned about Ursa's whereabouts, for example, some of the children just wish Martha would leave so they can get on with their game (24)—excusable for children, perhaps, but less forgivable when adults refuse to help, as when some neighborhood women remain compassionless (25) and the police impassive (36).

The most explicit refusal to cowitness for another is also the most cruel. Years later, when Martha desperately wants to reconnect to society, instead of incessantly trying to avenge her child's death, she confesses to her lover, Albert, that she gave Ursula an overdose of sleeping powder. He responds by rejecting her permanently: "If anything separates us even further, it's that. You've made me an accessory [*Mitwisser*] to your—act, against my will. . . . And please go. I don't want to throw you out, but I'm afraid of your further confessions" (158). *Mitwissen*, etymologically, not "to know," but "to know with," is the action at the heart of psychological cowitnessing. Thus Albert refuses to aid Martha precisely by refusing to be a *Mitwisser*.

Martha's own ineptitude can be viewed in at least two ways. As suggested above, numerous passages hint that by refusing the help some others are, in fact, willing to offer, she is selfishly refusing to be a surrogate witness. When her employer, Frau Hoffmann, comes to visit, for example, the older woman demonstrates her readiness to serve as listener-cowitness to Martha's testimony on Ursula's behalf: "You're forcing yourself to converse with me about things that don't concern you. Isn't that right? You can only think of your child. You shouldn't force yourself so. . . . You should cry. —This daze . . . I can't abide it" (51). But Martha cannot accept the other woman's sympathy and insists on keeping her pain—and Ursula's story—to herself: "I have to bear this alone . . . everything . . . for me" (52).[50]

On the other hand, Martha's failure or refusal to witness can also be interpreted as the consequence of her own victimization and should be therefore evaluated in the context of Martha's (and Ursa's) overdetermined status as other in Weimar society. Not only is Martha an outsider as a Jew born in an eastern province (14), but she is also an abandoned wife, a single parent, and a working woman, each a factor of varying importance in her ostracization by others and in her self-hatred.[51] Mother and daughter's "racial" difference is repeatedly foregrounded with reference to their skin color. Martha's skin carries an "ivory tone [*Elfenbeinton*]" and Ursula's is darker: "yellow, almost brown [*gelblich, fast braun*]" (18).[52] That their Jewishness has social consequences is amply illustrated throughout the course of the novel. The elder Mr. Wolg is particularly antisemitic in his diatribes against Martha. In pleading with his son not to marry her, he argues, "We live in the twentieth century, not in Jacob's tent. She sure looks right out of the Old Testament. Her name should be Leah, not Martha. Champagne on ice, you think? Not me: ice, sure, a big chunk. Jerusalem at the Northpole" (15).

But Martha's otherness is portrayed most frequently in linguistic exchanges in which she can't seem to communicate on the most basic level with those around her. Whether it is the young children who saw Ursa's abduction or the parents and neighbors she questions during her search, other Berliners do not seem to understand what Martha is asking:

"Tell me, you were playing with Ursula Wolg; where did you leave her?"
". . . with Ursula Wolg . . . ?"
"Yes, Ursa. I'm speaking German, no? [*Ich rede doch deutsch?*] Where is she?" (23; Kolmar's ellipses)

There is no reference whatsoever in the novel to Martha's having an accent and yet in this passage and in others, her difficulties are framed in terms of language. Berliners assume Martha does not understand their language, either because she is a "foreigner" or because she is mentally incompetent. Martha's own doubts about her comprehensibility are hinted at here through the use of a question mark where one might expect an exclamation point: *Ich rede doch deutsch?*

When Martha resumes her search for the missing child the morning after her disappearance, the narrator describes her as initially suspicious of everyone she sees (37). But when she then goes to ask folks for help, it is they who seem callously unsympathetic, if not hostile:

> she walked over to the lumberyard to ask the people who were carrying windowframes out of a shed, the worker who was sitting on some boards leisurely eating his breakfast. They shrugged their shoulders, merely shook their heads in amazement. No, they weren't even here anymore yesterday. Martha, who struggled on her way, didn't catch, that one said: "Who knows, if it's true. That one looks as if she weren't quite right up there [*als ob sie da nicht ganz richtig wäre*]." And he tapped himself on the forehead. (37–38)

People react to Martha as "*die Fremde*" (39) in every sense of the word: the "foreigner," as in "stranger," but also, "strange one," as in "crazy" or "weird."[53]

Martha's fate as other is only exacerbated by her status as mother of the victim, an alienation she acknowledges and even seems to cherish: "I . . . I am different" (52). Yet without access to the "same language" as those around her, Martha can neither find the perpetrator to Ursula's rape nor witness to this crime. Worst of all, in the process of being rejected by those whose aid she seeks, she becomes further traumatized, a state that results in her suicide.[54]

4. TEXTUAL WITNESSING

Attempts at witnessing among the characters are made known to us through the literary text, and it has been—and necessarily would be—impossible to discuss them without also discussing the way the text presents the story. A clue to the profundity of Ursula's pain resides in the indirect communication of her story to us, and a clue to Martha's childhood experience of sexual harassment as trauma is given by the lack of direct quotation of her recollection of the event and its aftermath. In this section, I focus explicitly on Kolmar's textual strategies and how they might be interpreted as signs of trauma. By proceeding in such a manner, I am replying to the text-as-statement by cowitnessing. Strictly speaking, the participants in the fourth circuit are the narrator and the narratee, and my interpretation of it belongs to the sixth circuit.

The novel's testimony is given in part by its narrative technique. Narrated in the third person with an internal, though not exclusive, focalization through Martha, the story presumably communicates to the narratee (and by extension to the reader) what happens as Martha comes to knowledge of events. But at crucial junctures the text abandons Martha's view, creating gaps. This textual strategy accords well with descriptions of trauma's "refusal to be simply located" (Caruth 1995a: 9). The lacunae in the text may mirror the lacunae created in the victim-character's psyche by traumatic events, but as we have seen in Maron's *The Defector*, we can also read them as the *text's* performance of trauma. Consequently, the narratee is not simply told what happened, because the text "cannot," or does not, simply offer a mimetic representation of trauma. What would this look like anyway?[55] Therefore, the reader's cognizance of the event—cowitnessing—involves registering gaps and fragments as analogues to traumatic symptoms (and again belongs to my sixth circuit). This activity could be considered the Talk counterpart of what in a psychoanalytic framework Caruth describes as "a new kind of listening, the witnessing, precisely, *of impossibility*" (1995a: 10).

Does circuit four flow here? Do the text and Kolmar as author witness more effectively than the characters in the novel? One must answer "yes," since as a reader of the story one understands that crimes have been committed and traumas suffered. And yet the obliquity of this testimony should be noted. Some textual strategies mimic the inarticulateness and displacement characteristic of trauma victims prior to successful cowitnessing. One sign of displacement or dissociation has already been identified as the novel's narrative mode: primarily, though not exclusively, internally focalized through the character of Martha, and yet not narrated in the first person.[56] That is to say, the world of the story is usually the world as viewed from Martha's perspective, but only occasionally through her voice or thoughts; the novel contains few direct quotations of her speech or instances of quoted interior monologue—"direct quotation" of her mental language. The choice not to use a first-person narrator to tell his or her own story may be interpreted as a choice made to control distance between the reader and the protagonist or to avoid certain kinds of information by avoiding inside views of the character. In this case, one of its effects is that Martha remains "*fremd*" to the reader, as well as to the other characters. One could also interpret Kolmar's stylistic decision as follows: the story cannot be told in the first person because it is a story about people who metaphorically cannot speak in the first person, as they do not fully understand what is happening to them—they have been traumatized—and then cannot speak clearly for themselves, at least not at certain moments. The narrative indirectness thus conveys Martha's as well as the text's (and therefore the readers') lack of access to her psyche.

Not surprisingly, narrative obstacles in this text occur at crucial dramatic junctures and around the most painful issues. In fact, none of the crimes are witnessed directly.[57] Consistent with the novel's general indirectness, the closest we come to the main crime is seeing its effect on others. And even then, narratees are not "told" and readers do not "see" what is before the characters' eyes. One of the most poignant instances of limited "sight" occurs when Martha finally discovers the body of her child. She enters an abandoned shed:

> There was a mattress, a red pillow cut open, out of which seaweed spilled. And there . . . She stared, for only a second, and didn't believe it. She didn't believe it. Then she slid screaming to the ground. [Martha groans over the child, finally picks it up and goes outside.]
>
> [The child] *was* breathing. She pulled her hand suddenly from under the backside it was supporting. Her hand was wet. It was full of blood. And suddenly she realized that her hand felt the naked legs of the child, not its underwear, not its panties. She lifted up the little skirt. Have mercy . . .
>
> She collapsed.
>
> She was blind from tears, she was deaf from her own sobbing. (39–40)

Twice in this crucial sequence the text withholds what Martha presumably sees. When we assume the role of sympathetic cowitness to the textual testimony in this passage, we "see" with Martha the scene in the shack, the old mattress, the slit pillow, the stuffing, but when her eye reaches the child, the text offers ellipses: "And there. . . ." Similarly, we "feel" with Martha the moisture, the bare legs, but when the skirt is raised we "hear" Martha's cry for mercy, and then we get silence, the ellipses again. I suggest that these ellipses serve to evoke the context of the production of the text: the experience of being traumatized. That is to say, in encountering Kolmar's ellipses, the reader encounters the inability to register what is before Martha's eyes but what she does not see, because she cannot fathom it. The text imposes gaps on its narratee (and by extension on its readers) the way that the shock of "seeing" her violated child inflicts blindness on Martha. For Martha, the sight of Ursa triggers trauma that blocks her vision. For readers to respond as cowitnesses they must recognize Kolmar's ellipses as the textual equivalent of that psychological experience. The ellipses mark the space to which, in Caruth's phrase, "willed access is denied" (1995a: 152). While these textual gaps might be considered quite conventional adherence to the decorum of the period, an additional and not incompatible interpretation would be that the text, too, is blinded by the shock—traumatized—and therefore neither witnesses to nor transmits to the narratee nor to readers the site of the transgression. However, readers should not "fill in" these gaps. Rather, as cowitnesses, they should notice the lacunae and register them as "raising the matter" of trauma.

Another type of evidence supporting a reading of this narrative-as-statement of trauma is that the text does not relay the story of the rape to its narratee the few times it is presumably narrated explicitly by characters. When, for example, the child speaks of the rape that night in the children's ward of the hospital, her words are never stated in the text, a scene I considered briefly above as failed cowitnessing on the part of the other children and the old woman who becomes Ursula's new roommate, but here considered also as an incomplete witnessing by the text to the narratee and consequently to the reader. We never find out what—however incoherent—the child was able to say "about this man" (54). Another partially suppressed source of information is a newspaper article about the rape, described enthusiastically by the owner of the local pub to Martha as "precisely, completely correctly described" (45).[58] Kolmar similarly omits a narration of the violation when the child arrives at the hospital; the text laconically states: "Martha didn't speak, the others delivered the word for her [*führten für sie das Wort*]" (40). We never hear "the word"—the sympathetic women's explanation of what happened. In other words, though a successful mimetic representation of the event is posited as a possibility—indeed as a fait accompli in the world of the story—it is not reproduced by the text's narrator for the narratee (and readers). During Martha's conversation with a lawyer whose aid she seeks in her search for the "murderer," the lawyer counters Martha's view by saying: " 'That isn't murder. It's—,' he quickly swallowed the word [*'Das ist nicht Mord. Es ist—,' er verschluckte hastig den Namen*]"

(96).[59] Presumably, the lawyer articulates the word "rape," but like another infamous rape in German literature, in Kleist's novella "Die Marquise von O . . . ," the text elides the crime—in this scene the mention of it—by merely giving us a dash.

As with linguistic indirection and euphemism on the part of characters referring to Ursula's rape, these kinds of gaps and silences could be attributed to decorum: an author simply doesn't describe the lacerated, bruised body of a five-year-old rape victim in a novel of this period.[60] But I am also suggesting a metonymic interpretation: that the text itself is performing trauma and therefore does not speak directly of the crime that generates its plot. I do not mean that Kolmar did not know what she was doing. Rather, I am suggesting that the numerous lacunae and forms of indirection in the story draw attention precisely to the impossibility of telling. By doing so, they point to the incommensurability of the crimes and to the presence of trauma, not just to that inflicted by an individual perpetrator on the child and metonymically on the mother, but also to a general pattern of urban violence perpetrated within the society depicted in the novel and—pointing ahead to circuit five—within the society in which the novel was written, against it weakest members. That Kolmar never released the text to find a response among her contemporaries (a short-circuiting of literary-historical witnessing) I would claim backs such a reading of *A Jewish Mother* as a story partially about ubiquitous violence in the capital of the Weimar Republic and general fear of testifying to it.

The existence of this pattern of trauma is further supported by the fact that all the characters in the novel have referents for what has happened to Ursula in their heads, though they do not (cannot?) articulate them. With the very first signs of the disappearance of the child, neighbors assume the worst, lamenting, "how can anyone do things to children *[wie bloß einer Kindern was antun kann]*" (27; see also 26, 33, 40).[61] Another factor connecting Ursula's story to ubiquitous violence in Weimar Berlin is indeterminate culpability: the criminal is never caught or even identified, and Martha's own guilt, particularly with regard to administering the sleeping potion, is never clearly argued for or against (143–44). This moral fuzziness facilitates extrapolating assignation of guilt and victimhood to Weimar Berlin society as a whole.[62] The society is perpetrator; the society is victim.

5. AND 6. LITERARY-HISTORICAL AND TRANSHISTORICAL-TRANSCULTURAL WITNESSING

For readers who want to Talk, Kolmar's technique, her use of indirection, euphemism, and elision, can be considered "deictics" in my extended sense, signaling the text's raising of the matter of trauma that seeks a respondent's answering of orientation to the exchange of witnessing. But, as I mentioned in my survey of the circuits, there was no involvement of contemporary readers during the Weimar Republic or in National Socialist Germany, since the novel was neither circulated nor published in Kolmar's lifetime. Literary-historical witnessing was short-circuited. It is up to later readers to witness to this fact.

The last type of communicative circuit involves understanding the way the novel in toto—that is, taken in its historical and cultural context—can testify about the violence of the Weimar Republic to its later readers, and these readers, in turn, to their contemporaries about violence in Weimar. Successful witnessing in this circuit consists partly in what I have attempted to do above, namely, learning "what happened," in the sense of noting both the incomplete previous attempts at witnessing and the absence of attempts altogether. Successful witnessing involves cognizance of all the events represented by the narrative: traumas within the text such as the marginalization of the child and her mother by society, the sexual crime against the child by a male perpetrator, the mother's sense that the child can never rejoin society because of the crime perpetrated against her, and consequently the mother's poisoning of her own offspring and the mother's eventual suicide. But a reader's testimony also involves being aware of the trauma of Kolmar and her text implied by the inability of both to witness fully to the crimes of the story during the Weimar Republic. Again, to cowitness, a current reader needs to (re)mark the absence of literary-historical witnessing (circuit five).

So let me begin to do just that by reviewing the publication history of the text. Kolmar began composing the novel in August 1930, shortly after her own mother's death. She completed it five months later, in February 1931. (Kolmar is presumed to have perished in Auschwitz in 1943.) As executor of her sister's estate, Hilda Wenzel agrees to the publication of the novel for the first time in 1965, when it appears under the title *A Mother*. The novel is reissued in 1978 with a slight variation of the title that appeared on the typescript: *A Jewish Mother*, as opposed to Kolmar's "The Jewish Mother." These facts raise several questions for me: Why did Kolmar turn to prose after years of (successfully) writing and publishing poetry? Why did she choose to write about an act as despicable as the rape of a young child? Why, having completed the novel, did she not publish it? After all, there were not yet any publishing restrictions for Jewish authors in 1931, though there were during the Third Reich when Kolmar's last volume of poetry is seized and turned into pulp (1938). Why did Kolmar's sister withhold this manuscript from publication for so long, though she let Karl Otten publish Kolmar's novella *Susanna* in 1959? Why, when Hilda Wenzel finally consented to publication, did she elide the word "Jewish" from the title, though it appears on the typescript?

There are probably no simple or even verifiable answers to these questions. And of course, the issues raised by these questions may or may not be related. Still, the mystery of the existence of the novel and the lack of its publication push one to wager answers. Presumably, Kolmar's choice of genre would be related to her choice of subject; a topic as big as this needs the breadth of a novelistic format. But this logic just leads to another of my questions: Why this subject? Eichmann-Leutenegger repeatedly emphasizes the impact of an abortion on Kolmar's life and work and specifically interprets the composition of *A Jewish Mother* as Kolmar's response to "the tragedy of unfulfilled motherhood" (1993: 23).[63] However, I do not count autobiography as a full and sufficient explanation of Kolmar's choice of subject, and I find Sparr's explanation that she was influenced by Fritz Lang's movie *M-Eine Stadt sucht einen Mörder* (1993: 81) at least as plausible. To my mind, as with cowitnessing to trauma in a clinical setting as well as noting the gaps within Kolmar's text, the point is to note the phenomenon, not to pin down one answer.[64] No extant letters elucidate Kolmar's choice not to (try to) publish the text immediately after she completed it. The explanation may be as banal as her dissatisfaction with her ability to express herself in prose.[65]

My theory about both choice of subject and withholding from publication as responses to Kolmar's own sense of increasingly ubiquitous violence in the Weimar Republic is backed by internal evidence like the behavior of characters in the novel that I have adumbrated above,[66] and to external evidence like the marginalization of minorities during the Weimar Republic or the increase in general violence, and sexual and racial crimes, as well as the plethora of other artistic works that similarly speak of traumatic events.[67] As for Hilda Wenzel's treatment of the manuscript, one could assume that she just didn't think the work was as good as her sister's poetry or the novella *Susanna*. In any case, her specific elision of the word "Jewish" from the title indicates that she was also concerned about the way readers would react to its Jewish protagonist and presumably to the racial dynamics of the story. Woltmann claims (without citation of her source) that Wenzel feared the original title could unleash antisemitic sentiments (1995: 285n. 151). If this is true, then it would reflect Wenzel's perception that the text could not testify in the postwar Federal Republic; it would extend, so to speak, the time period of the short-circuiting of contemporary witnessing.

As these sketchy comments demonstrate, I cannot offer definitive explanations for any of these mysteries. Yet to cowitness to Kolmar's trauma and to what I have posited as the trauma of myriad individuals in Weimar society, the reader-scholar needs to ask these questions, needs to articulate these prior attempts at witnessing, needs to at least name the short-circuits. The critic has to show how, in Felman and Laub's terms, a crisis of history was translated into a crisis of literature, and how Kolmar tried to witness to something in her society but could not do it fully because she too was a victim of that crisis (Felman and Laub 1992: xx). In other words, the incompleteness of Kolmar's testimony itself testifies eloquently, and I cowitness to that testimony by pointing out its incompleteness. Such action constitutes Talking with these kinds of texts.

In explicating other circuits as incomplete or failed testimonies, the reader-scholar at a historical-cultural remove is herself telling a story of trauma—even if it as unspecific as deducing the infliction of trauma by remarking its symptoms—and thereby facilitating the flow of testimony that the characters, text, and author try to give. This reader, as enabler of the text, bears witness to the crimes, though her completion of the process cannot be said to aid the original victims (by which I refer to Kolmar and not to Martha or Ursula, who obviously exist only on paper). Despite the lack of any personal psychotherapeutic healing, I follow Herman, Caruth, Minow, and others in believing that there is societal benefit to such narrative witnessing. For through the process of analysis, the reader-scholar becomes cowitness to a trauma that, precisely because it has yet to be fully witnessed, could be said to still exist, to be speaking through symptoms. To state this bluntly, if grossly: we have not fully appreciated the violence and antisemitism of the Weimar Republic if we remain unaware that at least one person (Kolmar) perceived it strongly enough to write this kind of novel and yet withhold it from publication.

I'd like to flesh out this point at least somewhat by invoking four historical moments and putting them into dialogue with one another:

1. Berlin, August 1938. The Jewish Book Publisher Erwin Löwe (Jüd-ischer Buchverlag Erwin Löwe) publishes a small volume of poetry titled *Woman and the Animals* (*Die Frau und die Tiere*). The poems are written by Gertrud Kolmar, but the name that appears on the volume is Gertrud Chodziesner, since Nazi regulations prohibit Jew-ish authors from using pen names. The book is seized within a few months and is made into pulp.

2. Stuttgart, 1959. Karl Otten includes Gertrud Kolmar's novella *Susanna* in a volume titled *The Empty House: Prose of Jewish Writers* (*Das leere Haus. Prosa jüdischer Dichter*).

3. Munich, 1986. The publisher dtv (Deutscher Taschenbuch Verlag, Ger-man Paperback Publisher) issues a volume called *Dictionary of German-Speaking Women Writers, 1800–1945* (*Lexikon deutsch-sprachiger Schriftstellerinnen, 1800–1945*). The cover artwork is a photo of Ger-trud Kolmar.

4. New York, 1993. Paragon House publishes *Different Voices: Women and the Holocaust*. Editors Carol Rittner and John K. Roth foreground their project by telling the life story of Gertrud Kolmar and by using her poems as epigraphs for the book as a whole and for the major sections of the book.

I've juxtaposed these four sets of historical events to help make a bridge between literature and history. They suggest to me how an individual, her generation, and subsequent generations are *entangled*, in this case in the traumas of German antisemitism and the legacy of the Holocaust. Kolmar's own lived tragedy is linked to those who needed to praise her in 1938 as "the most important Jewish poetess since Else Lasker-Schüler" (Kolmar 1970: 14).[68] After Kolmar's death in the Holocaust, Otten tries to reinsert her into postwar German consciousness by reminding his au-dience of what they have repressed: absent Jewish writers (1959: 603). And a few generations later, the (West) German editors of the dtv dictionary recuperate Kolmar for *German* literature through their use of her portrait. Rittner and Roth take her life story to teach *U.S. Americans* today the story of German antisemitism and persecution of European Jewry. The last three anecdotes support Caruth's hunch that "it may only be in future generations that 'cure' or at least witnessing can take place" (1996: 136n. 21).[69] And the exposure given to Kolmar's work through the activities of the dtv editors and Rittner and Roth are two small signs of her reintegration into literary canons—something that was just beginning to happen during her lifetime, before the Nazis actively forced out her and other German writers of Jewish heritage.[70] My acts of noting previous impediments to the reception of *A Jewish Mother*, even when I cannot fully account for them, add in some small way to the linkage between our world and Kolmar's. Because one response to noting that the fifth circuit is broken is to reread the text for some hints about the nature of the trauma that blocked its ability to witness to its contemporary readers, I will conclude by returning to Kolmar's novel.

One of the most obvious signs of Kolmar's partial witnessing can be found at the end of *A Jewish Mother*. Martha fantasizes that she has Ursa in her arms once again and confesses to her, "I once killed you, you joy; God is just: he who touches you must die." The mother then enters the water, pleasurably weighed down (in her mind) with the child, and the novel concludes: "Water splashed. The Spree closed and ran on" (161). But Martha's suicide is not the ultimate finale. After a blank space, the book ends with the reproduction of a "newspaper excerpt" describing "The Daily Accident" ("Der tägliche Unfall"). A twenty-eight-year-old man was apparently run over by a truck driver who had lost control of his vehicle. Although the man is rushed to the hospital, he "expired shortly thereafter from his severe injuries" (162).

Kolmar provides no explanation of the placement of this newspaper article and no prior mention of the victim, "Heinz Köfer of Charlottenburg"—at least not by name. Since Martha's perspective has been the controlling perspective of the novel, but Martha is dead at this point in the discourse, the relationship of this article to the rest of the novel is particularly mysterious; technically it cannot be something Martha saw or read. Given the dramatis personae of the preceding story, a reader might well wonder if this man is meant to be the elusive perpetrator of Ursula's rape and if the inclusion of the article is a way to communicate that he met his deserved death. However, if victims are avenged, if there is closure to this story, if there is healing for trauma, if God is just, as Martha dies believing, the text and Kolmar do not state this directly. As one critic suggests, making this connection is a "task for the reader" (Balzer 1981: 182). Yet no explicit instructions for making this connection are provided; nothing in the text proves, as another critic hypothesizes, that he is the perpetrator (Shafi 1991: 704; 1995: 194).

Indeed, the excerpt could be a way of demonstrating what kind of violence was deemed worthy (and by default unworthy) of mention. Martha's suicide does not merit an article, for example, whereas this accident does.[71] Kolmar may have been trying to tell us something about her society by demonstrating what it considered tragic and therefore who could be considered a victim. As Minow suggests in an analysis of contemporary North American society, to decide "whose suffering we care about" is also to "define ourselves and our communities" (1993: 1445). In the light of Wigren's warning to note when the analyst is "filling in the details that are not present in the original narration" (1994: 417), my point here about Kolmar's text and other narratives-of/as-trauma is precisely that readers must be aware that such connections remain *our* constructions, *our* hypotheses; self-consciously making these connections is also a part of readers' narrative witnessing. To return to another lesson from the psychotherapeutic community mentioned in the first part of this chapter, such hypotheses remain just that—we must remember that there is no verifiably correct or complete story of the trauma. My fifth and sixth circuits make this particularly apparent, since material could come to light that would change our current answers to any of the questions I have raised about why Kolmar did what she did.

I would like to conclude by offering my own coda about the negative valence of language and specifically of naming in Kolmar's novel. I have already suggested several times that by completing the literary communicative circuit, by being a genuine "listener" to the inscribed and extrapolated victims, the contemporary reader-scholar responds by producing a story of the trauma, not through a mastery of the facts but rather through a simple testimony to the short-circuits. Since Kolmar's is a story that helps us better understand the nature of society in a critical historical period, I would like to attribute an ethical value to such explications, especially for a society like our own that continues to struggle with discrimination, marginalization, and violence. Even though my valuation does not aid Kolmar in any way, it begins to restore the social order by addressing the harm and challenging the perpetrators, not directly, of course, but as with Clamence, by implicitly expressing the judgment that those things were wrong then and that we currently endorse a value system that considers such actions crimes.[72]

My final point, however, is that in an ironic twist, my ability to do what Ursula, Martha, the text, and even Kolmar cannot—name the crimes through my knowledge of the culture and its hegemonic discourse—makes me potentially complicit with the perpetrator, implicitly identified here as the articulate, if also violent, depersonalized Germany of the early twentieth century. Kolmar, like Atwood with her depiction of those cocky, insensitive twenty-second-century scholars or Faulkner with his of scientific Mr. Compson, warns us against this complicity through several hints about the negative power of language, and specifically of naming. Ursula's abductor, for example, is said to have called her by name (24), a sinister detail that is never commented on explicitly in the story, but one which, like his claim that her mother was calling her, must have convinced the child to go with him. Martha's relationship to language is of particular interest since she is portrayed as one of the verbally and otherwise disenfranchised of her society. She feels its power; to say something will make it come true. During a rare pause in her search for Ursula after the discovery of her disappearance, Martha stops to ask a gardener about a flower she has long admired:

"The rose . . . do you know what it's called?"
"The yellow one there? 'Melodie.' But it's written with a "y" at the end.
"Melody," she repeated quietly. And felt: My Ursa was a dark yellow rose.
"*Was?*" she thought shaking, "was . . .? My God, she *is*. She's still alive! I know it—I want to know it!" (25; Kolmar's ellipses)

Martha's fear that to put the event into words will make it come true causes her anguish in this early scene. That this thought is one of relatively few rendered in quoted interior monologue—in Martha's direct mental language—underscores its importance. Martha mobilizes "I know it" like a talisman against the previous, negative, articulated thought. In another manifestation of her belief in the power of language, Martha's fear of concretely describing her daughter's situation initially prevents her from going to the police (26). But as we have seen in the case of trauma in general, as well as in the examples of Martha's own child-hood sexual harassment and in the characters' avoidance of the word "rape," to *not* put the experience in words will not make it go away either.[73] The trauma must be narrativized for healing to take place. And yet, Kolmar seems to be warning us, this naming, this putting into words, this translation of traumatic memory into narrative memory involves danger. It seems to me that Kolmar might have agreed with Caruth's assessment of this danger as "the loss, precisely, of the event's essential incomprehensibility, the force of its *affront to understanding*" (1995a: 154) or with Culbertson's concern about the "distancing power of nam-ing" (1995: 180).

In narrative witnessing there is no specific patient whose relief can confirm for us the value of the story we construct or justify the diminu-tion of the force of trauma's affront to human comprehension, as there was for Janet and his patients or today for Wigren and Laub and theirs.[74] Whichever story we tell, we need to foreground the difference between it and the textual performance of the trauma. My reply in the form of this analysis does not have the power of Kolmar's novel. To avoid the hubris of Atwood's scholars, to acknowledge the deformation of the trauma, a reader-cowitness must be as self-conscious as possible about her narra-tive witnessing. She must remain aware, as Trezise urges, of "the differ-ence between implicit and explicit" (1997: 10), while creating another narrative that explicates the incompleteness of previous testimonies and also points to the "cost" of reconnecting the circuits. Whether the reader-witness can be counted successful will be determined by whether her own readers decide to Talk with the text, by whether they in turn witness to the crises of modern history articulated through Kolmar's *A Jewish Mother*, witness to crises of urban sexual violence enabled by the escalation and toleration of making the stranger the other. To return to Kolmar's cousin Walter Benjamin, the reader/cowitness, like the story-teller, will be judged by whether he takes the story of the trauma and "in turn makes it the experience of those who are listening to his tale" (1969: 87).

4

APOSTROPHE

Talk as Performance

This is not for you.

Jane Rule's enigmatic 1970 novel, *This Is Not for You*, opens with:

> This is not a letter. I wrote you for the last time over a year ago to offer the
> little understanding I had, to say good-by. I could have written again, but
> somehow your forsaking the world for the sake of the world left me
> nothing to say. Your vow of silence must also stop my tongue, or so it
> seemed. What a way to win an argument! Now I find I can't keep your
> vow, not having taken it. Each of us has his own way to God, I used to say;
> there is no direct relationship, except through Him. But also, in the last
> hour of an examination we were both writing, I disproved the existence of
> evil. You must have written on the nature of salvation, starting down one
> of my untaken roads as I started down one of yours. For a long time, we
> could call back and forth, offering insults and encouragement. Not now.
> This is not a letter. (3)

"This is not a letter," and yet it is discourse addressed to someone. The
paragraph, as the whole novel, is narrated by an "I" to a "you," pronouns usually signaling relationship and verbal exchange of some kind.
However, the paragraph announces that written interaction has already
stopped: *I wrote you for the last time over a year ago . . . to say good-by*.
Exchange—or impeding it—is a major theme introduced here. The "I"
and "you" had argued and corresponded in person and on paper for a
long time in the past, but then barriers to communication had been put
in the way—*your vow of silence*. Now the narrator rejects the idea that the
other's silence necessitates the narrator's silence—*I find I can't keep your
vow, not having taken it*. The narrator's use of the second person seems
to resume a calling back and forth, though there are no quotation marks
to indicate speech. The paragraph ends as it opens, with the exclusion

of one common option for written exchange—*this is not a letter*. The novel's first paragraph, like its title, seemingly initiates contact to shut it down; it calls, but paradoxically it claims not to address the one it calls—*this is not for you*.

Who is this "I"? Who this "you"? Is the "I" genuinely uninterested in exchange or is this posture a feint? Can the "you" hear this address? Is the addressee capable of responding to it? If so, will the addressee eventually respond? If not, why not? If "this" is not a letter, what is it? If it is addressed to "you," but not for "you," as the title sternly warns, for whom is it intended? Could there be more than one "you" involved?

Some of the answers to these questions quickly come into view for the reader. The novel's second paragraph offers clarification about the vows, the silence, and the breaking of the silence by the narrator: the "you" is a religious novice and the "I" has inherited "your" clutter and chooses "to remember" the past (4). The next paragraph discloses the gender of the two people involved, providing women's names for the "I" (Kate) and "you" (Esther). Information about the two women's acquaintance in college and their interaction in the years between college and Esther's entrance into the convent follows in mainly chronological order. Kate's narration continues to unfold as address to Esther, but almost exclusively to narrate past actions and to quote past conversations between the two and their circle of friends. Several hundred pages of such narration provide few clues to the mysteries raised by the narrative mode beyond those offered in the opening paragraphs; in fact, they even begin to make us feel as if this is merely an odd way to tell a story about the past.

It is only at the very end of the novel, when Kate's narration returns to the story time of the opening, her discursive present, that a connection between the "you-address that is not for you" and the story we've been reading emerges. In the present tense Kate reflects, "I suppose I can explain why all this began, though I don't know why it has gone on and on through these months of my living and the years of our life" (282). She then narrates one of the events of "these months," the visit of common friends Andrew and Monk to Kate in Athens, after Esther has begun her novitiate. Kate recounts a conversation with Andrew during which he finally asks:

"Were you in love with Esther, Kate?"
"Yes."

"She didn't know."

"Probably not," I said.

"Surely that's a failure masquerading as success."

"That's your decent answer," I said. (283)

Kate's amatory admission comes as no surprise to the reader, who has long ago figured out that Kate loves Esther. But the issue of that love being communicated or not to its object resonates now with the issues raised by the narrative mode.

When, immediately after quoting this (past) interchange with Andrew, Kate explicitly addresses Esther one more time, we see how plot and narrative mode merge:

> I am not guilty, and Joyce is right: it is a limited way to live. Yet I don't see how I could have afforded any other. It's a happy enough ending surely, even for me, vindicated of a crime I didn't commit, an evil I don't believe in. Andrew is right too: there may be something wrong with the argument, with the whole concept of self-sufficiency, but it has been expedient. If I have been incapable of loving you well enough, I've made a virtue of loving you badly. Pray for me if you will, Sister, beloved of God. This is not for you. (284)

With these final sentences, readers have answers to a few more questions: no, the "you" never answers back because there are no indications that this discourse, whatever it is, actually reaches Esther. The structural feature is reinforced by the explicit message. What Kate considers a "virtue" is her refusal to communicate her actual feelings: she can't be "guilty" of loving Esther because she has never even told her about it, much less acted on it. Kate is "vindicated," because Esther's cloistering means that she won't ever hear about Kate's feelings that are now being explicitly articulated.

Even if Kate's pre-Stonewall values, or at least diction ("vindicated," "crime," "evil"), do not accord with the values held by contemporary readers, we can appreciate the suitability of Rule's choice of narrative technique to express them. Precisely because her story is set in a time and society when lesbian relationships were not often openly enacted, Rule's choice, if not Kate's, seems perfect. Having a first-person narrator address someone who cannot be addressed, or more accurately, who theoretically can be addressed, but who won't hear the call and answer back, parallels feeling love for somebody and keeping the feelings to oneself.[1]

As the discursive instance precludes verbal reply, the interpersonal one precludes consummation, facilitating what Judith Roof calls lesbian "desire for desire."[2] Kate gets the satisfaction of telling without telling, of loving without exposure or exposing.

How can Kate have it both ways? The very act of addressing performs: to say anything at all, even "I'm not talking to you," is to create a relationship to the addressee, at least for the duration of the utterance. Kate's narration in the second person effects for Kate a rhetorical connection to Esther in a situation in which any kind of physical connection has been made impossible and any emotional connection socially risky. Furthermore, I suggest that "this is not for you" engages the reader in a way that "this is not for Esther" simply would not. For one thing, readers witness to the vocative force of Kate's address and keep listening for a reply from the addressee. Until the conclusion of the novel, we wonder if Esther will answer back. By narrating in the second person and refusing to disambiguate the genre of this discourse, Rule involves the reader on another level as well. In the context of the long story of the women's relationship, the most obvious interpretation of the novel's ending is as a confirmation of the way Kate has handled her desire for years: this (lesbian love I feel) is not for you (Esther) to share. If considered in the context of Kate's discourse, the same statement could mean: this (declaration of my love) is not for you (Esther) to hear. And in the context of novels as messages sent to readers, Rule's clever formulation can mean additionally: this (declaration of my love for Esther) is not for you (the reader) to overhear.[3] More specifically, in the context of the social climate of the period in which the novel was written, and in our still homophobic culture, Rule's title could even be warning potential readers that this (story of lesbian love) is not for you (the mainstream/straight/homophobic reader) to consume.

Readers don't have to choose between these interpretations because they are all invited by the narrative technique of Rule's text, a technique I propose we call *narrative apostrophe*, borrowing from the rhetorical figure for turning from one's normal audience to address someone or something who, by reason of absence, death, inanimateness, and/or mere rhetorical convention, cannot answer back. Though apostrophe has been discussed for a long time in the context of oratory and lyric, no one has remarked its systematic use in some recent narrative fiction in which a first-person narrator tells a story primarily through address to a you-character who does not reply.[4] Texts written in this mode, like Rule's novel, constitute an obvious if complex form of talk fiction, since orientation toward exchange (Talk) is always based on a fiction: that the "you" is animate and capable of response (whereas the "you" is absent, dead, or inanimate); that the message is not for readers, when it is, since readers read the book; that a specific actual reader is being called by the narrating voice in the text, whereas any reader could feel called by it. Recognizing both the vocative force of such discourse and the fictions on which it rests—that it is and is not for you—constitutes the Talk of narrative apostrophe. As I suggested in my first chapter, such a stance accords particularly well with other secondary oral genres, like talk shows, since apostrophes are meant to provoke response but not actual verbal reply. Apostrophic Talk seems to fulfill a need for connection in societies or situations in which actual face-to-face interaction is thwarted for various reasons.

My storytelling mode foregrounds the attitude of the listener. Proper orientation to exchange sustains the relationship to the storyteller and to the community that the story effects and affects. In narrative witnessing, the construction of the message takes center stage; speaker and listener as witness and cowitness must orient toward exchange so that a story of the trauma can flow. Narrative apostrophes draw attention to the mechanisms of orientation to exchange by putting into question the issue of who is involved: a speaker addresses someone who is (seemingly) being addressed to provoke response in someone else. As in my storytelling mode, pronouns of address once again function as deictics, as signals of the text-as-statement's orientation to exchange. But in my apostrophic Talk mode, readers' reply involves not so much the proper attitude of listening as the recognition that one is called both to identify and not to identify with this "you." I therefore associate the Talk of apostrophe with "performance" not merely to acknowledge the origins of my analogy in the public performances of speech and ancient oratory but also, and more importantly, to highlight the active role of readers. Readers' replies, I maintain, may function socially and politically in the societies in which these texts appear. A reader who orients to exchange with Rule's text can be said to be taking an antihomophobic stance by responding to "this is not for you," with "maybe" or "yes, it is."[5] Having introduced the basic issues at stake in this mode of talk fiction through Rule's brilliant matching of subject, setting, title, and narrative technique in *This Is Not for You*, I want to flesh out the dynamics of Talk as performance first by borrowing from rhetoric, linguistics, and philosophy to better explain how apostrophe moves those who "hear" it and then by illustrating additional cultural work that apostrophic Talk accomplishes in a series of diverse texts: Michel Butor's *Change of Heart* (*La Modification*), Günter Grass's novella *Cat and Mouse* (*Katz und Maus*), Julio Cortázar's short story "Graffiti," John Barth's short story "Life-Story," and finally the novel with which I launched my whole study, Italo Calvino's *If on a winter's night a traveler* (*Se una notte d'inverno un viaggiatore*).

Apostrophe and Address: Relationship, Reversibility, Identification

The term "apostrophe" as used by ancient rhetoricians is a capacious concept referring to a number of different situations. The Greek roots of the word describe the gesture common to them all: the preposition *apo*, meaning "away," and the verb *strophein*, "to turn."[6] The ancient use of the term most relevant to the definition of narrative apostrophe I'm developing here involves the act of an orator turning away from his normal audience—the judge(s)—to address another, whether adversary, a specific member of the jury, someone absent or dead, or even an abstract concept or inanimate object.[7] It is worth recalling that speaking to the judge(s) was a reality of the oratorical situation and that turning from that audience or addressing a specific individual in it was considered a departure from standard procedure (a "figure"). But even this sense of apostrophe covers many different kinds of departures, at least when measured against conversation. To cite the most obvious of these: singling out an auditor who is present versus addressing someone who is absent or dead, or addressing something that is inanimate. In the former, verbal reply would at least be conceivable, if forbidden by convention, but in the latter, reply is simply not possible. As far as my research can unearth, however, the ancients did not distinguish among types of apostrophes based on the ontological status of the apostrophized, presumably because the acts of turning and addressing were common to all. These acts, they insisted, furthered the orator's aims by impressing the audience of those individuals who actually hear (receive) the utterance. Quintilian, for example, comments that the apostrophic gesture "is wonderfully stirring [*mire movet*]" (396, 397). And Longinus marvels that change of person causes a "vivid effect" (200, 201). Both Quintilian and Longinus advocate use—though not overuse—of apostrophe to catch the attention of the audience and to move its members (see Quintilian 41–45 and Longinus 200–205). In other words, apostrophe is both double and duplicitous address because it is mobilized to provoke reaction—though not verbal reply—in those who hear it, not in those to whom it is explicitly addressed.

Even if their categories were broad and their distinctions fuzzy, the ancient teachers' examples are memorable and suggest different explanations for apostrophe's efficacy in moving the audience. To support his contention that apostrophes should not be excluded categorically from the exordium, the first part of a classical oration, Quintilian cites several instances in which the speaker turns from the jury to his physically present opponent. Quintilian explicates one of these, a brief passage from Cicero's *pro Ligario* in which the great orator turns from the judge Gaius Caesar to address Tubero, his accuser. Quintilian comments on Cicero's rhetorical choice:

> His speech would have been much less effective, if any other figure had been used, as will be all the more clearly realised, if the whole of that most vigorous passage "You are, then, in possession, Tubero, of the most valuable advantage that can fall to an accuser etc." be altered so as to be addressed to the judge. For it is a real and most unnatural diversion of the passage, which destroys its whole force, if we say "Tubero is then in possession of the most valuable advantage that can fall to an accuser." In the original form Cicero attacks his opponent and presses him hard [*pressit atque institit*], in the passage as altered he would merely have pointed out a fact [*hoc tantum indicasset*]. (43)

In the defense as delivered, Cicero enacts his relationship *to* Tubero before the audience's eyes. Auditors of a statement *about* Tubero's advantages would "merely" learn another fact about somebody, not witness the quality of the speaker's relationship to that somebody.[8] The "whole force" that would have been "destroyed" by not apostrophizing presumably derives from the idea of witnessing interaction (as opposed to hearing narration) and specifically from witnessing the intensity of the adversarial relationship between prosecutor and defender. That Cicero and Tubero are adversaries is a fact known from the outset, but presumably it is seeing this relationship "performed"—enacted before their eyes—that moves the audience.

Drama is also critical for Longinus, whose interest in apostrophe is similarly raised by its ability to move those who hear it, not to a specific judgment, but to a feeling of the sublime. Drawing on a wide variety of narrative texts, Longinus suggests that apostrophe "often makes the audience feel themselves set in the thick of the danger" (200, 201), as when the *Iliad*'s narrator apostrophizes the epic audience about the quality of a fierce battle: "You would say that unworn and with temper undaunted / Each met the other in war, so headlong the rush of their battle" (201; *Iliad* XV, l. 697). Longinus implies that because the narrator hypothesizes how the audience would describe the scene ("You would say that . . ."), they have seen it for themselves. The issue of being transported to another place is made more explicit by being thematized in Longinus's example from Herodotus's account of his travels in Egypt. Though writing mainly in the first person and sometimes in the impersonal, Herodotus occasionally narrates in the second-person singular, as in Book 29, from which Longinus quotes:

> "You will sail up from the city of Elephantine and there come to a smooth plain. And when you have passed through that place you will board again another ship and sail two days and then you will come to a great city, the name of which is Meroë." You see, friend, how he takes you along with him through the country and turns hearing into sight. All such passages with a direct personal application set the hearer in the centre of the action. (201)

Longinus describes the effect of the apostrophe by saying that Herodotus "takes you along with him." The audience members don't just "hear" about the place, they see it for themselves. Longinus implies that listeners take up the second-person singular pronoun as a call to themselves, that is, they identify with the "you," even though it is heard in the presence of many others who presumably also feel addressed. It seems purposeful to me that Longinus takes up apostrophe directly after describing the efficacy of the historical present; both transform a narrative into a current experience, "a vivid actuality" (201).

Based on even these limited examples, it is not hard to see why contemporary commentator Jonathan Culler has distinguished apostrophe from other figures by its troping "not on the meaning of a word but on the circuit or situation of communication itself" (1981: 135). In addition to the basic fact of address without verbal reply, surely the situations praised by Quintilian and Longinus of (a) turning to address another, with the intention of affecting those from whom the speaker has turned, and (b) feeling personally called by an address that could call anyone who hears it, count as odd communicative circuits. If those situations count as communication at all, we could say that there are multiple addressees or more than one trajectory of address operating simultaneously. To help us understand the issues of relationship, reversibility, and identification raised by the rhetoricians' examples, I continue with more recent accounts of that "preeminent sign of interaction": "you," expanding the discussion of the second-person pronoun presented at the end of chapter 1.[9]

Although I can offer no proof that such arguments were made in response to literary developments in their respective countries, it is curious that the work of both German philosopher Martin Buber and French linguist Emile Benveniste on the second person as the pronoun of relationship were published at particularly triumphant moments of the "anti-communicative" idea of *l'art pour l'art*: Buber's in 1923 at the height of German Modernism and Benveniste's in the 1950s during the gestation of the nouveau roman. Buber contrasts use of the second person, what he calls the ability to say *Du* (Thou), with use of the third person, insistence on saying *Es* (It). While the latter, according to Buber, reveals a notion of the world as something to be experienced, the former signals an attitude of being in relation with another subjectivity and thus of acknowledging another's personhood (1955: 9, 12). Benveniste's argument about "Relationships of Person in the Verb" can be heard as an echo, or confirmation, of Buber when he explains that, "When I get out of 'myself' in order to establish a living relationship with a being, of necessity I encounter or I posit a 'you,' who is the only imaginable 'person' outside of me" (1971: 201). It follows that to say "you" is to bestow personhood on the referent of the "you." U.S. American literary critic Barbara Johnson makes a similar point about rhetoric and relationship in the context of what many consider the most abstract of theoretical movements, Deconstruction, by formulating this principle in her article "Apostrophe, Animation, and Abortion" as "the ineradicable tendency of language to animate whatever it addresses" (1987: 191). Johnson shows how certain rhetorical strategies are not trivial pursuits, but matters of life and death, because of the relationships they create.

Address, animation, and relationship are inextricable. Even in Benveniste's narrowly grammatical terms, every use of the second-person pronoun necessarily implies a relationship to an "I": " 'you' is necessarily designated by 'I' and cannot be thought of outside a situation set up by starting with 'I' " (1971: 197). Only the grammatical first and second persons can actually be in relation to one another and thus merit the designation "person." The *I-you* pair belongs to "a *correlation of subjectivity*" (201), whereas the so-called third person is outside this correlation and expresses the "*non-person*" (198).[10] Benveniste expands this idea of intersubjectivity by describing the reversibility of first- and second-person pronouns:

> "I" and "you" are reversible: the one whom "I" defines by "you" thinks of himself as "I" and can be inverted into "I," and "I" becomes a "you." There is no like relationship possible between one of these two persons and "he" because "he" in itself does not specifically designate anything or anyone. (199)

For Buber, Benveniste, and Johnson, then, the mere use of the second person animates the other through recognition of the personhood of that other and hence of the possibility of relationship and interaction between speaker and interlocutor. Switching roles could be counted as a normal consequence of the attitude behind addressing another, acknowledgment of another's subjectivity. Cicero's "you" animates Tubero at a point when the audience is not expecting Tubero's subjectivity to be at issue, a point when, as Quintilian senses, their relationship is brought to life in front of the audience in a way that it would not be if Cicero reported on Tubero as "him," a third- or "non-person." Once Tubero has been "animated" through address, I surmise that the audience's attention is further stimulated because his (conventionally required) silence goes against the anticipated reversal of positions in the relationship between "I" and "you" inherent in the act of addressing. In other words, though Quintilian does not point to this issue, the forceful effect of apostrophizing on the audience must also partly derive from what in the light of these twentieth-century theories must be considered a peculiar, restricted enactment of relationship: Tubero is in the courtroom and hears what Cicero "says" to him, but he may not respond at that point, and thus the question of his "response" to Cicero's thrust, to this initial part of their "inter"-action, hangs in the air. Indeed, one could hypothesize that absence of the addressee's response raises the tension in those who hear the address and the silence, perhaps even making them feel the urge to respond themselves.

Another set of Benveniste's observations about the nature of pronouns will aid us in understanding the animational principle made explicit by Johnson and that is necessary for our pursuit of the effect of apostrophe. The first- and second-person pronouns, Benveniste explains, are empty signs that do not refer to any extrinsic reality but rather to the instance of enunciation; such pronouns (and other shifters like "this," "now," "here," and so forth) are used for "the conversion of language into discourse" (220). The first-person singular pronoun can be used by any speaker to refer to "the individual who utters the present instance of discourse containing the linguistic instance *I*" (218). Symmetrically, Benveniste defines the second-person singular as the "individual spoken to in the present instance of discourse containing the linguistic instance *you*" (218). "I" and "you" are thus empty signs made "full" (animated) through the instance of discourse. But I want to draw attention to an implication of this view of "I" and "you" that Benveniste doesn't mention—the "emptiness" of "you" (potentially) allows all who hear it to feel addressed; this appears to explain why hearers of "Homer's" and Herodotus's "you" respond as if themselves specifically addressed by it. Though such slippage only seems warranted in the absence of any other signs designating the addressee—a rare case—its very possibility may cause a *residual identificatory effect* in many (all?) uses of the second person. That is to say, every hearer's ubiquitous experience of being called "you" probably also contributes to the audience's "stirring" when Cicero apostrophizes Tubero—and Kate Esther. I suggest we refer to this as the "subliminal invitation" of the second-person pronoun. I will develop this point thoroughly, since it accounts for an important dimension of the Talk quality of my literary examples.

The first step in my argument derives from Benveniste's explanation of the advantage of having the empty sign "I": "If each speaker," Benveniste warns, "made use of a distinct identifying signal (in the sense in which each radio transmitting station has its own call letters), there would be as many languages as individuals and communication would become absolutely impossible. Language wards off this danger by instituting a unique but mobile sign, 'I,' which can be assumed by each speaker on the condition that he refers each time only to the instance of his own discourse. This sign is thus linked to the *exercise* of language and announces the speaker as speaker" (220). Here, as elsewhere in his work on pronouns, Benveniste implies a symmetry between "I" and "you." But I want to challenge the notion that "I" and "you" are equally "unique" and "mobile."

Though, as we have seen, Benveniste is careful to define the second person as "the individual spoken to in the present instance of discourse containing the linguistic instance *you*" (218), the pronoun itself cannot anoint an individual as addressee. One can become the speaker by uttering the word "I," but one cannot become the intended addressee by hearing "you." To put it otherwise, one individual cannot utter the "I" that makes another individual the speaker, but one individual can hear the "you" that makes another individual the addressee. In most Western languages at least, there has to be some element other than "you" in the utterance or in the communicative situation that makes clear which "you" is being addressed. The nonsymmetry of "I" and "you" is again instructive: "I" can *only* refer to the one speaking it unless additional information is given, as in quoting: *and then she said*, "I'm leaving." In the case of "you," a name (Tubero), a description (accuser), a tone of voice, a glance or glare, or a physical touch might all serve to designate "the individual spoken to." In the absence of such specifications, nothing prevents whoever hears the "you" from taking it up—from considering it as direct address—even though this hearing doesn't make her into the person the speaker intended to address.

Think of someone shouting "hey, you" in a crowded department store. Most people within hearing range will turn toward the voice, even if they have no reason to think someone could want to communicate with them, because, for example, they are strangers in town or because they haven't done anything wrong. Similarly, to borrow Benveniste's radio metaphor to make a different point: uttering "you" is more like a radio signal that is diffused into general airwaves and picked up by all radios within range of the signal than a telephone call that dials a specific number. To be sure, even in the case of a phone call, anyone in the house can pick up the receiver, so the caller must still ask for the person to whom she wants to speak. There is another commonplace situation that substantiates the claim that the pronoun "you" always carries an appellative force for whoever hears it, whether the speaker intends this or not. In the course of conversing, a speaker uses "you" in a generalizing way or to mean the speaker's self: "you hate to visit your parents when they're not taking your advice." A certain awkwardness arises instantaneously if the speaker realizes that she does not want to insinuate anything about the conversation partner with regard to this particular issue. So the speaker immediately corrects herself, replacing "you" with "I" or "one," hastily reformulating the previous statement by saying, "I hate to visit my parents when . . ." This familiar experience reveals our awareness of the potential for a listener to feel addressed despite accepted uses of "you" that do *not* signify the interlocutor. It seems that the only way to guarantee that a listener does not identify with the second-person pronoun is not to use it.[11]

Somewhere in time and space, the act of uttering "I" connects the sound to the individual utterer, even if we don't witness the act. But there is no complementary, necessary physical connection between the sound of "you" and the specific person addressed. For this reason, I suggest, "you" is a "more empty" and thus more available sign than "I." It is perhaps due to this structural looseness that individuals encountering "you" may feel a residual appellative force even where other signs indicate that they are not the designated addressee. I can now introduce explicitly the writing/reading situation that I will argue does not differ on this score from the oral—or, if it differs at all, may enhance the "emptiness" of the second person, since numerous potential ways of specifying the addressee are unavailable (glance, tone of voice, touch, and so forth). Reading "you" may even intensify this urge to feel addressed because of the physical act of holding in one's hands the paper or book that says "you," when you are the only "you" around at that instant. To consider again the specific case of apostrophe: if I am right about the "extra emptiness" of the second-person pronoun, one reacts strongly to apostrophe partly because hearing or reading vocative forms is common to both address and apostrophe. We all can easily become "you," because we so often do, feeling called into the relationship it creates, even when we don't wish to try it on, so to speak (as when we want to be left alone in the department store), or when we know it is meant for another (Tubero), or when we know it couldn't possibly be meant only for us since its lack of designation invites every other hearer to become "you" as well (as in the cases of reading the *Iliad* and Herodotus).[12]

By distinguishing between "addressees," "hearers," and "recipients," the field of conversation analysis implicitly recognizes the existence of this appellative force and the nonsymmetry of "I" and "you" I have derived from Benveniste's observations.[13] As introduced in chapter 1, conversation analysis reserves the term "addressee" for persons to whom speech is addressed; "hearer" for persons who physically hear the speech; and "recipient" for hearers who orient toward the speech (Goodwin and Heritage 1990: 291–92). In employing these terms here to understand the Talk of apostrophe, I suggest we add the term "respondent" to designate recipients who become speakers by verbally responding to the speech. (In technical parlance, they are just "speakers," now taking their turn.) In the baseline model of communication that Benveniste, for example, is working with, addressees are hearers who become recipients and then respondents. But analyses of spontaneously occurring conversation back up the theoretical considerations from above, indicating that these positions can be occupied in different combinations: most obviously, recipients must be hearers, but addressees are not necessarily hearers or recipients—since they may or may not hear the speech and may or may not orient to it—and hearers may become recipients even if they are not addressees. To return to the scenario of the department-store shout, presumably the speaker has a specific individual in mind as the addressee, but there are numerous hearers, most of whom become recipients by looking in the direction from which the shout comes. Those who ask, "Are you talking to me?" become respondents. Conversely, if the intended addressee is among the hearers and recognizes himself as "the individual spoken to," he still may choose not to become a recipient or respondent by not looking and not replying. If the speaker continues to shout, "hey you" and the addressee continues not to respond, we can imagine that more hearers might orient and even become respondents by offering a response themselves.

These terms help me do two things the ancient rhetoricians did not do: distinguish more clearly between types of apostrophe and account more fully for the efficacy of apostrophe. Why, in Quintilian's phrase, is it "wonderfully stirring"? In the example of Cicero and Tubero discussed by Quintilian, apostrophe is speech uttered to an addressee who is a hearer, in the presence of other hearers who are not addressees, but who are intended to become recipients by orienting (hearing and having an emotional reaction) to the address. Cicero speaks to Tubero, not so that Tubero will reply, but rather to effect an emotional reaction in Caesar, to sway him to Cicero's view of Tubero and the accusation. The same structure essentially applies to apostrophes uttered to absent, dead, or inanimate addressees, whose absence, death, or inanimateness—in short, their inability to be hearers—makes even more clear that the intention is not to initiate a dialogue with the addressees (create respondents), but to effect orientation in hearers of the apostrophe (create recipients). Using the terms of conversation analysis to create a separate definition of the apostrophes discussed by Longinus leaves us with speech constructed as address to an addressee so minimally specified as such, that any/all hearers can become recipients by identifying themselves with the addressee. Longinus claims that Herodotus intends for all of his readers to feel as if they are taking the trips he has taken.

In all its variants, apostrophic "you's" don't become "I's," perturbing the equation of addressees, hearers, recipients, and respondents operative in dialogue. In sum, *the mere utterance of "you" releases expectations in hearers about animation, relationship, and reversibility* that are foiled by whichever specific perturbations of the equation of addressees, hearers, recipients, and respondents that type of apostrophe effects.

As my own reader will have guessed by now, I want to use these definitions to set up general and specific relations to talk fiction. I have suggested before that apostrophe is a particularly obvious kind of talk fiction because it makes so apparent that it aims, not at dialogue, but at mediated forms of "interaction." Apostrophe would not count as exchange under colloquial definitions of conversation, but it does fulfill Goffman's ideas of statement and reply as well as mine of Talk. Hearers of apostrophe, like readers of its talk fiction variations, are not meant to verbally reply in the same circuit of communication as apostrophizers, but they are supposed to demonstrate attention to the matter raised by the speaker by having a response to the apostrophe, my technical sense of "reply." The "subliminal invitation" of "you" accounts for part of this response, as it promotes some level of identification between hearer-readers and apostrophized no matter the other circumstances. The content of the apostrophe and the type, that is to say, the ontological status of the apostrophizer and the apostrophized, will determine the amount of identification and the nature of orientation to exchange.

Apostrophic literary texts, like the replies they seek, do not fall into completely distinct groups but range along a spectrum of identification between actual readers and the "you." In other words, one end would resemble the oral situation of eavesdropping, where readers identify someone else as the addressee. The other would resemble conversation, where readers identify themselves as the explicit addressee.[14] Toward the eavesdropping side, I would place texts like Jane Rule's *This Is Not for You*, since the level of identification with the "you" on the part of the actual readers is likely to be fleeting and subordinate to other kinds of responses, like curiosity about the relationship between the apostrophizer and the apostrophized, who are both named, characterized, and acting out a specific story in a specific setting. The Talk of these texts most closely resembles the communicative situation of Cicero's apostrophe to Tubero discussed by Quintilian. Toward the other end of the continuum, I would place texts like Italo Calvino's *If on a winter's night a traveler*, where apostrophizer and apostrophized are unnamed and minimally characterized (at least initially) to maximize the level of identification between actual readers and the texts' "you." Longinus's examples from "Homer" and Herodotus can guide our understanding of Talk in these texts since readers have to be willing to consider themselves addressed. For actual readers to perform the role of the apostrophized, the narratee in these literary texts must necessarily be scripted as some kind of reader in the act of reading. Hence the possibilities of sustaining such narration are limited. Full occupation of either end of the spectrum falls outside the range of what I am including under my apostrophic mode, since this kind of Talk requires awareness of the *perturbations* of the conversational equation of addressee = hearer = recipient = respondent discussed above. My Talk is never actual exchange, as it is never only eavesdropping. The context of reading this kind of literary text implies that you can never be uniquely addressed, as you can never be completely free from interpellation. As a reader, apostrophic talk fiction is always simultaneously for you and not for you. That is to say, even at moments when the identification might feel strong, you are meant to notice that the role doesn't quite fit, and inversely, even when you feel like you are eavesdropping on something addressed to another, you are meant to realize that the message is intended for you too.

With this schema in mind I want to return to prose fiction. First I will present some literary-historical evidence for the effects of using the second-person pronoun through the example of actual readers' reactions to Michel Butor's 1957 "new novel," *Change of Heart*. Then I will illustrate the range of apostrophic Talk by presenting several texts that occupy different locations on the spectrum just proposed. I begin with Günter Grass's 1961 novella *Cat and Mouse*, which must be placed even closer to the "eavesdropping" pole of my continuum than Jane Rule's *This Is Not for You,* since it clearly starts out as a story about two named characters and contains only the intermittent use of apostrophe. Next I discuss Julio Cortázar's short story "Graffiti," which falls somewhere near the midpoint between the two poles, since on the one hand, there is a distinct story, and on the other, both apostrophizer and apostrophized remain unnamed, inviting readers to assume the narratee position. I close by considering two texts that try to effect complete reader identification by constructing (parts of) the story as actual contemporary reading experiences—John Barth's "Life-Story" and Italo Calvino's *If on a winter's night a traveler*, the novel that launched my search for talk fiction.

Reading Readers Reading Butor's *Change of Heart*

When Michel Butor's third novel, *La Modification* (*Change of Heart*),[15] pushed its way into the French literary scene in October 1957, one assumes its fate was as unknown to its author as the protagonist Delmont's is to himself when he pushes his way into the train compartment of the Paris-Rome express:

> You've put your left foot on the brass groove and with your right shoulder you try in vain to push the sliding door a little bit further.
> [*Vous avez mis le pied gauche sur la rainure de cuivre, et de votre épaule droite vous essayez en vain de pousser un peu plus le panneau coulissant.*]

Despite its banal plot of a bourgeois Parisian businessman trying (and failing) to leave his wife for his mistress, the novel received much initial critical praise, winning the Théophrast-Renaudot prize before the year's end.[16] It quickly became a commercial success as well and has remained the best-selling work of what was first referred to as *L'Ecole du regard* (the school of the look), then as the *nouveau roman* (the new novel).[17]

To understand what all the fuss was about, I want to briefly review the narrative mode of *Change of Heart*. As can be detected in the short quote above, Butor narrates the events of his protagonist's trip to Rome and back again in the present tense, using the pronoun *vous* (the French second-person plural/formal pronoun "you"). In contrast to *This is Not for You*, there are no explicit signs of the narrator, though many early reviewers understood, with or without having read Benveniste, that the existence of the "you" implied an "I."[18] The identity of Butor's you-protagonist is revealed slowly, even as the "you" performs very specific actions, like getting settled in the train compartment. In the fifth sentence of the novel, the grammar reveals that the second-person pronoun must refer to a single male.[19] Several paragraphs later, the initials on the suitcase are reported as "L. D.," and through the review of recent past events in his life, specifically through embedded quoted conversations, we eventually get his full name, Léon Delmont. There are no quotation marks surrounding the entire discourse nor paratextual features like Vikélas's or Wilson's prologues that offer some explanation of its source. Although initial readers didn't know what to call it, with few exceptions, they pointed to Butor's use of "you" (*vouvoiement*) as the feature of greatest interest.[20] In *La Nouvelle Revue française*, reviewer Dominique Aury referred specifically to Butor's "curious manner of *apostrophizing* his protagonist" (1957: 1147; my emphasis). I analyze Butor's novel under the category of apostrophe because like the classical rhetorical situation, pronouns of address are used to animate a being, but not to promote verbal response by that being. My goal is not to explicate the novel—that has been done well by others[21]—but rather to document what Butor's contemporary readers made of it, how, in a later critic's terms, the novel was not within the horizon of expectation of its initial readers (Netzer 1970: 76). To read readers reading *Change of Heart* is to encounter a diversity and intensity of response that confirms Quintilian's assessment of apostrophe as "wonderfully stirring."

A rush to praise the novel and its author provides a first sign that readers were "stirred." Literary critic Gaetan Picon remarked the rareness of journalistic accord: "For once the literary page of *Le Monde* and that of *France-Observateur* agree in praise of the young writer," suggesting the novel's "richness" and "ambiguity" ([Jan. 1958] 1961: 265–66). Another sign of strong reaction is the way Butor and his novel immediately became catalysts for assessing the current state of the French novel. Barjon rejoiced that "with Butor we finally have a writer on account of whom our narrative literature will recapture through new paths the originality and the vigor which have been missing from it for so long" (1958: 95). And *Arguments* (February 1958), *Le Figaro littéraire* (March 1958), and *Esprit* (July 1958) all staged and published debates on the subject. The very terms and scope of these discussions attest to an interest beyond what one might think a single book could raise, especially a book published in the same year as Robbe-Grillet's *Jealousy*, Claude Simon's *The Wind*, and the reissue of Nathalie Sarraute's *Tropisms*. What could have seemed new in such a context? What aroused such strong emotions and contradictory opinions?

As suggested earlier, clearly it was not the "plot." Rather, critics pointed to the use of "you" as a "completely new mode of narration" (Raillard 1968: 192), crediting Butor with its invention. For instance, Pingaud announced that "Michel Butor has happily added this third dimension to the universe of narration" (1958: 91); and Pouillon called "this second person plural which Butor has just given to novelists a find [*trouvaille*] in itself" (1958: 1105). That Butor had "invented" something new can be contested,[22] but the liveliness of contemporary reaction to his use of "you" cannot. Whether readers interpreted it as an address to actual readers, to the character, or, a position I hold, to both, the language with which they argued their views reveals a strong emotional response. Readers were caught in "the nets of you [*les rets du vous*]" (Leiris 1963: 288).

One rather obvious testimony to critics' fascination with Butor's use of "you" are the many responses to the novel written in the same mode. Barjon, whose enthusiasm for Butor and his novel has already been cited, addresses his own reader by saying, "You risk balking first at its sibylline title and the rather strange narrative tone which it proposes to us. But you would be wrong to follow that first impression, to sulk and stop there" (1958: 92). Michel Leiris begins his influential essay, "The Mythological Realism of Michel Butor" (which originally appeared in 1958 in

Critique and was included as an afterword in subsequent editions of the novel): "You have in your hands a brand new copy of *Change of Heart*, a novel signed Michel Butor. You leaf through the book and in the course of this little action you read a few paragraphs at random. What is it that strikes you first?" (1963: 287). We suspect the answer to Leiris's question before he finishes asking it. Leo Spitzer, the great analyst of style himself, could likewise not resist the temptation to write about this novel, albeit briefly, in the second person ([1961] 1970: 513).

In the most entertaining example of this phenomenon, *Le Monde*'s reviewer, Emile Henriot, "tells" the author what he thinks:

> But beware of sleepiness, Monsieur Butor! the extreme repetition leads to it, it's the principle of counting sheep for insomniacs. . . . When in your description of the trip you speak to us ten times, twenty times of the bead of blue light at the center of the ceiling lamp . . . I assure you that each time, one is tempted to write in the margin: *again!* or *enough, I already know that!* (1957: 7)

Henriot's use of the second person seems fitting, but I do not consider it merely stylistic contagion, that is, an imitation of Butor's style—Barjon's and Leiris's reviews come closer to the tone of *Change of Heart*. Rather, in formulating his book review *as a reply to the author* ("Monsieur Butor"; "I assure you"), Henriot demonstrates his orientation to an exchange one can only assume he experienced as initiated by the novel as "statement" in Goffman's sense. His description of the reading process, especially of wanting to write a response in the margin, provides evidence for my interpretation of it as Talk. I am particularly intrigued by his impatience with repetitions, a reaction I interpret as evidence that those who witness the apostrophe (readers) are urged toward reply in the face of absence of reply on the part of the specific "you." Though Henriot obviously knows he has read a novel about a character with a name who takes a specific series of actions, his review betrays the extent to which he has experienced the "you" as a call: he answers back.

When early readers turn explicitly to the question of the referent of Butor's "you," and therefore also of the "I" who must enunciate it, something Henriot does not do, there is an urgency about discovering a satisfactory answer that is revealed through the evocative language they use and their insistence on the obviousness and correctness of their position. Consider, for example, Luc Estang's review for *Pensée française*

(1958): "The question arises which could lead to endless discussions: who says 'you'? The novelist to his character? Without a doubt." In asking why the address is not therefore in the second-person informal nor for that matter in the first-person singular, Estang again answers emphatically and yet in a way that undermines his first answer:

> Intentional ambiguity, for sure. . . Personally, I end up feeling the efficacy [of this device] not in the novelistic realm strictly speaking, but in the poetic realm. It creates a kind of incantation and contributes, I believe, to the achievement of which any reader will be sensitive: the physical sensation of the movement of the train; I am there [*on y est*]! (56)

First, Estang emphatically insists that the "you" must refer to a character and, like Henriot, seems unaware of his theoretically unsound reference to the novelist as the vocal origin of a fictional text ("novelist to his character"). By the end, he implies that the effect of the use of "you" is to put the reader in the scene, an idea with which Longinus would no doubt be in agreement. But my point here is not so much what Estang argues or the coherence of it but rather how he argues, that is, the personalized and insistent form of his answer: "without a doubt," "for sure," "personally," "I believe." Though he does not explicitly reply to Butor as Henriot does, the passion of his analysis and particularly his sense of being interpellated (*on y est!*) constitute a response to the novel in the technical sense of Talk I have developed in this study.

A few more examples will suffice to show that no matter what position they held, critics argued forcefully; to use Quintilian's term, they were "stirred." Thus Bernard Pingaud in *Esprit*: "If one asks oneself who the 'you' is to whom the novelist addresses himself, the ambiguity of the device [*procédé*] appears immediately [*tout de suite*]. This 'you' is the protagonist of the novel, but it is also the reader" (1958: 98). Pingaud's "*tout de suite*" indicates how obvious he thought his interpretation should be to anyone who opens the novel. Leiris, too, implies that his interpretation will be apparent immediately to any reader: "*Change of Heart*, with the exception of a few passages, is written in the second person plural: it's you yourself, reader, whom the novelist politely seems to involve, and a few glances thrown at the printed lines while you cut the pages open suffice for you to feel in the presence of an invitation, if not a summons" (1963: 287).[23] Bernard Dort implies that there wasn't anything to interpret, stating simply, "Butor is addressing himself to each one of us" (1958: 123). And in my last example, Roland Barthes, one of the participants in the roundtable sponsored by *Arguments* mentioned earlier, called for a "literal" interpretation—as if there could be such a thing! "This use of *you* appears to me literal: it's that of the creator to the created, named, constituted, created through all of his actions by a judge and begetter" (1958: 6).

This brief survey has uncovered various stylistic features and common issues in critical discourse about *Change of Heart*—imitation of Butor's style, evocative rhetorical language, confusion of novelist and narrator, reader and narratee—that seem attributable at least in part to the pronoun of narration. Quite in contrast to Wayne Booth's dismissive comment that person is "[p]erhaps the most overworked distinction" in narrative theory (1961: 150), actual reader response to *Change of Heart* suggests that even when "you" has a name (like Butor's protagonist, Léon Delmont) and a specific story (a train trip from Paris to Rome and back again), the second-person pronoun wields power to move readers, evidently causing most of them to feel themselves addressed and/or to feel strong emotions about the experience of reading the address that creates an unusual relationship between the narrator and narratee. It is to the dynamics of "relationships" created by apostrophizing that I turn next.

Apostrophic Talk as Resuscitation in Grass's *Cat and Mouse*

I begin my survey of apostrophic texts near the eavesdropping pole of my spectrum, where, I have suggested, readers' urge to identify with the you-narratee is outweighed—though not completely extinguished—by curiosity about the drama that is being enacted before them. The intermittent use of apostrophe, perhaps even more so than the continual use of it, communicates the dynamics of the relationship between the apostrophizer and the apostrophized, because readers can observe the circumstances that trigger the resort to apostrophizing. This is precisely the case for readers of Günter Grass's 1961 novella *Cat and Mouse*, in which a first-person narrator, Pilenz, claims to tell a story about Mahlke, a boyhood friend in then-German Danzig before and during the Second World War. Pilenz frequently interrupts his narration to apostrophize Mahlke, even switching the personal pronoun referring to his former friend from third to second in mid-sentence. There are no quotation marks around these second-person passages, though, as in the German convention for writing letters, Grass capitalizes all personal and possessive pronouns referring to the addressee. I place Grass's text even closer to the eavesdropping end of the continuum than Rule's (and certainly closer than Butor's), since *Cat and Mouse* limits reader identification by supplying a name and a description of the apostrophized before any apostrophe is actually uttered.

Perhaps it is because Pilenz's apostrophes are embedded in a more traditional first-person narrative that the technique of *Cat and Mouse* did not attract the attention of Butor's *Change of Heart*. I do not mean that the novella went unnoticed. Grass had entered the German literary scene with a bang, if I may, when he published *The Tin Drum* in 1959, and readers and critics eagerly awaited his next effort.[24] They were not disappointed by this colorful story of German adolescents during the war. Focusing on the act of apostrophizing in *Cat and Mouse*, however, will lead to as yet un- or underexamined aspects of it. First, analysis of when Pilenz apostrophizes and what he says in those apostrophes will reveal how truly ambiguous his feelings for Mahlke were and still are.[25] Second, and just as important to my mind for an adequate appreciation of Grass's accomplishment, a consideration of how Pilenz's "you" implicates actual readers suggests that Grass is inviting Germans to examine their own role in the Second World War. But I, like Pilenz, mustn't get ahead of myself (1974: 64; 1994: 61). I need to review certain elements of the complicated plot to begin to clarify the significance of the apostrophes.

Approximately fifteen years after Joachim Mahlke's disappearance during the last year of the Second World War, Pilenz, a former schoolfriend, sets out to write the story of "cat and mouse." Pilenz has been urged to write by his confessor, Father Alban, and he displays some sense of a larger audience who might read his text, though he never directly addresses either of these audiences. In his writing, he recounts Mahlke's feats: summer explorations of a half-sunken minesweeper in the Danzig harbor, school (fashion trends, gym class, and most importantly the theft and eventual return of the Iron Cross of a visiting alumnus of their high school, a prank for which Mahlke is transferred to another school), and military service (Mahlke's affair with the training commander's wife, his discovery of an underwater partisan ammunition dump, his receipt of his own Iron Cross for destroying so many Russian tanks, and his desertion). Pilenz attributes all Mahlke's exploits to his friend's need to compensate for an obtrusive Adam's apple and to win the love of the Virgin Mary. Despite repeated claims that he is telling Mahlke's story, the adolescent Pilenz was not a distant observer to Mahlke's struggle for acceptance. In his narration Pilenz hints about undermining Mahlke. He draws a cat's attention to the movement of Mahlke's Adam's apple during a break in a ball game, scrutinizes him in church, and mimics his clothing and posture. Although the cat's attack serves as the symbolic frame of reference for their relationship, the act that compels Pilenz to write is his role in Mahlke's (final) disappearance, for it was Pilenz who suggested that Mahlke hide in the sunken minesweeper of their adolescent summer games, when Mahlke goes AWOL after being denied the privilege of other military heroes to speak to the students of his original high school. To Pilenz's knowledge, Mahlke never surfaces from that dive.

Pilenz wonders to what extent he is responsible for Mahlke's various decisions, declaring that he writes to exculpate himself: "I write, because that has to go [*ich schreibe, denn das muß weg*]" (my translation; 1974: 67; 1994: 64).[26] Pilenz claims in the same passage that he is in thrall to accurate historical reporting, but an examination of how he tells his story undermines his contention: events are elided or narrated multiple times in different versions or, most relevantly here, are reframed by being directly addressed to the absent Mahlke.[27] This apostrophizing, with its "ineradicable tendency . . . to animate whatever it addresses" (Johnson 1987: 191), allows Pilenz to change the most persistent historical circumstance of all: Mahlke's absence. By calling Mahlke into his presence, Pilenz resuscitates him—rhetorically anyway.

A cataloging of when Pilenz resorts to apostrophe shows that he usually addresses Mahlke after mentioning events in which his motives are the most dubious, because something he did hurt Mahlke, or because something Mahlke was doing caused his secret admirer Pilenz to feel snubbed. During many descriptions of Mahlke as particularly absorbed in an activity, for instance, in looking at "someone" other than Pilenz (most frequently, the Virgin Mary, Pilenz's most serious rival for Mahlke's regard), the narrator switches to apostrophe as if to attract his attention, as if to say "hey, look at me!"[28] Along similar lines, Pilenz sometimes apostrophizes to report actions that prove he was a true friend to Mahlke, for example, in buying him candles for his Marian devotions (1974: 75; 1994: 72), or in erasing an odious caricature of him from the classroom blackboard (1974: 30; 1994: 28).[29] Other apostrophes seem to be triggered by Pilenz's narration of scenes in which he refused to talk to Mahlke; that is, although he didn't talk to Mahlke at a point in the past when Mahlke might have appreciated a friendly contact, he apostrophizes him years later while writing about those moments. These apostrophes function as compensation for negligent past behavior.[30]

Pilenz does not resort to apostrophe, however, only to communicate his goodwill in the past or longing for his friend in the present. Apostrophes that provide evidence for Pilenz's friendship either through their explicit content or their placement are countered by others that "attack" Mahlke. Such apostrophes are particularly strong proof for the overall ambivalence of Pilenz's feelings, because the act of apostrophizing puts the two into relation but in these instances delivers a message of repulsion. (In this sense, they function similarly to Kate's statement, this is not for you.) In the most revealing of these passages, Pilenz describes graffiti Mahlke had carved into the latrine wall of a military camp the year prior to Pilenz's training in the same place: "Here the two syllables—no first name—were carved, or rather chipped, into a pine board across from the throne, and below the name, in flawless Latin, but in an unfounded, runic sort of script, the beginning of his favorite sequence: *Stabat Mater dolorosa . . .*" (1994: 84). I will go into this scene at length, since its rhetoric as well as its content reveal Pilenz's need to assert control over Mahlke as well as to cede power to him.

Mahlke's graffiti infuriated Pilenz in the past because even while "relieving" himself, he could not be free from Mahlke. The intensity of his emotion is still palpable years later when he writes about the scene through his "direct" upbraiding of Mahlke: "*you* gave me and my eyes no peace" (1994: 84; my emphasis). No matter what Pilenz does to distract himself in the latrine, perhaps the only private place in the camp, his eyes and mind are overwhelmed by Mahlke's "presence" and evidence of his love for Pilenz's rival, the Virgin Mary. I suggest that this scene inverts Pilenz's apostrophic gesture: Mahlke "calls" himself into Pilenz's presence through his graffiti, forcing Pilenz to play Mahlke's script without being able to respond.[31] The effectiveness of this strategy is underscored by Pilenz's reluctant admission that "Mahlke's text drowned out [*be-*

siegte] all the more or less wittily formulated obscenities" (1994: 84; 1974: 86). Grass's choice of the verb *besiegte* (defeated) emphasizes Pilenz's framework of competition, even of battle.

Pilenz concedes greater victory when he confesses that Mahlke's text was written so perfectly that it almost accomplished the vital task of converting Pilenz into a believer:

> What with the accuracy of the quotation and the awesome secrecy of the place, I might almost have got religion in the course of time. And then this gloomy conscience of mine wouldn't be driving me to do underpaid social work in a settlement house, I wouldn't spend my time trying to discover early Communism in Nazareth or late Christianity in Ukrainian kolkhozes. I should at last be delivered from these all-night discussions with Father Alban, from trying to determine, in the course of endless investigations, to what extent blasphemy can take the place of prayer, I should be able to believe, to believe something, no matter what, perhaps even to believe in the resurrection of the flesh. But one day after I had been chopping kindling in the battalion kitchen, I took the ax and hacked Mahlke's favorite sequence out of the board and *eradicated your name* [*und tilgte auch Deinen Namen*]. (1994: 84–85; 1974: 86–87; my emphasis)

The series of subjunctives stating what he would not have to do if he had become religious represents, of course, the things Pilenz has been doing and thinking ever since Mahlke's disappearance. The list culminates in what he would be able to do now if Mahlke's writing had effected a conversion then: "I should be able to believe, to believe something, no matter what, perhaps even to believe in the resurrection of the flesh." Pilenz wants desperately to believe in something, but especially in something religious. One connects this with the even younger Pilenz's intense observations of Mahlke in church, trying to understand what he is doing there, declaring at one point: "As often as I served at the altar, even during the gradual prayers I did my best, for various reasons, to keep an eye on you" (1994: 12). If one accepts Pilenz's logic that this whole story is about Mahlke only, these "various reasons" would be to document the other boy's obsession with the Virgin Mary. But if one widens Pilenz's frame to let in questions about Pilenz's motivations, one suspects that he is watching Mahlke to see if he can figure out how to believe, how to be comforted by the Church, as his friend seems to be. The adult Pilenz would particularly like to believe in resurrection, one might surmise, in order to be able to believe that Mahlke could be alive still—or once again. To be able to believe in Mahlke's presence would mean Pilenz's own salvation, both because he feels guilty about the role he played in Mahlke's life, and also because he loves and misses him.

Pilenz's need for Mahlke's resuscitation is so strong that he does the only thing available to him: he calls Mahlke into his presence rhetorically with an apostrophe. But the message he delivers in this apostrophe reveals his ambivalent emotions, especially his pent-up frustration. The adult Pilenz, searching for spiritual salvation, or perhaps needing to exonerate himself, like the jealous boy, Pilenz, in love with his believing friend, cannot let Mahlke save him, even if he thinks that friend embodies the only source of salvation: "I took the ax and hacked Mahlke's favorite sequence out of the board and *eradicated your name.*" At the very moment he could be saved, Pilenz destroys his potential savior by creating an absence, that is, by destroying the writing he had left behind. Yet in recounting his creation of this absence, Pilenz fills it in by apostrophizing. In murdering Mahlke symbolically, he resuscitates him rhetorically, simultaneously confessing his crime and trying to undo it.

Ironically, the blank spot created by Pilenz communicates Mahlke's message better than the original writing, and Pilenz finds himself more haunted by Mahlke than ever before:

> the empty patch of wood with its fresh fibers spoke more eloquently than the chipped inscription. Besides, your message must have spread with the shavings, for in the barracks, between kitchen, guardroom, and dressing room, stories as tall as a house began to go around, especially on Sundays when boredom took to counting flies. The stories were always the same, varying only in minor detail. About a Labor Service man named Mahlke, who had served a good year before in Tuchel-North battalion and must have done some mighty sensational things. (1994: 85)

The posture of Pilenz and Mahlke's other former schoolmates who are training in the same camp toward these "stories" is curious. They remain impassive until the point when hints of Mahlke's official recognition for his feats leak out. They then burst into a fit of confused storytelling, trying to claim a prior, and therefore somehow superior, connection to Mahlke (1994: 87).

Parallels can be drawn between the way Pilenz attempts (and fails) to control Mahlke by destroying his writing and the way Pilenz attempts (and I would argue fails) to rid himself of his rival permanently. Pilenz makes the writing in the latrine disappear, and he helps Mahlke to disappear physically when Mahlke decides to go AWOL, by suggesting he hide in the sunken minesweeper; Pilenz even offers to row him there.[32] Pilenz's problem, however, is that in both cases, Mahlke's "absence," the blankness on the latrine wall and the silence after Mahlke's dive into the wreck, trouble Pilenz more than his prior presence. There is a way in which seemingly exercising the greatest control over Mahlke puts Pilenz in thrall to Mahlke.

Pilenz reports that when Mahlke dives into the hatch on that blustery day, he immediately misses him and waits for a sign that Mahlke has arrived safely in his former hideaway of the radio shack: "Though we had not arranged for any signals, you might have knocked" (1994: 107). The resort to apostrophe indicates how intense the original experience was as well as how intense the remembrance of it is to the narrating self. Pilenz needs Mahlke now as he needed him then. The adolescent Pilenz becomes desperate; he bangs the deck with his fists and screams to Mahlke to resurface to retrieve the can opener. Mahlke does not respond: "Ever since that Friday I've known what silence is. Silence sets in when gulls veer away. Nothing can make more silence than a dredger at work when the wind carries away its iron noises. But it was Joachim Mahlke who made [*bewirkte*] the greatest silence of all by not responding to my noise [*indem er auf meinen Lärm keine Antwort wußte*]" (1994: 108; 1974: 110). Appropriately, in recounting this part of his tale, Pilenz does not resuscitate Mahlke by apostrophizing him. Pilenz credits Mahlke with superiority. As in assigning victory to Mahlke's graffiti in the latrine, here Pilenz says that Mahlke creates the *greatest* silence.[33] Furthermore, Pilenz credits Mahlke with the ability but not the volition to act, since a more literal translation of the last part of the passage would be, "he knew to make no answer to my noise."

With these pieces of evidence for Pilenz's growing awareness that his story and his life are in Mahlke's hands, readers can receive the full import of Pilenz's "conclusion." The last section of the novella begins with the question, "Who will supply me with a good ending [*Wer schreibt mir einen guten Schluß*]?" (1994: 109; 1974: 111). This question could be interpreted as another sign of Pilenz's inadequacies as a writer and of his reluctant conclusion that he cannot save himself by writing Mahlke's story. Having reached the point in story time when Mahlke is absent, Pilenz is not sure how to proceed. After describing the many ways in which the story of "cat and mouse" is not over for him, Pilenz asks another question. This one is addressed to Mahlke, for the narrator apostrophizes him one last time:

> Must I still add that in October 1959 I went to Regensburg to a meeting of those survivors of the war who, like you, had made Knight's Cross? They didn't let me into the hall. Inside, a Bundeswehr band was playing, or taking a break. During one such intermission, I had the lieutenant in charge of the door page you from the music platform: "Sergeant Mahlke is wanted at the entrance." But you didn't want to surface [*Aber Du wolltest nicht auftauchen*]. (my translation; 1974: 112; 1994: 109)[34]

As a question to Mahlke, this first sentence implies Pilenz's admission that Mahlke is the superior writer: Mahlke would know if he is supposed to narrate this incident or not. Concomitantly, it serves as a gesture of relinquishing control. Qualitatively, this is different from Pilenz's claims early in discourse time that his narrative is governed by Mahlke in the sense that Mahlke is his subject and his only subject and that he will limit himself to events in which Mahlke was a participant (for example, 1994: 15). Here he is asking Mahlke what he should write. This should remind readers of Pilenz's earlier comment (in relation to the purportedly central anecdote of the cat's attack): "If I only knew who made up the story, he or I, or who is writing this in the first place!" (1994: 76).

Pilenz's answer to the question he has just posed about who should write the ending comes in the form of "handing over" the narrative to Mahlke through apostrophe. Pilenz throws his own voice that would control Mahlke to Mahlke; he gives up control. He puts himself in the position of needing something from Mahlke, as in the scene on the barge where he needs Mahlke to respond to his furious knocking. Transferring the narrative to Mahlke in this final paragraph indicates Pilenz's recognition of Mahlke's superiority, as he recognizes that he needs Mahlke more than Mahlke needs him, both as author of the conclusion of the story and as author of Pilenz's salvation. The last sentence completes the change in Pilenz's mood and the shift in power that become more obvious after Mahlke's dive into the minesweeper and the cessation of his physical companionship to Pilenz. Its content reinforces the incarnation effected rhetorically by the apostrophe, "But you didn't want to surface," which implies that Mahlke is alive. He could have surfaced if he had chosen to, but he chose not to. By choosing not to surface, he denies Pilenz salvation.

Mahlke "lives," on the other hand, as long as he is apostrophized. By suspending his narration in the apostrophic mode, Pilenz indefinitely sustains his resuscitation of Mahlke. The logic of his writing strategy (analogous to his continued search for Mahlke among circus clowns, divers, and war heroes) is that it allows him to continue hoping that one day Mahlke actually will surface in the flesh and that Pilenz will be saved from his doubt about the truth of their relationship. The bittersweet quality of this ending as well as the frustration that permeates Pilenz's comments about writing reflect Pilenz's forced recognition that Mahlke has the upper hand. In recollecting the role Mahlke played in his life, Pilenz realizes that only Mahlke could have effected his salvation then (via his graffiti on the latrine wall) and only Mahlke can be the author of Pilenz's happiness or lack thereof now. The only thing Pilenz can do to help himself is to apostrophize Mahlke. But this resuscitation only works grammatically and not in the flesh. Furthermore, it involves a loss of control. For when the last apostrophe is uttered, he must surrender himself to the blankness of which Mahlke is master. Still, Pilenz's decision to suspend his narration in apostrophe, like Kate's to narrate her whole story in apostrophe, allows him to get what he wants: to continue hoping for salvation.[35]

This final apostrophe offers the most explicit example of how, I believe, Grass wanted readers to Talk with his text. Through my analysis of apostrophe in rhetoric and through historical reader response to Butor's *Change of Heart*, I have suggested that even in instances where the apostrophized has a name and a story, the audience that overhears that address is constrained to reply. As Quintilian argues about Cicero, the figure may be effective because the audience is more easily moved by witnessing the acting out of a relationship than by hearing it narrated. Additionally, as at least some evidence from readers of Butor implies, readers respond emotionally because they feel called by the "you." I have suggested that to Talk with apostrophic texts, readers have to be open to both types of listening and to both types of responses. As I hope to have convinced my readers above, actual readers of *Cat and Mouse* gain a deeper understanding of the relationship between Pilenz and Mahlke by paying attention to the complicated enactment of it. By noting when Pilenz switches to apostrophe, as well as by "overhearing" what Pilenz wants to say to Mahlke, one comes to understand Pilenz's combination of love and hate for his missing friend. I also want to argue that throughout the text, Grass is trying to reach his readers. Like his narrator, he "write[s] toward you [*schreibe in Deine Richtung*]" (my translation; 1974: 63; 1994: 61). Grass's choice of verb form in the very last apostrophe of the text particularly challenges readers to respond. In the sentence "You didn't want to surface [*Du wolltest nicht auftauchen*]," *wolltest* can be the (second-person singular) simple past indicative form of the verb "to want," but it can also be the present-tense subjunctive. Considering it a simple past, as in the translation and analysis above, I take it to apply to Mahlke. But as a subjunctive—"you wouldn't want to surface"—we could take it as Grass's challenge to his actual readers to consider their own actions vis-à-vis the same issues that are raised for Pilenz and Mahlke: What were readers' roles in the German war effort? What kind of ending to the story of Nazism do they want to write? When will they want to surface?

Interpreting the last apostrophe as a subjunctive addressing readers invites consideration of the political and social context of the novella's publication. Grass's metaphor of diving and surfacing is particularly appropriate for the period in which *Cat and Mouse* appeared (1961), a time when Germans had immersed themselves in economic reconstruction and had not yet "surfaced" to examine their own past. I take Pilenz-Grass's last question as a challenge to do so. To Talk with the text in this way is for *Cat and Mouse* to become more than an entertaining story about German adolescents during the war, more than a story about someone else dealing with a sense of guilt: it becomes a call to all Germans to reckon with the Nazi past. It is a testament to Grass's social conscience that he recognized the necessity of such a national reckoning years before the revelations of the Auschwitz trials and the violence of the student riots would shock the nation into looking back.[36] And it was literary genius to plant a seed for that reckoning with his use of apostrophe in *Cat and Mouse*.

Waging Political Resistance with Apostrophe
in Cortázar's "Graffiti"

Although the geographical and chronological leap between postwar Germany and the Argentine Dirty War may seem large, the artistic and political distance between Grass's *Cat and Mouse* and Julio Cortázar's short story "Graffiti" (1979) is small.[37] In terms of the spectrum sketched earlier, moving from Grass to Cortázar involves moving a bit further toward the "exchange" pole since the possibilities for readers to identify with the narratee are greater, the story being narrated almost exclusively in the second person, and the "you" and "I" remaining unnamed. I would place "Graffiti" somewhere near the middle, in the proximity of Butor's *Change of Heart*. Like Butor's, Cortázar's "you" performs a specific series of actions. But at the story's beginning there is a brief indication of the vocal origin of the narration in a first-person narrator, who reappears toward the end. Even though the discourse may seem more like a conversation between two inscribed characters (therefore needing to be placed closer to the eavesdropping end), I suggest that "Graffiti" invites even greater identification on the part of flesh-and-blood readers than *Change of Heart* by modeling such identification. That is to say, the plot concerns the act of responding to apostrophe by personally identifying with the "you." Of course neither Cortázar nor his unnamed narrator calls the structure of communication in the story "apostrophe." But I hope to demonstrate that the narrative mode of the story parallels the mode of drawing and looking at graffiti discussed in the story and that both parallel the kind of "statement" and "reply" I have outlined as my apostrophic mode of Talk. If one accepts my analogy between drawing and viewing graffiti on city walls and uttering and hearing apostrophe, one can then interpret the story as waging rhetorical resistance to a totalitarian regime by creating relationships through art. Communication and connection threaten the atomization on which the Argentine junta was relying to refigure the population into a "docile, controllable, feminine 'social' body" (Taylor 1997: 151). In "Graffiti," looking and listening, which automatically place people into relationship with one another, are ways of resisting this refiguration.

Cortázar's plot revolves around an unnamed you-protagonist who is referred to with second-person verb forms and the Argentine second-person singular informal/intimate pronoun *vos*. As in Butor's *Change of*

Heart, the protagonist's maleness is established through elements of the plot and even more unambiguously through grammatical revelation of gender.[38] The presence of a first-person narrator-apostrophizer is minimally announced in the first sentence by a present-tense verb, "I suppose [*supongo*]" (1980: 107; 1983: 33), but does not appear to play a role in the story until the end. This elusive "I" recounts how the you-protagonist enjoys defying "the menacing prohibition against putting up posters or writing on walls" (1983: 33–34) by creating chalk drawings in public places. The intent of this "you" is not overtly political; the graffiti most often consist of abstractions or innocuous representations of birds or intertwined figures. Only once do "you" inscribe words, their critical force mitigated by their nonspecificity: "It hurts me too" (34). Nevertheless, "your" drawings are washed away by the authorities almost as quickly as they appear. But until then "you" delight in their being seen by whoever passes them. "Your" pleasure increases when "you" realize that someone—a woman, "you" decide by the style—begins to answer "your" drawings with graffiti of her own, though "you" realize the risk increases for both of "you" as a result. One night, when "you" return to check if she has left an answer to one of "your" drawings, "you" hear sirens and see lights, glimpsing blue slacks and black hair being pulled, as she is hauled off. "Your" fear stops "you" from sketching for a while, but after a month "you" begin again, returning to the spot where she had left her first independently initiated message. "You" are surprised when they don't erase "your" drawing immediately, and "you" keep returning to it, to discover after several trips that she has drawn again: "From a distance you made out the other sketch, only you could have distinguished it, so small, above and to the left of yours. You went over with a feeling that was thirst and horror at the same time; you saw the orange oval and the violet splotches where a swollen face seemed to leap out, a hanging eye, a mouth smashed with fists" (38). At this point, the narrative thread of the story is broken as the narrator speaks in the first person for the first time since the opening sentence, interjecting herself and switching back from past to present tense: "I know, I know, but what else could I have sketched for you?" (38). We realize that the "she [*ella*]" we've been reading about is also the first-person narrator. The whole narrative has been the apostrophe of the woman graffiti artist to the "you" from the "hole [*hueco*]" in which she now hides her disfigured self.

The structure of enunciation at the main diegetic level, then, is that of a speaker who addresses someone she cannot talk to directly, someone who is not only "absent" but whom she may never have even seen.[39] This situation does not seem to preclude a sense of intimacy between the characters; I would go so far as to say it fosters it in this kind of society. Intimacy is created by the animating and relational power of apostrophe. "Graffiti" both tells of and itself enacts relationship and hence, in the context of the Dirty War, it performs resistance. The story proposes the apostrophic structure of communication that is not fully reciprocal, the "as if" structure of the addressee's potential response, as the most effective strategy against authoritarian repression.

How does this indirect address structure function? The story's opening suggests that the you-protagonist began his scribblings on the walls as a mere game (*un juego*). The narrator even comments that he wouldn't have liked the term "graffiti," because it was "so art critic-like" (34). It sounds too abstract, but it is insisted upon nonetheless—the story is called "Graffiti" after all—because abstraction is needed in the dangerous world of this junta. The protagonist's drawings—like untagged second-person pronouns—invite relationship in a society governed by a junta that is deadly serious about enforcing alienation. Like an apostrophic address, the seemingly nonpolitical drawings trope on the situation of communication, not on the meaning, to paraphrase Culler's definition of apostrophe (1981: 135).[40] The you-protagonist overcomes fear, "and every so often picked the time and place just right for making a sketch" (34). Just right, because if the places were more public, the sketches more explicit or more permanent, the risk of looking at them, much less of creating them, would be too great.

As abstract figurations in chalk in public, but not central, places, on the other hand, the graffiti allow the artist to "talk" without talking directly to anybody present, just like they allow the populace to look without directly looking: "Looking at your sketch from a distance you could see people casting a glance at it as they passed, no one stopped, of course, but no one failed to look at the sketch" (34). By their very existence, the graffiti speak defiance since everyone knows that nothing is allowed on public walls. And though no one—at least at first—responds by drawing back, the glances of passersby constitute some kind of connection made between the artist and other city dwellers. Merely the creation of the sketch and its few hours of "addressing" those who see it before it is erased allow something to open up for "you," something "like a very clean space where there was almost room for hope" (34). Beyond just benefiting the graffiti artist, these graffiti function like an antidote against what Taylor calls "percepticide," that complicated policing of the given-to-be-seen and the given-to-be-invisible that forces the population to collude with the violence around it (1997: 123). Many people see the drawings, though they pretend not to, just as many members of an audience can feel moved by—even identify with—an apostrophe without being given away, because, after all, nothing is being said to them directly.

Once the woman begins to draw next to the male protagonist's sketches, the act of drawing eventually functions even more explicitly as communication. But first the protagonist has to learn to read her graffiti. In the terms of my analysis, he has to learn to be the audience of the apostrophe:

> it amused you to find the sketch beside yours, you attributed it to chance or a whim and only the second time did you realize that it was intentional and then you looked at it slowly, you even came back later to look at it again, taking the usual precautions: the street at its most solitary moment, no patrol wagon on neighboring corners, approaching with indifference and never looking at the graffiti face-on but from the other sidewalk or diagonally, feigning interest in the shop window alongside, going away immediately. (33)

Initially, the protagonist doesn't "hear" the call; he doesn't realize that the woman's drawing is "addressed" to him. When he does make this realization, he responds, but in the oblique way that is necessary in this society: he "looked at it slowly," "approaching with indifference," "never looking face-on," "feigning interest" in something else. Once he has learned to "hear" the woman's drawings, they become "appeals," "questions," "a way of calling you," and "answers" (35). When he sees the first drawing that she puts up on her own, he "replies" immediately by drawing in turn, but it still takes him a few moments to register that she will be looking for his answer and will therefore return to her drawing (35). He is learning about conversational turn-taking in a visual form. Even though the text uses words we associate with dialogue, I would suggest that this graffiti-communication is more like the circuitous route of apostrophe than conversation, since "speaking," "listening," and "responding" do not proceed together (Chafe 1982: 37). For a brief time, the protagonist attempts to transform the apostrophe into direct address, to continue within the terms of my analogy, by trying to catch the woman in the act of drawing (35) or later in the act of looking at his reply (35–36). But he realizes that any woman passing by might be the artist (36); the you-address of the graffiti calls any and all of them. Therefore, the successful strategy continues to be sketching and looking solitarily, at solitary moments in solitary places. Such behavior is a kind of calling, like apostrophe, in the sure knowledge of *lack* of specific message, *lack* of immediate reply. The "gap" of graffiti provides enough safety to at least encourage attempts at communication. Of course it does not provide a foolproof shield, since one can indeed be caught creating a sketch or looking at one, as the male artist almost is the night he replies to her "first sketch all by itself" (35) and as the woman artist is when she tries to reply to the next independent sketch of the man (36).

Still, the success of this strategy is so great that the fateful attempted sketch that leads to the woman's arrest continues to "speak"—at least to him—even after the police have erased it: "enough remained to understand that she had tried to answer your triangle with another figure, a circle or maybe a spiral, a form full and beautiful, something like a yes or an always or a now" (36). The graffiti communicate through form ("answer your triangle with another figure") and with color, the "signature" by which the two recognize each other's messages ("that orange color that was like her name or her mouth"; 36). These graffiti thus affirm the relationship: "yes"; project it into the future: "always"; and insist on its current function: "now."

The acts of apostrophizing function similarly. To address, as to draw in this story, is to bring into relationship. The parallel between drawing and apostrophe is made most explicit when the male protagonist replies to the woman's first independent message to him (as opposed to her previous graffiti as responses to his drawings). First he draws an answer, confident that she will understand it: "a quick seascape with sails and breakwaters; if he didn't look at it closely a person might have said it was a play of random lines, but she would know how to look at it" (35). Then, in what I count as one of the most important passages of the story, he resuscitates her in his apartment: "That night you barely escaped a pair of policemen, in your apartment you drank glass after glass of gin and you talked to her, you told her everything that came into your mouth, like a different sketch made with sound [*como otro dibujo sonoro*], another harbor with sails, you pictured her as dark and silent, you chose lips and breasts for her, you loved her a little" (1983: 35; 1980: 109). This scene contains a *mise en abîme* of the apostrophic act that is the narrator's discourse. In other words, this passage describes an embedded apostrophe. The need and desire for relationship is so strong that the male graffiti artist "talks" to the absent other. The very act of apostrophizing allows him to change the status quo by animating her, by bringing her into his presence. Whereas previously, sketches are like words, here words are like sketches: "you talked to her . . . like a different sketch made with sound." The Spanish original emphasizes the inversion and the parallel: "*como otro* dibujo sonoro," a "sound sketch." Both the drawings and the apostrophes promote relationships. In this scene, the animation is so complete, the relationship so palpable: "you loved her a little." Apostrophe thus effects—even if temporarily—the connection the regime would prohibit. In this sense, the most private act functions as a public act; the protagonist's imagined lovemaking performs political resistance.

Returning to the level of the narrator's discourse, we see again the parallel between drawing and apostrophizing and can interpret both as resistance. The narrator's apology for her last sketch, "I know, I know, but what else could I have sketched for you?" (38), reveals her dilemma about having used "direct address," to continue in the metaphor of my analysis and the story. We recall that the woman artist-narrator had resorted to a more mimetic representation of her physical condition (the swollen face with hanging eye and smashed mouth) as opposed to the more abstract visual invitations to "conversation" and relationship. Her doing so, I suggest, signals among other things that she needs to step out of this particular circuit of communication. As indirect as the previous graffiti may have been, her current state provides proof of how efficacious a strategy it was—the exchanges of the two artists threatened the regime that arrests and tortures her, writing on her, for having written on/to the city.[41] Despite the state's attempt to control her, she does draw one more time to say good-bye, but more importantly in the context of resistance, to say "continue": "In some way I had to say farewell to you and at the same time ask you to continue" (38). She uses the last image she draws to "say" and to "ask." Her hope "that you were making other sketches, that you were going out at night to make other sketches" (38) is a way of ending her own active resistance and yet continuing it through him and his activity. The political charge of her request is underscored by her repetition of it as well as by the ambiguity of the phrase "other sketches." She might just be asking him to continue drawing additional sketches, and this act alone, as we have seen, is counted as subversive by the government and the populace, but she might also mean "other," as in "other kinds of sketches." In either case, we need to notice that despite her own retreat from drawing, she has not stopped her political activity. The apostrophe to the male graffiti artist that constitutes the whole story is uttered *after* she has been tortured. Thus she hasn't given up as much as she has changed forms of transmission. Furthermore, her suspension of her narration in the apostrophic mode suspends the peculiar apostrophic structure of statement and reply. Like Pilenz's final apostrophe to Mahlke, Cortázar's narrator addresses the male graffiti artist as if he always might reply; as if he always might be drawing, thereby perpetually resisting the prohibition against communication.[42]

To be sure, the ending and specifically the narrator's admission that she had fashioned the you-protagonist—"I had imagined your life" (38)—could be interpreted as an erasure of everything that has gone before. There was no communication, no relationship, there may not even have been a single other person putting up graffiti. There was just her imagining a specific male individual drawing the graffiti she was seeing in the city, her imagining a relationship with him, even her embedding the act of imagining—her imagining him fashioning her during that night of fearful, drunken, erotic reverie (35), and her imagining him imagining her when she is at the police station (36–37). The reader is forced to consider whether the connection between the "I" and the "you" is "only" grammatical, "only" rhetorical.

However, if we choose to read this story as apostrophic Talk, we can interpret this closing admission as a *mise en abîme* of reading second-person fiction. Readers, too, have been imagining both of the artists' lives up to this point. Following the model of audience response to apostrophe proposed above, as actual receiver of the story one will interpret the message as targeted to two addressees. In listening as if one were the specified addressee, the apostrophized other of the narrator, one is positioned to feel the emotional force of the relationship that is created between the "I" and "you." As a hearer-recipient, one is moved by witnessing the apostrophe's animation and is persuaded to the narrator's view of the relationship: it did exist. Furthermore, the narrative mode—the use of untagged second-person pronouns—invites slippage between these two positions, thus eliciting the potential involvement of anyone who will take up the available pronoun, anyone who will consider himself called by the narrator's "you," anyone who will look at the graffiti, in the metaphor of the story. As the narrator's emotional allies and surrogate recipients for the message, readers feel addressed and will then "draw" by recognizing that they are supposed to feel addressed and called into action. The episode in which the you-protagonist apostrophizes the woman artist and "loves her a little" models such slippage, models Talk. It is an allegory of the narrative's/narrator's hope that the inscribed reader-viewer becomes a real reader, that the "you" becomes a real and available agent able to share love, as in the inscribed scene, and able to wage acts of protest, as in the story as a whole. The scene is an allegory of a reading that had consequences. If we imitate it, we Talk with "Graffiti," and graffiti can continue to function as resistance.

I want to conclude this section by considering how Cortázar's gesture in writing this story when and how he did also constitutes a kind of apostrophic Talk. Like many of Cortázar's short stories, "Graffiti" cannot be precisely dated, but it was written sometime in the late 1970s, inspired by the cruelty of the Argentine military dictatorship's Dirty War (Prego 1990: 15–16; Peavler 1990: 89–90). As far as my research can uncover, the story, dedicated to Catalan artist Antoni Tàpies, first appeared in a French art journal in French translation, juxtaposed to reproductions of Tàpies's vibrant artworks in multimedia: oil paint, cord, wood, cardboard, fabric, sand (*Derrière le Miroir*, May 1979). Half a year later, in November 1979, the Spanish original was published in a journal in Washington and Paris.[43] "Graffiti" was anthologized in Cortázar's volume of short stories *Queremos tanto a Glenda* (We Love Glenda So Much), published in Mexico the next year (1980). The English translation appeared in 1983, shortly before Cortázar's death in 1984. I mention the dedication to Tàpies because it seems to me that on the level of the whole text, "Grafitti" functions as an apostrophe; it is addressed literally and figuratively to this artist: "A Antoni Tàpies" ("To/For Antoni Tàpies"). I doubt it was merely the resemblances between Tàpies's art and graffiti that prompted the dedication, or even the friendship between the two artists who had spent so much time and energy protesting the dictatorships in their respective beloved homelands. More importantly, I suspect, Cortázar was trying to foreground the political role of art, specifically its ability to bring people together to remember and transmit knowledge that dictators would rather bury.

Shamefully, to my mind, Cortázar's "Graffiti" has received almost no literary critical attention. This neglect appears to be due to the story's subject. As a work written in response to an actual political situation, it has been deemed polemical by numerous Cortázar scholars and thus aesthetically inferior.[44] Although she does not discuss Cortázar's text, performance theorist and Latin American scholar Diana Taylor sees the issue of art and political violence differently. Painfully aware of "the traps and complexities of representing political violence" (1997: 145), Taylor nonetheless concludes that artists have no choice but to try to represent it, scholars but to try to analyze it:

> *Not* representing real political violence and atrocity only contributes to its legitimization and perpetuation. Rather than *whether* we should attempt such an undertaking, the question is *how* to represent this violence, how to think and write about these bodies? What do these invisible bodies *mean*? Who determines that meaning? How are we being asked to respond to these representations that make conflicting tugs on us as witnesses, spectators, artists, activists, and scholars? How do we hold onto the significance of the "real" body even as it slips into the symbolic realm through representational practices? (147)

Though my analysis has only begun to address some of these questions, I believe it helps us appreciate the act of witnessing to the Dirty War Cortázar performs in and through "Graffiti." Cortázar never mentions any specific place, city, or time, nor does he include any specific political issues whatsoever. Neither of the main characters has a name or even any real distinguishing features. It is nonspecificity, however, that allows readers to identify with the position of the story's narratee, its "you." That the story first appeared during the Dirty War, but in French in France, and then in the Spanish language but not in Argentina, seems to me to enact another kind of apostrophe. Cortázar "calls," but not in a way that asks for a direct reply or one that specifies an addressee (citizens of Argentina?), who could then be arrested and tortured. His choices of narrative technique and of publishing underscore Cortázar's conviction about the efficacy of indirection, at least for the particular struggle in Argentina, an efficacy that he illustrates through the story itself.[45]

I maintain that rhetorical choices like Cortázar's use of the second person always have real consequences for readers, who after all, are agents in the real world. In talking about his own choice to narrate *Change of Heart* in the second person, Michel Butor helps me to see more clearly what is at stake in the apostrophic act: "We are in a situation of instruction; it's no longer only someone who possesses the word as an inalienable property, irremovable, like an innate faculty which he contents himself with exercising, but also it's someone to whom one gives the word [*on donne la parole*]" (my translation; 1961: 942). This "giving of the word" is the apostrophic gesture par excellence. Those who "give the word"—God, orator, poet, author, or narrator—wield power by controlling the other, but they also risk losing control by giving life and voice to the other, as "Graffiti's" narrator does when she addresses "you" and Cortázar us. What they gain by taking that risk is the possibility of provoking response, of succeeding to animate, of rousing to action. Those who choose to "hear the word"—Adam, orators' audiences, narratees or readers—reply by being brought into a relationship-conversation, though it may not be to their liking and in any case is not under their control. Cortázar could not know what people inside or outside Argentina would do with his story in 1979, nor could he know what we would do with it today. But he could and did draw the sketch in the hope that someone would know how to read the lines.

Can You Perform Barth's "Life-Story" and Calvino's *If on a winter's night a traveler*?

The analyses presented so far have suggested several ways in which actual readers are invited to cross borders between the world of the texts and the world in which they live. These border crossings are instigated by the appellative force of the second-person pronoun and are made easier or more difficult by various factors promoting reader identification with that particular "you." I have now come to the point along my spectrum that is as close to conversational exchange as apostrophic Talk can come. Reader response to identify with the "you" seems almost as inevitable as Longinus claims, when he says that apostrophe sets the hearer in the center of the action (201). Except, rather than putting the reader into the scene of the text in the way Longinus claims Herodotus does or in the way Luc Estang describes his experience of feeling like he was in the train when reading *Change of Heart*—"*on y est!*; I am there!"—it's as if the text steps into the world of the reader, seeing what s/he does and forcing her/him to admit: "yes, I'm here." It is now time to explain my qualifications, my own "as if's," my insistence that such texts can get only so close to conversation and no closer and that readers need to remain aware of the gap preventing full identification. In short, it is time to return to the novel that originally prompted me to consider whether readers and texts can Talk, Italo Calvino's *If on a winter's night a traveler*.

The first words you read are:

> You are about to begin reading Italo Calvino's new novel, *If on a winter's night a traveler*.
> [*Stai per cominciare a leggere il nuovo romanzo* Se una notte d'inverno un viaggiatore *di Italo Calvino*.] (3)[46]

Although I have argued for at least subliminal reader identification with any of the unmarked "you's" presented so far in this chapter, I now need to suggest that Calvino's "you" promotes a qualitatively different urge to identify. This is the opening of the book, readers have Calvino's novel of this title in front of their eyes, and they are beginning their perusal of it. The text addresses *you* with no sign of quotation marks or a name connecting it to somebody else. I have yet to encounter a flesh-and-blood reader who didn't report a sense of being startled when reading this line.

However, if one pauses a moment over this first sentence, one realizes that it doesn't quite fit the situation of the actual reader of *If on a winter's night a traveler*, who *has already begun* to read the novel, and is *not about to begin* it.[47] What if we are reading the novel years after its publication? Then it is no longer Calvino's "new novel" (Phelan 1989: 134).[48] For the truly attentive reader, what this opening line effects is both a seduction to feel addressed *and* a realization that the call is not quite accurate. In the terms of conversation analysis introduced earlier, the addressee is constructed as a reader, and therefore all readers are hearers who are invited to become recipients. This resembles the apostrophes analyzed by Longinus. In Goffman's framework, the matter raised by the text-as-statement concerns the very issue of reading, and the orientation to this matter, the "reply," is the self-conscious performance of the role of you-narratee by hearer-readers. To Talk with the text, one allows oneself to be seduced, while recognizing that the seduction succeeds because one is playing the role of the seduceable.

To better understand this kind of performance, we need to consider what constitutes complete identification of actual readers with the "you." I propose to call this limit case the "irresistible invitation" of the second-person pronoun, as opposed to the merely "subliminal" one discussed earlier. I suggest that there are some (if few) sentences that when read would necessarily constitute the actualization of the utterance by any reader. The most obvious example would be the statement, You are reading this sentence. To read it is to do what the sentence says you are doing. You can't resist it; if you read it, you are accomplishing what it says. Elsewhere I dubbed such sentences "literary performatives," in homage to Oxford School philosopher J. L. Austin's concept of the performative.[49] You will recall that Austin describes performatives as utterances in which to say something is in fact (at least in part) to do that something: for example, "I promise" or "I bet." Although Austin's performative can occasionally be executed without actually speaking (for instance, betting by putting money in a slot machine; 1962: 8), "literary performatives" can only be actualized by reading. A sentence like "you are dead," which if read is not "performed," and if "performed" cannot be read, would fall outside my rubric, as would any of the second-person statements we have looked at so far in this chapter.[50] In those texts I have suggested that the reader feels a subliminal sense of being addressed by the inherent appellative force of second-person pronouns and can choose to reply to the text-as-statement by identifying more fully with the "you" and feeling the force of the relationship with the "I" who utters that "you." In literary performatives where the irresistible invitation is operative, readers don't have a choice but to respond by doing what the address says—unless they stop reading, in which case they're completely outside "hearing range" anyway. The involuntariness of executing literary performatives contrasts with the consciousness, even the deliberate will to identify with the "you" of apostrophic Talk, to perform it. Indeed, it is the self-conscious effort required to perform the role of the inscribed "you" that made me place my apostrophic mode third in this survey of modes of Talk organized by the complexity of reader response. In what follows, I will argue that the existence of the literary performatives promotes apostrophic Talk, and therefore, despite what might otherwise appear as the unfortunate closeness of the terms, I will continue to designate reply to the apostrophes I am describing as "performance."

Before returning to consider if and how readers can perform Calvino, I'd like to demonstrate the existence of literary performatives by looking at a published literary text (as opposed to my fabricated sentence above). John Barth's "Life-Story," a highly self-reflexive short story about a writer trying to write a story about a writer who suspects that his own life might be a fiction, breaks into the following tirade three-quarters of the way through:

> The reader! You, dogged, uninsultable, print-oriented bastard, it's you I'm addressing, who else, from inside this monstrous fiction. You've read me this far, then? Even this far? For what discreditable motive? How is it you don't go to a movie, watch TV, stare at a wall, play tennis with a friend, make amorous advances to the person who comes to your mind when I speak of amorous advances? Can nothing surfeit, saturate you, turn you off? Where's your shame? (127)

Barth's narrator subsequently refers to this passage as a "barrage of rhetorical or at least unanswered questions" (127), but I maintain that two particular questions remain "unanswered" only as long as they remain unread. Just perusing the lines "You've read me this far, then? Even this far?" generates affirmative responses to them. This is Goffman's "statement" and "reply" indissolubly linked, as if the text catches us in the act of what we are actually doing.[51] However, the rest of this passage would not qualify as literary performatives by my definition. Though they are in the second person, references to activities like going to the movies and playing tennis imply a cultural frame of reference that might not make sense—much less apply—to a given reader. Similarly, a reader could choose not to see himself in the characterization of "dogged, uninsultable, print-oriented bastard" or feel any sense of shame.

If the phenomenon is so ephemeral, its utilization so unsustainable, why am I bothering to introduce it at all? Because its existence—even the possibility of its existence—shapes reader response to all unmarked uses of the second person: *literary performatives promote learning how to Talk with apostrophic texts*. I do take myself to be addressed by Barth. I squealed with pleasure when I read this passage for the first time and smile despite myself every time I reread it. Though I am not claiming to have been fully aware of what went on for me that first time I read "Life-Story," I now surmise that the completeness of the fit at the moment of reading the literary performatives causes a jolt, the jolt of absolute recognition, which then engages a stronger vigilance about levels of identification. This stronger vigilance makes readers both more aware of what doesn't fit and also more aware that the text is playing the game of trying to make a fit. Ultimately, I would argue that "getting" Barth's entire passage requires the reader to step into the role that is created for the you-narratee by the text, remaining aware that one is in fact playing a role, in this case, a role of the persistent, voracious reader who won't let the writer "end." Giving such a response constitutes Talking with this text.

Outfitted with knowledge about literary performatives, I can now reengage Calvino's "great novel of reading," as Susan Winnett has called it (1990: 506). Even without making comparisons to Austin's performative, several critics have noticed the discrepancy between the actual reader's situation and that of the you-narratee initially and subsequently. But they have not registered what literary performatives help me perceive as Calvino's strategy to create this misfit.[52] The opening move quoted above is the first such intentional misfit. Once one perceives that misfit with regard to one's own situation, I suggest, one can posit a characterized reader, the you-narratee, for whom this statement is fully felicitous. The further I read, the clearer it becomes that Calvino's novel is not about me, a real reader, but rather about a reader-protagonist who reads a series of book fragments. The story of this reader serves as a frame around the book fragments that are reproduced in Calvino's text. This reader is initially designated only with the informal singular pronoun "you" (*tu* in the original Italian) and subsequently also by the capitalized word "Reader" (Lettore). The necessary "I" who tells this you-Reader what he is doing in the present tense remains unnamed and uncharacterized.

And yet, precisely because the story of this Reader is so thoroughly about reading, actual readers find themselves alternating between concentrating on the "you" as character and recognizing themselves in the text. Occasional literary performatives promote this identification by flesh-and-blood readers with the inscribed "you." At the beginning of the second chapter, for example, the narrator states, "You have now read about thirty pages [*una trentina di pagine*] and you're becoming caught up in the story. At a certain point you remark: 'This sentence sounds somehow familiar. In fact, this whole passage reads like something I've read before'" (25). As an actual reader of these lines it is true that one has read "about thirty pages"; in both the Italian original and the English translation this statement appears on page 25. "*Una trentina*" is a looser term than "about thirty," and so I can accept this as a statement about the twenty-five pages read. Hence this counts as a literary performative.[53] On the other hand, any specific reader may or may not have been getting caught up in the story. For those who have, the sense of complete identification with the "you" may last through the end of the sentence. But it is highly unlikely that any actual readers say to themselves at this moment, "This sentence sounds somehow familiar." And so these readers lapse into the strategy of positing a you-protagonist for whom these other statements do apply. For most of us flesh-and-blood readers, there is a rapid alternation between "reading *about* life" and "reading *as* life"—by which I mean reading as what is happening to us at the moment of reading ("you have now read about thirty pages"). As I proposed about reading Barth, the exact "fits"—the literary performatives—can promote greater awareness about what fits and what doesn't, but also about the text's strategy to create those fits. Therefore, I would like to proceed by considering features that determine degrees of identification with "you," moving from aspects of Calvino's novel that promote the widest possible reader identification with "you" to those that more unambiguously restrict such identification. Then I will consider what Calvino's purpose might be in making actual readers self-conscious about the process of reading his novel.

As suggested by my previous quotations from *If on a winter's night a traveler*, actual readers and the characterized "you" share the activity of reading. In fact, the Reader and the actual reader both read fragments of novels with the same titles. At the moment the narrator of the frame story reports that the Reader begins a new novel (usually under the illusion that he has found the continuation of the last one he was reading), actual readers turn the page and find a segment with the same title. Any reader of Calvino's novel is reading some of the same material that the Reader-protagonist is reading.[54]

Also inviting identification with the "you" of the frame story are the narrator's several strategies revealing how little he knows about "you" and implying that he is everyman—or rather every reader. (My apparent tolerance for the sexist generic will become clearer below, where I argue that the narratee is, in fact, a male reader, "a general male you" [141].) In the opening sequence, the narrator encourages "you" to get comfortable for settling down to read Calvino's new novel by proposing many possible reading positions: "Find the most comfortable position: seated, stretched out, curled up, or lying flat. . . . In an easy chair, on the sofa, in the rocker, the deck chair, on the hassock. In the hammock, if you have a hammock" (3). The narrator is ignorant about the type of furniture "you" have in the space in which "you" find "yourself." Presumably, one of the options listed will appeal to an actual individual reader who will then experience pleasure, perhaps in the plethora of options but perhaps more particularly in discovering the one that applies to the position s/he is in at that moment. Such a discovery does not constitute the execution of a literary performative, however, since, most importantly, it does not apply to every reader but also because, as in the novel's opening sentence, there is a chronological discrepancy (presumably you are already in that favorite reading position, not in the act of finding it). Still, the passage might solicit a moment of recognition for some readers: that's me; I'm in that position. And this sense of being able to locate features of one's own experience in the fiction may promote one's general sense of performing the text. This use of inventories also underscores the fact that many possibilities do *not* fit, diminishing that reader's sense of being uniquely addressed but enhancing awareness of playing a role, since some of those misfits will apply to other readers trying to perform the same text. Such awareness can be likened to that of early radio listeners or listener-viewers of talk shows who sense that they are part of a large audience responding to the call of the host to "you listeners out there."

Calvino's narrator sometimes promotes identification by describing a specific experience presumably almost every reader has had or could imagine having. One scenario that seems widely applicable is of being in a bookstore and feeling accosted by books one is not planning to buy but feeling pressured to buy them because they fall into categories like "the Books You've Been Planning to Read For Ages," "the Books You Want To Own So They'll Be Handy Just In Case," "the Books That Fill You With Sudden, Inexplicable Curiosity, Not Easily Justified" (5).

An analogous appeal to every reader, characterized or flesh-and-blood, is made through gnomic pronouncements about reading. A salient example occurs in the opening of the fourth chapter of the frame story: "Listening to someone read aloud is very different from reading in silence. When you read, you can stop or skip sentences: you are the one who sets the pace. When someone else is reading, it is difficult to make your attention coincide with the tempo of his reading: the voice goes either too fast or too slow" (68). This passage, which continues in a gnomic manner for another paragraph, is relevant to the characterized reader in the frame story because he has just been read to. But its aptness is not limited to him on this occasion or specifically to his recent reading experience; it is apparent to actual readers as well. This is the "you" that can mean "I," "you," "one," "anyone." In other words, the "you" of this passage could refer to the novel's Reader and to any reader of Calvino's novel, as well as to anyone—any "you"—who reads. It could even refer to the narrator, enhancing a sense of commonality between speaker and listener. All such gnomic pronouncements contribute to a sense of being addressed by the text and therefore of being able to perform it, though perhaps less than the strategies looked at so far.

Similarly contributing to identification between actual reader and inscribed reader is the extent to which the latter remains uncharacterized. The narrator does not give his narratee a name, neither a proper name, nor in the first chapter a generic title.[55] The narratee is evoked only through the second-person singular informal pronoun and second-person singular verb forms. (Italian, like Spanish and Greek, does not need to include a grammatical subject.) On the other hand, nonspecificity, as in Barth's story, seems unsustainable in an involved narrative context; to build a plot, options must be chosen and other options excluded. This is precisely what happens in Calvino's frame story. In the second chapter, additional characters are introduced, including "*una signorina*" whom the narrator quickly dubs "la Lettrice" (29; meaning, literally, the reader [female gender] but translated by Weaver into English here and elsewhere as "the Other Reader"). At this moment the narrator christens his addressee "Lettore" (Reader). But as if to stave off—or distract us from?—the inevitable concretization and thus limitation that even this generic title confers, the narrator comments, "Who you are, Reader, your age, your status, profession, income: that would be indiscreet to ask. It's your business, you're on your own" (32). The narrator seems to be recognizing the reader-protagonist's autonomy, not only with regard to the developing attraction to the newly introduced female reader but also with regard to his personality—he could be anybody, have any personal history, and hence, it is implied, "you" could be *you*, the actual reader.

This is not the stance of a traditional omniscient narrator, whom we usually think of as exercising complete control over, or at least having full knowledge of, his characters. But Calvino's narrator, like the narrator of Barth's "Life-Story," frequently confers on the inscribed reader the kind of autonomy that belongs to actual readers. These narrators mix narrative levels by projecting commonalities with you-characters onto *you*, the flesh-and-blood reader. In Calvino's highly self-reflexive fiction, we get a statement that this is the narrator's explicit intention: "This book so far has been careful to leave open to the Reader who is reading the possibility of identifying himself with the Reader who is read; this is why he was not given a name, which would automatically have made him the equivalent of a Third Person, of a character . . . and so he has been kept a pronoun, in the abstract condition of pronouns, suitable for any attribute and any action" (141). The narrator could be paraphrasing Benveniste when he comments on the availability of an untagged second-person pronoun for any listener. Add a name and this potentiality diminishes—though readings of *Change of Heart* suggest that it does not entirely disappear. On the one hand, Calvino's narrator recognizes, as we had to in discussing the opening line, the existence of multiple readers ("the Reader who is reading"; "the Reader who is read")—that is to say, "you" does not exactly equal *you*. On the other, he claims that it is possible for the actual reader to identify with the inscribed Reader.

It is time to confront this claim directly. What factors work against "reader-Reader" identification? Why am I insisting that to Talk with this text is to feel both an urge and a refusal to identify? Calvino's inscribed "you," cued or not by a mere pronoun, becomes a characterized entity whose actions do not coincide precisely with those of the actual reader, despite occasional literary performatives that he and we execute, despite the narrator's claim just presented. The "you's" actions, rather, constitute a plot of their own, a plot about searching for the novels that the "you" is prevented from reading to conclusion. The you-Reader's pursuit of reading material is likened explicitly and implicitly to conquering a woman (for example, 9, 33) and is coupled with pursuit of a particular woman, the "signorina" mentioned above, a female reader, the Lettrice, who, in contrast to the Lettore, is given a name: Ludmilla. Although going into the details of these hunts would distract from my own pursuit of apostrophic Talk, the sexualized plot offers an important hint about an issue intimately connected to the possibilities of reader-Reader identification, namely exclusion by gender. To take up this issue is to reveal the selectivity of the quotes I have analyzed so far. It is also to take up an issue at the heart of Calvino's novel: gender relations in contemporary (Western) society.

Although the first and second person are technically considered to be nongenderized forms in most Indo-European languages, as soon as "I" or "you," ("*io*" or "*tu*") becomes part of a sentence, gender is likely to come quickly into play. Philosopher Elizabeth Beardsley has proposed the term "linguistic genderization" to describe the phenomenon of "requiring a sex distinction in discourse about human beings, in such a way that to disregard the sex distinction produces a locution which is incorrect (where genderization is formal) or inappropriate (where genderization is informal)" (1977: 117; see also 1973–74: 285). Beardsley further differentiates between "referential" and "characterizing" genderization, where the former describes the revelation of gender in all terms that *refer* to a human being and the latter are those that *characterize* people (1977: 117). How highly inflected a language is correlates with the amount of either type of genderization. The contrast between English and Italian, for example, becomes obvious when we compare Calvino's text with its English translation. Whereas Calvino can write "*una cliente*" (1979: 28) and automatically communicate that the person being introduced is a woman, his translator, Weaver, must add an extra phrase to convey the same information: "another customer, a young lady" (1981: 28). (As in other Romance languages, Italian verbal predicates, adjectives, and definite and indefinite articles can reveal gender.) The word for "customer" is the same for both genders in both languages, but the Italian indefinite article indicates a woman, whereas the English does not exhibit referential genderization in this case.

With genderization in mind, let us reconsider the novel's opening:

> You are about to begin reading Italo Calvino's new novel, *If on a winter's night a traveler*. Relax. Concentrate. Dispel every other thought. Let the world around you fade. Best to close the door; the TV is always on in the next room. Tell the others right away, "No, I don't want to watch TV!" Raise your voice—they won't hear you otherwise—"I'm reading! I don't want to be disturbed! [*Sto leggendo! Non voglio* essere disturbato!]" (1981: 3; 1979: 3; my emphasis)

I proposed above that the initial sentence, though it is not technically a literary performative because of the verb tense ("You are about to begin"), does promote identification. One experiences the surprise of being "seen" by the text. This experience continues to occur intermittently, alternating with our recognition of the novel as "about" a characterized reader whose reading adventures and our own occasionally overlap. This overlap may enhance our own general willingness to identify; we may let our sense of the distinctions between reality and fiction, between what is genuinely happening to us and what is "happening" to a character, blur.

But will all readers be equally willing to identify? Are there some factors that might make differences between the inscribed "you" and the reader particularly apparent? What happens to an actual female reader when she continues beyond the opening sentence to "Raise your voice— they won't hear you otherwise—'I'm reading! I don't want to be disturbed!' "? Perhaps she can identify if she's reading the novel in English. But if she reads the original Italian, she may feel more excluded than addressed. For although the novel's opening sentence did not exhibit referential genderization, just a few lines later the participle "disturbato," and the many that follow it, indicates that the "you" is a man.[56] So that even if Calvino's narrator intends to leave open to *any* reader the possibility of identifying by not specifying the characterized "you's" age, status, profession, and income, gender can't be avoided; it is grammatically encoded in Italian, as it is in most Western languages.[57]

What are the consequences of this? Linguist Sally McConnell-Ginet explains that "grammar provides a way to superimpose communication of social messages on utterances whose main purpose is something else"

(1980: 15). In the case of *If on a winter's night a traveler*, the actual female reader can't proceed past the first page without realizing that she can't be called by the exact words she reads. To perform the text she will have to pretend that she can be by reading as a man.[58] Specifically, she will accept the male participles and other references to "*tu*, Lettore" as a "generic masculine," a masculine form that supposedly applies to all human beings.[59] To have the experience of feeling addressed, actual women readers of this text will have to do "additional mental processing to transform the initial literal interpretation into one that includes them" (Crawford and Chaffin 1986: 16).

But, it is precisely "additional mental processing" that I contend is generated by the alternation of intermittent literary performatives and the other prods to identification. Therefore, we could say that the female reader is in the best position to play the game to win, to perform the text. She will perhaps recognize most quickly that the text is simultaneously for and not for her—to return to Jane Rule's title. Of course, the "ideal reader" of this and other apostrophic texts can be a biological woman or a man as long as she or he adopts this duplicitous stance of identifying and not identifying.

This stance is absolutely necessary to "performing" Calvino, to understanding the larger pattern in the novel of making claims that its structure contradicts—a pattern into which the question of reader identification falls and a pattern that clues us in to what Calvino might be saying about contemporary relationships between men and women. I need to return to a few more of my selectively constructed quotations to elucidate what I believe is Calvino's specific intent—to have readers reflect on gender relations. I mentioned above that although the "you" is left without a name throughout the novel, he does receive the generic title of "Reader [Lettore]," at a certain point—at the moment of the introduction of the female reader. When the narrator baptizes the female client in the bookstore as the "Lettrice," he designates the heretofore bare "you" as the "Lettore": "And so the Other Reader [Lettrice] makes her happy entrance into your field of vision, Reader [Lettore], or, rather, into the field of your attention" (1981: 29; 1979: 29). Even though the genderization of the "you" from the onset was linguistically unavoidable, Calvino "refutes" the normal practice of using the masculine singular noun as the universal—*lettore* as the singular for any reader—by deploying it only at the moment when he can offer the counterweight of a female noun. This is not to suggest that the novel's particular plot of heterosexual pursuit is any less heterosexist but rather to offer evidence that readers should be wary about taking that plot at face value.

As with seemingly every issue related to reading, this self-conscious novel eventually reflects on women readers. I refer to the narrator's direct address to the Lettrice, the Other Reader, in the seventh chapter of the frame story:

> What are you like, Other Reader? [*Como sei*, Lettrice?] It is time for this book in the second person to address itself no longer to a general male you, perhaps brother and double of a hypocrite I, but directly to you who appeared already in the second chapter as the Third Person necessary for the novel to be a novel, for something to happen between that male Second Person and the female Third, for something to take form, develop, or deteriorate according to the phases of human events. (1981: 141; 1979: 142)

The narrator's contention here about the construction of a relationship defies the linguistic logic of verbal person, which, as we have seen Benveniste argue, can only occur between an "I" and a "you." The correctness of Benveniste's position and the contradictions of the narrator's claim become even more apparent if we consider the continuation of this passage in which the narrator further explains his motivations. I now quote in full a passage I had quoted earlier only in part:

> This book so far has been careful to leave open to the Reader who is reading the possibility of identifying himself with the Reader who is read: this is why he was not given a name, which would automatically have made him the equivalent of a Third Person, of a character (whereas to you, as Third Person, a name had to be given, Ludmilla), and so he has been kept a pronoun, in the abstract condition of pronouns, suitable for any attribute and any action. Let us see, Other Reader, if the book can succeed in drawing a true portrait of you, beginning with the frame [*cornice*] and enclosing you from every side, establishing the outlines of your form. (1981: 141–42; 1979: 142–43)

As already mentioned, the narrator contends that not giving the "you" a name facilitates identification by the actual reader with the inscribed reader. But Ludmilla has been given a name, implying that the actual reader is not meant to identify with her. The irony of this passage, of course, is that the narrator makes such an argument in a mode that resuscitates the Lettrice by talking *to* her and objectifies the Lettore by talking *about* him.[60]

In the continuation of this passage, the narrator makes his most spurious claim of all: "For a second-person discourse to become a novel, at least two you's [*due tu*] are required, distinct and concomitant, which stand out from the crowd of he's she's and they's" (1981: 147; 1979: 148). However, despite the seeming symmetry of the pair, "Lettore" and "Lettrice," it is simply not the case that this novel is narrated to two "you's." The Lettrice is only addressed directly in the singular at three points in the novel, all in the seventh chapter, and two of those instances in passages without story content. There are two other passages in a true second-person plural, the first when the Lettore and the Lettrice become lovers (154) and the second at the very end, when they are in bed as husband and wife.[61] This last scene provides adequate evidence to counter the narrator's claim about narrating to two "you's":

> Now you are man and wife, Reader and Reader [*Ora siete marito e moglie, Lettore e Lettrice*].[62] A great double bed receives your [*le vostre*] parallel readings.
>
> Ludmilla closes her book [Ludmilla *chiude il suo libro*], turns off her light, puts her head back against the pillow, and says, "Turn off your light, too. Aren't you tired of reading?"
>
> And you say [*E tu*], "Just a moment, I've almost finished *If on a winter's night a traveler* by Italo Calvino." (1981: 260; 1979: 263)

The first paragraph resuscitates the Lettrice—after more than a hundred pages since the first and only time she is addressed—by using a true second person, here in the plural ("Now you are [*Ora siete*]"; "your [*le vostre*]"). But in the next sentence she is objectified again, written of in the third person ("Ludmilla closes . . ." [Ludmilla *chiude*]). The last paragraph returns the focus explicitly to the male "you," where it has been for the vast majority of the novel ("And you say . . ." [*E tu*]). Thus despite the mise-en-scène of the double bed and the declared equality of "parallel readings," in this second-person discourse that supposedly requires two "you's," "distinct and concomitant," the marginalization of one of those "you's" is palpable. Indeed, it is so palpable that I submit it is intended to draw our attention to the inequality of the addressees, just as genderization, chronological discrepancies, inventories, and generalizations in other passages are intended to draw our attention to both the gaps preventing and the similarities inviting full identification between ourselves and the inscribed "you."

In an interview with Italianist Gregory Lucente, Calvino admitted to entertaining the hope that literature "could and would intervene in reality" (1985: 248). Reading Calvino's novel as apostrophe, that is, as discourse that calls us indirectly, causing us to reflect on the act of calling itself—who is called, how they are called, when they are called—invites us to be self-reflexive about our reading practices, as it invites us to be self-aware about how gender relations are inscribed in language. In the last scene, Calvino presents a parody of a novelistic ending with its teleological and conjugal satisfactions, "And they lived happily ever after." We should be as self-conscious about the last invitation to identify as about the first—"And you say, 'Just a moment, I've almost finished *If on a winter's night a traveler* by Italo Calvino' "—by acknowledging the irony of reading an entire novel about the seeming nonexistence of endings and yet feeling so satisfied about now concluding. We should read the issue of address in a similar manner. We might like to believe that this story could be our story. Or, we might like to believe that this story has nothing to do with us because we are not male or because even if we are, we refuse to identify with one who acts the way this one does. But only when we realize that this narrative talks to one "you," a "you" who is male, heterosexual, and sometimes sexist, *and* only when we realize that we in fact have some things in common with this "you"—like the near fit of the last sentence—are we performing Calvino's text.

This is the lesson I eventually learned from reflecting on the contrast of my first reaction to *If on a winter's night a traveler* with that of my former student: I wanted to have nothing to do with Calvino's younarratee, and he identified so completely that he felt exhilarated by reading his own story. Performing the text, I decided, involves understanding what produces each of these urges and then trying to feel them both simultaneously. At the heart of each of these urges is the second person: I wanted to read it as an eavesdropper, he as an intended addressee. The rubric of apostrophe led me to imagine a double stance in which I heard both types of "you" at once. This in turn helped me understand why so many texts written in the second person might have appeared in the late twentieth century, in a secondary oral age that has also been called a postmodern one, in Linda Hutcheon's sense of "self-conscious, self-contradictory, self-undermining statement." For Hutcheon, the postmodern stance is "rather like saying something whilst at the same time putting inverted commas around what is being said. The effect is to highlight, or 'highlight,' and to subvert, or 'subvert,' and the mode is therefore a 'knowing' and an ironic—or even 'ironic'—one. Postmodernism's distinctive character lies in this kind of wholesale 'nudging' commitment to doubleness, or duplicity" (1989: 1). The necessarily duplicitous address of apostrophe helps me appreciate the performance, the "putting in of the inverted commas," the hearing of the message "this is for and not for me" required to Talk with the postmodern texts I have examined in this chapter.

5

INTERACTIVITY
Talk as Collaboration

In June 1995 the *New York Times Magazine* published a spoof by Michael Rubiner called "T. S. Eliot Interactive." Next to an image that at first glance looks like the illuminated capitals of medieval manuscripts but on closer examination consists of the famous poet's head mounted on a (computer) mouse, Rubiner intones:

> Let us go then
>> *Click on one*
>> you and I
>> the three of us
>> just the men
>
>> *Click on one*
>> When the evening is spread out against the sky
>> When the morning is spread out against the sky
>> Around noon
> Like a patient etherized upon a table;
> Let us go,
>
>> *Click on one*
>> through certain half-deserted streets
>> through the souks of Marrakech
>> through the fourth dimension
> The muttering retreats
> Of restless nights (62)

Although Rubiner's rewriting of "The Love Song of J. Alfred Prufrock" is neither a computer hypertext nor a work of prose fiction, I'm launching this chapter with it because I believe it begins to hint at why interactivity might be considered both the apotheosis and the endgame of talk fiction.

This is why I am including interactivity in this study and yet relegating it to a short chapter.

On the one hand, recent computer technologies facilitate "orientation to exchange." Rubiner's "Click on one" reminds us that hypertexts—which, I provisionally define as a database format in which information related to that on a display can be accessed directly from the display—not only present options among which readers can choose but also provide a mechanism for reply in a most concrete way. With a control key, a mouse, a touch screen, or a joystick, the reader of an actual hypertext can physically register his or her choice among several possible segments of text. In many hypertexts, though not in Rubiner's paper version, that specific choice in turn triggers a specific continuation. Digital data processing makes possible not only a chain of "statements" and "replies" but also additional readings—texts—produced by selecting different segments and thereby creating different sequences. Hypertext allows readers to make so many decisions about what appears on the screen that, as I have suggested in this chapter's subtitle, this kind of Talk might be considered "collaboration" between those who develop the computer program and those who use it.

On the other hand, for the same reasons, computer technology raises the issue of whether interactivity can be thought of as part of the same phenomenon as Talk in narrative literature. Who are the participants? Does the computer itself figure as part of the "enacted capacity" of the speaker or of the respondent? How about the hardware and software developers? In hypertext systems or interactive video games where the tools for programming can be accessed, is there any way to justify keeping the categories of speaker and respondent or writer and reader distinct? If there isn't, it follows that there is no justification for thinking in terms of exchange between them. What about the "text"? To consider Rubiner's parody one last time, does the "Click on one" belong to the statement? to the reply? to neither? to both? And if we move now to actual hypertexts, which "store information in electronic codes rather than in physical marks on a physical surface" (Landow 1992: 18)? What is the "text" to be analyzed as Talk? As Bolter points out, "The bits of the text are simply not on a human scale. . . . If you hold a magnetic or optical disk up to the light, you will not see text at all. . . . There are so many levels of deferral that the reader or writer is hard put to identify the text at all: is it on the screen, in the transistor memory, or on the disk?" (1991: 42–43). Furthermore, with advances in digital processing, many hyper*text* environments are actually hyper*media* environments in which even the simulacrum of words on the screen is subordinated to sound and image or in which words may not play a perceptible role at all. Late-twentieth- and early-twenty-first-century technologies that create "virtual reality," or, as expert Brenda Laurel prefers to call it, "immersion technology," beg the question Can we justify talking about a text, much less about Talk in prose fiction? Many intelligent people have written about interactive technologies, and some even focus on how these new technologies affect notions of literature. My readers who would like to pursue the subject in a fuller and more technological manner must be referred elsewhere (see especially Aarseth 1997; Landow 1997; Morse 1998; and Turkle 1995). I am not a technology whiz and purposely refrained from trying to become one so that I could approach interactive technologies as exclusively as possible from a Talk framework.

Therefore, rather than break out of the parameters of my book altogether, I'd like to shrink my perspective once again by suggesting that despite the implications of technology for such concepts as author, text, reader, and so on, much of what counts today as interactive literature still resembles something like a story that the person sitting in front of the screen reads/views/hears. Because so many procedures involving computers are referred to today as "interactive" and because I have yet to come across any definition of "interactive story," I propose to limit my remarks to hypertexts (hypermedia, CD-ROM, and video games) that have a narrative structure, namely, that represent at least two real or fictive events or situations in a time sequence (Prince 1982: 4). The role of the person interacting with the hypertexts may involve manipulation of the representation, events, or time sequence of the narrative. While there is not space here to enumerate all the things I am hoping to exclude through this definition, I will mention one: previously published literary works that are loaded into hypertext systems so that "students" can read the work, look up background information on the author, and check vocabulary and editions: "Hypertext Faust," for instance.[1] In these types of hypertexts, the user is manipulating information about the narrative, not the events in the narrative. On the other hand, I would include hypertexts whose format consists of original or previously published stories that "readers" can order or reorder or write or rewrite.

I will proceed from here and conclude my study by describing some of these "interactive stories" and the extent to which they Talk. I have selected and arranged my examples to give a sense of the variety of hypertext stories and the increasingly complicated role of the reader in producing them. However, even when the technologies at issue are not fully tapped, they provide for so many ways of engaging response that I do not pretend to exhaustively typologize interactive literature. There are simply too many things in cyberspace. Furthermore, there will doubtless be numerous hypertexts created and circulated in the time between the writing and the publication of this book. My goal here, therefore, is to shed some light on the idea of interactive Talk from the perspective of narrative literature, not from the perspective of computer engineering. Before turning to examples of interactive stories that are currently circulating, I want to consider one more text that, like Rubiner's spoof, falls outside my definition and yet provides a kind of training ground for understanding the Talk of hypertext.

"Assembling" Cortázar's *Hopscotch*

Julio Cortázar's 1963 novel *Rayuela* (translated into English as *Hopscotch*, 1966) has been called an ancestor of hypertext,[2] labeled, for example, a "protohypertext" (*www.duke.edu/eng169s2/group3/dnorris/intro.html*) and a "paper hypertext" (*web.uvic.ca/~ckeep/hflo117.html*), and even scholars who have not considered it in the light of hypertext have remarked the active role of the reader, suggesting that readers participate in the assemblage of the novel (Simpkins 1990: 61). Like any other "print" novel, it appears between two covers with a predetermined number of pages (155 chapters in three sections for a total of 573 pages in the American translation, an Avon paperback edition). The title of the book, as many of its numerous constituent parts, foregrounds the idea of a game and, with its concomitant active role for the reader, of turn-taking. Following the title and copyright pages, *Hopscotch* presents a Table of Instructions (*Tablero de dirección*) that amplifies the gaming idea introduced by the title: "In its own way, this book consists of many books, but two books above all."[3] The narrator proposes the first book as that which is read "in a normal fashion," by beginning with the first chapter and reading through chapter 56.[4] The narrator adds that chapter

56 ends with "three garish little stars" standing for "The End," permitting the reader to "ignore what follows with a clean conscience." With this comment the narrator privileges the second book that is created by "beginning with chapter 73 and then following the sequence indicated at the end of each chapter." In other words, the reader is to discover the shape of the book in the process of reading. Nonetheless, the narrator provides a list of the chapter sequence "in case of confusion or forgetfulness." The Table of Instructions concludes by pointing to an additional navigational tool: "Each chapter has its number at the top of every right-hand page to facilitate the search" (Cortázar 1975: 5).

Although Cortázar's novel could be productively analyzed for its theories about readers and reading,[5] I want to restrict this discussion to how *Hopscotch* makes the procedures of reply explicit, something it shares with most hypertexts. The first "move" of Cortázar's text-as-statement is the Table of Instructions described above, proposing these two readings and the existence of others. Actual readers must then decide which one they will pursue. I suggest that in no matter which order readers move through the book—start to the end of chapter 56, the suggested "hop-scotched" order, last page to first, or any variation thereof—the readers' turning of the pages can function as "reply" to the matter that has been raised by this initial move on the part of the narrator-text. To be seen as an "answering of some kind to a preceding matter that has been raised," the physical action of turning the pages must be accompanied by consciousness of doing so in a certain order that readers' have elected—even if they are proceeding in a "normal fashion."

Self-consciousness about the order one chooses to read is reinforced by the existence of the chapter number on each right-hand page. These chapter numbers function like deictics in Prince's sense, introduced in my introduction to this study, as "any term or expression which, in an utterance, *refers to the context of production* of that utterance" (1987: 18; my emphasis). Although readers do not write the words on the pages of *Hopscotch* (the way they do in some portions of some hypertexts), the chapter numbers "call" readers to remind them of the narrator's statement in the Table of Instructions: in choosing the order in which to read the already composed pages, readers produce the very book they are reading, at least from the narrator's perspective. The chapter numbers placed at the close of each chapter directing readers to the next chapter in the narrator's recommended order (for example: [-56]) similarly remind all readers—those who reply to them by turning to that chapter and those who do not—that they are responsible for the order in which they read. The hyphen in particular suggests to readers that they are building a chain of chapters in their own heads, a chain that ultimately is the book they have read. Of course, readers can read the pages of any book in any order. But by composing the chapters as relatively coherent units, by foregrounding the issue of chapter sequence with the comments in the Table of Instructions, and by providing readers with constant reminders of the choices they are executing, Cortázar's novel asks readers to orient to their own decisions about reading order. Those who do so orient, Talk with *Hopscotch*.

I want to pause over the "second" reading proposed in the Table of Instructions because it offers some additional insights into turn-taking and Talk in actual hypertext readings. At a basic level, reading *Hopscotch* (and other hypertexts) means reading differently. Following the narrator's preferred order makes apparent an undermining of the linearity that organizes the reading process of traditional books. To be sure, linearity is not completely abandoned in *Hopscotch*, as it is not completely abandoned in hypertext. For this reason, Landow proposes the terms "multilinear" or "multisequential" rather than "nonlinear" or "nonsequential" for hypertext, remarking, too, that, "Although conventional reading habits apply within each lexia [a term borrowed from Barthes's *S/Z* to mean "blocks of text" within a hypertext], once one leaves the shadowy bounds of any text unit, new rules and new experience apply" (1992: 4).[6] This description suits Cortázar's novel well.

On the macrolevel of the whole book, the hopscotched reading neither begins at the beginning nor ends at the end nor even goes every place in between. Rather, one commences with chapter 73, then moves to the first chapter, then to the second, then to chapter 116. Readers peruse the very last pages of the book (chapter 155) less than halfway through the hopscotched sequence (though readers would only realize how far along they are by looking at the chart in the Table of Instructions, a point to which I will return below). Chapters 1 through 56 are eventually read in sequential order (with many other chapters inserted in between); and yet there are numerous foilings of any expectation the hopscotched order raises. For example, a fairly regular alternation of chapters from the third part of the book with the first is "interrupted" by a long string of later chapters; or chapter 55 is altogether absent from this second order. Even reading strictly linearly within chapters is put into question at one point, since proceeding from line to line in chapter 34 simply doesn't produce sense (202–8). After reading this way for a few moments, readers discover that skipping every other line creates one narrative (a "clumsy novel," of the kind the protagonist's girlfriend reads) and that stringing together the skipped-over lines creates another (the protagonist's thoughts while presumably skimming the clumsy novel). After making this discovery, readers still have to decide how to make their way through the chapter: whether to read all of one text and then return to read the other, for instance, or whether to follow a few lines of one and then back up to follow a few lines of the other. (I tried to read two lines at a time, attempting to follow both sequences at once, but had to abandon this quickly since I just couldn't keep track of the sense of each while looking at both.) In any case, the pattern breaks down at chapter's end, where the novel being read ends before the protagonist's thoughts and the very last paragraph demands line-to-line reading once again.

The hopscotched reading raises expectations about the relationship between the order and the content of the chapters only to then undermine them. The chapters of the third section (subtitled "Expendable Chapters") read in the first part of the sequence are mainly philosophical considerations, almost like epigraphs. But just when one begins to think, aha, there's a pattern to the hopscotching—an alternation of narrative content in the early chapters with reflective passages in the later ones— one discovers narrative content, even new characters, in those supposedly dispensable later chapters.

Perhaps the most important disorientation and attendant self-consciousness promoted by the hopscotched sequence is about the "size" of the book itself. Even though, as I have already stated, there are a set number of pages between the two covers of the book, the novel is long enough and the chapters numerous enough that when reading in the hopscotched order, readers never really know how much of the book they have finished and how much lies ahead without checking the listing of the entire sequence on the Table of Instructions page. Even this chart is long enough that readers would have to reconstruct it in numerical order to be sure that it includes every chapter (which, again, it does not).

The "end" of the entire (hopscotched) sequence makes most apparent to readers this idea of the flexibility of the size of the book as well as of the importance of their own role, for it sends readers ping-ponging between chapters 131 and 58. That is to say, the deictic at the end of chapter 131 ([-58]) sends readers to chapter 58 where the deictic at the end ([-131]) sends them back to chapter 131 and so on. The book doesn't conclude on its own; to put this idea in terms of Talk, the text-as-statement never stops displaying orientation to an answering to follow. *Readers* have to consciously decide to ignore this particular matter if they want to finish reading the novel. If readers consult the Table of Instructions they find:

-131-58-131-

In my framework of the text as Talk, this last hyphen indicates that readers get to take the last turn by returning to reread chapters, by deciding to stop adding to the "chain" and stop reading, or perhaps by deciding to write additional chapters.

Like the first decision about "which book" within *Hopscotch* to read or the last about how to end one's conversation with the novel, the hopscotched reading is designed to make readers aware of the amount of control they exercise when reading. I disagree with analyses like Simpkins's that claim, "by pretending to waive his control over the reader, Cortázar tries to deceive the reader into following his guidance to the text" (1990: 66). Although I can speak with certainty about only my own experience, the hopscotched order promoted my sense of independence. Immediately after deciding to read in the hopscotched order, I had to decide if and when I was going to read the pair of epigraphs to the book that follow the Table of Instructions—there are no directives about the epigraphs. I also remember thinking early on that the mental bridges I made between chapters were facilitated by the exigencies of getting there. Locating the next chapter in the sequence provided a pause in which I could reflect on what I'd just read and wonder about what I was about to read. Again, one can pause over any moment in any book, but the process of finding the next chapter in Cortázar's novel automatically provides the time for readers to do so. And readers can take as much time as they want to get there. Responding to the statement of the text by flipping to the recommended next chapter in the sequence also afforded the opportunity to create my own path through the book by stopping to read or reread something along the way that wasn't "prescribed." Even when, in contrast, I tried to follow directions exactly—in the metaphor of hopscotch, I tried to jump directly to the correct square—I found myself reflecting on my own actions, not on the book's control over them. The few times I actually succeeded in turning directly to the start of the aimed-for chapter, I felt a little thrill, a thrill I would liken to the surprise of executing a literary performative as discussed in the previous chapter. But these magical moments cannot be programmed by the author the way literary performatives can. Jumping "precisely," like choosing not to jump or not to jump yet or to stop along the way, is a reply of the reader. From the perspective of Talk, readers' interaction with the parts of the text makes Cortázar's work an interesting progenitor of hypertext more than his linking of multiple texts (the chapters in *Hopscotch*, the lexias in hypertexts). Let me turn now to how "readers" ("visitors," "players") take their turns in various hypertexts by selecting the sequence of lexias, by writing new lexias, and by redesigning elements of the program that produces the narrative.

Interactive Talk as Sequencing

Like Cortázar's novel *Hopscotch*, the issues of which textual segments—lexias—will be read and in what order are at the heart of the Talk of many interactive stories. In the world of websites, in particular, reader-visitor activity mainly consists of selecting and sequencing things to be read. A typical example of an interactive story on the Web is "Biochip5's and wDSZ06C's The Phantom Tollbooth Interactive Story" (located at: *www .geocities.com/Times Square/Fortress/2435/phantomtoll-main.html*). Based on Norton Juster's beloved children's book *The Phantom Tollbooth* (1961), this website offers visitors the opportunity to play the role of the novel's protagonist and to make their way through a series of adventures (based on part of the novel) by choosing specific actions at specific points. In terms of Talk, the "statements" of the hypertext involve presenting a lexia narrating a specific amount of action and offering choice icons that will in turn trigger specific lexias. Visitors' "replies" involve reading the lexia and using the mouse or other device to indicate one choice among the two or three offered at any point. This triggers the subsequent statement of the hypertext and so on. With this overview in mind, I'm going to describe this initial hypertext example in detail in order to coordinate the terminology of Talk used in this study with the terminology of interactive computing. Subsequent descriptions will just mention features that differ from this basic model.

Making one's way to a website is a process that I'm assuming is familiar to my readers. To extend to computing an observation made by Chafe about writing and reading, the process requires elaborate resources external to the bodies of users (1994: 43–44). Once one has made one's way to the welcome page of the "Phantom Tollbooth" website, the hypertext offers its first statement in the form of an underlined command: "Click this text to start the story." There are two dimensions to this statement that reveal its "orientation to some kind of answering to follow." The first is the appellative force of the second-person pronoun, which in this instance is revealed through the imperative mode, and the second is the underlining, a convention of hypertext. Underlining signals that another lexia can be accessed from that place. The actual message reinforces the idea that the hypertext-as-statement is seeking an answering. By using the computer mouse or keys to place the cursor—that graphic element Landow calls the representation of the reader's presence in the text (1992: 44)—anywhere on this underlined portion, visitors will see an image of a small hand. I consider the appearance of this hand the hypertext's reply to the visitor moving the cursor to a location where exchange can occur. The appearance of the next lexia is the hypertext's reply to the visitor clicking with this hand, and so on. In other words, *hypertext facilitates the multiple turns characteristic of ordinary conversation.*

This specific hypertext's next turn begins with a short paragraph telling about Milo (the novel's protagonist) and his decision to go to "Dictionopolis . . . having no idea of what he was getting into." The next paragraph announces: "That's where we'll stop for now. In the rest of this story, you are going to be Milo. If you're ready to go on, let's Continue with the story." This time the explicit verbal instruction to visitors about how to take their turn ("Click this text to start the story") is replaced by the more implicit verbal invitation to continue the Talk ("let's continue"); the underlining again indicates that the matter raised is the issue of clicking. So far, I would suggest, the clicking functions like the turning of pages when reading: if you want to get the next segment, you have to click. But in hypertext, it is even harder than in *Hopscotch* to know what is coming next. One doesn't "see" how much text—or rather how many statements of the hypertext—lies ahead. One only sees one screen at a time.[7]

Once visitors have responded by clicking, the next lexia of the "Phantom Tollbooth" appears, this one narrated in the second person, present tense: "You find yourself driving along a country highway, and looking back, see no trace of the tollbooth or your house." That visitors are supposed to identify with "you" is reinforced by the end of this lexia (as well as the part of statement in the previous lexia: "you are going to be Milo"): "You now have a choice: Drive along the road paying careful attention, or lay back and relax." This sentence is followed by a small blank space and then:

Choice #1
Choice #2

The matter that has been raised by the text this time is selection of narrative action. Visitors' next turn involves (a) making a choice ("drive and pay careful attention" or "lay back and relax"), (b) coordinating the choice laid out in the lexia and the specific deixis indicating how to make the reply: Choice #1 or Choice #2, (c) physically manipulating the cursor over the desired choice, and (d) actually selecting that choice by clicking. If visitors select the first choice, the hypertext produces another lexia filled with "your" adventures in Dictionopolis, including finding a dog named Tock, exploring a Word Market, and meeting a creature called a Spelling Bee (all are plot and character elements from the novel). Reading through the paragraph, the visitor will arrive at another binary choice: "Trust the Spelling Bee or Don't trust him," and then a confirmation that "The choice is yours" followed again by: Choice #1 or Choice #2.

To backtrack: if a visitor decides to opt for the second original choice ("lay back and relax"), the text also replies to the visitor's turn, but in rather a different tone, seeking a slightly different kind of answering: "Don't you want to try something new?!! Get your fat rear in gear and press the 'Back' button on your browser just above the location!" In other words, instead of giving a new sequence in the narrative, the visitor is berated for having made a bad choice and is instructed on how to take a turn that will result in facing the previous options once again. Or to put it another way, in a turn somewhat analogous to *Hopscotch*'s ping-ponging between chapters 131 and 58, the "Phantom Tollbooth" website is looking for an answering that involves continuation of the Talk.

The actual mechanism recommended for taking one's turn at this stage is not the underlining but the "back" arrow found in the options menu (computer functions) of most websites, above the web address of the site being visited ("location").[8] This kind of deixis may involve no words at all but just the image of the arrow, or the arrow may be labeled "back." There is even another way to take one's turn: specific lexias can be accessed directly by using a web address for that exact segment of text.[9] That is to say, here, as in most hypertexts, visitors have some choice about not only sequencing but also the physical procedure for taking their turn. The number of possibilities depends on the actual web design (something usually not under visitors' control), as well as on visitors' knowledge of how to use the technology to access the lexias.

When visitors who have opted for the "relax" choice respond to the matter that has been raised by returning to the previous set of options—one must return or quit playing altogether—that previous "statement" of the hypertext will look the same, with one difference. The deictic of the choice they had originally selected (Choice #2) now appears in red. Though this detail may seem trivial (and may not be registered by casual users of hypertext), it is important for an analysis of the hypertext as Talk, because this change in color represents the hypertext's reply to the visitor's previous turn. Computer technology makes possible not only multiple turns but also "reply specific" multiple turns. Visitors who chose the first choice will never see the screen saying "Get your fat rear in gear" nor will they see "Choice #2" highlighted in red unless they backtrack (at which point they will see "Choice #1 highlighted in red) and select this other option.

Subsequent turns in the "Phantom Tollbooth Interactive Story" function similarly. One choice (in which "you," the protagonist, demonstrate desire to opt for action) tends to trigger a lexia that advances the plot, and the other a lexia that berates "your" choice and sends "you" back to the previous options to make another, a better choice. If you move back, there is a "trace" that you have been there before in the form of the deictic for your previous choice that appears in red. As the "Phantom Tollbooth" unfolds, there are sometimes three options and sometimes an amount of narrative in the lexia triggered by a "bad" choice. Short of choosing to terminate your visit early by signing off, any path through the site—in Talk terms, continuing to reply to the hypertext's statements—will eventually get all visitors to a concluding lexia that narrates your triumph over the demons and your return home: "CONGRATULATIONS! YOU HAVE COMPLETED 'The Phantom Tollbooth Interactive Story' THE END." In other words, all possible paths through the story lead to the same concluding lexia.

Like Cortázar's novel, the "Phantom Tollbooth Interactive Story" has a set number of lexias. Some readers of Cortázar will end up reading every page by following their own order (remember, neither the narrator's "first book" or "second book" actually leads to a reading of every page), and, similarly, some visitors to the "Phantom Tollbooth" site can figure out how to make choices that will allow them to see every lexia. But no matter which order you read *Hopscotch*, the actual words on the page are the same, though, naturally, they may have a different significance for a reader depending on when they are read. Depending on the choices visitors select in "Phantom Tollbooth," however, what is seen *can* change, even if only slightly. I am trying to spell out this point very clearly, because though the changes and their significance in this particular example may seem trivial, the technology of hypertext allows visitor-readers' replies to impact what appears on the screen. This is, of course, one reason they are referred to as "interactive."

There is another feature of the "Phantom Tollbooth Interactive Story" that I'd like to mention because it is typical of many interactive stories, at least on the web. The welcome page announcing the title and inviting visitors to orient to the matter that has been raised by clicking to start the story, also invites visitors to write to the website designers: two e-mail addresses are included. While the exact nature of the response desired is not indicated, these addresses function to invite interaction between designer and visitor, "writer" and "reader." This proposal to correspond could be thought of as just an updated version of any reader writing to the author—Henriot to Butor, for instance—since it occurs in another circuit of communication. But when there are hot links (links that can be directly accessed from the screen one is looking at) to the home pages of the web designers, as there are here and in many other interactive stories on the Web, the interaction between "author" and "reader" becomes much more direct and the issue of the boundaries of the "text" becomes much more complicated. My next example spells out some of the complications of invited "contact" between web designers, visitors, and the "story" itself.

Interactive Talk as Co-Writing

Visitors to "Gav and Peloso's Interactive Story" (*http://www.nuc.berkeley*
.edu/~gav/wayfarence/welcome.html) are offered some initial information on the welcome page of the website that indicates how this story
differs from ones like the "Phantom Tollbooth." As in any hypertext,
visitors have the opportunity to move about in multiple ways. But here,
visitors are also invited to write lexias: "This is a *moderated* [their em-
phasis] Choose-your-own-adventure type of story where YOU [their
bold] get to write the story. Follow the story as it grows and grows, taking
up much needed hard drive space. You can even copy down the story
location [their underlining and highlighting in blue] and come back to it
at a later date, to see how it's grown." On this initial page visitors are also
told that the site was started on August 21, 1995, and that it currently
(more than five years later) has 18,138 episodes (as of 5 December 2000);
this number increased regularly during the time I tracked the site (approximately one and a half years). After giving a brief overview of the
site, I'd like to focus on what visitors are actually being invited to do
or not do, that is, on what constitutes turn-taking within this interactive story and, specifically, to what extent such moves can be considered "co-writing."

While the "Phantom Tollbooth Interactive Story" is short and simple
enough to describe essentially all its parts, "Gav and Peloso's Interactive
Story" is so large that a review of the entire website is simply impossible.
I have already described most of the welcome page, which also includes
the links to the website's sponsor and to the home pages of the two
"authors," who significantly label themselves "programmer/designer"
(Gav, Darren Bleuel) and "conceptual designer" (Peloso, Chris Peloso).
Other links include a "story location" page, which explains how to directly access a particular part of the story, in order, for example, to return
to an episode and see how that strand of the story developed subsequent
to your last visit; and a "Story Writer's Guide" page, which explains the
guidelines for submissions of episodes. The vast amount of space on the
hard drive, as the welcome page puts it, is taken up by the thousands of
segments of this "adventure" story. Although it is theoretically possible
to follow all the story lines, it is humanly impossible; there are simply too
many, and they are being added to constantly. Turning to the kernel of
the site, to how it all begins, however, will give some indication of what

kinds of narrative unfold and, most importantly for our purposes here, of how visitors "reply."

Setting the story in process involves turns for hypertext and visitors similar to those described for the "Phantom Tollbooth." The welcome page contains an initial statement of the hypertext—"So, Start the Story!"—that, through the imperative and the underlining, indicates that visitors should reply by clicking. The hypertext's next turn offers a short text with two images: on the left what looks like a door with some light coming through under it, and on the right a chair with buttons and an electric cord. The text reads:

> Our story begins . . .
>
> You wake up from a disturbingly sleepless night a bit peckish and even more groggy. Your mind hasn't quite jumpstarted today, but you manage to pull yourself out of bed anyway. Perhaps, you think, a spot of caffeine will do the trick. Maybe then, you'll wake up enough to remember what it was you were supposed to do today, or at least recognize where you are.
>
> Rubbing the sleep stuff out of your eyes, you vaguely become aware of your surroundings. It's a relatively spare room, sporting only a chair and a bed for furniture. There is also a closed door, leading . . . well, somewhere to be sure.
>
> What would you like to do?
>
> Go through the door
>
> Sit in the chair[10]

As in the "Phantom Tollbooth," the underlining indicates the hypertext's orientation to a reply. Visitors display their orientation to this matter that has been raised by clicking on one choice or the other. But unlike our previous example, in this interactive story both options (sometimes there are three) will lead to a new lexia with narrative content, which in turn will offer options leading to new lexias with narrative content. That is to say, the story continues to branch, and each branch produces a narrative sequence. Visitors can of course move "backward" and then to another branch by using the back arrow or the lexia addresses that have been discussed above (and are also explained at the site link called "story location"). Though, again, there are theoretically a concrete number of ways to move through the site, the number of lexias is large enough that an actual visitor to the site has the impression of creating her unique story through the particular sequence she is selecting.

If visitors continue to move forward by making choices, they will eventually get to a screen that confirms the impression of "going where no one has gone before"; it reads: "This portion of the story does not exist! You may, if you wish, write this portion of the story. If so, simply fill out the form below. Otherwise, press the 'Back' button on your web browser to return to the story and pick a different choice. Or return to the Welcome Page and start over." At this point, the hypertext displays orientation to an answering of a different sort, offering visitors the option to make their next move by actually writing the continuation of the thread of the story they have been following (through the previous choices they have selected in their previous turns). How to take a turn of this kind is described in relative detail, both in the continuation of the lexia quoted in part above and in a link mentioned previously called "Story Writer's Guide." In addition to technical information, like using a double carriage return to indicate a new paragraph or not trying to embed a link to another website, the guide includes legal information ("all submissions become the property of Darren Bleuel and Chris Peloso to do with as their evil minds see fit—nothing personal") and stylistic suggestions ("keep it real"; "don't portray the opposite sex as empty airheads or willing hunks"; "don't contradict previous links"). Two categories particularly impinge on interactivity: "Stick to the Genre" and "The Reader's Choices." Under the former, the web designers admonish potential co-writers to write the correct amount, not too much, not too little, and even more importantly, to continue the narrative mode by using second person, present tense. About this mode, Gav comments: "Maybe some day, I'll start up a new storyline, but this one is written in the second person and present tense to make it seem like the story is happening to YOU and that it is happening NOW. This means don't write 'I opened the sarcophagus.' Instead write 'You open the sarcophagus.'" Similarly, when offering guidelines about how to frame the "Reader's Choices" that should appear at the conclusion of the episode, Gav suggests coming up with an action "the reader can take"; he spells this out:

> Good Choice: Look for your leather bomber jacket
> Bad Choice: You find your leather bomber jacket

One can chuckle about the pedantic tone or about the adolescent examples, but as we have seen in the previous chapter and in the previous example of hypertext, Gav's narrative decisions invite reader identification in a way that writing in other modes simply wouldn't. Furthermore, the actual number of writers contributing to this site confirms that this formula elicits response. In a final section of the Writer's Guide, visitor-co-writers are invited to e-mail Gav in cases where they wish to participate even more fully, that is, if they wish to break out of the pattern by including extra choices, graphs, different colors, links to other websites, or circular links.

"Reply" in the form of writing an episode is important to my notion of Talk not just because it represents another kind of "turn" that visitors can take but also because it must be seen as even more participatory than sequencing. Furthermore, it affects our notions of "author," "text," and "reader." Once visitor-co-writers have composed their episode, the interaction continues, so to speak, though not in the instantaneous format we have been considering so far. Visitors submit their episodes at the website and then can quit the website, return to its beginning, or backtrack. If they have replied by writing, they will have to check at a later date to discover if the hypertext has Talked back, that is, to see if their episode has been incorporated into the interactive story and if others have responded to it by writing additional episodes.

To be sure, the original designers and maintainers of this site retain a certain authorial role since they review all potential additional lexias and their attendant departures from the guidelines. And yet, I submit that "Gav and Peloso's Interactive Story" takes "exchange" to a new level. Its founders welcome new portions of text, feedback, and suggestions about even the design of the site. The vast majority of its thousands of lexias have been written by visitors to the site, not by its original designers. Lexias acknowledge the idea of co-writing by prominently featuring the names (code or real) and the e-mail addresses (if desired) of the people who have submitted the episode directly above the text they have written. The inclusion of e-mail addresses in particular invites contact between any visitors to the site with the co-writers, potentially creating an even stronger sense of collaboration among those who have interacted with the story.

There are numerous communities organized around a story in cyberspace today, sometimes clearly identifiable through a website or chatspace and sometimes more loosely affiliated through random e-mail contact. Some of the larger communities have formed around television soap operas, where the latest turn in the plot, introduction of a new character, or departure of a familiar one is evaluated or where desires for future developments are expressed. Such communities have also become a conduit for the last type of interactivity I have space to consider here, where aficionados of a particular video game exchange not just opinions about the game but actual pieces of its design. I will return to this type of communal interaction after introducing the idea of Talk in video games.

Interactive Talk as Co-designing

"Gav and Peloso's Interactive Story" website is constructed so that visitors cannot directly add episodes or make changes to the hypertext but rather must pass their suggestions through the keepers of the site. A recent trend in video-game technology takes interaction further by allowing access to the actual tools for creating the worlds and stories in the program and thereby allowing "players" to literally co-design the game. Though I am quickly reaching the end of my own competence, I want to include this phenomenon, because if computer technology in general has provided for the apotheosis and endgame of Talk, this particular development provides for the apotheosis of the apotheosis and the endgame of the endgame. At a point when the size of the video-game industry has reached the size of the movie industry in the United States (Rothstein 1994: 1), I clearly cannot present any kind of overview of Talk in video games. So I will continue as I did above by presenting one example that sheds some light on the general issues.

Like many video games, "Unreal" (published by GT Interactive) requires particularly elaborate computer equipment to access all dimensions of the game.[11] Similarly elaborate are the procedures for loading the game onto your equipment via a CD-ROM. If you succeed in these procedures (which one would analyze in a more computer-centered discussion of video games than this one), you will be confronted with the popular video-game genre of "kill or be killed," also referred to as "hack and slay" (Turkle 1995: 181), in which your role is to survive by killing off every creature that would like to kill you. There is a back story that sets up the particular scenario of why you are engaged in this mortal combat. As a prisoner in a space ship that was on route to a penal colony, you crash on a mysterious planet. Emerging from the wreckage, you see a spectacularly dramatic landscape, including sky, mountains, and water; however, most of the flora and fauna are out to kill you. Luckily, some of the creatures you encounter do want to help you. The default version (if one doesn't modify the structure of the game—more on this below) ends with you escaping the planet, but in a craft that doesn't have enough fuel to break out of the planet's orbit.

Even though what appears on the computer screen is strikingly different from what appears on the screen when arriving at a website of the kind we have looked at above—note the addition of sophisticated moving images and sound and the absence of printed words—the basic principles of playing the game resemble the basic principles of moving through an interactive story at a website, though turn-taking usually happens at an exponentially faster pace. The game presents its statement in the form of moving images and sound. Players reply by manipulating the mouse and clicking, and the game replies with more moving images and sound. (The game can also be configured to be played with a joystick or just the keyboard.) Players' presence in the game is not marked by an arrow or a straight blinking line but rather by perspective—what one sees on the screen is shown from your, the protagonist's, viewpoint, including various objects with which players can affect what goes on in the world of the game. For example, as you are trying to escape the vehicle that crashed here, you see and can seize (by moving the mouse) a "dispersion pistol"; other weapons that become available to you include rocket shooters and grenades. When you click to fire, the game responds with the image and sound of a speeding bullet or rocket, followed by the attendant effects on whatever you were aiming at. Shooting across a canyon will produce a different image, sound, and result than shooting into a building. The principles of multiple turns and of specific replies to players' specific replies are not only operative here, but operative by many degrees of magnitude. These "degrees of interaction" become additional elements for interaction between player and game. By taking a turn that involves hitting keys to open the options menu, a player can alter some aspects of the visual or audio dimensions of the world of the game, as well as the characters within it. Using the same options menu, one can change the speed with which the Talk, the taking of turns, proceeds. If players take a turn that involves reducing the speed of the action, the game replies not only by proceeding more slowly but also by adding frames to smooth the animation—hence my assessment of video games like this one as a culmination of the idea of Talk.

I contend that what I have described so far still falls within the realm of Talk because the basic principle of turn-taking is operative, albeit with a responsiveness that some would argue exceeds that of my model, face-to-face human interaction. My assessment of games like "Unreal" as the endgame of talk fiction, on the other hand, comes from a different aspect of the experience. Via part of the software called "Unreal Ed," the Unreal level editor, players can point and click their way to creating their own world with their own creatures. You start with a three-dimensional grid to which you import geometric shapes. Then you can build up your world by giving those shapes properties like height, radius, translucency, texture, and so on. You can populate the world you have created with opponent creatures or you can program this world for combat between yourself and other human opponents moving in the world you have created. In terms of the definition of narrative I introduced at the beginning of this chapter, "players" act more like authors—in this context, game co-designers—by changing not only the sequence but also the events, the characters, and the representation of all of this. Potentially, the only aspect that stays the same is the skeletal plot of trying to kill one's adversaries. Although from a computer programming point of view there may be technical reasons to consider the variations fundamentally related, from a literary point of view, this bare plot is not enough to justify consideration of players' versions as the same "text" as the "text" they first bought.[12]

I return now to the "communities" mentioned at the end of the last section because these cybercommunities can provide opponents against whom you can play on-line or from whom you can receive "pieces" for the world you have created (see websites such as *unreal.org* or *unreal-nation.com*). At the core of it, the same translation of language into digital computer code that allows for the recombination of lexias in hypertext allows for the trading of new monsters or new landscapes of "Unreal." I offer two observations about this activity of using the "Unreal Ed" and trading what you produce with it: first, this on-line interaction can be looked at as a new shape of human experience of the kind that McLuhan predicted technology would engender (1964: 302).[13] Second, it effectively transforms the notions of "an" "author," "a" "text," "a" "reader" to a point where we can no longer consider it in the framework of Talk I have developed in this study.[14]

Although huge amounts of money and talent are being expended to develop an interactive product that would attract a broader and larger audience, the verdict of both experts and the public is still out. In an interview about one of the first interactive movies, a so-called interfilm ("I'm Your Man," 1992, produced by Controlled Entropy Entertainment of Manhattan), Bran Ferren, head of Associates and Ferren, a Long Island company that develops technology for the entertainment industry, said, "If what you're trying to accomplish is telling a story and entertaining, you don't necessarily want people determining choices. That's why you have a director and producer" (as quoted in Grimes 1993). On the other hand, Denise Caruso, one of the technology correspondents for the *New York Times*, suggests that interactive (video) games have had such great commercial success precisely because of "people determining choices." As Caruso argues the point: "your actions have a material, measurable effect on what happens next. You do something, the game responds, and you react to its response. The result is dramatic tension—an emotional, absorbing relationship between you and the game that feels real because the outcome is unscripted and unpredictable" (1996). What seems necessary for the future development of interactive entertainment, according to Mike Ribero, executive vice president of marketing for Sega of America, is to tap other emotions besides the competition that structures almost every interactive video game (as quoted in Caruso 1996).[15]

I submit that the novels and stories considered in this study have done just that. Talk fiction taps numerous emotions through a format that creates absorbing relationships between you and the text. The variety of replies—whether a sense of responsibility to pass on stories that sustain communities of my storytelling mode, or of helping to enable testimony to trauma of my witnessing mode, or of performing a role with which one can and cannot identify of my apostrophic mode—leads me to believe that literary Talk produces distinctive kinds of pleasure. These pleasures ensue in part from recognizing the cultural work that writing and reading accomplish, and they assure me that prose fiction won't be disappearing anytime soon.

Notes

PREFACE

1. Douglas Biber points out that whereas for twentieth-century linguists speech is considered primary over writing, the lay view is that written, literary language is true language (1988: 6). Robin Lakoff reports on fears of the triumph of illiteracy because of the resurgence of the oral and suggests that nothing of value will be lost by it (1982: 257, and my discussion of Lakoff in chapter 1). The work of Sven Birkerts illustrates this paranoia. And then there are academic views that not only take the end of print culture as a given, but celebrate it (e.g., Case 1996). Mitchell Stephens's recent study, *The Rise of the Image, The Fall of the Word* (1998) offers hope of a more balanced assessment of shifts from literacy, particularly toward the visual, which can't be my subject here.

2. Marshall McLuhan's idea of the whole world as a single global village has been rightly criticized for glossing over real differences—especially with regard to access to technology—that exist in various places. While specifically aiming not to ignore cultural differences, I use McLuhan's phrase to emphasize that there is indeed no place on earth today that has not been touched in some way by technology. In this sense, all cultures of the world do participate in secondary orality, though, granted, not in the same fashion. As Brian Stock puts it, "Societies do not evolve at the same rate nor in the same way under the influence of given media of communications" (1990: 9).

3. I have argued this point more fully in Kacandes 1997: 9.

4. The standard phrase is "talk in interaction," that is to say, the role of talk in accomplishing interpersonal tasks. I modify the phrase to reveal one of its premises: that talk itself is interactive.

5. Whereas Nobel literary prizes have been awarded to two Greek poets, George Seferis (1963) and Odysseus Elytis (1979), no Greek novelist has been so distinguished.

1. SECONDARY ORALITY

1. On the idea of conversation as the foundation for other forms of communication, see Mannheim and Tedlock 1995: 1; Nofsinger 1991: 2, 4–5, 107; Zimmerman and Boden 1991: 18; Goodwin and Heritage 1990: 289; Chafe

1994: 41, 49. The polemical idea that all language is produced dialogically is anathema to certain branches of linguistics that consider the individual actor to be the source of the parole and language to flow from active speaker to passive recipient. Goodwin and Heritage finger Saussure for bracketing out "the interactive matrix that constitutes the natural home for language" (285). Despite his inclusion of the conative function, Jakobson's model, commonly cited by literary scholars, also propagates a notion of active addresser and passive addressee (1960).

2. For a helpful overview of Goffman's rich career, see Burns (1992).

3. West and Zimmerman (1982) and Goodwin and Heritage (1990) offer concise reviews of the development of conversation analysis and its basic principles.

4. For a convincing explanation of why such statements are so unnatural, that is to say, why we are highly unlikely to ever hear a sentence like this in spontaneous conversation, see Chafe 1994: 17, 84, 108.

5. On the idea of language games, see, for example, Wittgenstein's *Blue and Brown Books* (1969: 77). Discussions of Wittgenstein's notion can be found in Baker and Hacker (1980: 47ff) and Harris (1988: 25–26). For an early use of the concept by Goffman, see *Encounters* (1961: 34–36); for a full deployment of the idea to understand talk, see *Forms of Talk* (1981, esp. 24).

6. Of course, there could be intermediate outbursts of applause or catcalling that register response to part of the "statement."

7. See Jenny Mandelbaum's concept of "shared storytelling" (1987; 1989; also Nofsinger 1991, esp. 160ff).

8. See Goodwin and Heritage 1990:291. The list of such specifications is almost endless, but some examples include Goffman on radio, which will be discussed below (1981: 197–327); Greatbatch and Heritage on the television news interview (Greatbatch 1988; Heritage and Greatbatch 1991); Hopper on telephone conversations (1992); Atkinson and Drew on talk in judicial settings (1979); Byrne and Long (1976) or West (1984) on patients and doctors; and Whalen and Zimmerman on citizen calls to the police (1990).

9. The use of e-mail is now changing the nature of interpersonal communication once again. However, e-mail should not be viewed as a simple return to written communication. Sherry Turkle, among others, shows how e-mail and the related interaction in MOOs (multiuser domains or dimensions [MUDs] of the Object Oriented variety) must themselves be regarded as a new form that makes use of written and oral communication strategies (1995).

10. On the dependence of secondary orality on literacy, see Ong 1982: 136. Although it is not directly relevant to this discussion, the global dissemina-

tion of communication technologies allows some cultures and subcultures to jump from a primary to a secondary orality without themselves passing through a fully literate phase. Also, some commentators are beginning to speak of a "new literacy" or of a "post-textual literacy," by which they want to reference the way digital processing has proliferated the circulation of images and (nonverbal) sound that future educated classes will need to be familiar with as well (Markoff 1994).

11. Chafe never mentions braille, but my assumption is that touch would function similarly to sight in his argument.

12. For a caveat on the dichotomy spontaneous/nonspontaneous, see Lakoff 1982: 241.

13. Recent fossil research into the size of the hypoglossal canal suggests that humans may have developed the ability to speak even earlier than previously assumed—as early as 400,000 years ago, perhaps 350,000 years prior to any known human drawing (Wilford 1998).

14. From playing certain video games, some children have learned to shoot accurately without ever having held an actual gun in their hands. In at least one of the cases of school violence in the United States in the late 1990s, the student gunman is known to have never fired a gun before the day he stole a pistol and fired eight shots, hitting eight people and killing three of them. According to Dave Grossman, a former Army officer, professor at West Point and the University of Arkansas, and author of *On Killing: The Psychological Cost of Learning to Kill in War and Society* (1995), "when Michael Carneal was shooting, he fired one shot at each kid. He simply fired one shot at everything that popped up on his screen." To appreciate the effectiveness of video games as teacher, Grossman offers the comparison to professional law-enforcement officers who on average hit fewer than one in five shots (as quoted in Caruso 1999). Though I would argue that even this chilling example should not lead us into the trap of categorically condemning recent technologies—it takes a very long time for changes in mental hard-wiring to be passed on to large portions of the human population—we ignore their effects at our peril.

15. This phrase serves as the subtitle for Ong's 1982 book *Orality and Literacy*. For his hypotheses about the way writing structures consciousness see 78–116; on the psychodynamics of orality, see 31–77.

16. It is interesting to note that Marconi, the inventor of radio, envisioned it as a superior alternative to the telephone for "point-to-point communication." It took about twenty-five years for its broadcasting potential to be fully realized (Douglas 1987: xvi).

17. As quoted in Douglas 1987: 308. It is fascinating to me that some late-twentieth- and early-twenty-first-century commentators are making similar claims for the latest round of communication technology. Citing such innovations as caller identification for screening phone calls and internet software that allows downloading without banner advertising, *Boston Globe* columnist John Ellis predicts, "Soon all of us will have technology that will allow us to block out all messages and interruptions we choose not to tolerate" (1999: 45).

18. Jane Shattuc mentions that while doing research for her book, *The Talking Cure: TV Talk Shows and Women*, all she had to do was enunciate the words "talk show," and her interlocutors would react strongly (1997: vii).

19. On the other hand, I don't want to deny the existence of some more direct technological influence, for example, that of the telephone and telephone answering machine on Mariella Righini's *La Passion, Ginette* (1983) and Nicholson Baker's *Vox* (1992).

20. On the age children (babies) learn to view television, see Allen 1992b: 132 and Lemish 1987: 33–57. I find it particularly revealing about U.S. society that more households now have television sets than telephones. For these and other statistics on numbers of viewers of television in the United States and around the world, see Allen 1992a: 1. Given that in a single day 3.5 billion hours around the world will be devoted to watching television, Allen's assessment that "except for oral storytelling, television is the most prolific and important narrative medium in the world today," seems a reasonable hypothesis (1992a: 1, 26). As an example of intermedia influence, see E. L. Doctorow's argument about the way demands of the film industry have changed the length of contemporary novels (1999).

21. In radio, of course, the announcer is making it possible for listeners to know what's happening at a game they cannot attend and see for themselves. Action override on television as well as viewers in a stadium listening to a radio broadcast of the game they are watching make apparent the additional value of being part of a group that shares a given experience. In these instances the announcers' superior knowledge of the players and the game may further enhance watching the game as an end in itself, but it also bonds two consciousnesses that are experiencing the same thing (see Chafe 1994: 281).

22. On direct address in cinema, see Lawrence 1994.

23. This is not surprising given that Goffman's data derive mainly from the 1950s and early 1960s, the period that gave birth to the form the broadcast industry calls talk radio. Though Goffman does not remark it, radio prior

to the 1950s rarely "involved audience participation apart from letters read and responded to on the air" (Munson 1993: 7).

24. Goffman does mention parenthetically the existence of "phone-in" shows and even remarks the strengthening of the effect of direct address through the image of the announcer/host looking into the camera, but he does not discuss the television talk show genre directly (1981: 235–36).

25. Munson points out that relative to other forms of radio, talk radio is an expensive format (1993: 3). But the form began to flourish, despite its expensive production cost, when stations and sponsors realized its attractiveness to potential advertisers precisely because a lot of people were listening. According to James Ledbetter (1998), commercial radio is the most profitable communications medium in America today, with profits in the range of 30 percent (as opposed to 8–12 percent for newspapers and 1–2 percent for books). In the (expensive) world of television, the talk show is relatively cheap to produce and reaps huge profits (see Shattuc 1997: 16, 66).

26. See Morse 1985; Heritage and Greatbatch 1991; Kozloff 1992: 80.

27. Consider, for example, the continued popularity of the *Oprah Winfrey Show* even after she moved away from sensationalist topics—which some critics have claimed is the only attraction of talk shows.

28. In any case, it is the reason I will not take up the content of the shows here; for such analyses see Levin 1987; Munson 1993; Laufer 1995; Shattuc 1997.

29. Morse even calls it a "fictional form of dialogue" (1985: 15), though I would suggest that this formulation effaces the reality effect.

30. Consider the case of Jenny Jones's talk show in which the show was held responsible for manipulating a guest in ways that lawyers claimed led to him murdering a gay man who revealed his attraction to him on the show (see Bradsher 1999).

31. Putting Habermas's notion of the public sphere more fully into dialogue with Ong's analysis of the transition from literacy into secondary orality would probably produce fascinating results; unfortunately, I can only suggest it here.

32. Radio and television developed their very forms on the basis of commercial logic to encourage mass consumption. As Allen bluntly explains: "Within the context of American commercial television, at least, the principal aim of broadcasting is not to entertain, enlighten, or provide a public service; it is to make a profit. . . . The economic value of this system, measured strictly in terms of revenues generated by broadcasters, is more than $25 billion per year in the United States alone" (1992a: 17). An interesting development is the promotion of "serious" literature by television,

most notably, through talk-show host Oprah Winfrey's "book club." Although exact "before and after" figures are hard to come by, Bayles suggests that generally, "every book [Oprah] has recommended has experienced a significant bump in sales, and many have become runaway best sellers" (1999). Carvajal reports that writer Melinda Haynes's first novel received a second printing of 750,000 copies (up from an initial printing of 6,800) after *Mother of Pearl* was designated Oprah's summer 1999 book selection.

33. Goffman 1981, McLuhan 1964, and Munson 1993 all comment explicitly on the critical role played by the invention of the microphone, which could pick up the nuances of the human voice.

34. Lakoff's definition of oral coincides well with Ong's: participatory mystique, the fostering of a communal sense, and a concentration on the present moment (Ong 1982: 136).

35. Lakoff is well aware that there are nonspontaneous oral forms of discourse and spontaneous written ones, but she builds her argument on the dominant associations we have developed with writing and speech (1982: 241).

36. In addition to the characterizations of Ong, Chafe, and Goffman considered above, see Philipsen's idea of the "communal function" (1989: 79).

37. As far as my research can uncover, the term "narratee" was introduced by Gerald Prince in his study "Notes toward a Categorization of Fictional 'Narratees'" (1971). Gérard Genette appears to have come to the same term at approximately the same time, using the French equivalent, *narrataire,* in "Discours du récit" (1972: 265). In the foundational 1966 volume of *Communications*, Roland Barthes (18–19) and Tzvetan Todorov (146–47) describe the function within narrative that the term "narratee" is meant to cover, but without using the term.

38. I follow Shlomith Rimmon-Kenan's suggestion that we not think of narrators as "absent" or "present" but rather as characterized by different forms and degrees of perceptibility (1989: 89). Prince offers the terms "primary" and "secondary" to distinguish between narratees who hear or read the entire narration and those who hear only part (1973: 187–92).

39. Goffman's suggestion to think about participants in communication as "enacted capacities" rather than necessarily single, distinct, embodied individuals could address the concerns of Rimmon-Kenan (1989: 88), Suleiman (1981: 92) and Warhol (1989: 30) about "implied authors" and "implied readers," since as "enacted capacities," "implied authors" and "implied readers" would not need to be "consistently distinguished" from real authors, narrators, real readers, and narratees (Rimmon-Kenan 1989: 88).

40. Julio Cortázar's novel *Hopscotch* leads Scott Simpkins to a similar observation (1990: 61). I will take up this case in chapter 5.

41. This issue returns us to an earlier observation that the participants in Talk are not symmetrical. While a real reader can regard a move as an answering, my participant-narrator obviously cannot. Since authors are sentient beings, it is at least theoretically possible to discover whether they would consider a particular reply as an answering, whereas narrators cannot even theoretically be consulted.

42. Landow makes a similar point when raising the issue of cultural changes that will occur in response to the invention of hypertext (1992: 30–31).

43. See Feather 1985, 1988; Plumb 1982; Raven 1992; McKenzie 1976, to name just a few.

44. See also Tedlock 1983, Duranti 1986, Haviland 1986.

45. As I stated in my preface, I am trying to offer an alternate way of looking at the development of twentieth-century narrative literature. Therefore, I am using "post-Modernist" here not as a reference to a literary style or period but rather as a shorthand for what came after the (Modernist) triumph of a noncommunicative conception of literature.

46. Exceptions include highly characterized first-person narrators who self-consciously set out to tell a story of someone they have known, for example, Serenus Zeitblom's account of his friend Adrian Leverkühn in Thomas Mann's *Doktor Faustus* (1947).

47. For other efforts to expand the traditional notion and concept of deixis, see Green 1995. My thanks to David Herman for bringing this volume to my attention.

48. I will mainly use the term "second person" due to its familiarity and as a matter of convenience to indicate the "pronoun of address." As several of the studies of individual texts show, it is sometimes the third-person pronoun and sometimes the first-person inclusive that invites exchange. See Fludernik 1993: 219 and 1994a: 286.

49. Naturally, the activity is more complicated than this; I will lay out the many factors involved in playing Calvino's game in chapter 4.

2. STORYTELLING

1. This is reply not in the sociolinguistic sense of reply introduced in my previous chapter, but in African American scholar Robert Stepto's intertextual sense of whole texts that "answer the call of certain prefiguring texts" (1991: x).

2. I treat this fascinating communicative situation of apostrophe in chapter 4.

3. The idea of the Talking Book as a trope probably needs even further investigation to determine how widespread a cultural realm actually relies on it. In my own haphazard reading I have come across one even earlier scene of

an illiterate German watching a monk read that has several common features, although obviously not the dimension of race (see Grimmelshausen, *Die Abenteuer des Simplicissimus* 1669).

4. For information about versions of the tale of the Talking Book, see Carretta's notes to Equiano (1995: 254–55). And for additional information as well as a more sustained argument about the use of the anecdote as a trope in early African Anglo-American writing, see Gates (1988: 127–69).

5. I quote from the Newport, Rhode Island, reprint of 1774 based on the original printed in Bath (American Antiquarian Society Readex Microprint; Worcester, Mass., 1959: 16–17).

6. I would count Modern Greek literature as a minor literature in the context of European literature, and African American literature as a minor literature in the context of Anglo-American literature. See Kacandes 1990; Jusdanis 1991; Jones 1991.

7. Although this is not an explicit task I assign myself here, this argument intervenes in previous debates about African American and Modern Greek literature and about sentimental literature in general that count bridges to extratextual realities and relations as signs of inferior literary production. In showing how these texts' use of reader address serves a relational agenda, I am implicitly arguing for the creative power and inherent worthiness of these novels and their projects.

8. The Greek war for independence from the Ottoman Turks is usually considered as beginning in March 1821, with the Metropolitan of Patras Germanos's call for an uprising in the Peloponnesus, and as concluding with the 1829 Treaty of Andriople, which ends the Russo-Turkish war and obliges the Ottomans to accept the decisions of the Conference of London concerning Greece. Within the novel, Lukís recounts initial violence in Smyrna in 1821 that precedes the Russo-Turkish war and forces the Greek population mainly to flee and then battles in the islands of the eastern Aegean for the next three years.

9. For this reason I disagree with Beaton's characterization of the novel and its role for Modern Greek literature (1994: 60–61).

10. Vikélas 1881a: 198; 1881b: 231. Future references to and quotations from the novel will be to Gennadius's English translation (1881b). I will refer to the Greek original (1881a) only when the exact sense is not communicated clearly enough by Gennadius. Transcriptions of the Greek follow the guidelines of the *Journal of Modern Greek Studies*. Lukís's marriage to Déspina at the end of his narrative is one of several examples of complying with a literary convention that also serves an extraliterary, cultural, communal agenda.

11. Gennadius translates this as "you," of course, since by the late nineteenth century, English no longer employs the intimate second person ("thou") in common speech and writing (see Brown and Gilman 1960: 265–66).

12. On addressee as "peer," see 1881b: 19–20; on reaching the younger generation, see 1881b: 117–18.

13. See, for example, Warhol 1995: 67.

14. The idea of connection expressed here is foregrounded by the preceding passage in which Lukís describes the sense of solidarity that Greeks in his part of the Ottoman empire (the eastern Aegean islands) felt with the insurgents who staged the first naval revolts in distant (western) areas.

15. One thinks again of Chafe's contention that a major difference between oral and literate communication is simultaneity vs. disjuncture of production and reception (1982: 37 and 1994: 42–43).

16. In quoting this passage I am following the typesetting of the original Greek text where Vikélas places the first apology about digressions in one paragraph and then this idea about reader protocol in another. Gennadius groups the first two sentences quoted here with the previous paragraph, starting a new paragraph with the idea of the child and nurse. I follow Vikélas's original structure since it better reveals the linking of digression and reader address.

17. Warhol's analysis of engaging narrators is again relevant here (1989).

18. My thanks to Mary Lou Kete for this point.

19. This request reveals how much Lukís understands about reading, in this case about the power of readers' imaginations.

20. See Longinus's analysis of this phenomenon (1927: 201). I take up Longinus and the idea of placing the reader in the narrated scene in chapter 4.

21. As I mentioned in my preface, Greek culture has known writing for millennia, and in Lukís's mercantile expatriate community, we can assume most people are literate. But oral communication had traditionally been used for the most valued (cultural) information.

22. Indeed this conceit is an integral part of the rise of the novel form. See *Robinson Crusoe* (1719), *Pamela* (1740–41), and *Clarissa* (1748–49) for a few examples from the English tradition, or *The Scarlet Letter* (1850) from the American. E. T. A. Hoffmann's "Die Abenteuer der Sylvesternacht" (1814), or Chamisso's "Peter Schlemihls wundersame Geschichte" (1814) are examples from a continental tradition.

23. The veritable explosion of Modern Greek prose fiction in the late nineteenth and early twentieth century should not be linked directly to Vikélas or to this novel; rather, it should be considered part of a widespread call for Greek nation-building at this time.

24. See Gates 1983: xxiv–lii; Bell 1987: 47; White 1993: 41–45; Stern 1995.

25. See, in particular, Gates's comparison of *Our Nig* to Baym's analysis of sentimental novelistic features (1983: xli–li). More recent discussions, however, challenge Gates's assessment. Stern maintains, for example, that *Our Nig* "must no longer be seen in exclusively sentimental terms" (1995: 447) and even argues, convincingly in my view, that "Wilson takes aim at domestic sentimentalists" (449). Stern produces much evidence for its closer kinship to gothic fiction. Mitchell, too, sees similarities to gothic novels (1992: 8).

26. Almost a century earlier Gronniosaw felt similarly compelled to write and sell his personal story only at the point when he could no longer support his family in another way (1774: 3).

27. Gates suggests that the most remarkable feature of this preface is Wilson's anticipation of objections to her text by Northern abolitionists. "Hers is not meant to be an attack on Northern whites at all." Rather, she can (safely) criticize her white, Northern mistress because that mistress was "imbued with *southern* principles" (1983: xxxv). While I share Gates's admiration for the way Wilson juggles her attacks on Northern racism with mitigation of offense to abolitionists, in my view, she most definitely intends to criticize *Northern* white abolitionists for *Northern* behavior.

28. It is unclear to me why Gates assumes this writer is a man (xx). If anything, we might assume this writer is a woman, since the other two endorsers are women.

29. See White 1993, esp. 34–38. White also makes it clear that Wilson could not characterize them as abolitionists in her text because that would present too much of a risk to herself from the still-living Hayward family members.

30. Eric Gardner's preliminary research on original readership for *Our Nig* offers some support for my hypotheses (1993: 227, 241).

31. There is clearly much more to be said on the subject, including Jack's use of the term and the narrator's specific comment: "How different this appellative sounded from him; he said it in such a tone, with such a rogueish look!" (70).

32. White makes a similar point (1993: 40).

33. This is, of course, one of the examples eluded to earlier of the word "nigger" being used by whites in a derogatory manner.

34. To be sure, much more could be said about Christians and Christianity in the text.

35. Gardner's preliminary research uncovered no original black owners of *Our Nig* (1993: 240). Gardner also points out that there were few blacks in Milford, New Hampshire, where the most (traceable) copies were sold

(233). On the other hand, Boston, the town in which it was printed, did have a growing black community that was literate, but it had no proven readers of *Our Nig* (244).

36. In the wedding ceremony of the Eastern Orthodox Church the couple dons crowns, in current custom usually looking like wreaths, which symbolize their new roles as king and queen of creation. Although originally published in 1963, Tachtsís's novel achieved fame with its second edition (by Ermís) in 1970 (1985a). There have been two published English translations: one by Leslie Finer first published in Great Britain as *The Third Wedding* (1966) and another by John Chioles published in Greece as *The Third Wedding Wreath* (1985b). Quotations and references in my text will refer to the Chioles translation since it sticks closer to the original; I include page numbers to the Ermís Greek edition (1985a) only when there is a point that cannot be discerned in the translation.

37. See my comments on Greek oral storytelling in the preface, as well as in Kacandes 1992; also Tannen 1980, 1982a.

38. Ong's analysis of conflict in oral culture is relevant here. Specifically, he suggests that "oral or residually oral cultures strike literates as extraordinarily agonistic in their verbal performance and indeed in their lifestyle" (1982: 43).

39. See Nofsinger's point that conversation is a way through which we make relationships (1991: 162) and Mandelbaum's similar arguments about the function of storytelling (1987, 1989).

40. I have placed in brackets an addition Chioles makes to the original, explaining for the English-speaking reader who Spanoúdis was.

41. I don't think it's coincidental that these scenes take place at a food distribution center. Food and stories, the linking implies, are vital to life, especially in a city where tens of thousands of people had recently died of famine. And both food and stories, in this society at least, come through relationship with other people, who, like Ekávi, have already learned the lesson that what people *do* is more important than who they supposedly are. (Ekávi had learned to judge people by their character, not their reputation or wealth, through the behavior of her supposed friends when her husband deceives her and abandons her for her own cousin, 75–91.)

42. In Ong's terms, "orality situates knowledge within a context of struggle" (1982: 44).

43. The complete integration of so many anecdotes into one life story makes it difficult to pinpoint beginnings—or endings for that matter. In the retrospection of her narrative, Nína actually identifies an earlier incident when Dimítris is arrested as the accessory to a murder as "a kind of prelude, a

sort of dress rehearsal of the breakdown that [Ekávi] was to experience for the last time during the Occupation," for Nína experiences a cessation in Ekávi's flood of stories (1985b: 165). But since in the "final performance" Ekávi and Nína trade roles, I contend it is this sequence that readers experience as the beginning of Ekávi's end.

44. Because Dimítris has had so much trouble with the law, he feels that his sister has betrayed him by marrying a policeman, whom—merely by virtue of his profession—he considers his persecutor. Ekávi understands this logic, but first tries to defend her daughter to her son, especially since the marriage has already taken place.

45. Within a Christian framework, this mention of three days foregrounds a resurrection.

46. In the original Greek, "they," the subject of the sentence, isn't even specified with a pronoun; it's just implicit through the third-person plural verb form; and "what" they did is equally unspecific, the Greek "aftá" meaning merely "those things." So Ekávi's answer to Nína's question about what she should tell Thódoro is particularly ambiguous.

47. See, for instance, the passage in which Nína has the listener ask her why she didn't have an abortion when she found out that her husband was cheating on her with her own brother (48).

48. We first learn the date (1999) in the outer frame from the communal "we" (10) but then also from a reference Cocoa makes within one apostrophe to where they are and to a day when they were there together before George's death—a day when Cocoa heard voices telling her, You'll break his heart (223). Information about the island and its history is given throughout the book but most explicitly in parts of the paratext: a map, a family tree, and a bill of sale for Sapphira.

49. I put words such as "conversations," "overhear," and "say" in quotation marks because none of what George and Cocoa say transpires audibly, yet the narrator tells us that we readers "hear" it.

50. The paratext, like the communal "we" of the narrating voice, is an important aspect of the revoicing performed by *Mama Day*. The paratext is, as we have already discussed, a critical part of nineteenth-century slave narratives. The content of the documents Naylor includes emphasizes that blacks here are authorizing themselves. Furthermore, I read Naylor's communal "we" as a revoicing of the singular first person of so many by now canonical texts in African American literature, such as Johnson's *Autobiography of an Ex-Colored Man*, Wright's *Black Boy*, and Ellison's *Invisible Man*. It's as if Naylor is saying: enough of the individual, now it's time for the community to tell its story.

51. Fowler suggests a somewhat similar emphasis, but she frames the novel more negatively as revealing "the destructive powers of possessive love" (1996: 101).

3. TESTIMONY

1. Benjamin's observations about the effects of modern battle resonate with Freud's, whose encounters with soldiers who fought in the Great War pushed him to connect war neuroses and accident neuroses, developing in the process a formal theory of trauma (see Caruth 1996: 58–67).
2. My term "witness narrative" should not be confused with Cohn's term "witness biography" (1989: 21n. 13; see also N. Friedman 1955: 1174–75) nor with Stanzel's term "peripheral narration" (1984: 205–9) in which a first-person narrator tells the story of someone she knew or knows. Witness narratives as I am defining them here are not necessarily narrated in the first person.
3. As we saw at the beginning of this chapter, Benjamin, a cultural commentator, had connected similar interpersonal and mass phenomena decades earlier. It took the medical and, specifically, the psychoanalytic community quite a while to achieve this same insight. I follow Brison (1999) and Herman (1992) in limiting my investigation to traumas intentionally inflicted—that is, by other humans—since they affect survivors' sense of self and therefore of interpersonal relations in particular ways.
4. See also Herman 1992: 121; Caruth 1993: 24 and 1996: 11; Frederick 1987.
5. Janet's stature in the early twentieth century can be gleaned from the fact that it was he, not Freud, who delivered the inaugural lectures for the opening of the new buildings of the Harvard Medical School in November 1906. (Janet 1965 is a facsimile of the 1929 edition of these lectures, originally published in 1907.) Although Janet's work was largely forgotten during the middle of the twentieth century, there has been renewed interest in him due to the way neurobiology has borne out in great part his schema for how trauma works.
6. The phrase *idée fixe* goes back at least half a century before Janet starts to use it for this technical psychological phenomenon (see entry for "*idée fixe*" in *Le Grand Robert de la langue française* 5 [1989]: 343). For Janet's usage, which is at first much more general and becomes more restricted, see 1889: 428–35; 1898: 2; 1911: 239–312; 1925: 596.
7. Brison has objected to Caruth's analysis of trauma as "unclaimed" or "missed" experience, suggesting that "at least in the case of a single traumatic event, the event is experienced at the time and remembered from that time, although the full emotional impact of the trauma takes time to

absorb and work through" (1999: 210). Brison agrees with Janet, Caruth, Wigren, and others that the absorbing and working through are facilitated by narrating to supportive others.

8. For a few of Janet's discussions of Irène's case see 1911, 1925, 1928, 1965. Van der Kolk and van der Hart also recount Janet's work with Irène (1995; esp. 160–64).

9. English translation by van der Kolk and van der Hart 1995: 161, from Janet 1928: 207–8. There is a slightly different version of Irène's protestations in Janet 1965: 38.

10. The terms *fabula* and *sjuzet* come from Russian formalism. Narratology offers a plethora of terms to express the distinction between what is commonly called in English "story" and "discourse"; see Genette's "story" and "narrative" (1980: 27) and Rimmon-Kenan's "story" and "text" (1989: 3).

11. Janet's formulation seventy years prior is strikingly similar (as quoted in van der Kolk and van der Hart 1995: 170–71).

12. Leys disagrees with van der Kolk and van der Hart's assessment of the role of the recovery and narration of traumatic memory in Janet's actual treatment of hysterics (1994: 658–60). For the strides that neurobiology has made in understanding the processing of traumatic memory, see van der Kolk and van der Hart 1995: 174, and M. Friedman et al. 1995. For recent psychotherapeutic approaches, see Foy 1992; Wigren 1994; Kleber et al. 1995; Marsella et al. 1996.

13. Irène told Janet, "I'm afraid when you make me remember that. It's a fear I can't get over" (1911: 541). One striking illustration from more recent clinical and lay literature about overcoming fear and telling the story, as a result of proper social support, comes from Agate Nesaule's *A Woman in Amber* (1997). As a child, Nesaule was one of millions of persons displaced from their homes in Eastern Europe (in her case Latvia) toward the end of World War II. In several opening scenes of her memoir, it becomes clear that Nesaule can only "tell" when she feels that she is genuinely safe with a completely interested interlocutor, like her lover, John, or her therapist, Ingeborg. John, for example, requests to hear about her childhood by saying, "I really want to know. Please tell me" (9). Ingeborg notices and wonders about Agate's sadness, displaying an attention and calm acceptance that make Agate feel safe enough to tell (23–24).

14. Note the difference in trying to tell this kind of "story" from the ones that needed to be passed on in texts of my storytelling mode. Even if some of the events in Ekávi's life or of those leading to the death of George are traumatic in the colloquial sense, they are accessible and concrete to those

involved in a way that stories of trauma are not—perhaps precisely because they found genuinely interested listeners.

15. I want to draw particular attention to my choice of the word "enabler" rather than the word "addressee," which is used in accounts of communication such as Jakobson's (1960: 353), in order to reference the special kind of nonpassive listening noted above in psychotherapeutic accounts of witnessing to trauma. Hartman, commenting on Laub's work, describes listening as "the midwife role" (1996: 153), another metaphor that indicates that this role is one of enabling a process.

16. About the psychoanalytic process, Laub even says, "hardly anything of all this gets explicitly said in words" (Felman and Laub 1992: 63). Van der Kolk and van der Hart report on the research of Southwick and colleagues who use injection of yohimbine to induce people with PTSD to "immediately access sights, sounds and smells related to earlier traumatic events" (1995: 174). Consider, too, Leys's observation that Janet did not restrict himself to the positive construction of stories, but also used hypnosis to access and excise events (1994: 658–62).

17. In the case of the last two circuits, a researcher might uncover relevant literary-historical material outside of the novel itself that leads to interpreting the text-as-statement of trauma.

18. My use of the prefix "trans" (transhistorical/transcultural) is meant to refer to the otherness of these reader-cowitnesses in this most distant (from the trauma) circuit of witnessing, not to some kind of superior or universal ability to "know" the trauma. It may well be their distance, however, that allows such readers to recognize a literary phenomenon as a sign of historical trauma.

19. Robert Jay Lifton, another prominent analyst of trauma, even suggests that World War II and the Holocaust are "a certain kind of survivor reaction . . . to World War I" (Caruth 1995b: 139–40).

20. The messiness of this intertwining is useful to me, since it counteracts some of the seeming impropriety of using a framework as organized as a typology of circuits to approach a phenomenon as inscrutable as trauma.

21. Focalization refers to "the relationship between the 'vision,' the agent that sees, and that which is seen" (Bal 1985: 104), and as Bal points out, who sees is not necessarily the same agent as the one who speaks (101). This passage is narrated in the third person, but we "see and hear" what Stephen sees and hears.

22. In another example of these connections, the narrator ponders her childhood linkage of a Jewish boy and "the white snake" (1980: 135–36).

23. Wolf's novel was first translated into English with the infelicitous title "A Model Childhood." While the German word "Muster" of the original title is polysemous and allows for both the ideas of a "model" and a "pattern," it is clear from the text that any idea of "model" is meant ironically.

24. Though the Handmaid never names her addressee, there are numerous hints—for example, her chagrin about an illicit affair—that she addresses herself to her husband Luke, who had been separated from her when the family was trying to escape Gilead (224–25), before she was forced to become a handmaid.

25. Kartiganer describes the novel as Faulkner's "supreme attempt to realize the paradoxical dream of maintaining a hold on the past while achieving a creative autonomy in the present" (1995: 53).

26. Gerald Langford, collator of the original manuscript and the published book of *Absalom, Absalom!* emphasizes that Faulkner altered his original design to give Quentin a much bigger role, indeed to make him the "pivotal figure" (1971: 3).

27. Brooks, too, remarks this shift, saying that "Quentin enters the Sutpen *story* through the meeting with Henry at Sutpen's Hundred" (1984: 296).

28. Weinstein makes a similar observation about Compson's detachment (1974: 139–40). See also Brooks 1984: 291.

29. On the intensity of seeing without processing, Michael Herr comments about his experiences as a Vietnam War correspondent: "The problem was that you didn't always know what you were seeing until later, maybe years later, that a lot of it never made it in at all, it just stayed stored there is your eyes" (1978: 20). On the paradoxical operation of "seeing" trauma, consider also Caruth 1996: 28–29.

30. We are reminded again of Langford's discovery that many of Faulkner's revisions of *Absalom, Absalom!* move Quentin center stage, transforming him from one of four narrators who just "report" to "the pivotal figure" (1971: 3). Brooks calls Quentin "the better artist of the narrative plot" (1984: 296). I want to shift the emphasis yet a bit further, suggesting that Quentin's role is testimonial, not just structural or aesthetic.

31. Laub and other members of the psychotherapeutic community warn against listeners losing their sense of self. Although the listener "has to feel the victim's victories, defeats and silences, know them from within," says Laub, that listener must also retain separateness to fulfill his or her function as an enabler. Listeners must "not become the victim," lest they risk their own traumatization (Felman and Laub 1992: 58). In a context at once more literary and philosophical, Trezise describes how, in Charlotte Delbo's *None of Us Will Return,* the invitation to readers to witness by identifying is

coupled with a "challenge to the very possibility of such identification" (1997: 11).

32. I discuss this phenomenon more thoroughly in the next chapter.

33. According to Lottman, Camus's biographer, this final paragraph was added to the novel at the urging of Jean Bloch-Michel, a friend of Camus's who feared that otherwise the ending of this novel would sound too much like the ending of *The Stranger* (1979: 563).

34. Janet describes traumatic symptoms as "one of the consequences of inadequacy of action at the time when the event took place" (1925: 663). And he discusses generally the concept of changing an element in the traumatic world of the sufferer in a chapter called "Treatment by Mental Liquidation" (1925: 589–698). See also van der Kolk and van der Hart 1995: 175–79.

35. Depending on the identity of the reader, such an act would complete circuit five (for Camus's contemporary readers) or circuit six (for later or foreign readers).

36. For additional facts about the development of the Camus-Sartre debate and rupture, see also Lottman 1979: 495–507. Lottman offers as well the recapitulation of some contemporary (1956) interpretations of *The Fall* as a "long-delayed reply" to Sartre's 1952 attack on Camus (565).

37. See Alcoff and Gray 1993: 263 who warn similarly against readers/analysts setting themselves up as the experts who know better than the victim.

38. See Byland 1971: 62–72; Balzer 1981: 165–66; and Lorenz 1993. Shafi's approach to the prose texts distinguishes itself somewhat, since she reads them as allegories of the artist, though she, too, strives to illuminate the life through the texts (1991: 691; 1995: 189–214). It is symptomatic that a dictionary entry on Kolmar as late as 1993 does not even mention her dramatic or prose works (see Dick and Sassenberg 1993: 219–20).

39. I will discuss the titling of this book again when I take up the issue of publication. I note here that the novel was written quickly in 1930–31 and first published posthumously in 1965. The first page of Kolmar's typescript does not bear a title (see reproduction in Eichmann-Leutenegger 1993: 117), but the title must have been indicated by Kolmar as "Die jüdische Mutter" ["The Jewish Mother"] somewhere else—on a title page?—in the typescript (see Woltmann 1995: 155). In any case, Kolmar's sister Hilda insisted on the name *Eine Mutter* [*A Mother*] when the novel first appeared in 1965 (Kösel Verlag), since she feared the original title could encourage antisemitism (Woltmann 1995: 285n. 151). The second (1978), and all subsequent editions, as far as I know, have been published with the title *Eine jüdische Mutter* [*A Jewish Mother*]. The question of the protagonist's relationship to

Judaism is a complicated one that should not be given inadequate treatment here. The analysis that follows, however, reads Kolmar's Jewish protagonist and her daughter as marginalized by their society and as self-consciously aware of their difference from those around them because of their Jewish background.

40. All quotations from the novel are given in my own translation. The page numbers in parentheses refer to the (German) Ullstein Tachenbuch edition of 1981. Kolmar's language has a strange tone to a German ear. It may sound antiquated to some, but I hear it as awkward. Kemp calls it a late-Expressionist style (as quoted in Woltmann 1995: 157), and Smith says it lacks confidence and is inconsistent (1975: 30). I think the tone is one sign of the text's performance of trauma, so my translations try to render both the sense and something of the stilted tone. A competent English translation of the novel and of Kolmar's novella, *Susanna*, came to my attention after this chapter was drafted (Kolmar 1997). Since exact linguistic formulations are important to my analysis, I have retained my translations, which stay closer to the original than the published translation.

41. The DSM-IV emphasizes that PTSD can be caused by harm to oneself or by witnessing or learning about unexpected death or harm to a "family member or close associate" (1994: 424). Caruth describes the trauma to the parent of a dead child as the trauma of the necessity and "impossibility of a proper response" (1996: 100).

42. An inside view of a child's inability to witness verbally to events to which her body is testifying so glaringly is given in Dorothy Allison's painful novel of incest, abuse, and abandonment, *Bastard Out of Carolina*; see especially the interaction between the twelve-year-old protagonist and the sheriff at the hospital after the child has been beaten and raped by her stepfather (1992: 295–98).

43. In German, the words for "child" and "girl" have a neuter gender (*das Kind, das Mädchen*), so the use of "it" and "its" is not necessarily unusual. And yet, there are other choices (e.g., "she" and "her"). Therefore the use of "it" helps underscore Ursula's inanimateness. The word *doch* (here translated as "still") to indicate Martha's previous thought—presumably that the child is dead and therefore not breathing—is one sign that much of the novel's discourse is filtered through Martha's consciousness. In narratological terms, Martha is the focalizer. This aspect of the text is significant for my fourth category, textual witnessing, and will be discussed below.

44. Wigren observes that "trauma victims are often actively silenced" (1994: 417).

45. Culbertson's (adult) analysis of and testimony to her own sexual violation as a young child grapple with this problem of putting bodily trauma into words in a way that communicates the dilemma to others (1995).

46. Again, on the issue of "seeing" and trauma, refer to Herr 1978: 20, and Caruth 1996: 28–29.

47. We do not know Lucie's background. However, it would be consonant with the antisemitic dynamics of the novel if Lucie, as a German-Gentile child, can speak and name the crime, and Martha, the German-Jewish child, cannot.

48. One should also consider this scene under the rubric of my fourth circuit, additionally interpreting the indirection and euphemism as deictics calling for a reply of cowitnessing to the text-as-statement of trauma.

49. These issues of diction are relevant to circuit four as well. Wigren notes how it was initially impossible for two of her patients to name what had happened to them. To heal, Wigren's patient Hugh needed to learn to say that he had lost his leg, a fact for which he had corporeal proof, yet one that he had not processed before starting therapy. Similarly, Kathi could not call what had happened to her sexual abuse (1994: 418–21).

50. See, too, Martha's refusal of sympathy and aid from her parents-in-law (49) and her repeated rebuffs of her neighbor's succor (e.g., 42–43).

51. Any number of the essays in the chapter on "The Rise of the New Woman" in *The Weimar Republic Sourcebook* (Kaes et al. 1994: 195–219) could be read for Weimar attitudes toward single and working women. For example, shortly before Hitler's takeover (approximately when Kolmar was writing *A Jewish Mother*), commentator Alice Rühle-Gerstel laments that before the new woman "could evolve into a type and expand into an average, she once again ran up against barriers . . . and she therefore found herself not liberated, as she had naively assumed, but now doubly bound" (218). For the complexities of Jewish self-hatred, especially with regard to German Jews, see Gilman 1986: 270–308, and for interpretations of Kolmar's view of her Jewishness, see Lorenz 1993 and Colin 1990.

52. Though "Elfenbeinton" is light and not necessarily derogatory in and of itself, it did connote "Eastern," and therefore what would have been considered at the time *racial* difference.

53. It is on the basis of such evidence that I cannot agree with Shafi that Martha's isolation is by choice (1995: 202).

54. Many mental health professionals have tried to raise awareness of the dangers of secondary traumatization (Felman and Laub 1992: 57–58). Commenting on society's lack of understanding and support for victims, Frieze observes that "society tends to have rather negative views of victims of both

sexes" (1987: 118), and Frederick comments that victims "may be treated as if they are mentally ill on the one hand, or have factitious symptoms on the other" (1987: 84; see also 74). Wigren, too, comments on the frequent tragedy of trauma victims being denied the social contact they need to recover (1994: 417).

55. Caruth speaks relevantly of trauma's "indirect relation to reference" (1996: 7).

56. Although they do not use narratological terminology or draw the same conclusions, Balzer (1981: 172) and Sparr (1993: 82) also note that *A Jewish Mother* is rendered primarily from Martha's perspective.

57. The one "crime" that is narrated directly in the novel is Martha's administration of the sleeping powder to her child. But this is the transgressive act that remains the most ambiguous ethically. It is interesting to note that Martha keeps waiting for someone to appear at the moment she prepares the fatal draft, someone who would seemingly prevent her from carrying through with her plan (59). Even though the specter of "Medea" is raised in one early flashback (8), the text never directly charges Martha with infanticide. Despite the fact that *Martha* comes to consider herself Ursula's murderer, it remains unclear whether Ursula would have died even without the sleeping powder. One hint to the moral valence of Martha's act resides in a conversation with her husband years earlier that Martha recalls after Ursula has died—but, interestingly, before the text relates Martha's administration of the sleeping powder, an issue of narrative order that accords with the indirect textual witnessing. It seems that the couple had read a newspaper report of a mother who had killed her own son because of his homosexual liaisons. Friedrich Wolg found this mother inhuman and her action unconscionable. Martha, in contrast, says she understands her: "When one loves one's child, one can do anything. One can let oneself be killed by it. And one can also kill it" (56–57).

58. In a separate paragraph, the text does reproduce some excerpts from the article. In accordance with the overall pattern of focalization, the words rendered are presumably the words Martha's consciousness is actually able to take in when Frau Roßkaempfer thrusts the newspaper toward her. But the words we read by no means constitute enough of an explanation of what happened to warrant the barkeeper's assessment of "precisely, completely correctly described" (45).

59. Note Kolmar's choice of the word *Name*, which implies naming, rather than just *Wort*. I take this as a subtle reminder of the power of naming a crime explicitly. For more on this power, see the conclusion of this chapter.

60. One exception that springs to mind are the vivid descriptions of violence done to characters in Döblin's 1929 novel *Berlin Alexanderplatz*, though there, too, fascinating indirections are employed alongside more explicit narration, for instance, the Newtonian language in the flashback to Ida's beating (85–86) and the biblical refrains from Ecclesiastes interjected into the depiction of Mieze's murder (see esp., 310–17). In terms of decorum, perhaps it makes a difference that crimes in Döblin's novel are perpetrated mainly against adult women (and some men), whereas in Kolmar's the central crime is perpetrated against a very young girl.

61. The function of newspaper crime-reporting in shaping the consciousness of the populace in this novel as well as in other novels of the period warrants a separate study, one that I believe would elucidate and support my larger thesis of ubiquitous trauma in Weimar Berlin.

62. For this reason, I do not think it was frivolous for Kolmar's American translator to have changed the title to *A Jewish Mother from Berlin*. Although they do not point to the same kind of evidence, Smith and Shafi recognize a critique of urban life in Kolmar's novel (Smith 1975: 32–33; Shafi 1995: 204).

63. Documentation of this supposed abortion has not been published to my knowledge, but the verification of its occurrence seems to have come from Kolmar's sister Hilda. Smith also remarks on the "child-loss fantasies that plagued the author throughout her life" and that find expression in this novel and in many of her poems (1975: 31–32).

64. It should be noted that Lang's movie could be analyzed similarly to my analysis of *A Jewish Mother*. It, too, testifies to violence perpetrated against the marginalized in Weimar society.

65. Much is made over Kolmar's comment to Hilda in a letter that what she is writing is " 'just' prose, not verse" (5 March 1942 in Kolmar 1970: 136). But I think Kolmar's quotation marks around "just," together with the fact that she is reporting about a story she is writing under abominable conditions, should make us more cautious about drawing conclusions about the author's general evaluation of her prose writing (contrast my view with Shafi's 1995: 189).

66. In addition to Ursula's rape and the fact that all the neighbors seem to have in mind precedents for violence against children, one could mention Martha's discovery of antisemitic literature in the living room of the home in which her lover Albert Renkens lives (153–54).

67. The documentation of the Weimar period as violent is legion. On marginalization of minorities see, for example, Hancock 1991 and Milton 1992 on Roma-Sinti. On general urban violence and sexual crimes, see Linden-

berger and Lüdtke 1995 (esp. the essays of Crew, Rosenhaft, and Brücker) and Tatar 1995. As for artistic treatments, I have already raised the obvious examples of Döblin's *Berlin Alexanderplatz* and Lang's movie *M*. One shouldn't ignore visual artists such as George Grosz and Otto Dix, to name just two of the most prominent.

68. For more on the relationship between Lasker-Schüler and Kolmar, see Lorenz 1993.

69. On why there is such interest in remembering the Holocaust now, at such a historical distance from the events themselves, see Felman and Laub 1992: 84. See, too, Hartman 1996, esp. 1–14; Flanzbaum 1999; and Novick 1999.

70. An additional, if small, indication of Kolmar's increasing popularity is that in recent years, entire panels on Kolmar were included in the annual meetings of the German Studies Association and the Modern Language Association in the United States.

71. My thanks to Monika Kallan for pointing this out.

72. On making the bridge between individual trauma and the society in which it occurs, see Herman 1992 and Minow 1993.

73. For more on the power of language, see the scene in which Martha first begins to rethink her decision to give Ursula sleeping powder; she tries to undo the thought by saying out loud, "No!" (144).

74. I do not mean to exclude the possibility that an individual writer or reader might receive psychic relief from writing or reading such a story.

4. APOSTROPHE

1. There are several situations within the novel that could be applied to the overall discourse situation. For instance, at one point Kate reflects that perhaps her current writing is so easy because of previous letters she'd written to Esther to which she received no answer (176). Similarly, the narrative mode can be likened to the period in their relationship when Esther poses questions to Kate on postcards from abroad with no return address (206–7). And toward the conclusion of the novel, Kate describes her behavior as a "private séance" (281).

2. Judith Roof explicates Rule's novel as "the paradox of a desire fulfilled by its unfulfillment, by remaining a desire, a question. Paradoxically, then, in its nonfulfillment, the desire for desire is fulfilled" (1991: 169). While I do find Roof's assessment of Kate supported by a more thorough reading of the novel than either she or I provides, what I ultimately miss in Roof's analysis is attention to how the narrative technique, what I describe below as "narrative apostrophe," effects this desire for desire.

3. Roof makes a similar point (1991: 169). See, too, Barbara Johnson's brilliant analysis of the idea of "not for you" in Adrienne Rich's poem "To a Poet" (1987: 195–96).

4. I have adapted the phrase "narrative apostrophe" from classical philologist Elizabeth Block, who uses the phrase only to describe the Homeric and Vergilian narrators' addresses to characters and to the epic audience (1982: 8, 11, 13). Brian McHale uses the term "narratorial apostrophe" just for the former (narrators to characters 1984–85: 100). Heinrich Lausberg, the compiler of one of the most comprehensive handbooks of literary rhetoric, does connect the figure of apostrophe with reader address in prose fiction, though there is no indication that he applied apostrophe to—or was even aware of the existence of—texts narrated primarily in the second person (1960: 379; 1998: 339). To my knowledge, I was the first scholar to connect the figure of apostrophe with such texts (Kacandes 1990; 1993; 1994). On the other hand, there is a lengthy tradition of general critical interest in second-person narration aroused by the increasing number of novels and stories written in this mode (for a list of such texts and of scholarly work about them, see Fludernik 1994b). In 1965 Bruce Morrissette identified "narrative 'you'" as a new literary genre. Prince helped the study of such texts along by coining the term "narratee," the person to whom the narrative is addressed (1971, 1973). Genette seems to have come to the French equivalent (*narrataire*) at approximately the same time (1972) and later coins the phrase *narration à la deuxième personne* (second-person narrating) to describe whole texts written in this mode (1983: 92). Fludernik offered a clear definition for the phenomenon as "fiction that employs a pronoun of address in reference to a fictional protagonist" (1993: 217), also clarifying that the term "second person fiction" is a misnomer of sorts, since in several languages pronouns of address are not necessarily the second person (1993: 219). Evidence that literary critics have hardly finished with the subject is offered not only by this chapter but also by the studies of Capecci (1989); Richardson (1991); Wiest (1993); and an entire issue dedicated to the subject in *Style* (1994, 28.3). My own approach is distinguished from these by my use of the structure of apostrophe to account for the way narrating with a pronoun of address *inevitably involves the audience of actual readers*.

5. My thanks to Robyn Warhol for this graceful formulation.

6. Thus one application of the term was reserved for any strategy that involves changing the subject, or in Quintilian's words, that "divert[s] the attention of the hearer from the question before them" (book 4, section 2.38 in vol. 3, p. 398). See also Lausberg on metabasis (1960, 1998, section 848).

7. For definitions of apostrophe see Block (1982: 8–9); Lausberg (1960, 1998, sections 762–65); and Perrine (1975). All draw heavily on Quintilian's explanation (1960; esp. book 4, section 1.63–70 in vol. 3, pp. 396–99; and book 9, section 2.38–39 in vol. 2, pp. 41–45), as well as on that of "Longinus" (sections 26–27; 1982: 200–205). Henceforth, I will refer parenthetically just to page numbers in the Loeb Classical Library editions of Quintilian and Longinus.

8. This distinction is emphasized through the grammar of the original Latin. The verb form Quintilian uses to describe what happens by apostrophizing is the present indicative, signaling the hard reality of Cicero's act, whereas the verb form Quintilian uses to describe the hypothetical situation (no apostrophe) is the pluperfect subjunctive, diminishing the act through distance from reality and the present. My thanks to James H. Tatum for this point.

9. The phrase, "preeminent sign of interaction," is Ann Banfield's (1982: 120); see also McHale (1983: 19; 1987: 223).

10. It should be noted that Benveniste makes these points in the service of arguing the lack of symmetry between the so-called three grammatical persons. Providing convincing evidence from numerous languages, Benveniste shows that the third person really refers to what is absent and therefore unavailable to be considered in its personhood. Even in the case of third-person forms used for direct address (e.g., the current German *Sie*-form or the more antiquated *Er*-form), Benveniste argues the impersonal nature of the usage: the third person "can serve as a form of address with someone who is present when one wishes to remove him from the personal sphere of 'you'" by reasons of respect (His Majesty) or of scorn, "which can annihilate him as a person" (1971: 200).

11. For additional evidence that this is the case, see Schiffrin's analysis of the phrase "you know" in American English as "[enlisting] the hearer as an audience" (1987: 284).

12. See Culler (1981: 135) and Warhol (1989: vii), who mention embarrassment and annoyance experienced by most readers of the apostrophic "you."

13. Banfield distinguishes between addressees and hearers (1982: 120, 128, 129), but as far as I know only the field of conversation analysis maintains a tripartite division.

14. In a previous proposal for a typology of uses of the second person (Kacandes 1994: 335–37), I used "reversibility" between the "I" and "you" as the criterion of organization; in that instance I was trying to account for a much wider range of texts and techniques.

15. First English translation by Jean Stewart, published in 1959 by Simon and Schuster. All translations in this section are my own from the original French reviews of the novel.

16. As Bernard Dort commented, the idea of a man choosing between his wife and mistress is "a hackneyed story" (1958: 121). Butor admitted as much, though he thought of this as an aesthetic advantage, not a hindrance. "The banality of this theme served me well," Butor explained to Paul Guth in an interview shortly after the appearance of the novel: "It's the subject of three-quarters of contemporary novels. Therefore I was able to project some original light on it" (Guth 1957: 4).

17. Emile Henriot first used the phrase "Ecole du regard" to refer to similarities between Claude Simon, Alain Robbe-Grillet, and Michel Butor (1957: 7). For a history of the term "nouveau roman," see Sturrock (1969, esp. 1–2). On the popularity of *La Modification* see Raillard (1968: 192); Van Rossum-Guyon (1970: 41); and Lydon (1980: 100).

18. Pingaud, for example, comments that "every *you* presupposes a hidden *I*" (1958: 98; see also Krause 1962: 59). There are, in fact, a few instances of "I" toward the conclusion of the novel, but these can be interpreted as quoted interior monologue and need not represent the sudden appearance (and then disappearance) of the enunciator of the discourse.

19. The sentence begins: "*Si vous êtes entré dans ce compartiment.*" In French, as in other Romance languages, participles and adjectives after the verb "to be" must agree with the number and gender of the subject. Here "*entré*" is singular and male. Revelation of gender and number through grammar is critical to my reading of Calvino's text and will be taken up below.

20. One of these early dissenters is Pierre de Boisdeffre who insisted in his December 1957 review for *La Revue de Paris* that "nothing in *Change of Heart* testifies to any innovation in the realm of the novel." In making this judgment, he appears to have interpreted the narrative mode as an interior monologue, thereby dismissing it as "absolutely no longer a novelty" (171).

21. Particularly insightful studies include Leiris (1963), Morrissette (1965), Passias (1970), Van Rossum-Guyon (1970), Steinberg (1972), and Quéréel (1973).

22. In great part because of the publication of *Change of Heart* much research has been done on this mode. And while intermittent uses of the second person (excluding dialogue) have appeared in Western literature at least as far back as "Homer's" poignant apostrophes to heroes at Troy and to the faithful Eumaios in Ithaca, even sustained narration in the second person— something Bruce Morrissette credits Butor with inventing (1965)—goes

back much further than Butor's "experiment." I count Hawthorne's short story "The Haunted Mind" (1835) as the earliest literary example of an entire narrative told in the second person (that is, with no explicit signs of a first-person narrator); in Europe, the Austrian writer Ilse Aichinger should be acknowledged for exploiting the mode brilliantly in her story narrated from death to birth entirely in the second person, "Spiegelgeschichte" ["Mirror Story"] (1947). Fludernik cites the interesting nonfictional example of the French Duke of Sully's memoirs *Les Oeconomies royales* (1662), in which the Duke's (Maximilien de Béthune's) four servants at his behest write a history of his life and tell it to him, addressing him in the act (1994a: 297–98). That the discourse situation continues to fascinate is confirmed by a recent use of it in the French movie *The Dreamlife of Angels* (*La Vie revée des anges*), in which one of the protagonists writes in the diary of the girl in whose room she is squatting: "You have been in an accident. Your mother is dead. You are in a coma in the hospital."

23. Leiris is referring to the practice of book publishing in France (and elsewhere): one needs to cut open the pages of a new book in order to read it.

24. Grass had already published poetry and some drama. He won the coveted prize of "Gruppe 47" in 1958 based on prepublication readings from *The Tin Drum*, his first major commercial success.

25. Most critics assume the story is essentially about Mahlke, disregarding the discourse (including apostrophizing) that relates it. Reddick, for example, plots his analysis around stages in *Mahlke's* development (1974). Other critics who assume one can talk about Mahlke without reference to Pilenz's relationship to him include Leonard (1974: 26), Miles (1975: 86), and Piirainen (1968: 10–11). Notable exceptions include Rimmon-Kenan (1987: 179) and Keele (1988: 66), who argue that the real story is about Pilenz and his relationship to Mahlke. Still, Rimmon-Kenan relegates Pilenz's acts of apostrophizing to a footnote, creating what appears to be an airtight murder case against him (179). A few other critics notice that Pilenz addresses Mahlke, but they do not analyze the act for what it reveals about the relationship (Bruce 1966, Behrendt 1969, Schwarz 1971, Botheroyd 1976, Neuhaus 1979, Gerstenberg 1980).

26. The standard English translation by Ralph Manheim is generally very good, capturing well the idiosyncratic narrating style of Pilenz and the slang of the schoolkids. Occasionally, however, as in this passage, he takes liberties that obscure the point I am trying to make.

27. The most notable example of Pilenz's "renarrations" is how it came to pass that the cat jumps on Mahlke's throat (see the novella's opening). From other hints about this event in the novella, it appears that the third and last

version of the story is closest to the truth, that is, that Pilenz grabbed the cat and showed it the sleeping Mahlke's moving Adam's apple.

28. This might remind us of Johnson's analysis of Shelley: that he apostrophizes the wind "not in order to make it speak but *in order to make it listen to him*" (1987: 187; my emphasis). As for Pilenz's jealousy, its particular manifestations (attention to Mahlke's Adam's apple, to his penis, to anyone who shows interest in him or in whom Mahlke shows interest—like the Virgin Mary) clearly point to homoerotic feelings. This is a fascinating aspect of the novella, but one for which I don't have space to present all the evidence.

29. I disagree with Rimmon-Kenan (1987: 180), Ryan (1983: 98), and Ziolkowski (1972: 247), who interpret Pilenz's act of erasing the image as insincere, aggressive, and even a symbolic murder. The image expressed such ridicule of Mahlke, and Mahlke himself reacts so angrily, that one can only assume its disappearance was a relief to him and that he would have been grateful to whoever had erased it.

30. See, for example, the quotation of a conversation by all the boys about what Mahlke's problem might be. At the moment the boys tell Pilenz to ask him what's up, the narration of the scene breaks off, and, instead of reporting a conversation between himself and Mahlke that took place in the past, Pilenz apostrophizes him in the present moment of the discourse (1974: 21–22; 1994: 20). Similarly, in narrating the first time an alumnus hero gives a speech to the boys at the high school, Pilenz reports Mahlke's words of distress in discovering that the requirements for receiving a Knight's Cross have been increased. But instead of quoting his own words of comfort to Mahlke, Pilenz's narration breaks off (reinforced by a blank space between this paragraph and the next), and when his discourse resumes, it is in apostrophe to Mahlke, as if to make up for not having reassured him then (1974: 42; 1994: 40).

31. Compare this to several scenes in which Pilenz apostrophizes Mahlke and then puts words into his mouth by imagining what Mahlke was thinking. In the most striking instance of this use of apostrophe, Pilenz has Mahlke think that everyone is staring at his Adam's apple (1974: 43; 1994: 40–41). It is interesting to note that the quoted hymn in the latrine scene is itself an apostrophe to the Virgin Mary; in that context, Pilenz plays audience to Mahlke's call to the Virgin.

32. There are numerous additional details that incriminate Pilenz, like the fact that, at the moment Mahlke dives into the wreck, Pilenz has his foot on the can opener that Mahlke will need in order to open his provisions, or that he

promises Mahlke that he will return the same evening, whereas he returns a full day later.

33. The German verb "bewirken" is more emphatic than the translator's choice of "made" since it denotes "effecting," "causing," or "producing an effect."

34. Manheim takes numerous liberties with this passage. Although he conveys the events, he does not convey the rhetorical strategies that, in my opinion, are so crucial to a proper understanding of the passage and to a great extent of the book. For example, he turns the initial question into a statement "I may as well add . . ."; and he uses two sentences to render Grass's brilliantly crafted single final sentence: "But you didn't show up. You didn't surface." In addition to spelling out the ambiguity of Grass's formulation where "surfacing" references both the dive of the last time Pilenz saw Mahlke and his contemporary hope that Mahlke will surface out of the crowd, he misses Pilenz's attribution to Mahlke of volition: you didn't *want* to surface. This is important to my point that Pilenz concedes that Mahlke, not he, is in charge.

35. In this regard, *Cat and Mouse* functions like the apostrophe in Gwendolyn Brooks's poem "The Mother"; in Johnson's analysis: "As long as she [the persona] addresses the children, she can keep them alive, can keep from finishing with the act of killing them" (1987: 192).

36. It was through publication of the protocols of the trials of numerous personnel associated with the death camps at Auschwitz in 1965–66 (known in Germany as the "Frankfurter Prozesse" because the trials were held in Frankfurt) that most Germans had the brutality and bestiality of Nazi behavior forced into their consciousnesses. Peter Weiss used the trial transcripts to create his brilliant, if damning, play, *The Investigation* (*Die Ermittlung*). See, too, Alexander and Margarete Mitscherlich's analysis of German postwar society, *The Inability to Mourn* (*Die Unfähigkeit zu trauern*) (1967; 1975). Although there were numerous prods for widespread student unrest in 1968, calling the older generation, and specifically, the government and students' parents, to a reckoning with the Nazi past was certainly one of them. See, for example, numerous interviews with children of Nazis who were students in the late 1960s in Sichrovsky's *Born guilty* (*Schuldig geboren*) (1987; 1988). Many analysts would count a true reckoning with the Nazi past as occurring only with the historians' debate (*Historikerstreit*) of the 1980s (see Maier 1988, Evans 1989, and Baldwin 1990). And some would argue that such a general accounting has yet to occur.

37. The original title of Cortázar's story is "Grafitti." However, to avoid confusion, I will use its "English" spelling (which coincides with the original Italian) throughout. All quotes will be from the excellent English transla-

tion of Gregory Rabassa (1983), with mention of the original Spanish only to point out features that are not transmitted by the English.

38. I will take up this phenomenon in the analysis of *If on a winter's night a traveler*, pausing here only to mention that in Spanish, as in Italian and Greek, the conjugated form of the verb is sufficient to indicate the number and person of the subject of the sentence. This leaves room for some ambiguity, since, for example, in the third person, the verb, unlike the pronoun, will not in and of itself reveal gender. Adjectives or participles that are in agreement with the subject, however, will do so.

39. The text hints that the impetus for the woman's construction of the man's actions may have stemmed from an actual encounter. When the woman is being arrested, the mise-en-scène implies not only that he saw her but also that she may have glimpsed him running toward her, prevented from reaching her (and sure arrest) only because of the "fortuitous" interference of a car (36). One can presume the arrestee's wonderment at the stranger's risky behavior and that it may have prompted her to assume that he was the graffiti artist whose drawings she'd been seeing and answering.

40. Compare Susan Stewart's analysis of graffiti (in nontotalitarian states) as a "crime in mode of production . . . not a crime of content" (1987: 174).

41. Roemer also notices this inversion (1995: 26). Though she doesn't discuss Cortázar's story, Taylor describes torture as an act of double inscription by the state, writing bodies into the nationalist narrative and writing on bodies to turn them into cautionary messages for those on the outside (1997: 152).

42. See Culler on the way apostrophizing creates a timeless present (1981: 149).

43. The story's second publication (in *Sin censura*, Periódico de Información Internacional, Washington-Paris) was also illustrated, according to Prego (1990: 269n. 3), but since I was unable to locate what must have been the inaugural issue of this periodical I cannot confirm my suspicion that the images were those of Tàpies.

44. With regard to the story's critical neglect, consider Alazraki's article on Cortázar's recent short stories in which he literally mentions every story in *We Love Glenda So Much* except "Graffiti" (1983). Note, too, the absence of "Graffiti" from Yovanovich's chapter on Cortázar's short fiction (1991). Oddly, even a study of "La novela hispanoamericana en segunda persona" (Gnutzmann 1983) does not cite the story, though its author does discuss Cortázar and other short stories, albeit not those as short as "Graffiti" (e.g., Fuentes's "Aura"; 106). The only analyses I have been able to find that do more than merely mention the story appear in Peavler's mainly excellent overview of Cortázar's career (1990: 90–91), though there it is under the

rubric of "The Realistic"—a group he deems "less satisfying aesthetically" (93); and in Röhl-Schulze's general study of alienation in recent Argentine fiction (1990: 236–37). Röhl-Schulze makes several interesting points but draws a conclusion opposite mine that the form proves lack of communication and thus "failure" and "alienation." The glass is half-empty from her point of view and half-full from mine. A tantalizing but very short essay by Roemer begins to adumbrate some similar positions to those I take here (1995).

45. In the only statement I could find by Cortázar on this story, he comments on its mechanism of horror that, like Kafka's *Trial* or Orwell's *1984* or his own "Segunda Vez," is about "el horror sin causa definible, sin causa precisable" (as quoted in Prego 1990: 189). That indirection had become an unavoidable modus vivendi for Cortázar is apparent in remarks he made in Mexico in 1983 about (still) being in exile: "I have always been interested in returning to Argentina. What happens is that in Argentina there was and still is a government that is very interested in my not returning. And as I have the well-deserved reputation for being crazy but not stupid, I have taken care not to return to Argentina at a time when I could have entered without problem because no one would have impeded me, but I am sure that I would not have left alive. . . . If anyone wants to return to Argentina, it is the person speaking to you. I am profoundly Argentine, and I always will be" (as quoted in Zamora 1983: 64n. 15).

46. Calvino's novel was originally published in 1979 as *Se una notte d'inverno un viaggiatore*; the English translation by William Weaver appeared in 1981. Quotations will be provided mainly from the English translation but also from the original when grammatical features of the Italian are of interest.

47. Note that for her analysis, Claudia Persi Haines translates the opening words as "you are starting to read" (1984: 43). This provides for a more felicitous utterance, since it is true that the flesh-and-blood reader is "in the process," that is, is "starting to read." But this is an inaccurate translation of the original; the Italian idiom "*stare* + *per* + infinitive" refers to imminent action, not to progressive action. Therefore Weaver's translation "You are about to begin" (3) is more precise.

48. On the other hand, see Tani, who suggests convincingly that Calvino is punning on the literary-historical term "Nouveau Roman" ("New Novel") (1984: 133), a pun that wouldn't be invalidated with time.

49. Austin's foundational lectures on the performative were delivered at Harvard in 1955 and were subsequently published in 1962 by two disciples (Urmson and Sbisà) as *How to Do Things with Words*. On the idea of the

"literary performative," see Kacandes 1993. Note that in revisiting my own argument, I have decided to restrict my application of the term "literary performative" to only those utterances that are necessarily enacted when read by any reader.

50. I owe this striking counterexample to Carol Mullen (1987: 10).

51. Note that this is one example of how talk fiction undermines Chafe's contention that writing is desituated. In Barth's passage the "immediate physical and social situation" (Chafe 1994: 44) in which the text is received *does* matter.

52. See Davies (1981), LeClair (1982), Lively (1982), and Updike (1981), especially with regard to their exasperation. Wood warns his reader not to "[convert] all its apparent misses into clever hits" (1981: 25); while Mullen (1987), Phelan (1989), Salvatori (1986), myself—and Tani (1984), in a more limited way—base our analyses on the assumption that the actual reader is supposed to notice the misfit and use it as a goad to reflect on one's reading strategies. This is what I like to think Calvino was referring to when he said, "the reader is meant to see himself at the same time that he reads the book" (my translation; interview with DiMeo 1981: 11).

53. Someone with a higher demand for precision than I have could consider this a misfit similar to the opening line. Or, if one does not follow the standard practice of reading from beginning to end and in jumping around lands on this line, then, too, it would be infelicitous.

54. I say only "some" of the same material, because the Reader's fragments occasionally seem longer than ours. With regard to the first novel—*If on a winter's night a traveler* (the title of our entire novel but also the title of the first novelistic fragment we and the Reader start to read)—the Reader is described by the narrator as reading repeating signatures (the technical publication term), and whereas we get a description of him reading the repeating signatures, we do not read the repetitions ourselves. Davies sees this as a defect, attributable to the high costs of printing. He thinks Calvino should have insisted with Einaudi (the Italian publisher) on actually reprinting the pages of the first incipit (1981: 773). But Davies misses the point that this is one of many techniques that force us to recognize the difference between our reading and the Reader's.

55. This is my hybrid from Brown and Ford's terms "title" and "generic first name" (1964: 236). Calvino's "Reader" is (humorously) a kind of occupational title that also functions like a generic first name (Brown and Ford's "Bud" and "Mack")—hence my combination: "generic title."

56. Phelan is led astray by Weaver's English translation when he claims that use of the second person allows Calvino to address both sexes (1989: 135). This

is not an accurate assessment of the original Italian text. For the same reason, Marie-Laure Ryan's argument about the "gender morphing" of the narratee-reader needs to be modified (1999: 134).

57. I noted above a similar phenomenon in the opening of Michel Butor's *La Modification* and in Cortázar's "Graffiti." English does not reveal gender so readily; in Beardsley's terms, it does not exhibit universal referential genderization (1977: 117). Remarkably, the first-person novel *Sphinx* by Anne Garréta (1986) never reveals the gender of the narrator, a grammatical coup for a French text.

58. Although Judith Fetterly does not discuss second-person texts per se, she was the first to comprehensively describe the process of immasculation that occurs when women read. Compare her comments on women reading American fiction with what I have pointed out above: "In such fictions the female reader is co-opted into participation in an experience from which she is explicitly excluded; she is asked to identify with a selfhood that defines itself in opposition to her; she is required to identify against herself" (1977: xii). Schweickart comments similarly that "a crucial feature of the process of immasculation is the woman reader's bifurcated response. She reads the text both as a man and as a woman. But in either case, the result is the same: she confirms her position as other" (1986: 50). For this reason, Weaver's translation of "Lettrice" as "Other Reader" strikes me as particularly apt, even though it is not literal.

59. For an overview of discussions of the phallocentric claim that "he" and "man" are generic appellations for "person," see Smith (1985: 48–53). See also Baron (1986, esp. 139–41); Lakoff (1975, esp. 43ff); MacKay (1983, esp. 39); McConnell-Ginet (1979, esp. 78–80); and Martyna (1983).

60. Although it might seem at first glance that the narrator wants to further objectify the Lettrice through specification (that is, the opposite of keeping her in the abstract condition of pronouns), his intent to resuscitate her is further emphasized by his pun on the word "frame." To put her in the frame would be to put her into the story of the Reader for the first time, since in this particular novel with embedded novels, the diegesis is the *cornice*, the frame. In a second-person narrative, to put someone into the story is to address him or her. And this the narrator is finally doing with Ludmilla.

61. I have to disagree with the many critics who consider the two readers on equal footing; see Tani who refers to them as a "team of detectives" (1984: 130), or Haines, who calls them "two kindred spirits" (1984: 49), or Orr who describes their reading as "a dynamic activity performed together" (1985: 218). By paying close attention to the text it is possible to discover that they

do very few things together; furthermore, several passages that would appear to refer to both the Lettore and the Lettrice are actually focalized through the male reader, thus we often have the formulation "you and Ludmilla" (91) rather than a true second-person plural. Some instances when an actual second-person plural form is used turn out to be the Lettore's fantasies, e.g., when he imagines kissing Ludmilla in the professor's office (72).

62. A more accurate translation of the Italian would be "husband and wife," though Weaver's translation ("man and wife") supports my argument that readers are meant to pick up on the larger issue of sexism.

5. INTERACTIVITY

1. See *http://schiller.dartmouth.edu/hr/* (or e-mail Otmar.K.Foelsche@dartmouth.edu) to access the numerous German classical texts in "Annotext," a multimedia environment for teaching texts (1989–) for use on the Macintosh in connection with HyperCard. Prepared texts, special glossaries, and other materials exist for Goethe's *Faust, Part I* and *Die Leiden des jungen Werther*, Lessing's *Minna von Barnhelm*, and Lenz's *Die Soldaten*, among others.

2. Most accounts of hypertext trace the idea of nonlinear access of textual material to a 1945 article by Vannevar Bush in the *Atlantic Monthly* that predated digital computers. These same accounts credit Ted Nelson with coining the term "hypertext" in 1965. Various research teams were actively engaged in developing hypertext systems in the 1960s and 1970s. However, systems for microcomputers don't appear until the 1980s: Brown University's "Intermedia" in 1985, and Apple's "HyperCard" and Schneiderman's "HyperTies" for PC in 1987.

3. It is interesting to note that Cortázar added a sentence after this in the second Spanish edition, making it even more explicit that the reader is supposed to choose one of these two books: "El lector queda invitado *a elegir* una de las dos posibilidades siguientes:" (Cortázar's emphasis). This sentence was not added to subsequent publications of the English translation.

4. The attentive reader will already become wary, because concluding at chapter 56 would mean not reading about one third of the book; this would not be "normal."

5. For example, one could analyze what has become a rather infamous passage in chapter 79 about "female readers," who are "limited," and "male readers," who can function as "accomplices" of the author (406).

6. See, too, Whalley, who talks about "the myth of linearity," or how, in the light of hypertext, so-called traditional texts get set up as "purely linear" when in fact such texts can be written "to weave an entirely non-linear pattern of association in the reader's mind" (1993: 9).

7. There are hypertexts that allow for viewing more than one lexia at a time, but this is not the case here.

8. Similar arrows can be designed into the website itself.

9. Specific lexias and websites can be "bookmarked" by the browser so they can be easily and directly accessed at another time.

10. There is a certain similarity of tone, character, and action set up by this first lexia that reminds me of Jay McInerney's 1984 second-person novel, *Bright Lights, Big City*. Several strands of "Gav and Peloso's Interactive Story" continue in this vein: young man, addicted to fast living and drugs, searches for adventure, finds it hollow and his life a waste, etc. I note, however, that at least one of the strands—I don't claim to have seen them all—quickly makes it clear that the you-protagonist is a woman.

11. My own limited understanding of "Unreal" was greatly enhanced by an article about it (Herz 1998) and by e-mail and phone contact with several aficionados of the game found on-line who generously described to me their experiences of playing "Unreal," but who prefer to remain anonymous. My choice of "Unreal" as opposed to some of the even more popular games, like "Quake" has to do with the fact that, to my knowledge at least, it was the first commercially successful game to make the reprogramming or redesign of it relatively easy for nonprogrammers by including editing tools.

12. One of my informants explained that he was involved with a group of "Unreal" players who designed a "jetpack" so that players could fly instead of run. This would not cause the game to "break out" of my Talk framework. But the same informant told me that he had friends who had used the Unreal editor, the game "engine," to create a completely different kind of interactive experience, like a virtual tour of Notre Dame. That tour would have no narrative relationship to "Unreal," in my view, and thus would not be a "reply" to a move of the original game as "statement." It is an interaction, but not one that fits within the framework I have developed in this book.

13. I suggest that MUDs (multiuser domains or dimensions) and MOOs (MUDs of the Object Oriented variety) similarly represent a new category of experience. For this reason and because there is such fine work that tries to describe this experience (Turkle 1995; Haynes and Holmevik 1998), I will not pursue the genre here.

14. See Turkle for insightful comments on how related technologies affect personal identity (1995).

15. To be sure, there are some interactive games that already "tap other emotions besides competition" (Caruso 1996). One that should be cited here is "Ceremony of Innocence" (produced by Real World) in which the reader-player's reply involves moving the mouse not to harm or kill an opponent but to manipulate fantastic images painted on envelopes or cards. Once one "finds the key" to these images, the envelope opens or the card turns over and reader-players can read the next installment of a story. I hasten to note that it could be argued that the reader-player's actions do not in and of themselves involve the representation, the events, or the time sequence of that story and thus may not meet the criteria I used to restrict this consideration of Talk in hypertext. Furthermore, the game is based on the previously published "Griffin and Sabine" (book) trilogy of Nick Bantock (1991, 1992, 1993). In this context, I would like to mention an Australian project called "Juvenate," which at the time of this writing was not yet widely circulating, but which specifically takes as its goal departure from cinematic and video game experience. In terms of emotions, its vague "plot" involves exploring myths about illness. See Hutchinson 2000.

Works Cited

Aarseth, Espen J. 1997. *Cybertext: Perspectives on Ergodic Literature*. Baltimore: Johns Hopkins UP.

Alazraki, Jaime. 1983. "From *Bestiary* to *Glenda*: Pushing the Short Story to Its Utmost Limits." *Review of Contemporary Fiction* 3: 94–99.

Alcoff, Linda, and Laura Gray. 1993. "Survivor Discourse: Transgression or Recuperation?" *Signs: Journal of Women in Culture and Society* 18, no. 1: 260–90.

Allen, Robert C. 1992a. "Introduction to the Second Edition: More Talk about TV," 1–30. In Allen 1992c.

——. 1992b. "Audience-Oriented Criticism and Television," 101–37. In Allen 1992c.

——. ed. 1992c. *Channels of Discourse, Reassembled: Television and Contemporary Criticism*, 2nd. ed. Chapel Hill: U North Carolina P.

Allison, Dorothy. 1992. *Bastard Out of Carolina*. New York: Plume-Penguin.

Atkinson, J. M., and P. Drew. 1979. *Order in Court: The Organisation of Verbal Interaction in Judicial Settings*. London: Macmillan.

Atwood, Margaret. 1986. *The Handmaid's Tale*. Boston: Houghton Mifflin.

Aury, Dominique. 1957. "Notes, le roman, Michel Butor: *La Modification*." *La Nouvelle Revue française* 60: 1146–49.

Austin, J. L. 1962. *How to Do Things with Words*. Ed. J. O. Urmson and Marina Shisà. Cambridge: Harvard UP.

Baker, G. P., and P. M. S. Hacker. 1980. *Wittgenstein: Meaning and Understanding*. Oxford: Blackwell.

Baker, Nicholson. 1992. *Vox*. New York: Vintage.

Bakhtin, Mikhail Mikhailovich. 1981. *The Dialogic Imagination: Four Essays*. Ed. Michael Holquist. Trans. Caryl Emerson and Michael Holquist. Austin: U Texas P.

——. 1986. *Speech Genres and Other Late Essays*. Ed. Caryl Emerson and Michael Holquist. Trans. Vern W. McGee. Austin: U Texas P.

Bal, Mieke. 1985. *Introduction to the Theory of Narrative*. Toronto: U Toronto P.

Baldwin, Peter, ed. 1990. *Reworking the Past: Hitler, the Holocaust, and the Historians' Debate*. Boston: Beacon.

Balzer, Bernd. 1981. "Nachwort." In *Eine jüdische Mutter*, by Gertrud Kolmar, 163–82. Frankfurt am Main: Ullstein.

255

Banfield, Ann. 1982. *Unspeakable Sentences: Narration and Representation in the Language of Fiction*. Boston: Routledge and Kegan Paul.

Bantock, Nick. 1993. *The Griffin and Sabine Trilogy*. San Francisco: Chronicle.

Barjon, Louis. 1958. "Les Prix littéraires." *Etudes* 296: 92–95.

Baron, Dennis E. 1986. *Grammar and Gender*. New Haven: Yale UP.

Barth, John. 1968. *Lost in the Funhouse*. New York: Doubleday.

Barthes, Roland. 1958. "Il n'y a pas d'école de Robbe-Grillet." *Arguments* 6: 6–8.

———. 1966. "Introduction à l'analyse structurale des récits." *Communications* 8: 1–27.

———. 1970. *S/Z*. Paris: Seuil.

———. 1974. *S/Z: An Essay*. Trans. Richard Miller. Preface by Richard Howard. New York: Hill and Wang.

Bauman, Richard, and Joel Sherzer, eds. 1974. *Explorations in the Ethnography of Speaking*. Cambridge: Cambridge UP.

Bayles, Martha. 1999. "Imus, Oprah and the Literary Elite." *New York Times Book Review*, 29 Aug., 35.

Beardsley, Elizabeth Lane. 1973–74. "Referential Genderization." *Philosophical Forum* 5: 285–93.

———. 1977. "Traits and Genderization." In *Feminism and Philosophy*, ed. Mary Vetterling-Braggin, Frederick A. Elliston, and Jane English, 117–23. Totowa, N.J.: Rowman and Allanheld.

Beaton, Roderick. 1994. *An Introduction to Modern Greek Literature*. Oxford: Clarendon.

Behrendt, Johanna E. 1969. "Auf der Suche nach dem Adamsapfel. Der Erzähler Pilenz in Günter Grass' Novelle *Katz und Maus*." *Germanisch-romanische Monatsschrift* 50: 313–26.

Bell, Bernard W. 1987. *The Afro-American Novel and Its Tradition*. Amherst: U Massachusetts P.

Benjamin, Walter. [1936] 1977. "Der Erzähler. Betrachtungen zum Werk Nikolai Lesskows." In *Gesammelte Schriften*. Vol. 2, ed. Rolf Tiedemann and Hermann Schweppenhäuser, 438–65. Frankfurt am Main: Suhrkamp.

———. 1969. "The Storyteller: Reflections of the Works of Nikolai Leskov." In *Illuminations: Essays and Reflections*, ed. and intro. Hannah Arendt and trans. Harry Zohn, 83–109. New York: Schocken.

Benveniste, Emile. 1966. *Problèmes de linguistique générale*. Vol. 1. Paris: Editions Gallimard.

———. 1971. *Problems in General Linguistics*. Vol. 1. Trans. M. E. Meek. Coral Gables: U Miami P.

Biber, Douglas. 1988. *Variation across Speech and Writing*. Cambridge: Cambridge UP.

Birkerts, Sven. 1994. *The Gutenberg Elegies: The Fate of Reading in an Electronic Age*. New York: Fawcett Columbine.

Block, Elizabeth. 1982. "The Narrator Speaks: Apostrophe in Homer and Vergil." *Transactions of the American Philological Association* 112: 7–22.

Boden, Deirdre, and Don H. Zimmerman, eds. 1991. *Talk and Social Structure: Studies in Ethnomethodology and Conversation Analysis*. Cambridge: Polity.

Bogosian, Eric. 1988. *Talk Radio*. New York: Vintage.

Boisdeffre, Pierre de. 1957. "Une Révolution qui fait long feu." *Revue de Paris* 12: 170–71.

Bolter, Jay David. 1991. *Writing Space: The Computer, Hypertext, and the History of Writing*. Hillsdale, N.J.: Lawrence Erlbaum.

Booth, Wayne. 1961. *The Rhetoric of Fiction*. Chicago: U Chicago P.

Botheroyd, Paul F. 1976. *Ich und Er: First and Third Person Self-Reference and Problems of Identity in Three Contemporary German-Language Novels*. The Hague: Mouton.

Bradsher, Keith. 1999. "Talk Show Ordered to Pay $25 Million After Killing." *New York Times*, 8 May, A10.

Brinker-Gabler, Gisela, Karola Ludwig, and Angela Wöffen. 1986. *Lexikon deutschsprachiger Schriftstellerinnen: 1800–1945*. Munich: Deutscher Taschenbuch Verlag.

Brison, Susan. 1999. "The Uses of Narrative in the Aftermath of Violence." In *On Feminist Ethics and Politics*, ed. Claudia Card, 200–225. Lawrence: U Kansas P.

Brooks, Peter. 1984. *Reading for the Plot: Design and Intention in Narrative*. New York: Vintage.

Brown, Robert, and Marguerite Ford. 1961. "Address in American English." In *Language in Culture and Society. A Reader in Linguistics and Anthropology*, ed. Dell Hymes, 234–50. New York: Harper and Row.

Brown, Roger, and Albert Gilman. 1960. "The Pronouns of Power and Solidarity." In *Style in Language*, ed. T. A. Sebeok, 253–76. Cambridge: MIT UP.

Bruce, James C. 1966. "The Equivocating Narrator in Günter Grass's *Katz und Maus*." *Monatshefte* 58: 139–49.

Buber, Martin. [1923] 1955. *Ich und Du*. Cologne: Hegner.

Burns, Tom. 1992. *Erving Goffman*. London: Routledge.

Butor, Michel [1957] 1963. *La Modification*. Paris: Les Editions de Minuit.

———. 1959. *Change of Heart*. Trans. Jean Stewart. New York: Simon and Schuster.

———. 1961. "L'Usage des pronoms personnels dans le roman." *Les Temps modernes* 16: 936–48.

Byland, Hans. 1971. *Zu den Gedichten Gertrud Kolmars*. Ph. D. Diss., University of Zürich.

Byrne, P. S., and B. E. Long. 1976. *Doctors Talking to Patients*. London: HMSO.

Calvino, Italo. 1979. *Se una notte d'inverno un viaggiatore*. Torino: Einaudi.

———. 1981. *If on a winter's night a traveler*. Trans. William Weaver. San Diego: Harcourt Brace Jovanovich.

Camus, Albert. 1956a. *La Chute: récit*. Paris: Librairie Gallimard.

———. 1956b. *The Fall: A Novel*. Trans. Justin O'Brien. New York: Vintage, by arrangement with Alfred A. Knopf.

Capecci, John. 1989. "Performing the Second Person." *Text and Performance Quarterly* 1: 42–52.

Carretta, Vincent. 1995. Introduction to *The Interesting Narrative and Other Writings*, by Olaudah Equiano, ix–xxviii. New York: Penguin.

Caruso, Denise. 1996. "Interactive Media Must Tell a Compelling Story to Draw People In." *New York Times*, 20 May, D7.

———. 1999. "Digital Commerce." *New York Times*, 26 Apr., C4.

Caruth, Cathy. 1993. "Violence and Time: Traumatic Survivals." *assemblage* 20: 24–25.

———. ed. 1995a. *Trauma: Explorations in Memory*. Baltimore: Johns Hopkins UP. Originally published as two special issues on "Psychoanalysis, Culture and Trauma" of *American Imago* (1991) 48, no. 1; 48, no. 4.

———. 1995b. "An Interview with Robert Jay Lifton." In Caruth 1995a, 128–47.

———. 1996. *Unclaimed Experience: Trauma, Narrative, and History*. Baltimore: Johns Hopkins UP.

Carvajal, Doreen. 1999. "Exorcising Demons through Fiction: A Middle-Aged Writer Goes from a Trailer to Talk-Show Fame." *New York Times*, 8 Sept., B1.

Case, Sue-Ellen. 1996. *The Domain-Matrix: Performing Lesbian at the End of Print Culture*. Bloomington: Indiana UP.

Chafe, Wallace L. 1982. "Integration and Involvement in Speaking, Writing, and Oral Literature." In Tannen 1982b, 35–53.

———. 1994. *Discourse, Consciousness and Time: The Flow and Displacement of Conscious Experience in Speaking and Writing*. Chicago: U Chicago P.

Chamisso, Adelbert von. [1814] 1975. "Peter Schlemihls wundersame Geschichte." *Sämtliche Werke*. Vol. 1: 13–67. Munich: Winkler Verlag.

Chatman, Seymour. 1978. *Story and Discourse: Narrative Structure in Fiction and Film*. Ithaca: Cornell UP.

Cohn, Dorrit. 1978. *Transparent Minds: Narrative Modes for Presenting Consciousness in Fiction*. Princeton: Princeton UP.

———. 1989. "Fictional versus Historical Lives: Borderlines and Borderline Cases." *Journal of Narrative Technique* 19, no. 1: 3–24.

Colin, Amy. 1990. "Gertrud Kolmar. Das Dilemma einer deutsch-jüdischen Dichterin." In *Literatur in der Gesellschaft. Festschrift für Theo Buck zum 60. Geburtstag*, ed. Frank-Rutger Hausmann, Ludwig Jäger, and Bernd Witte, 247–57. Tübingen: Narr.

Conrad, Joseph. [1902] 1988. *Heart of Darkness. An Authoritative Text. Backgrounds and Sources. Criticism*. Ed. Robert Kimbrough. 3rd ed. New York: Norton.

Cortázar, Julio. [1963] 1988. *Rayuela*. Ed. Andrés Amorós. Madrid: Ediciones Cátedra.

———. [1966] 1975. *Hopscotch*. Trans. Gregory Rabassa. New York: Avon.

———. 1979. "Graffiti." Trans. Laure Guille-Bataillon. *Derrière le Miroir* 234: 1, 3, 6, 8.

———. 1980. "Grafitti." In *Queremos Tanto a Glenda*, 107–11. Mexico City: Nueva Imagen.

———. 1983. "Graffiti." In *We Love Glenda So Much and Other Tales*. Trans. Gregory Rabassa, 33–38. New York: Alfred A. Knopf.

Crawford, Mary, and Roger Chaffin. 1986. "The Reader's Construction of Meaning: Cognitive Research on Gender and Comprehension." In *Gender and Reading: Essays on Readers, Texts, and Contexts*, ed. Elizabeth A. Flynn and Patrocinio P. Schweickart, 3–30. Baltimore: Johns Hopkins UP.

Culbertson, Roberta. 1995. "Embodied Memory, Transcendence, and Telling: Recounting Trauma, Re-Establishing the Self." *New Literary History* 26, no. 1: 169–95.

Culler, Jonathan. 1981. "Apostrophe." In *The Pursuit of Signs: Semiotics, Literature, Deconstruction*, 135–54. Ithaca: Cornell UP.

Davies, Russell. 1981. "The Writer Versus the Reader." Rev. of *If on a winter's night a traveler*, by Italo Calvino. *Times Literary Supplement*, 10 July, 773–74.

Delbo, Charlotte. [1965] 1995. "None of Us Will Return." In *Auschwitz and After*, trans. Rosette C. Lamont; intro. Lawrence L. Langer, 1–114. New Haven: Yale UP.

Deleuze, Gilles, and Félix Guattari. 1986. *Kafka: Toward a Minor Literature*. Trans. Dana Polan. Foreword by Réda Bensmaïa. Minneapolis: U Minnesota P.

Dick, Jutta, and Marina Sassenberg, eds. 1993. *Jüdische Frauen im 19. und 20. Jahrhundert. Lexikon zu Leben und Werk*. Reinbek bei Hamburg: Rowohlt Taschenbuch Verlag.

DiMeo, Philippe. 1981. "Celui qui se tient derrière tous ceux qui écrivent." *Quinzaine littéraire* 346: 11–12.

Döblin, Alfred. [1929] 1961. *Berlin Alexanderplatz: Die Geschichte vom Franz Biberkopf*. Munich: Deutscher Taschenbuch Verlag.

Doctorow, E. L. 1999. "Quick Cuts: The Novel Follows Film into a World of Fewer Words." *New York Times*, 15 Mar., B1.

Dort, Bernard. 1958. "La Forme et le fond." *Cahiers du Sud: Epreuves du roman* 344: 121–25.

Douglas, Susan J. 1987. *Inventing American Broadcasting, 1899–1922*. Baltimore: Johns Hopkins UP.

DSM-IV. 1994. *Diagnostic and Statistical Manual of Mental Disorders*. 4th ed. Washington, D.C.: American Psychiatric Association.

Du Bois, W. E. B. [1903] 1961. *The Souls of Black Folk: Essays and Sketches*. Greenwich, Conn.: Fawcett.

Duranti, Alessandro. 1986. "The Audience as Co-Author: An Introduction." *Text: An Interdisciplinary Journal for the Study of Discourse* 6, no. 3: 239–47.

Eichmann-Leutenegger, Beatrice. 1993. *Gertrud Kolmar. Leben und Werk in Texten und Bildern*. Frankfurt am Main: Jüdischer Verlag.

Ellis, John. 1999. "Prepare to Merge: The Technological Revolution Will Change Almost Everything in Its Path." *Boston Globe Magazine*, 23 May, 12ff.

Equiano, Olaudah. [1789] 1995. The Interesting Narrative *and Other Writings*. Intro. and Notes by Vincent Carretta. New York: Penguin.

Estang, Luc. 1958. "Couronnes et bandeaux." *Pensée française* 17: 55–57.

Evans, Richard J. 1989. *In Hitler's Shadow: West German Historians and the Attempt to Escape the Nazi Past*. New York: Pantheon.

Faulkner, William. [1936] 1987. *Absalom, Absalom!* The Corrected Text. New York: Vintage.

Feather, John. 1985. *The Provincial Book Trade in Eighteenth-Century England*. Cambridge: Cambridge UP.

———. 1988. *A History of British Publishing*. London: Routledge.

Felman, Shoshana, and Dori Laub. 1992. *Testimony: Crises of Witnessing in Literature, Psychoanalysis, and History*. New York: Routledge.

Fetterley, Judith. 1977. *The Resisting Reader: A Feminist Approach to American Fiction*. Bloomington: Indiana UP.

Flanzbaum, Hilene, ed. 1999. *The Americanization of the Holocaust*. Baltimore: Johns Hopkins UP.

Flint, Christopher. 1998. "Speaking Objects: The Circulation of Stories in Eighteenth-Century Prose Fiction." *PMLA* 113, no. 2: 212–26.

Fludernik, Monika. 1993. "Second Person Fiction: Narrative YOU as Addressee and/or Protagonist. Typological and Functional Notes on an Increasingly Popular Genre." *Arbeiten aus Anglistik und Amerikanistik [AAA]* 18, no. 2: 217–47.

———. 1994a. "Introduction: Second-Person Narrative and Related Issues." *Style* 28, no. 3: 281–311.

———. 1994b. "Second-Person Narrative: A Bibliography." *Style* 28, no. 4: 525–48.

———. 1996. *Towards a "Natural" Narratology*. London: Routledge.

Fowler, Virginia C. 1996. *Gloria Naylor: In Search of Sanctuary*. New York: Twayne.

Foy, David W. 1992. *Treating PTSD: Cognitive-Behavioral Strategies*. New York: Guilford.

Frederick, Calvin Jeff. 1987. "Psychic Trauma in Victims of Crime and Terrorism." In *Cataclysms, Crises, and Catastrophes: Psychology in Action*, ed. Gary R. VandenBos and Brenda K. Bryant, 55–108. Washington, D.C.: American Psychological Association.

Friedman, Matthew J., Dennis S. Charney, and Ariel Y. Deutch, eds. 1995. *Neurobiological and Clinical Consequences of Stress: From Normal Adaptation to Post-Traumatic Stress Disorder*. Philadelphia: Lippincott-Raven.

Friedman, Norman. 1955. "Point of View in Fiction: The Development of a Critical Concept." *PMLA* 70: 1160–84.

Frieze, Irene Hanson. 1987. "The Female Victim: Rape, Wife Battering, and Incest." In *Cataclysms, Crises, and Catastrophes: Psychology in Action*, ed. Gary R. VandenBos and Brenda K. Bryant, 109–45. Washington, D.C.: American Psychological Association.

Gardner, Eric. 1993. " 'This Attempt of Their Sister': Harriet Wilson's *Our Nig* from Printer to Readers." *New England Quarterly* 66, no. 2: 226–46.

Garfinkel, Harold. 1967. *Studies in Ethnomethodology*. Englewood Cliffs, N.J.: Prentice-Hall.

Garréta, Anne. 1986. *Sphinx*. Paris: Bernard Grasset.

Gates, Henry Louis Jr. 1983. Introduction. In Wilson, xi–lv.

——— . 1988. *The Signifying Monkey: A Theory of African-American Literary Criticism*. New York: Oxford UP.

Genette, Gérard. 1972. "Discours du récit: essai de méthode." In *Figures III*, 65–278. Paris: Seuil.

———. 1980. *Narrative Discourse: An Essay in Method*. Trans. Jane Lewin. Ithaca: Cornell UP.

———. 1983. *Nouveau Discours du récit*. Paris: Seuil.

———. 1997. *Paratexts: Threshold of Interpretation*. Trans. Jane E. Lewin. Foreword by Richard Macksey. Cambridge: Cambridge UP.

Gennadius, John. 1881. Preface. In Vikélas 1881b, v–xxiv.

Gerstenberg, Renate. 1980. *Zur Erzähltechnik von Günter Grass*. Heidelberg: Carl Winter Universitätsverlag.

Gilman, Sander L. 1986. *Jewish Self-Hatred: Anti-Semitism and the Hidden Language of the Jews*. Baltimore: Johns Hopkins UP.

Gnutzmann, Rita. 1983. "La Novela hispanoamericana en segunda persona." *Iberoromania* 17: 100–120.

Goffman, Erving. 1961. *Encounters: Two Studies in the Sociology of Interaction*. Indianapolis: Bobbs-Merrill.

——. 1981. *Forms of Talk*. Philadelphia: U Pennsylvania P.

Goodstein, Laurie. 1998. "Readers Turning to Thrillers Depicting Spiritual Rapture." *New York Times*, 4 Oct., A1.

Goodwin, Charles. 1986. "Audience Diversity, Participation and Interpretation." *Text* 6, no. 3: 283–316.

Goodwin, Charles, and John Heritage. 1990. "Conversation Analysis." *Annual Review of Anthropology* 19: 283–307.

Gordimer, Nadine. 1979. *Burger's Daughter*. New York: Penguin.

Grand Robert de la langue française. 1989. 2nd ed. Montreal: Le Robert.

Grass, Günter. [1961] 1974. *Katz und Maus: Eine Novelle*. Darmstadt: Hermann Luchterhand Verlag.

——. 1994. "Cat and Mouse." Trans. Ralph Manheim. In *Cat and Mouse and Other Writings*, ed. A. Leslie Willson with a foreword by John Irving, 3–109. New York: Continuum.

Greatbatch, David. 1988. "A Turn-Taking System for British News Interviews." *Language and Society* 17, no. 3: 401–30.

Green, Keith, ed. 1995. *New Essays in Deixis: Discourse, Narrative, Literature*. Amsterdam: Rodopi.

Grimes, William. 1993. "When the Film Audience Controls the Plot." *New York Times*, 13 Jan., C15.

Grimmelshausen. [1669] 1967. *Der Abentheurliche Simplicissimus Teutsch*. Ed. Rolf Tarot. Tübingen: Max Niemeyer Verlag.

Gronniosaw, James Albert Ukawsaw. [1770] 1774. *A Narrative of the Most Remarkable Particulars in the Life of James Albert Ukawsaw Gronniosaw, an African Prince, as Related by Himself*. Newport, R.I. [Worcester, Mass.: American Antiquarian Society Readex Microprint, 1959]. Microfiche.

Grossman, Dave. 1995. *On Killing: The Psychological Cost of Learning to Kill in War and Society*. Boston: Little Brown.

Guth, Paul. 1957. "Un Révolutionnaire du roman 1926–57: ou les modifications de Michel Butor." *Le Figaro littéraire*, 7 Dec., 1, 4.

Haines, Claudia Persi. 1984. "The Visible Reader/The Invisible Writer." *Italian Quarterly* 25: 41–51.

Hancock, Ian. 1991. "Gypsy History in Germany and Neighboring Lands: A Chronology Leading to the Holocaust." In *The Gypsies of Eastern Europe*, ed. David Crowe and John Kolsti, 11–30. Armonk, N.Y.: Sharpe.

Harris, Roy. 1988. *Language, Saussure, and Wittgenstein: How to Play Games with Words*. London: Routledge.

Hartman, Geoffrey H. 1996. *The Longest Shadow: In the Aftermath of the Holocaust*. Bloomington: Indiana UP.

Havelock, Eric A. 1986. *The Muse Learns to Write: Reflections on Orality and Literacy from Antiquity to the Present*. New Haven: Yale UP.

Haviland, John. 1986. " 'Con Buenos Chiles': Talk, Targets and Teasing in Zinacantán." *Text* 6, no. 3: 249–82.

Haynes, Cynthia, and Jan Rune Holmevik, eds. 1998. *High Wired: On the Design, Use, and Theory of Educational MOOs*. Ann Arbor: U Michigan P.

Henriot, Emile. 1957. "*La Modification* de Michel Butor." *Le Monde* 13 Nov., 7.

Heritage, John. 1984. *Garfinkel and Ethnomethodology*. Cambridge: Polity.

Heritage, John, and David Greatbatch. 1991. "On the Institutional Character of Institutional Talk: The Case of News Interviews." In Boden and Zimmerman, 93–137.

Herman, Judith Lewis. 1992. *Trauma and Recovery*. New York: Basic.

Herr, Michael. 1978. *Dispatches*. New York: Avon.

Herz, J. C. 1998. "Holding the Reins of Reality." *New York Times*, 25 June, E4.

Hoffman, Ernst Theodor Amadäus. [1814] 1957. "Die Abenteuer der Sylvesternacht." In *Poetische Werke*. Vol. 1: 305–41. Berlin: Walter De Gruyter.

Holquist, Michael. 1985. "Bakhtin and the Formalists: History as Dialogue." In Jackson and Rudy, 82–95.

Hopper, Robert. 1992. *Telephone Conversation*. Bloomington: Indiana UP.

Hutcheon, Linda. 1989. *The Politics of Postmodernism*. London: Routledge.

Hutchinson, Andrew. 2000. "*Juvenate*: Getting Lost in the Interface of Interactive Narrative." Paper given at annual conference of Society for the Study of Narrative Literature, 9 Apr., Atlanta, Ga.

Hymes, Dell. 1962. "The Ethnography of Speaking." In *Anthropology and Human Behavior*, ed. T. Gladwin and W. C. Sturtevant, 13–53. Washington, D.C.: Washington D.C. Anthropological Society.

——. 1974a. *Foundations in Sociolinguistics: An Ethnographic Approach*. Philadelphia: U Pennsylvania P.

——. 1974b. "Ways of Speaking." In Bauman and Sherzer, 433–51.

Ingersoll, Earl G., ed. 1990. *Margaret Atwood: Conversations*. London: Virago.

Jackson, Robert Louis, and Stephen Rudy. 1985. *Russian Formalism: A Retrospective Glance. A Festschrift in Honor of Victor Erlich*. New Haven: Yale Center for International and Area Studies.

Jakobson, Roman. 1960. "Closing Statement: Linguistics and Poetics." In *Style in Language*, ed. Thomas A. Sebeok, 350–77. Cambridge: MIT UP.

James, Henry. [1907–9] 1962. *The Art of the Novel*. Intro. R. P. Blackmur. New York: Charles Scribner's Sons.

Janet, Pierre. 1889. *L'Automatisme psychologique*. Paris: Alcan.

——. 1898. *Névroses et idées fixes*. Vol. 1. Paris: Alcan.

——. 1911. *L'Etat mental des hystériques*. 2nd ed. Paris: Alcan.

——. 1925. *Psychological Healing: A Historical and Clinical Study*. Vol. 1. Trans. Eden and Cedar Paul. New York: Macmillan.

——. 1928. *L'Evolution de la mémoire et de la notion du temps*. Paris: Editions Chahine.

——. [1907] 1965. *The Major Symptoms of Hysteria: Fifteen Lectures Given in the Medical School of Harvard University*. 2nd ed. New York: Hafner.

Johnson, Barbara. 1987. "Apostrophe, Animation, and Abortion." *A World of Difference*, 184–99. Baltimore: Johns Hopkins UP.

Johnson, James Weldon. [1912] 1960. *The Autobiography of an Ex-Coloured Man*. Intro. Arna Bontemps. New York: Hill and Wang.

Jones, Gayl. 1991. *Liberating Voices: Oral Tradition in African-American Literature*. Cambridge: Harvard UP.

Joyce, James. [1922] 1986. *Ulysses*. The Corrected Text. Ed. Hans Walter Gabler, Wolfhard Steppe, and Claus Melchior. New York: Random House.

Jusdanis, Gregory. 1991. *Belated Modernity and Aesthetic Culture: Inventing National Literature*. Minneapolis: U Minnesota P.

Juster, Norton. [1961] 1989. *The Phantom Tollbooth*. Illus. Jules Feiffer. Appreciation by Maurice Sendak. New York: Random House.

Kacandes, Irene. 1990. "Orality, Reader Address, and Anonymous 'You.' On Translating Second Person References from Modern Greek Prose." *Journal of Modern Greek Studies* 8, no. 2: 223–43.

——. 1992. "The Oral Tradition and Modern Greek Literature." Laografia: *A Newsletter of the International Greek Folklore Society* 9, no. 5: 3–8.

——. 1993. "Are You In the Text?: The 'Literary Performative' in Postmodernist Fiction." *Text and Performance Quarterly* 13: 139–53.

——. 1994. "Narrative Apostrophe: Reading, Rhetoric, Resistance in Michel Butor's *La Modification* and Julio Cortázar's 'Graffiti.'" *Style* 28, no. 3: 329–49.

——. 1997. "German Cultural Studies: What Is at Stake?" In *A User's Guide to German Cultural Studies*, ed. Scott Denham, Irene Kacandes, and Jonathan Petropoulos, 3–28. Ann Arbor: U Michigan P.

Kaes, Anton, Martin Jay, and Edward Dimendberg, eds. 1994. *The Weimar Republic Sourcebook*. Berkeley: U California P.

Kartiganer, Donald. 1995. "An Introduction to the Last Great Short Story." *The Oxford-American,* May/June: 51–53.

Keele, Alan Frank. 1988. *Understanding Günter Grass*. Columbia: U South Carolina P.

King, Debra Walker. 1997. "Harriet Wilson's *Our Nig*: The Demystification of Sentiment." In *Recovered Writers/Recovered Texts: Race, Class, and Gender in Black Women's Literature*, ed. Dolan Hubbard, 31–45. Knoxville: U Tennessee P.

Kleber, Rolf J., Charles R. Figley, and Berthold P. R. Gersons, eds. 1995. *Beyond Trauma: Cultural and Societal Dynamics*. New York: Plenum.

Kleist, Heinrich von. [1808] 1977. "Die Marquise von O . . ." In *Sämtliche Werke und Briefe*. Vol. 2, ed. Helmut Sembdner, 104–43. Munich: Carl Hanser.

Kolmar, Gertrud. [1955] 1960. *Das lyrische Werk*. Munich: Kösel-Verlag KG.

——. 1970. *Briefe an die Schwester Hilde (1938–1943)*. Munich: Kösel-Verlag.

——. [1965] 1981. *Eine jüdische Mutter: Erzählung*, 2nd ed. Afterword by Bernd Balzer. Frankfurt am Main: Ullstein.

——. 1991. "Zwei Briefe an Walter Benjamin." *Sinn und Form* 43: 122–24.

——. [1959] 1993. *Susanna*. Afterword by Thomas Sparr. Frankfurt am Main: Jüdischer Verlag.

——. 1997. *A Jewish Mother from Berlin: A Novel; Susanna: A Novella*. Trans. Brigitte M. Goldstein. New York: Holmes and Meier.

Kozloff, Sarah. 1992. "Narrative Theory and Television." In Allen 1992c, 67–100.

Krause, Gerd. 1962. *Tendenzen im französischen Romanschaffen des zwanzigsten Jahrhunderts. Nouveau Roman—Traditioneller Roman*. Frankfurt am Main: Verlag Moritz Diesterweg.

Lakoff, Robin Tolmach. 1975. *Language and Woman's Place*. New York: Harper Colophon.

——. 1982. "Some of My Favorite Writers Are Litcrate: The Mingling of Oral and Literate Strategies in Written Communication." In Tannen 1982b, 239–60.

Landow, George P. 1992. *Hypertext: The Convergence of Contemporary Critical Theory and Technology*. Baltimore: Johns Hopkins UP.

——. 1997. *Hypertext 2.0, Being a Revised, Amplified Edition of Hypertext: The Convergence of Contemporary Critical Theory and Technology*. Baltimore: Johns Hopkins UP.

Langford, Gerald. 1971. *Faulkner's Revision of* Absalom, Absalom! *A Collation of the Manuscript and the Published Book*. Austin: U Texas P.

Laufer, Peter. 1995. *Inside Talk Radio: America's Voice or Just Hot Air?* New York: Carol.

Lausberg, Heinrich. 1960. *Handbuch der literarischen Rhetorik: Eine Grundlegung der Literaturwissenschaft*. Munich: Max Hueber Verlag.

——. 1998. *Handbook of Literary Rhetoric: A Foundation for Literary Study*.

Foreword by George A. Kennedy. Trans. Matthew T. Bliss, Annemick Jansen, and David E. Orton. Ed. David E. Orton and R. Dean Anderson. Leiden, Netherlands: Brill.

Lawrence, Amy. 1994. "Staring the Camera Down: Direct Address and Women's Voices." In *Embodied Voices: Representing Female Vocality in Western Culture*, ed. Leslie C. Dunn and Nancy A. Jones, 166–78. Cambridge: Cambridge UP.

LeClair, Thomas. 1982. "Fiction Chronicle: January to June, 1981." *Contemporary Literature* 23: 83–91.

Ledbetter, James. 1998. "Radio Clash: How Can Public Radio Survive in a Private Market?" Talk given at annual conference of the Modern Language Association, 28 Dec., San Francisco, Calif.

Leiris, Michel. [1958] 1963. "Le Réalisme mythologique de Michel Butor." In Michel Butor, *La Modification*, 287–314. Paris: Minuit. Originally appeared in *Critique* 129: 99–118.

Lemish, Dafna. 1987. "Viewers in Diapers: The Early Development of Television Viewing." In *Natural Audiences: Qualitative Research of Media Uses and Effects*, ed. Thomas Lindlof, 33–57. Norwood, N.J.: Ablex.

Leonard, Irène. 1974. *Günter Grass*. Edinburgh: Oliver and Boyd.

Levin, Murray Burton. 1987. *Talk Radio and the American Dream*. Lexington, Mass.: Lexington Books.

Leys, Ruth. 1994. "Traumatic Cures: Shell Shock, Janet, and the Question of Memory." *Critical Inquiry* 20, no. 4: 623–62.

Lindenberger, Thomas, and Alf Lüdtke, eds. 1995. *Physische Gewalt: Studien zur Geschichte der Neuzeit*. Frankfurt am Main: Suhrkamp.

Lively, Penelope. 1982. "Stories and Echoes." Rev. of *If on a winter's night a traveler*, by Italo Calvino. *Encounter* 58: 74–81.

"Longinus." [1927] 1982. "On the Sublime." Trans. W. Hamilton Fyfe. In *Aristotle XXIII: The Poetics. "Longinus," Demetrius*, 119–254. Cambridge, Mass.: Loeb Classical Library.

Lorenz, Dagmar C. G. 1993. "The Unspoken Bond: Else Lasker-Schüler and Gertrud Kolmar in Their Historical and Cultural Context." *Seminar: A Journal of Germanic Studies* 29: 349–69.

Lottman, Herbert R. 1979. *Albert Camus: A Biography*. New York: Doubleday.

Lubbock, Percy. [1921] 1957. *The Craft of Fiction*. New York: Viking.

Lucente, Gregory L. 1985. "An Interview with Italo Calvino." *Contemporary Literature* 26: 245–53.

Lydon, Mary. 1980. *Perpetuum Mobile: A Study of the Novels and Aesthetics of Michel Butor*. Edmonton: U Alberta P.

MacKay, Donald G. 1983. "Prescriptive Grammar and the Pronoun Problem."

In *Language, Gender, and Society*, ed. Barrie Thorne, Cheris Kramarae, and Nancy Henley, 38–53. Rowley, Mass.: Newbury.

Maier, Charles. 1988. *The Unmasterable Past*. Cambridge: Harvard UP.

Mandelbaum, Jenny. 1987. "Couples Sharing Stories." *Communication Quarterly* 35: 144–70.

——. 1989. "Interpersonal Activities in Conversational Storytelling." *Western Journal of Speech Communication* 53: 114–26.

Mann, Thomas. 1947. *Doktor Faustus: Das Leben des deutschen Tonsetzers Adrian Leverkühn erzählt von einem Freunde*. Frankfurt am Main: S. Fischer Verlag.

Mannheim, Bruce, and Dennis Tedlock. 1995. Introduction. In Tedlock and Mannheim, 1–32.

Markoff, John. 1994. "The Rise and Swift Fall of Cyber Literacy." *New York Times*, 13 Mar., A1.

Maron, Monika. 1986. *Die Überläuferin: Roman*. Frankfurt am Main: S. Fischer Verlag.

——. 1988. *The Defector*. Trans. David Newton Marinelli. London: Readers International.

Martyna, Wendy. 1983. "Beyond the He/Man Approach: The Case for Nonsexist Language." In *Language, Gender, and Society*. Ed. Barrie Thorne, Cheris Kramarae, and Nancy Henley, 25–37. Rowley, Mass.: Newbury.

Marsella, Anthony J. et al. 1996. *Ethnocultural Aspects of Posttraumatic Stress Disorder: Issues, Research, and Clinical Applications*. Washington, D.C.: American Psychological Association.

McConnell-Ginet, Sally. 1979. "Prototypes, Pronouns and Persons." *Ethnolinguistics: Boas, Sapir and Whorf Revisited*, ed. Madeleine Mathiot, 63–83. The Hague: Mouton.

——. 1980. "Linguistics and the Feminist Challenge." In *Women and Language in Literature and Society*. Ed. Sally McConnell-Ginet, Ruth Borker, and Nelly Furman, 3–25. New York: Praeger.

McHale, Brian. 1983. "Unspeakable Sentences, Unnatural Acts." *Poetics Today* 4: 17–45.

——. 1984–85. " 'You Used to Know What These Words Mean.' Misreading *Gravity's Rainbow*." *Language and Style* 17–18: 93–118.

——. 1987. *Postmodernist Fiction*. New York: Methuen.

McInerney, Jay. 1984. *Bright Lights, Big City*. New York: Vintage.

McKenzie, D. F. 1976. "The London Book Trade in the Later Seventeenth Century." Chicago: Newberry Library.

McLuhan, Marshall. 1964. *Understanding Media: The Extensions of Man*. London: Routledge and Kegan Paul.

Miles, Keith. 1975. *Günter Grass*. London: Vision.

Milton, Sybil. 1992. "Nazi Policies toward Roma and Sinti, 1933–1945." *Journal of the Gypsy Lore Society,* 5th ser. 2: 1–18.

Minow, Martha. 1993. "Surviving Victim Talk." *UCLA Law Review* 40: 1411–45.

Mitchell, Angelyn. 1992. "Her Side of His Story: A Feminist Analysis of Two Nineteenth-Century Antebellum Novels—William Wells Brown's *Clotel* and Harriet E. Wilson's *Our Nig.*" *American Literary Realism* 24, no. 3: 7–21.

Mitscherlich, Alexander, and Margarete Mitscherlich. 1967. *Die Unfähigkeit zu trauern. Grundlagen kollektiven Verhaltens*. Munich: Piper.

——. 1975. *The Inability to Mourn: Principles of Collective Behavior*. Trans. Beverley R. Placzek. New York: Grove.

Moerman, Michael. 1988. *Talking Culture: Ethnography and Conversation Analysis*. Philadelphia: U Pennsylvania P.

Morrissette, Bruce. 1965. "Narrative 'You' in Contemporary Literature." *Comparative Literature Studies* 2: 1–24. Repr. and expanded in *Novel and Film: Essays in Two Genres*, 108–40. Chicago: U Chicago P, 1985.

Morse, Margaret. 1985. "Talk, Talk, Talk: The Space of Discourse in Television News, Sportscasts, Talk Shows, and Advertising." *Screen* 26: 2–15.

——. 1998. *Virtualities: Television, Media Art, and Cyberculture*. Bloomington: U Indiana P.

Mullen, Carol Ann. 1987. "An Investigation of the Second Person Narrative Address in Works by Camus, Calvino, and F. Barthelme." Senior Honors Essay. Harvard College.

Munson, Wayne. 1993. *All Talk: The Talkshow in Media Culture*. Philadelphia: Temple UP.

Naylor, Gloria. 1988. *Mama Day*. New York: Vintage.

Nesaule, Agate. 1997. *A Woman in Amber*. Harmondsworth, England: Penguin.

Netzer, Klaus. 1970. *Der Leser des Nouveau Roman*. Frankfurt am Main: Athenäum Verlag.

Neuhaus, Volker. 1979. *Günter Grass*. Stuttgart: J. B. Metzlersche Verlagsbuchhandlung.

Newton, Adam Zachary. 1995. *Narrative Ethics*. Cambridge: Harvard UP.

Nofsinger, Robert E. 1991. *Everyday Conversation*. Newbury Park, Calif.: Sage.

Novick, Peter. 1999. *The Holocaust in American Life*. Boston: Houghton Mifflin.

Ong, Walter J. 1982. *Orality and Literacy: The Technologizing of the Word*. London: Methuen.

Orr, Marilyn. 1985. "Beginning in the Middle: The Story of Reading in Calvino's *If on a winter's night a traveler.*" *Papers on Language and Literature* 21: 210–19.

Otten, Karl, ed. 1959. *Das leere Haus. Prosa jüdischer Dichter.* Stuttgart: Cotta Verlag.

Passias, Katherine. 1970. "Deep and Surface Structure of the Narrative Pronoun *Vous* in Butor's *La Modification* and Its Relationship to Free Indirect Style." *Language and Style* 9: 197–212.

Peavler, Terry J. 1990. *Julio Cortázar.* Boston: Twayne.

Perrine, Laurence. 1975. "Apostrophe." In *Princeton Encyclopedia of Poetry and Poetics*, ed. Alex Preminger. London: Macmillan.

Phelan, James. 1989. *Reading People, Reading Plots: Character, Progression, and the Interpretation of Narrative.* Chicago: U Chicago P.

Philipsen, Gerry. 1989. "Speech and the Communal Function in Four Cultures." In Ting-Toomey and Korzenny, 79–92.

Picon, Gaeton. 1961. "Exemples du Nouveau Roman." In *L'Usage de la lecture.* Vol. 2: 265–70. Paris: Mercure de France.

Piirainen, Ilpo Tapani. 1968. *Textbezogene Untersuchungen über "Katz und Maus" und "Hundejahre" von Günter Grass.* Bern, Switzerland: Verlag Herbert Lang and Cie.

Pingaud, Bernard. 1958. "Je, vous, il." *Esprit* 26: 91–99.

Plumb, J. H. 1982. "Commercialization and Society." In *The Birth of a Consumer Society: The Commercialization of Eighteenth-Century England*, ed. Neil McKendrick, John Brewer, and J. H Plumb, 263–334. Bloomington: Indiana UP.

Pouillon, Jean. 1958. "A Propos de *La Modification.*" *Les Temps modernes* 13, nos. 141–44: 1099–1105.

Pratt, Marie Louise. 1977. *Toward a Speech Act Theory of Literary Discourses.* Bloomington: Indiana UP.

Prego, Omar. [1984] 1990. *Julio Cortázar (la fascinación de las palabras).* Montevideo: Ediciones Trilce.

Prince, Gerald. 1971. "Notes toward a Categorization of Fictional 'Narratee.' " *Genre* 4: 100–105.

——. 1973. "Introduction à l'étude du narrataire." *Poétique* 14: 178–96.

——. 1980. "Introduction to the Study of the Narratee." In *Reader-Response Criticism: From Formalism to Post-Structuralism*, ed. Jane P. Tompkins, 7–25. Baltimore: Johns Hopkins UP.

——. 1982. *Narratology: The Form and Functioning of Narrative.* New York: Mouton.

——. 1987. *A Dictionary of Narratology.* Lincoln: U Nebraska P.

Quéréel, Patrice. 1973. La Modification *de Butor.* Paris: Hachette.

Quintilian. [1921] 1960. *Institutio Oratoria.* Trans. H. E. Butler. Bilingual ed. Cambridge, Mass.: Loeb Classical Library.

Raillard, Georges. 1968. *Butor*. Paris: Gallimard.

Raven, James. 1992. *Judging New Wealth: Popular Publishing and Responses to Commerce in England, 1750–1800*. Oxford: Oxford UP.

Reddick, John. [1974] 1975. *The "Danzig Trilogy" of Günter Grass. A Study of* The Tin Drum, Cat and Mouse *and* Dog Years. London: Secker and Warburg.

Richardson, Brian. 1991. "The Poetics and Politics of Second-Person Narrative." *Genre* 24: 309–30.

Righini, Mariella. 1983. *La Passion, Ginette*. Paris: Grasset.

Rimmon-Kenan, Shlomith. 1987. "Narration as Repetition: the Case of Günter Grass's *Cat and Mouse*." In *Discourse in Psychoanalysis and Literature*, ed. Shlomith Rimmon-Kenan, 176–87. London: Methuen.

———. 1989. *Narrative Fiction: Contemporary Poetics*. London: Routledge.

Rittner, Carol, and John K. Roth, eds. 1993. *Different Voices: Women and the Holocaust*. New York: Paragon.

Roemer, Danielle M. 1995. "Graffiti as Story and Act." In *Folklore, Literature, and Cultural Theory. Collected Essays*, ed. Cathy Lynn Preston, 22–28. New York: Garland.

Röhl-Schulze, Barbara. 1990. *Einsamkeit, Entfremdung und Melancholie in der zeitgenössischen argentinischen Literatur (1955 bis zur Gegenwart). Mit einer Zusammenfassung in spanischer Sprache*. Cologne: Böhlau.

Roof, Judith. 1991. "'This Is Not for You': The Sexuality of Mothering." In *Narrating Mothers: Theorizing Maternal Subjectivities*, ed. Brenda O. Daly and Maureen T. Reddy, 157–73. Knoxville: U Tennessee P.

Rothstein, Edward. 1994. "A New Art Form May Arise from the 'Myst.'" *New York Times*, 4 Dec., B1.

Rubiner, Michael. 1995. "T. S. Eliot Interactive." *New York Times Magazine*, 18 June, 62.

Rühle-Gerstel, Alice. [1933] 1994. "Back to the Good Old Days?" In Kaes, Jay, and Dimendberg, 218–19.

Rule, Jane. [1970] 1988. *This Is Not for You*. Tallahassee: Naiad.

Ryan, Judith. 1983. "Resistance and Resignation: Günter Grass' *Cat and Mouse*." In *The Uncompleted Past: Postwar German Novels and the Third Reich*, 95–112. Detroit: Wayne State UP.

Ryan, Marie-Laure. 1999. "Cyberage Narratology: Computers, Metaphor, and Narrative." In *Narratologies: New Perspectives on Narrative Analysis*, ed. David Herman, 113–41. Columbus: Ohio State UP.

Sacks, Harvey, Emanuel Schegloff, and Gail Jefferson. 1974. "A Simplest Systematics for the Organization of Turn-Taking for Conversation." *Language* 50, no. 4: 696–735.

Salvatori, Mariolina. 1986. "Italo Calvino's *If on a winter's night a traveler*: Writer's Authority, Reader's Autonomy." *Contemporary Literature* 27: 182–212.

Schiffrin, Deborah. 1987. *Discourse Markers*. Cambridge: Cambridge UP.

Schwarz, Wilhelm Johannes. 1971. *Der Erzähler Günter Grass*. Bern, Switzerland: Francke Verlag.

Schweickart, Patrocinio P. 1986. "Reading Ourselves: Toward a Feminist Theory of Reading." In *Gender and Reading: Essays on Readers, Texts, and Contexts*, ed. Elizabeth A. Flynn and Patrocinio P. Schweickart, 31–62. Baltimore: Johns Hopkins UP.

Shafi, Monika. 1991. "Gertrud Kolmar: 'Niemals "die Eine" immer "die Andere"': Zur Künstlerproblematik in Gertrud Kolmars Prosa." In *Autoren damals und heute: Literaturgeschichtliche Beispiele veranderter Wirkungshorizonte*, ed. Gerhard P. Knapp, 689–711. Amsterdam: Rodopi.

———. 1995. *Gertrud Kolmar: Eine Einführung in das Werk*. Munich: Iudicium Verlag.

Shattuc, Jane M. 1997. *The Talking Cure: TV Talk Shows and Women*. New York: Routledge.

Sherzer, Joel. 1992. "Modes of Representation and Translation of Native American Discourse: Examples from the San Blas Kuna." In *On the Translation of Native American Literatures*, ed. Brian Swann, 426–40. Washington, D.C.: Smithsonian Institution P.

Sichrovsky, Peter. 1987. *Schuldig geboren: Kinder aus Nazifamilien*. Cologne: Verlag Kepenheuer and Witsch.

———. 1988. *Born Guilty: Children of Nazi Families*. Trans. Jean Steinberg. New York: Basic.

Simpkins, Scott. 1990. " 'The Infinite Game': Cortázar's *Hopscotch*." *Journal of the Midwest Modern Language Association* 23, no. 1: 61–74.

Smith, Henry A. 1975. "Gertrud Kolmar's Life and Works." In *Dark Soliloquy: The Selected Poems of Gertrud Kolmar*. Trans. Henry A. Smith, 3–52. New York: Continuum.

Smith, Philip M. 1985. *Language, the Sexes and Society*. Oxford: Blackwell.

Sparr, Thomas. 1993. "Nachwort." In *Susanna*, by Gertrud Kolmar, 65–91. Frankfurt am Main: Jüdischer Verlag.

Spitzer, Leo. 1961. "Quelques Aspects de la technique des romans de Michel Butor." *Archivum Linguisticum* 13: 171–95. Repr. in *Etudes de style*, 482–531. Paris: Gallimard, 1970.

Stanzel, Franz K. [1979] 1982. *Theorie des Erzählens*. Göttingen: Vandenhoeck and Ruprecht.

——. 1984. *A Theory of Narrative*. Trans. Charlotte Goedsche. Cambridge: Cambridge UP.

Steinberg, Günter. 1972. "Zur erlebten Rede in Michel Butors *La Modification*." *Vox Romanica* 31: 334–64.

Stephens, Mitchell. 1998. *The Rise of the Image, The Fall of the Word*. New York: Oxford UP.

Stepto, Robert. 1986. "Distrust of the Reader in Afro-American Narratives." In *Reconstructing American Literary History*, ed. Sacvan Bercovitch, 300–322. Cambridge: Harvard UP.

——. [1978] 1991. *From Behind the Veil: A Study of Afro-American Narrative*. 2nd ed. Urbana: U Illinois P.

Stern, Julia. 1995. "Excavating Genre in *Our Nig*." *American Literature* 67, no. 3: 439–66.

Sterne, Lawrence. [1759–67] 1967. *The Life and Opinions of Tristram Shandy, Gentleman*. Ed. Graham Petrie. Intro. Christopher Ricks. Harmondsworth, England: Penguin.

Stevenson, Robert Louis. 1887. "Talk and Talkers." In *Memories and Portraits*, 144–90. New York: Charles Scribner's Sons.

Stewart, Susan. 1987. "Ceci tuera cela: Graffiti as Crime and Art." In *Life after Postmodernism: Essays on Value and Culture*, ed. John Fekete, 161–80. New York: St. Martin's.

Stock, Brian. [1990] 1996. *Listening for the Text: On the Uses of the Past*. Philadelphia: U Pennsylvania P.

Sturrock, John. 1969. *The French New Novel: Claude Simon, Michel Butor, Alain Robbe-Grillet*. London: Oxford UP.

Suleiman, Susan R. 1981. "Of Readers and Narratees: The Experience of *Pamela*." *L'Esprit créateur* 21: 89–97.

Swift, Graham. 1983. *Waterland*. New York: Washington Square Press.

Tachtsís, Kóstas. 1967. *The Third Wedding*. Trans. Leslie Finer. London: Alan Ross.

——. [1963] 1985a. *To tríto stefáni*. Athens: Ermís.

——. 1985b. *The Third Wedding Wreath*. Trans. John Chioles. Athens: Ermís.

Tal, Kali. 1996. *Worlds of Hurt: Reading the Literatures of Trauma*. Cambridge: Cambridge UP.

Tani, Stefano. 1984. *The Doomed Detective: The Contribution of the Detective Novel to Postmodern American and Italian Fiction*. Carbondale: Southern Illinois UP.

Tannen, Deborah. 1980. "A Comparative Analysis of Oral Narrative Strategies: Athenian Greek and American English." In *The Pear Stories: Cognitive, Cul-*

tural, and Linguistic Aspects of Narrative Production, ed. Wallace L. Chafe, 51–87. Norwood, N.J.: Ablex.

———. 1982a. "The Oral/Literate Continuum in Discourse." In Tannen 1982b, 1–16.

Tannen, Deborah, ed. 1982b. *Spoken and Written Language: Exploring Orality and Literacy*. Norwood, N.J.: Ablex.

Tatar, Maria. 1995. *Lustmord: Sexual Murder in Weimar Germany*. Princeton: Princeton UP.

Taylor, Diana. 1997. *Disappearing Acts: Spectacles of Gender and Nationalism in Argentina's "Dirty War."* Durham: Duke UP.

Tedlock, Dennis. 1983. *The Spoken Word and the Work of Interpretation*. Philadelphia: U Pennsylvania P.

Tedlock, Dennis, and Bruce Mannheim, eds. 1995. *The Dialogic Emergence of Culture*. Urbana: U Illinois P.

Ting-Toomey, Stella, and Felipe Korzenny, eds. 1989. *Language, Communication, and Culture. Current Directions*. Newbury Park, Calif.: Sage.

Todorov, Tzvetan. 1966. "Les Catégories du récit littéraire." *Communications* 8: 125–51.

Tompkins, Jane P. 1980. "The Reader in History: The Changing Shape of Literary Response." In *Reader-Response Criticism: From Formalism to Post-Structuralism*, ed. Jane P. Tompkins, 201–32. Baltimore: Johns Hopkins UP.

Trezise, Thomas. 1997. "Trauma and Testimony in Charlotte Delbo's *None of Us Will Return*." Paper given at annual conference of the American Comparative Literature Association, 13 Apr., Puerto Vallarta, Mexico.

Turkle, Sherry. 1995. *Life on the Screen: Identity in the Age of the Internet*. New York: Simon and Schuster.

Tziovas, Dimitris. 1989. "Residual Orality and Belated Textuality in Greek Literature and Culture." *Journal of Modern Greek Studies* 7: 321–35.

Updike, John. 1981. Rev. of *If on a winter's night a traveler*, by Italo Calvino. *New Yorker*, 3 Aug., 90–93.

Van der Kolk, B. A., and Onno van der Hart. [1991] 1995. "The Intrusive Past: The Flexibility of Memory and the Engraving of Trauma." In Caruth 1995a, 158–82. First published in *American Imago* 48, no. 4: 425–54.

Van Rossum-Guyon, Françoise. 1970. *Critique du roman. Essai sur* La Modification *de Michel Butor*. Paris: Gallimard.

Vikélas, Dimítrios. [1879] 1881a. *Lukís Láras*. Athens: Parnassós.

———. 1881b. *Loukis Laras*. Trans. John Gennadius. London: Macmillan.

Warhol, Robyn. 1989. *Gendered Interventions: Narrative Discourse in the Victorian Novel*. New Brunswick: Rutgers UP.

———. 1995. "'Reader, Can You Imagine? No, You Cannot': The Narratee as

Other in Harriet Jacob's Text *Incidents in the Life of a Slave Girl.*" *Narrative* 3, no. 1: 57–72.

Weinstein, Arnold L. 1974. *Vision and Response in Modern Fiction*. Ithaca: Cornell UP.

Wenzel, Hilda. 1960. "Nachwort." In Kolmar 1960, 595–607.

West, Candace. 1984. *Routine Complications: Troubles in Talk between Doctors and Patients*. Bloomington: Indiana UP.

West, Candace, and Don H. Zimmerman. 1982. "Conversation Analysis." In *Handbook of Methods in Nonverbal Behavior Research*, ed. K. R. Scherer and P. Ekman, 506–41. Cambridge: Cambridge UP.

Whalen, M. R., and Don H. Zimmerman. 1990. "Describing Trouble: Epistemology in Citizen Calls to the Police." *Language in Society* 19: 465–92.

Whalley, Peter. 1993. "An Alternative Rhetoric for Hypertext." In *Hypertext: A Psychological Perspective*, ed. C. McKnight, A. Dillon, and J. Richardson, 7–17. New York: Ellis Horwood.

White, Barbara A. 1993. " 'Our Nig' and the She-Devil: New Information about Harriet Wilson and the 'Bellmont' Family." *American Literature* 65, no. 1: 19–52.

Wiesel, Elie. 1977. "The Holocaust as Literary Inspiration." In *Dimensions of the Holocaust: Lectures at Northwestern University: Elie Wiesel, Lucy S. Dawidowitz, Dorothy Rabinowitz, Robert McAfee Brown*, annotated by Elliot Lefkovitz, 5–19. Evanston: Northwestern UP.

Wiest, Ursula. 1993. " 'The Refined, though Whimsical Pleasure': Die You-Erzählsituation." *Arbeiten aus Anglistik und Amerikanistik (AAA)* 18: 75–90.

Wigren, Jodie. 1994. "Narrative Completion in the Treatment of Trauma." *Psychotherapy* 31, no. 3: 415–23.

Wilford, John Noble. 1998. "Ancestral Humans Could Speak, Anthropologists' Finding Suggests." *New York Times*, 28 Apr., A1.

Wilson, Harriet E. [1859] 1983. *Our Nig; or Sketches from the Life of a Free Black, in a Two-Story White House, North. Showing that Slavery's Shadows Fall Even There*. Intro. and notes by Henry Louis Gates Jr. New York: Vintage.

Winnett, Susan. 1990. "Coming Unstrung: Women, Men, Narrative, and Principles of Pleasure." *PMLA* 105: 505–18.

Wittgenstein, Ludwig. 1969. *Blue and Brown Books*. 2nd ed. Oxford: Blackwell UP.

Wizisla, Erdmut. 1991. "Deine Teilnahme wäre eine viel tiefere" [Commentary to Gertrud Kolmar, "Zwei Briefe an Walter Benjamin"]. *Sinn und Form* 43: 125–28.

Wolf, Christa. [1976] 1979. *Kindheitsmuster*. Darmstadt: Luchterhand.

——. 1980. *Patterns of Childhood*. Trans. Ursule Molinaro and Hedwig Rappolt. New York: Farrar, Straus and Giroux.

Woltmann, Johanna. 1995. *Gertrud Kolmar: Leben und Werk*. Göttingen: Wallstein Verlag.

Wood, Michael. 1981. Rev. of *If on a winter's night a traveler*, by Italo Calvino. *New York Times Book Review*, 21 June, 1, 24–25.

Woolf, Virginia. [1925] 1953. *Mrs. Dalloway*. San Diego: Harcourt Brace Jovanovich.

Yovanovich, Gordana. 1991. *Julio Cortázar's Character Mosaic: Reading the Longer Fiction*. Toronto: U Toronto P.

Zamora, Lois Parkinson. 1983. "Movement and Stasis, Film and Photo: Temporal Structures in the Recent Fiction of Julio Cortázar." *Review of Contemporary Fiction* 3: 51–65.

Ziolkowski, Theodore. 1972. *Fictional Transfigurations of Jesus*. Princeton: Princeton UP.

Zimmerman, Don H., and Deirdre Boden. 1991. "Structure-in-Action: An Introduction." In Boden and Zimmerman, 3–21.

Zwicky, Arnold M. 1974. "Hey, Whatsyourname!" *Papers from the Tenth Regional Meeting, Chicago Linguistic Society*, 19–21 Apr., 787–801. Chicago: Chicago Linguistic Society.

Index

abolitionists. *See* Wilson, Harriet: critique of abolitionists by

absent addressee. *See* Goffman, Erving: on present-absent addressees

action override, 14

addressivity (Bakhtin), xiii

adjacency pair, 4, 5. *See also* conversation analysis; turn-taking system

aesthetic attitudes toward novel, 26

African American culture, 34, 36, 38–39; and literature, 226 n.6 n.7, 230 n.50. See also *Mama Day*; slave autobiography; Wilson, Harriet: *Our Nig*

Aichinger, Ilse: "Spiegelgeschichte" (Mirror Story), 244 n.22

Allen, Robert C., 15, 222 n.20, 223 n.32

Allison, Dorothy: *Bastard Out of Carolina*, 236 n.42

analepsis, 124

Angelou, Maya, 61

Anna Karenina (Tolstoy), 67

"Annotext," 251 n.1. *See also* hypertext

answering. *See* Goffman: on statement and reply

apostrophe, 74, 76–77, 103–6, 141–96; definitions of, xvi–xvii, 146, 149; effects of, 147–49

applause, xiii, 5–6, 13, 77–78, 229 n.6

Argentine Dirty War. *See* Cortázar, Julio: "Graffiti"

Arguments, 159, 162

art for art's sake, xiv, 28–29, 149, 225 n.45

Atwood, Margaret: *The Handmaid's Tale*, 105–6, 117–19, 139, 140

Aury, Dominique, 158

Auschwitz, 69, 116, 133; trials, 171, 246 n.36

Austin, J. L.: *How to Do Things with Words*, 183, 185, 248 n.49

Bakhtin, Mikhail Mikhailovich, xii, 33, 87–88. *See also* addressivity

Bal, Mieke, 233 n.21

Balzer, Bernd, 138

Banfield, Ann, 242 n.9 n.13

Barjon, Louis, 159, 160

Barth, John: "Life-Story," 146, 157, 184–85, 186, 189

Barthes, Roland, 162, 202, 224 n.37; *S/Z* 202

Beardsley, Elizabeth, 190. *See also* linguistic genderization

Benjamin, Walter, 89, 96, 98, 99, 115, 120, 140, 231 n.1 n.3; "The Storyteller," 89–90, 140

Benveniste, Emile, 31, 149–54, 158, 189, 193, 242 n.10

Biber, Douglas, 219 n.1

"Biochip5's and WDSZO6C's The Phantom Tollbooth Interactive Story," 205–9, 210, 211. *See also* hypertext

Birkerts, Sven, 219 n.1

Bliven, Bruce, 13

Block, Elizabeth, 241 n.4

Bogosian, Eric, 17, 18

Boisdeffre, Pierre de, 243 n.20

Bolten, Juy, 198–99

Booth, Wayne, 28, 162

Brison, Susan, 231 n.3 n.7

Brooks, Gwendolyn: "The Mother," 246 n.35

Brooks, Peter, 234 n.27 n.30

Buber, Martin, 88, 149–50

Butor, Michel, 181, 243 n.16 n.17; *Change of Heart*, xvii, 146, 157–62, 163, 170, 172, 181, 189, 209

call-in, 15. *See also* radio; talk show

Calvino, Italo, 195; *If on a winter's night*

Index

In the Frontiers of Narrative series:

Talk Fiction: Literature and the Talk Explosion
by Irene Kacandes